PARIS
IN THE
THIRD REICH

PARIS
IN THE
THIRD REICH

A HISTORY OF THE
GERMAN OCCUPATION, 1940-1944

BY DAVID PRYCE-JONES
MICHAEL RAND, PICTURE EDITOR

Holt, Rinehart and Winston
New York

Copyright © 1981 by David Pryce-Jones

All rights reserved, including the right to reproduce this book or portions thereof in any form.

Published by Holt, Rinehart and Winston, 383 Madison Avenue, New York, New York 10017.

Published simultaneously in Canada by Holt, Rinehart and Winston of Canada, Limited.

Library of Congress Cataloging in Publication Data
Pryce-Jones, David, 1936–
     Paris in the third Reich.

     Includes bibliographical references and index.
     1. World War, 1939–1945—France—Paris.
2. Paris—History—1940–1944. I. Title.
D802.F82P376   940.53′44′361   80-21256
ISBN: 0-03-045621-5

First Edition

Printed in the United States of America
10 9 8 7 6 5 4 3 2 1

Photo Credits

Black-and-white photographs:

Camera Press Ltd.: p. 13

Private collection: p. 69.

Roger Schall: pp. 4, 7, 9, 10, 11, 14, 15, 17, 20, 21, 23, 25, 27, 29, 32–33, 40, 41, 49, 52, 54, 55, 56, 57, 58, 59, 60–61, 74, 75, 76, 77, 78, 79, 80 (all), 81, 84, 85, 91, 95 (both), 96, 97, 99, 101, 102, 103, 106, 108, 109, 132, 133, 134, 158, 159, 170, 171, 198, 199, 203, and 205. All copyright © Roger Schall.

Pierre Vals: pp. 163 and 208–09.

André Zucca: pp. 65, 100, 107, 110, 111, 115, 119, 121, 122, 123, 127, 130–31, 137, 139, 161, 166, 175, 176–77, 182, 184, 185, 189, 191, and 273. All copyright © André Zucca—Tallendier—Magnum Distribution.

Color photographs:

All color photographs are by André Zucca, Copyright © André Zucca—Tallendier—Magnum Distribution.

Contents

Sixteen pages of color photographs follow page 150.

Acknowledgments

While I was working on this book, a number of people were extremely generous to me, and among them was M. Henri Amouroux, now perhaps the foremost authority in France on the German occupation. He immediately asked what he could do to help, opened his files, and produced a list of names of men and women with whom I ought to be in touch. His mastery of the subject and his pleasure that others were interested in it were certainly an encouragement to me.

Those whom I interviewed put themselves to a lot of trouble to answer a stranger's question, "What did you do in the war?" Not all were quoted in the end, but I am grateful to everyone for what I learned from them (not least, if indirectly, for the few who refused to have anything to do with me, and the odd one or two who consented to be interviewed, only to repudiate afterward what they had said. One saw that although the passions of the last war may seem banked down, they are easily fanned again). Herbert Eckelmann and Gerhard Heller were kind enough to allow me to use their unpublished diaries. Madame Simone Mittre unstintingly made available documents and pamphlets from her Fernand de Brinon archive.

Among those who wish to remain anonymous for fear of giving unspecified offense were two friends in particular, one who helped me with introductions in Germany, and another with whom I stayed during repeated visits in Paris. I would like to thank Alain and Annette Bourrut-Lacouture for the loan of a valuable book; Hans Coudenhove; Philippe Daudy; Nicholas Deakin; Frau Lisbeth Epting and Frau Puth Epting, who obtained for me a copy of Alice Epting-Kullmann's *Pariser Begegnungen*; Alfred Fabre-Luce; Joachim Fest; John Gross, for researches into Corinne Luchaire; André Halimi, who put on a special showing of his film *Chantons sous l'occupation,* as well as presenting me with a copy of his excellent book of that title; Professor Artur Henkel of Heidelberg; Serge and Beate Klarsfeld; Michael Klett; Michèle Lapautre; Herbert R. Lottman; Michael R. Marrus; Fritz Molden; Albert Speer; Mrs. James Teacher; Professor Georges Wellers. From Tom Wallace, the book's editor, came the original idea, as well as much support for which I am also grateful. I should like to thank librarians and staff at the libraries that I used, mainly the Bibliothèque de Documentation Contemporaine at Nanterre University, the Centre de Documentation Juive Contemporaine (or CDJC, for short, when documents in its archives are quoted), the Imperial War Museum, the Institut für Zeitgeschichte in Munich, the London Library, and the Wiener Library.

Finally I have an interest to declare that in May 1940, when I was a small child, it so happened that I found myself with my mother's family at their house, Royaumont, some thirty kilometers north of Paris. The exodus to the south and the subsequent period spent in the Vichy zone are among my earliest memories. When at Christmas 1945 the French and English members of my family were once again united at Royaumont, there lay by the side of the road at the house's entrance a burnt-out tank. I can still see its white Allied markings, but whether Americans or Englishmen or Free French had died in it I cannot say.

Glossary

Abbreviations

CGQJ	Commissariat Générale aux Questions Juives
CNE	Comité Nationale d'Ecrivains
CNR	Conseil National de la Résistance
DNB	Deutsches Nachrichten Büro (official news agency)
FFI	Forces Françaises de l'Intérieur (Free French)
FTP	Francs-Tireurs et Partisans
LVF	Légion des Volontaires Français
MSR	Mouvement Social Révolutionnaire (Deloncle party)
NRF	*Nouvelle Revue Française*
PCF	Parti Communiste Français
PPF	Parti Populaire Français (Doriot party; its newspaper, *Le Cri du Peuple*)
PQJ	Police aux Questions Juives
RNP	Rassemblement National Populaire (Deat party; its newspaper, *L'Oeuvre*)
RSHA	Reichssicherheitshauptamt, the German police and security apparatus under Himmler, with the SS and SD among its components
SD	Sicherheitsdienst. Amt VI of the RSHA responsible for external security
SOE	Special Operations Executive
SOL	Service d'Ordre Légionnaire
STO	Service de Travail Obligatoire
UGIF	Union Générale des Israélites en France

German organizations and personnel

German Embassy	Otto Abetz, ambassador, 1940–44
	Rudolf Schleier, minister, 1940–44
	Ernst Achenbach, counselor, 1940–43
German Institute (Deutsche Institut)	Dr. Karl Epting, director 1940–44
Kommandant von Gross-Paris	General Alfred von Vollard-Bockelburg, June–August 1940
	General Ernst von Schaumburg, August 1940–September 1943
	General Hans von Boineburg-Lengsfeld, September 1943–July 1944
	General Dietrich von Choltitz, August 1944

Militärbefehlshaber
(German Military
Governor)

General Alfred von Streccius, July 1940

General Otto von Stülpnagel, October 1940–February 1942

General Heinrich von Stülpnagel, February 1942–July 1944

General Karl Kitzinger, August 1944

German Security Forces

Standartenführer Helmut Knochen, commanding SD, June 1940–August 1944

General Karl Oberg, Höherer SS und Polizeiführer, May 1942–August 1944

I. THE OCCUPATION

1 The Harvest of 1940

aris, in a tumultuous history, had been conquered by invaders and stormed by its own revolutionaries, but Thursday, June 13, 1940, was nonetheless a day quite without precedent. For the city was ominously silent, deserted. There were no crowds, nobody on the shuttered streets except a few stragglers in French uniforms, a few looters too. Traffic, the metro, commerce, the radio and newspapers, the usual activities of a great city, had all been suspended. Of the nearly five million inhabitants of Paris and the surrounding Seine department, some three million had fled. That this was war, and not some natural catastrophe or plague, was revealed only by token sandbagging of the famous monuments so integral to the nation. Late in the afternoon, smoke blotted out the sky, as black haze arose from several fuel storage depots that had been set on fire to prevent them from falling into enemy hands. To the remaining citizens indoors, the darkness augured what was to come.

That night, under a flag of truce, two French officers and a trumpeter met German delegates a few kilometers north of Paris, at Sarcelles. Under the threat of imminent conquest, Paris had already been declared an open city and, according to international convention, it would not be defended but handed over with due process. Advance German patrols were already peacefully penetrating into the northern suburbs, and by five o'clock on the morning of the fourteenth, infantry was marching in columns of three toward selected key points, including the railway stations and the city center. A French colonel, with two or three of his men, attempted to set up a machine-gun post at the Porte d'Orléans, but a dutiful police inspector prevented this single recorded attempt at resistance. A senior officer in the Garde Républicaine, Comte Georges Benoit-Guyod, noted in his diary how orderly the Germans were as they took over fully equipped barracks and three-ton trucks abandoned there. At one moment he found a couple of Germans aiming submachine guns at him, but at the words *"Gendarmerie française"* he was allowed to pass and even received a bow which he took for politeness. Altogether the enemy troops, he decided with reluctant admiration, were in calm control.

In the skeleton of the captured open city, seven municipal councillors were to be found, along with a few notables, such as Professor Rouchy, head of the university; Achille Magny, *préfet* of the Seine department; and Roger Langeron, *préfet* of police. The latter, writing in his diary for that day, expressed the feeling of the general public, *"L'affreuse chose s'est realisée"* (The terrible thing has happened). "An immense, an interminable defile of motorized troops has begun to cross Paris," as Langeron described it. "They are coming from Saint-Denis and from the northern suburbs and in the direction of Montrouge. First motorcyclists with sidecars, in their leather overcoats. Then the weight of the armor, of tanks. The streets are virtually empty, and the majority of houses are shuttered." By midmorning, Langeron and Magny had received a German emissary and were answering a summons to be at the Crillon Hotel, as though for some sort of privileged social occasion. There, in the silk-lined reception rooms, they were introduced to General Bogislav von Studnitz, temporarily military governor of Paris: "monocle, little moustache, with a slightly old-

Nothing so dramatically represented the German presence as the ubiquitous swastika flags, here flying over the requisitioned Hotel Continental.

fashioned cavalry officer air about him," as Langeron wrote. Champagne was gracefully offered and accepted. By then, swastika banners were already flying over the ministries, the Chambre des Députés, the Sénat, and other public buildings.

Across the street from the Crillon, on the corner of the Place de la Concorde, was the American embassy; there neutrality still prevailed, although Ambassador William C. Bullitt stared at the Germans with dismay, even anger. On his staff was Robert Murphy, who thought "there had never been anything like the eerie atmosphere" of the German takeover. Beforehand he had been helping people to leave, not always successfully—as in the case of the Grand Rabbi of Paris, who at first had intended to stay, but changed his mind so late that he was turned back by the incoming Germans. Standing on the sidewalk outside the embassy that morning, Murphy was approached by a lieutenant, who detached himself from the passing convoys to ask Murphy to recommend a suitable hotel. It was not long before Bullitt sent Murphy over to the Crillon. There he too was enjoying General von Studnitz's champagne when one of the dozen staff officers in attendance suddenly exclaimed, "Murphy! What are you doing here?" He proved to be an old friend from Bavaria. By the end of July, the company agreed happily, the war would be over.

Across the river, in the rue de Grenelle, the Russian embassy was obliged to welcome the Germans in as allies, thanks to the pact which Hitler and Stalin had signed the previous August. The Soviet ambassador, Bogomolov, seems to have believed in its sincerity, although a member of his staff by the name of Ivanov was later picked as a scapegoat for the embassy's friendliness toward the Germans and was liquidated. In any case, Vyacheslav Molotov, the Russian foreign minister, sent Hitler a telegram of congratulations upon the capture of Paris.

Setting the seal on the military triumph of the hour, General Kurt von Briesen, commanding the Nineteenth Division, took the salute toward midday at an impromptu victory march of his men down the Champs-Elysées. Like his senior officers, he was mounted, and it was observed that the general occasionally stood up in his stirrups out of plain excitement. Later, he hastened out by car to Versailles and there, in Louis XIV's Galerie des Glaces, decorated with the Iron Cross those who had earned it on the campaign.

No time was wasted while settling in. Not only were French installations occupied immediately and field bivouacs established, but all over the city the quartermaster general's staff was following General von Studnitz's example and requisitioning hotels. For obvious reasons, there would be no other tourists; moreover, these hotel rooms were paid for from the first day to the last. At lunch on that Friday, June 14, many a German soldier had the sight of clean linen and a properly laid table, luxuries suspended since the opening of the blitzkrieg.

Thousands of cooks and waiters and maids and bellboys suddenly found themselves—like Langeron and Magny with their drinks—called upon to take an attitude toward their conquerors, and once taken, by simple reflex mostly, the attitude was unlikely to change. Yesterday's fears jostled with today's astonishment and relief, and meanwhile a job had to be done, a service performed, a key or a concierge produced. Their parading over, many of the Germans left their new quarters to see quite where it was that they had finished up, to photograph the sights, especially the Arc de Triomphe and the Tomb of the Unknown Soldier, irresistibly heightening the impression that they were some kind of mass tourists. A well-known brothel, the Chabanais, encouraged by such business-as-usual normality, hung a notice on its front door: "The house will reopen at three o'clock."

Rather than submit so passively to national humiliation, sixteen Parisians preferred to commit suicide, among them the mayor of Clichy, Maurice Naile, who had left the Communist party after the Russian-German pact, and Comte Thierry de Martel, head of the American Hospital. A few more took this escape route in the days to come, including Ernst Weiss, an émigré novelist and a student of Freud's. Otherwise no violent encounters marked this stark moment, no sabotage, no violence or rapes. Paris, far and away the greatest of Hitler's prizes, smoothly but assuredly assumed its place in the Reich that was intended to last a thousand years.

Only thirty-five days earlier, when the blitzkrieg in the West had begun, such a feat of arms had been imaginable to no more than a very small number of professional strategists or commentators who had observed Hitler's Germany at first hand. To write them off as alarmists had been easier than the alternative, which was to vote for massive arms expenditure. Had not Marshal Pétain, eighty-four years old but France's most prestigious military man and a symbol of victory in World War I, been writing as late as 1939 that an invasion of France was possible only if the French allowed themselves to be lulled to sleep? Three million men, reputed to be a fighting force without equal, had been mobilized since August 1939. Why should Paris be defended with more than sandbags when the fortifications of the Maginot Line stretched for several hundred impregnable kilometers from Switzerland up to Belgium? Only thirty-five days earlier, the theaters in Paris had been crowded, white ties were still worn, there were dancing and trips abroad and summer plans, and British officers on leave in Paris were smiled at. True, England and France had declared war in the first place to uphold their treaties to defend Poland, and Poland had died in three weeks without a finger being raised to help her in the West. Dreadful as the Polish fate was at the hands of the Germans, at least it couldn't happen here, which put most consciences into abeyance—the very phrase *drôle de guerre,* or phony war, had something flip about it. So the news of the German attack of May 10 did not at first alarm. At that stage self-satisfied politicians and generals were still listened to and trusted.

Within three days the Germans had crossed the Meuse and cut to pieces the Ninth Army under General Corap. Twenty-four more hours and the Second Army under General Huntziger was broken. The road to Paris lay open. Already by May 16, the French army, and therefore the government too, had lost control of the war. Bizarre countermeasures were offered: a government not notable for piety attended Mass at Notre-Dame, and holy relics were paraded. The prime minister, Paul Reynaud, invited Marshal Pétain to join the cabinet, though as it turned out, this intended effigy of national unity evolved within days into Reynaud's own successor. The rhythm of disaster accelerated: the Belgian capitulation, the tail-between-the-legs evacuation of the British Expeditionary Force at Dunkirk, the bombing of the Paris airports on June 3, Italy's declaration of war against France on June 10.

"I felt the German advance like a personal threat," someone as rational as Simone de Beauvoir could write on June 9. "There was only one idea in my head . . . not to be caught like a rat in occupied Paris." Panic stirring in the gut, the *grande peur,* swept almost all before it. If complacency had been exaggerated beforehand, so now was folly. In ministries and government offices, papers and archives were either burnt in full view of the frightened public, or hastily evacuated on hundreds of trucks, or even, in the worst cases, abandoned to the incoming troops. Caretakers alone were left behind in all departments of the administration. In museums little remained except objects like the Winged Victory of Samothrace, too heavy to be crated up and packed off in a hurry. Official Paris disintegrated during the night of June 10; its destination was Bordeaux, with the further possibility of evacuation by

6

A party of officers following the example of Hitler, who also paused on this terrace to admire the Eiffel Tower.

sea. In government cars with escorts, the President of the Republic, Albert Lebrun, and Jules Jeanneney, President of the Senate, preceded Reynaud, who was accompanied by General Charles de Gaulle, recently promoted but virtually unknown outside political circles (where his determination to make a stand against the Germans seemed more a personal quirk than a realistic alternative). Marshal Pétain and his wife also took the roads south.

The average citizen lost no time following the example of his government, and by June 11 the exodus from Paris was unstoppable, pell-mell. Few cared why, how, or where they fled, so long as they could be elsewhere. Apartments, offices, pets, obligations of all sorts, were abandoned. Factory production lines had simply been switched off—airframes, brand-new trucks, and weapons made by Hotchkiss and Potez and Renault and other suppliers of the French army were shortly to be incorporated lock, stock, and barrel into the German war machine. In one instance nurses administered fatal injections to hospital patients too old or ill to be moved.

As early as May 30, at dawn, the Duke of Windsor had left, without so much as a word to Major Metcalfe, the aide-de-camp who had been with him since the abdication—and who now had to make his way alone to Bordeaux. The Windsors' house, 85, boulevard Suchet, was in fact looked after by a German caretaker and handed back in 1944 in perfect order. The Aga Khan left for Switzerland, and so did James Joyce. The international set—Daisy Fellowes, Sir Charles and Lady Mendl, Elsa Maxwell, Peggy Guggenheim, Princess Winnie de Polignac (neé Singer)—disappeared. Gertrude Stein and Alice B. Toklas left their apartment and their pictures and went to Culoz, near Annecy, where they were lucky to survive the war. Distinguished Parisians who were to spend the war in America included the filmmaker René Clair and the famous actor Louis Jouvet, and Jean Renoir, André Maurois, St. John Perse, Fernand Léger, and the composer Darius Milhaud. Vladimir Nabokov escaped to New York on the last liner out ahead of the incoming Germans. Prince George of Greece left—his house was to be requisitioned. Marc Chagall, André Malraux, Louis Aragon, Henri Matisse, Roger Martin du Gard, and André Gide left and were to spend the war in the unoccupied zone, though Gide was to go one stage further still, to Tunis. In his diary for June 14 Gide comments, "Hitler has played the hand in a magisterial way. . . . The tragic light of events has revealed the profound decay of France, which Hitler realized only too well. Incoherence on all sides, lack of discipline, claims of chimerical rights but failure to accept obligations." Ten days later, listening to Pétain's broadcast, he asked rhetorically, "Is it not enough that France is defeated? Must she be dishonored as well?" By September 5 he was to write, "To come to terms with yesterday's enemy is not cowardice but wisdom; as well as accepting what is inevitable."

Among the few in positions of authority who stayed put were Cardinals Beaudrillart and Suhard, the former about to become an enthusiastic collaborator praying in public for the Germans, the latter on the contrary one of the first to have his apartments searched. Abel Hermant, like Cardinal Beaudrillart a member of the Académie Française, and a passionate collaborator as well, also stayed and soon was writing an article explaining, "Oh! I did not do it on purpose. It was no more out of calculation than out of heroism that I remained in the open city. Once more it was a question of habit."

Another writer, Paul Léautaud, had watched the *sauve-qui-peut* with no desire to do more than keep the record as usual in his diary, a well-known chronicle of the times which he had been publishing in dribs and drabs in the literary magazine *Mercure de France* ever since he first made a reputation back in the 1890s. Now seventy,

Numbers of German soldiers were observed to have taken their cameras on the blitzkrieg.

he was a crotchety little man who habitually wore an idiosyncratic soft hat when he went out and a bonnet when he stayed at home, and who gloried in prejudices which were shared more generally than he knew: a dislike of democracy, England, and the Jews, and a grudging approbation of the way Hitler's Germany was setting about things. About the exodus of June 11, he wrote, "Along the entire length of the boulevard Saint-Michel, an uninterrupted flow of people is leaving Paris with the most varied means of transport: cars crammed with luggage, heavy trucks loaded with people and suitcases, people on bicycles, others pushing a small hand cart, with a dog tied underneath on a lead, huge country carts going as fast as two or three plow horses can pull them, loaded with bales of hay upon which sit old peasant women (certainly coming from departments most recently under threat). One of these carts even had half a dozen cows in the rear, apparently in the last stages of exhaustion. On the edge of the pavements, a number of people with cases, waiting for transport of every kind, others shoving as much into their cars as possible. . . . At midday, boulevard Saint-Germain, same spectacle. Rue Dauphine, luggage all over the pavements, trucks loading up. Shops shut. Some are leaving with nothing more elaborate than a pram."

Two days later he could see, and enjoy, what Paris had become. "Empty: that is exactly the word. Shops shut. The odd passerby. The rue de Châteaudun deserted. Same thing around the Opéra, avenue de l'Opéra, and the streets off it. All buildings

Like so many tourists, German soldiers after the 1940 campaign swarmed into shops in search of goods unobtainable at home.

have their doors closed. . . . The *grands boulevards* in the direction of the Madeleine, on the far side from the corner of the rue Drouot, as far as the eye could carry, absolutely deserted, all the shops closed. And the silence!"

Clogging the roads westward and southward, or spilling into Normandy and Brittany, inextricably mingled into shattered units on the retreat, exposed to dive bombing and shelling, this civilian rout was a parallel to the military catastrophe. The two million prisoners captured by the Germans matched the number of refugees, and if as many as forty thousand civilians died (according to estimates), then casualties in battle were only between two and three times as great. For weeks afterward distraught announcements appeared in newspapers all over the country about babies who had been lost, or found without means of identification.

The exodus was not finally sorted out before the end of the summer. All along it had played into the Germans' hands; it allowed their performance its soldierly elegance. For when those who had experienced these events resumed their lives under occupation, had not their conduct, their whole moral bearing, been conditioned by so much abject fear and humiliation?

The government, doomed already to bear responsibility for the loss of Paris and a military defeat which left the entire country exposed to the invaders, had no time to lose before deciding where the national interest lay. One of those choices which are properly called historic had to be made: either to withdraw from metropolitan

10

Auxiliary helpers—known as *Blitzmädchen* to the Germans, and sometimes as "gray mice" to the French—here shopping in the Magasins du Printemps department store.

France, rallying in colonial North Africa and carrying on the war from there, or to sue for an armistice. In terms of personalities, Paul Reynaud embodied the former course of action, Marshal Pétain the latter. The exodus from Paris seems to have established in Pétain's mind the hopelessness of resistance; he had seen for himself the misery suffered by the population. In his view, to quit the territory of France was to deliver the nation to its enemies, even to forfeit its soul—a preconception not shared by the Polish, Czech, or Dutch governments, for example, nor indeed by General de Gaulle. Before the German entry into Paris, Pétain was already insisting on an armistice and nothing but an armistice. The rivalry between him and Reynaud was total but brief. Both threatened to resign, until on June 16 Reynaud did so, by which time he was in a minority in his own cabinet. That very night Pétain, in office only a matter of hours, asked the Spanish ambassador, Felix de Lequerica, to ascertain Hitler's terms for an armistice. The following morning, acting on rumor, Pétain ordered the arrest of Georges Mandel, who had been minister of the interior in the dissolved government and who remained convinced, with Reynaud, that the war should be pursued at whatever cost. Mandel was Jewish. Some sort of denunciation had been made that Mandel had been planning an armed coup against the new government: the absurdity was such that Mandel was released almost at once, with a written apology from Pétain. The incident was a forewarning for those able to look facts in the face.

The terms for armistice were not dishonorable. France would maintain a government of its own in the southern two-fifths of the country, from then on referred to as the *zone libre,* or *zone non-occupée.* Hitler calculated, probably correctly, that this maintenance of an apparently independent government would be face-saving for the French; more important, it would inhibit the English from seizing French colonies, and thereby strengthening their own position in the Mediterranean. Equally, the French fleet did not have to be transferred to the German navy, and a small standing army was tolerated. The costs incurred by the Germans in the zone which they had occupied would have to be paid by the French: 400 million francs a day (sufficient, the French estimated when they argued for a reduction, for an army of eighteen million men), and this disproportionately large sum was to remain a matter of contention. An armistice commission was set up at Wiesbaden, the town where a similar French-run commission had sat after World War I. At its head was Dr. Hemmen, a banker and economist. In fact the volume and the increasingly political nature of the commission's business was such that Hemmen soon effectively transferred his office to Paris, where it was gradually submerged into the rest of the German administration. As for a peace treaty, this would follow the defeat of England, when the ambitions of the Reich's geopolitics could be finally satisfied.

The armistice was signed on June 22, at Compiègne. There, in the forest, some thirty miles from Paris, Marshal Ferdinand Foch, once Pétain's commander in chief, had received the German generals who surrendered after World War I. The railway carriage in which this former meeting had taken place had been preserved as a national monument. To oblige the French to reenact the scene, with the roles reversed, was exactly the kind of revenge Hitler relished. When he arrived at the forest clearing and stood outside the carriage, he could not hide his joy from the photographers commemorating this peak of his career. Present with him were General Wilhelm Keitel, his chief of staff, Goering, Hess, and Ribbentrop—the latter was one of the few Nazi leaders never to set foot in Paris itself during the occupation. All returned after the ceremony to a field headquarters set up at the village of Bruly.

Although Hitler's inner feelings toward France had been spontaneously revealed at the armistice signing, his outward behavior was circumspect. The next morning, when it was still dark, he left Bruly to fly into Le Bourget, accompanied by two of his adjutants, Colonel Rudolf Schmundt and Major Gerhard Engel, General Keitel, Otto Dietrich, who was responsible for press propaganda in Germany, as well as those associates with whom he enjoyed airing his artistic pretensions, the architects Hermann Giesler and Albert Speer and the sculptor Arno Breker. In his memoirs, *Im Strahlungsfeld der Ereignisse,* Breker has described how he had been summarily fetched from Germany without warning and deposited at Bruly. Once in Paris, Hitler's party was met by Colonel Hans Speidel, who for just eight days had been chief of staff to the military governor and had been ordered to act as guide because of the expert knowledge he had acquired before the war as assistant military attaché in Paris. The itinerary, Speidel says in his memoirs, included the Opéra, the Madeleine, Place de la Concorde, the Arc de Triomphe, avenue Foch, Trocadéro, the Eiffel Tower, Ecole de Guerre, Les Invalides and its courtyard, the German embassy, the Palais Luxembourg, Notre-Dame, the Tuileries, the Place Vendôme, and finally Montmartre. It was a tour of famous sites which any of his own soldiers-turned-sightseers might have made.

Hitler and his convoy of open cars covered the ground rather fast, between a quarter to six and half past eight. The Opéra particularly appealed to Hitler's nineteenth-century taste; he revealed that he had studied its plans. The janitor, Pierre Théodore, known as Glouglou, was the only member of the staff at hand to receive

Hitler so soon after dawn, and, on a Sunday at that, Glouglou duly switched on the stage lighting and then refused a tip with a dignity which struck the German party—the poor man had a heart attack soon afterward and died in the course of the following year. Hitler lost himself in thought at Napoleon's tomb in Les Invalides—gratifying historical comparisons were no doubt running through his mind. Settling more scores, during the excursion he gave instructions to destroy the statue of General Mangin, one of the World War I commanders; it was leveled three days later, along with a memorial to Edith Cavell, the British nurse shot in 1915 by a German firing squad. "I am grateful to fate," he said in Breker's hearing, "to have seen this town whose aura has always preoccupied me. At the beginning of hostilities I gave orders to the troops to find a way around Paris and to avoid fighting in its periphery. For it is our responsibility at several levels to preserve undamaged this wonder of Western civilization. We have succeeded." A few bystanders, mostly at Le Bourget airport, had recognized Hitler, with appropriate degrees of shock—Langeron even claimed to have had him followed by gendarmes, which seems unlikely in the circumstances. Never in his life, then, did Hitler have a meal in Paris or enter a private house. Nor was he to return again to the city which he claimed set standards for Berlin to surpass.

Hitler was in Paris only once, for a matter of hours, on June 23, 1940.

This expedition was all that survived of an earlier impulse to hold a monster victory parade, laid aside because it would only alienate the French and, worse, expose the fiction of the armistice. For the armistice contained its own logic, working brilliantly to German advantage, as the French were to discover without delay. First of all, within the German zone an administrative decree hived off two northern departments and placed them under the rule of the military governor in Brussels. Then the entire coastline was defined as a military area and blocked off to nonresidents. Alsace and Lorraine, for whose disputed ownership so many men had died in successive wars, passed separately under the jurisdiction of German *gauleiters,* exactly like any other part of the Reich. In case there remained any doubt about whether or not this amounted to annexation, the two provinces were Germanized, and the tens of thousands of people who did not opt for German citizenship (which entailed military service for the men) were forcibly expelled into the unoccupied zone during the course of the summer.

France had been effectively partitioned. The economic and social difficulties built into the situation meant that decision making, down to small particulars, had to reside with the Germans. Furthermore, the demarcation running right across France between the occupied and unoccupied zones could be treated as a proper boundary, with customs and police posts, and if need be all manner of special permits to cross could be demanded for people as well as for goods. Fuel or food might be withheld at will. Total closure could be threatened. A month was to pass before train links were reestablished, and yet another month before open postcards were permitted between zones. As the French delegation at Wiesbaden heard from Dr. Hemmen, the demarcation line served like the curb on a horse, to be tightened or relaxed according to the horse's behavior.

Under these pressures, the so-called free zone was bound to be far from free in reality. Though its inhabitants did not have to deal with Germans in their daily lives—and so were rid of the chief irritant or inconvenience of the occupied zone—none of them could fail to perceive how limited French initiatives had become. German approval or at least toleration was the requisite for the government's internal and external measures. As head of state, Pétain's position was defined by his refusal, or inability, to see this central fact for what it was. Pétain believed himself to be

13

rescuing what he could from the national collapse. It was an illusion. From the outset, his prestige was useful to the Germans; his very name entailed the stability and obedience without which their ends could not be achieved. Time would prove brutally to Pétain that it was his sincerity which had made him such a dupe. Like Neville Chamberlain, the British prime minister, who had similarly believed in the possibility of accommodating rationally to Hitler's demands, he had been accustomed to a world in which certain standards were taken for granted, whereby what public men said corresponded to what they did. In a totalitarian setting he was easily manipulated. He was talking about honor. Hitler was talking about power.

During the first week of July, Pétain and the politicians and job hunters scuttled from Bordeaux, which was felt to be unsafe, and settled instead upon Vichy, of all places, hitherto a tranquil spa with poor communications and poor facilities. Hotels had to be taken over for accommodation and offices, exactly as the Germans were forced to do in Paris. The corridors of power had a comic improvisation about them. Few people had a clear idea of what was demanded of them, or how to proceed. On the initiative of Pierre Laval, the National Assembly met in the local casino and took a step without precedent in a democracy: it voted for its own extinction. Instead Pétain was to have plenipotentiary powers; he could rule by decree, he could appoint ministers, and accordingly he rewarded Laval by making him vice-president and heir-apparent for the time being.

A self-made man, a lawyer, socialist when it suited him, former foreign minister, interlocutor with Stalin over the Franco-Russian Pact of 1935, Laval was very much a between-the-wars politician, for whom democracy was essentially a bargaining ring

14

among traders. Rightly he believed that he had the skills to argue any case, no matter how often or how confusingly he changed tack. Had he been less sure that every man has his price, he might perhaps have been more ruthless, but cleverness seemed to him to produce better results than violence. Like Reynaud before him, he was confident that he could exploit Pétain, keep him as "a vase on the mantelpiece" in his telling expression. Holland, Belgium, Poland, Czechoslovakia, he saw, had simply been subordinated to German military authority. He was convinced—and here he and Pétain were in accord—that for the time being France would receive more lenient treatment than these other conquered countries if its own nominal government could be interposed between the population and the German authorities. Force majeure was bound to impress someone of Laval's temperament, and he expected to cede to Hitler's inevitable demands, but he hoped that expediency and deviousness and subservience would mask or mitigate the basic weakness of France. An area of bargaining—perhaps even a holding action—would be thus created, which he imagined suited his talents and had tantalizing personal prospects as well. In justifying himself, Laval could point out with truth that hundreds of thousands of people from the occupied zone, including refugees, Jews, and Communists, all variously menaced by the Germans, had found in the Vichy zone a refuge of some kind. Moreover, the degree of goodwill shown by the French, Laval calculated, would serve its purpose when a peace treaty came to be drawn up after the ultimate German victory, which did not appear in doubt. Then France might emerge on some sort of footing with Germany while Poland, Holland, and the rest of the Reich satellites would receive nothing but the heel of the jackboot. So although Vichy was theoretically the French capital now, and Paris no more than a truncated city the wrong side of the demarcation line, it was to Paris that Laval went immediately in order to contact the Germans. He was the first to realize that the Third Republic was dead.

Pétain and the men around him were not sorry to see Laval busy elsewhere. They were conservative in outlook; he was a radical. In order to regenerate a France that would be a fit match for Germany, a "national revolution" was ordained at Vichy. Its catchwords were *work, family, fatherland*. Semimilitary ideals of discipline and sacrifice were to be fostered. There were uniforms for everyone—shorts for boys in youth movements and blue shirts for a Legion of ex-servicemen—and as much military music and martial activity as were possible without either pathos or provoking the Germans. Anthems were composed to Pétain. Paul Claudel wrote him an ode; Sacha Guitry arranged for dozens of distinguished people to contribute to a patriotic album in his honor. Photographs of Pétain in a selection of five poses were sold by the million—the old face under its kepi gazed everywhere, the skin amazingly pinkish, the eyes rheumy but paternal and sagacious. Vichy trappings may have been fascist, but the spirit was more generally *vieille France*—in a word, right-wing. The men who built and supported the Vichy regime were those who most naturally should have resisted the Germans, since for years they had been claiming to possess the monopoly of patriotism and nationalism. Instead, patriotism and nationalism had come to be harnessed to surrender to the Germans. Though Vichy might seem like a marshal's dream come true, what the regime really represented was the complete desertion of national and traditional values.

Those who continued to believe in such values could find a focus for them nowhere except in the defiance of General de Gaulle. On June 18, de Gaulle had begun broadcasting from London, where he had retreated after a few hectic days in Bordeaux. He called for volunteers, or Free French, to carry on the war. Ironically de Gaulle had been on friendly terms with Pétain, but now the two men passed sen-

German soldiers viewing Montmartre in 1941.

tences of death upon each other. Everyone began accusing everyone else of betrayal. In the small town of Riom, Vichy was eventually to stage show trials of those held responsible for the disaster of 1940: notably Léon Blum, Edouard Daladier, General Maurice Gamelin. Soon it became obvious that the defendants were arguing not about their guilt as warmongers but about how they might have defeated the Germans. Hitler intervened to complain about this scandal. Proceedings were suspended.

It was not in courtrooms that public opinion was thrashed out, but in bars, on the streets, even in the press—although that now had official censors at Vichy. If what had happened was the fault of traitors, then did those traitors wear French, German, or English uniforms? Alternatively it was the fault of the fifth column, of too much wine and too few munitions, of profiteers, of the two hundred families and the capitalist trusts supposedly in control of all the funds. It was the fault of decadence, of André Gide (who consequently could no longer be allowed to deliver a public lecture), or of paid holidays for the working classes; or it was the fault of the perfidious Anglo-Saxons for looking after their own interests, of Winston Churchill and President Roosevelt, neither of whom sent help. It was the fault of democracy, of elected representatives who were so many jobbers, of the Communists, of the Freemasons, and behind them an even more mysterious force known as the *synarchie,* whose tentacles were sought out high and low in Vichy, via such disparate elements as the Banque Worms, Jean Bichelonne, the technocratic minister of production, and Pierre Pucheu, minister of the interior (he later defected to General de Gaulle, who promptly put him before a tribunal and had him shot). It was the fault of the extreme right, who really did prefer Hitler to Blum, as they had boasted before the war, and who were now emerging in their true fascist, pro-German colors. Nobody looked inward much into self and society, lest laziness be found at the center as well as vainglory and ineptitude at every level. The enemy had won through greater daring, strength, and efficiency, backed by a totalitarian system which could be met only by responses of a higher moral order. Instead, this was the hour for scapegoats, alibis and recriminations, conspiracy, and above all, self-preservation.

The case of Glouglou at the Opéra was out of the common run, but each and every Parisian was in the same predicament of having to decide what to do, how to behave, in the confrontations now unavoidable in daily life. The first German whom Paul Léautaud spotted was opposite the main gate to the Luxembourg, being instructed in the use of the public telephone by a French policeman. Léautaud hardly reacted: "It had no effect on me whatsoever." A rather more sociable writer, André Thérive, viewed the German occupation with an equal lack of distress—eighteen months later he was to join a party of writers on a propaganda tour of Germany. In his diary he told a literary story of someone he called L. (initials for fear of identification are a prominent feature of the period) on his way to lunch with a poet in the rue de Vaugirard. Spotting two unexpected soldiers and wondering who these might be, he asked a policeman, who informed him. "Oh, I thought they might be Dutch," said L., continuing to his luncheon.

Georges van Parys, one of the most popular dance-band leaders, was hardly more emotional. "*Eh bien,* it's most odd; for three days now I've been circulating among these green uniforms, and I hardly dare write down the fact: it doesn't shatter me. . . . To be in Paris among them neither surprises me nor makes me uneasy. No reflex of embarrassment or revolt. I won't be going about boasting of it, naturally. Nobody would understand."

Yuki Desnos, wife of Robert Desnos, both central figures in upper-bohemian circles, has described in her memoirs how the first sight of the Germans and their swastikas made her legs so wobbly that she had to sit down on the terrace of Maxim's. There, without ado, a German naval officer took a chair next to her, ordered champagne, and proposed that she should drive off with him to Rouen. "There I was having shared some champagne with the enemy. Oh, *zut alors!* But it was the gospel truth that he had a way with him, that admiral did." She went on to add, "Having been so afraid, the people of Paris, regaining confidence, began to tease the invaders harmlessly, nicknaming them *'haricots verts'* or *'les Frises.'* . . . For their part, the Fritzes called back with rather more malice, *'Vou, gross filou'* and *'Oh! la! la!'* After the agony of defeat, a kind of euphoria reigned."

L'Illustration, the mass-circulation weekly—one of the few papers to survive from before the war, although suitably collaborationist under a new editor, Robert de Beauplan—caught the general mood when it summed up the German soldiers as "handsome boys, decent, helpful, above all correct." *La Gerbe,* one of the newly created papers, had sent a reporter, André Bellier, out on his bicycle to cover the events of June 14, and he wrote: "There was some fraternizing with the Fridolins [yet another piece of slang]. Some were laying it on a bit thick. In the rue Lafayette, during a march, a big, stout woman couldn't hold herself back. She kept it up all the time: 'Oh, what lovely-looking men! And their horses! Oh! So they haven't had a bite to eat for ten years, and will you just have a look at these lovely men! And the trucks! And the motorbikes! So they have no gasoline? And nothing to fight with? We've been had good and proper.' In the end I saw she was going to clap. I was obliged to tell her, 'Watch it, lady, watch yourself. Some of our boys are dead. . . .'" However, Elise, wife of the writer Marcel Jouhandeau and depicted in a series of his books as

The stands at Auteuil reserved for German soldiers.

Everyone who was anyone went to the races, according to Serge Lifar. At Longchamps, the Kommandant von Gross-Paris occupied the official box of the French President.

a kind of legendary monster, was once watching a similar procession, only to be asked by another lady if the goosestep was not typically barbarian. Elise answered that she had been a ballet dancer and knew a difficult exercise when she saw one. "Try and goosestep yourself, Madame," she added, "and you'll soon be on your backside."

The Germans, as amorphous as they were busy, lost no time creating their own atmosphere, their own surroundings: they were erecting white signposts with black lettering everywhere to direct military traffic; they were requisitioning empty houses and buildings, making a beeline for anything English-owned. Posters appeared on the walls showing a uniformed and obviously Aryan soldier, gazing with sentimental tenderness at a child in his arms, above the slogan: *"Populations abandonnés, confiez-vous au soldat allemand"* (You have been abandoned. Put your trust in the German soldier). Were Parisians to identify themselves with a forlorn child? This piece of propaganda pierced deeper into the subconscious than any other throughout the occupation, memorable, perhaps, for the way it both goaded and soothed.

Museums, post offices, banks, and the metro were back in service without much delay. Although clocks had been brought forward one hour to correspond to the Greater Reich time, already by July 5 the curfew had been extended to eleven o'clock, and soon it was to be midnight. Outside restaurants the telltale signs of *"Hier spricht man deutsch"* had replaced "English spoken." Germans made themselves at home in cabarets and nightclubs, like Don Juan, Eve, Chez Elle, and the famous Tabarin and the Lido, all of them in full swing only a fortnight after the armistice. It was perfectly possible for French and Germans alike to stay there until five in the morning, when the curfew was lifted.

Education, suspended just before the annual exams, was reorganized with efficiency, so that as early as July 18, the *préfet de police* Langeron was writing in his diary that approximately seven hundred schools were reopening, and seven big lycées and numerous primary schools. The Institut Pasteur, he observed, was back at work, as were the Ecole des Beaux-Arts, the Ecole des Langues Orientales, the Conservatoire de Musique, the Musée de l'Homme, and the Palais de la Découverte.

The exchange rate had been fixed at twenty francs to the Reichsmark, although the Berlin stock exchange quoted slightly over seventeen, and therefore any transaction in the shops was a bargain. Items like clothes, especially gloves, and food and drink of a quality long since unobtainable in Germany, vanished from display.

As German scout cars and trucks rumbled purposefully through streets without other traffic, French traffic police saluted them, according to new orders, in the way their German counterparts did. The eagerness to oblige seemed a telling little symbol of who were the masters now. If soldiers struck up a conversation with French bystanders they uttered platitudes like *"Krieg kaput, gut. Krieg nicht gut."* Did that require an answer? Should a Frenchman who spoke German pretend not to, when asked a question? Or was it a matter of principle to give a misleading answer? Or, on the contrary, to give a particularly polite and comprehensive answer, to show that French manners remained what they had always been, even in the presence of Germans? Was it in order to stare as another squad came goose-stepping along behind its fifes and drums, for ceremonial duties outside one of the requisitioned hotels? Should one put one's fingers in one's ears when a platoon out on a training march passed singing the *"hallis"* and *"hallos"* of some typical song? Did one move aside for a German walking on the pavement, or instead try to maneuver him into stepping down? If one of them gave up his seat on the metro to a lady, ought she to accept? What if the telephone rang, and there was some German friend or acquaintance from before the war asking if he could pay a visit? Was it all right to have him in the

A jockey weighing in; he happens to have the Gaullist Croix de Lorraine on his owner's colors.

house in uniform, or only on condition that he changed out of uniform, or had he better be allowed no nearer than a café? How individuals responded was a matter of temperament and hazard, though later their lives were sometimes to turn on such imponderables.

Simone de Beauvoir, who was shortly to settle down in the Bibliothèque Nationale to read Hegel, felt that in general she had been condemned to rot away. On July 1, she wrote, the café where she had been sitting was invaded by tarts, "so much so, indeed, that it's like walking into a brothel." She left for a tour of the city by herself. "Followed the Seine most of the way back. People swimming and boating in the Grand-Jatte: holiday atmosphere, though somewhat oppressive. When the car stopped close to a bridge a German soldier there threw us a bar of chocolate from a truck. Some of them were standing beside the road, chatting very cheerfully with a group of pretty girls. 'There'll be plenty of little Germans on the way soon,' the driver remarked to me. I've heard this phrase a dozen times, never with a hint of censure attached to it. 'It's just human nature,' said the driver. 'You don't need to talk the same language for that.' I haven't seen the symptoms of real hatred in anyone yet."

The day after these fraternizings, Sacha Guitry happened to return from his exodus into the unoccupied zone, bringing with him the elderly philosopher Henri Bergson. Actor, dramatist, impresario, libertine, a husband five times over (Yvonne

23

Printemps was one wife), Guitry incarnated the flamboyant style of entertainment for which the Paris theater had been famous for so long. In order to discover what he might appropriately do next, on July 3 he saw Roussy, the *recteur* of the Académie, who was standing in for the absent minister of education, and also the German authorities. Encouraged by them to return to the stage, by the end of the month he had put on a play about the scientist Pasteur, in which the words *"Vive la France"* were spoken. Guitry claimed to be exercising his profession and, more than that, defending the values he stood for. Virtually the only other play on in Paris was Michel Duran's *Nous ne sommes pas mariés,* which had opened at Les Ambassadeurs on July 11. *La Gerbe* reviewed it with sarcasm: "In these serious times, the spectator is confronted with an agonizing dilemma: is it better to deceive one's wife discreetly, or to make her openly unhappy by desiring another woman? And after this we shall probably feel rubbed up the wrong way and shriek at the tops of our voices when accused of being frivolous!" Business-as-usual proved that fighting was over and done with for good; consequently the staging of plays was to the German advantage. Occupation and normality were shown to be one and the same thing. Would it then have been more suitable to give no public performances of any kind? So drastic a solution was never contemplated: nobody at the time argued that a complete close-down would be preferable to the German manipulation and exploitation of entertainment. When driven to defend himself after the liberation, Guitry declared with some passion that the only thing which distinguished him from everyone else dealing with Germans was that he was prominent and talented. As for frivolity, *La France au Travail,* one of the new papers, in its issue of September 25 made a pun that immediately entered folklore. Albert Willemetz was the French Irving Berlin or Ivor Novello, and the paper said of his new operetta, "We may have lost Metz and other towns but we have Willemetz, and that's a consolation."

During the autumn, when the theater as a whole was once again in full swing, the season's successes included a comedy by Armand Salacrou, *Histoire de rire,* and two plays by Jean Anouilh, *Le Bal des voleurs* and *Léocadia.* Both authors were in Paris throughout the war. The Opéra reopened on August 24 with *The Damnation of Faust.* Hervé le Boterf's book *La Vie parisienne sous l'occupation* is an exhaustive (not to say exhausting) summary of every kind of artistic manifestation during the period, and he states that box office receipts for this performance were ten times those of June 5—also that in the four years of occupation the Germans alone purchased opera tickets to the value of six and a half million francs. Four days later, on August 28, the ballet company at the Opéra, under the new direction of Serge Lifar, gave *Coppélia.*

Meanwhile the stock exchange was functioning again (and continued to do so until the liberation), and by mid-October so were virtually all institutions down to the Sorbonne, the Ecole Normale Supérieure, the exclusive Jockey Club, and the racecourses at Longchamp and Auteuil. It was at the races, according to Serge Lifar, that everyone who was anyone went to be seen, whether they were young German officers or the Paris smart set.

So although Paris had been turned inside out, like an old coat, it proved to be made of much the same material as before. If some of the prominent names were absent, plenty were left to take stock of one another. Marie-Laure de Noailles (née Bischoffsheim, daughter of a Jewish banker and, as a patron of the arts, the backer of Luis Buñuel's film *L'Age d'or*) had remained in her house all along. German soldiers would have requisitioned it and made off with her splendid Goyas had she not received a document from Ambassador William Bullitt claiming that the property

A film entitled *The Rothschilds* is on the program in this *Soldatenkino,* to which civilians are forbidden entrance.

was American. Serge Lifar had stayed in her house while the Germans entered Paris, whereupon he was swamped with offers of work—in 1942 alone he was to visit Germany three times—and Hitler, Goebbels, and Goering were variously to receive him with admiration and flattery. Comte Etienne de Beaumont, another social figurehead and a patron of the arts and of artists, also kept open house for French and Germans while angling to become director of the Opéra. José-Maria Sert, the designer and artist who had been at the forefront of every avant-garde for fifty years, had a berth in the Spanish diplomatic service (nominally ambassador to the Vatican), and he remained in Paris, together with his wife, Misia. "The largesse he dispensed in his lordly way was in brutal contrast to the deprivations suffered by almost everyone else," write the biographers of Misia Sert; "nevertheless, it was very much welcomed by his friends." One of these friends, Boulos Ristelheuber, recorded in his diary one such typical evening, with the Duc d'Harcourt and Coco Chanel as guests, the latter going into a long tirade against the Jews. "Fortunately she was sidetracked when everyone agreed that Catherine d'Erlanger's emeralds are nothing but bits of green bottles. . . ."

Botti, the Italian ambassador, was prominent in the diplomatic corps, which was now reduced mostly to representatives of countries friendly to the Axis, for instance Hungary and Rumania and Bulgaria. The neutrals as a rule maintained consulates.

25

A Brazilian attaché, Souza da Dantas, was fashionable, and the Swedish consul general, Raoul Nordling, acted as a go-between with the German authorities, coming into his own at the close of the occupation. At the Mexican embassy was the cosmopolitan multimillionaire Charles de Beistegui. Another South American with diplomatic privileges was the playboy Porfirio Rubirosa, who married the film star Danielle Darrieux in 1942 and was notorious for all-night parties where Django Reinhardt played jazz otherwise unacceptable to the German ethos. The British embassy became a furniture repository, and three thousand British subjects, nannies and grooms for the most part, had been rounded up and had to endure the war in a special internment camp at Saint-Denis, where the main complaint was boredom; but those over the age of sixty-five were released, so that an elderly Englishman like Edward Gordon Craig lived unharmed. This grand old man of the theater spent the war in Paris writing a book. Antonin Artaud, another trend-setting theorist of drama, was shut up in an asylum, but after his release was to be found wearing sandals and no socks in all weather. Balenciaga, Nina Ricci, Paul Poirier, Lucien Lelong, Jacques Fath, Dior, continued the traditional haute couture. Coco Chanel was to hole up in the Ritz with an aristocratic German officer; she scarcely emerged from her ivory love nest except to go on a dubious mission to Spain, neither quite cocotte nor quite spy. Paul Valéry continued to lecture on poetry at the Collège de France. Georges Duhamel and Simenon and Jacques de Lacretelle, Léon-Paul Fargue and Marcel Jouhandeau and Jean Giraudoux, went on writing as before (when a book of his was banned, Duhamel declared to his censor that it was impossible to do such a thing to one of the national glories like himself). Colette and Jean Cocteau were neighbors in the Palais Royal, both hard at work, neither hesitant about contributing to the collaborationist press. In *La Gerbe*, on December 5, 1940, Cocteau published an "Address to Young Writers," which contained more rhapsody than sense. "A prodigious task solicits you. . . . Think, write, adore, start little magazines. Put on plays. Trample over us. I am a specialist in destiny and its mysteries, believe me. Seize your chance. It's here." Among eminent scholars who remained were Paul Hazard and Fernand Lot, who was a Communist.

Georges Braque was in Paris throughout the war, lying low, though exhibiting, notably at the Salon d'Automne of 1943. Pablo Picasso also returned after the exodus from his seaside villa in the unoccupied zone to his studio on the Quai Saint-Augustin, and never left Paris again during the war. André Derain, Charles Despiau, Maurice de Vlaminck, Foujita, were there, and Marie Laurençin, who took to bartering her pictures for food.

Composers in Paris included Olivier Messiaen, teaching at the Conservatoire, and the young Georges Auric, who was also writing reviews of music in the newspapers. Music was a sphere in which German supremacy could be acknowledged quite naturally. Jean Bérard, artistic director of the recording company Pathé-Marconi and a leading light in the Paris musical world, explained in a public lecture in 1941 how "since the armistice I have spent—if I add up all my visits—nearly three months in Germany," in order to conclude that "Fascist and Hitlerian doctrines are today championing civilization." The pianist Lucienne Delforge was eager to strike the heroic pose too, typically writing in *Paris-Midi* on April 19, 1941, "I hear voices telling me that France is in her death throes, Paris is dead. These voices are wretched in their corrupted love. These voices are lying and envious. These voices are false." Paris under the Germans, she thought, was being invigorated; collaboration, she said, meant "Mozart in Paris." Alfred Cortot, in spite of his age still in the top flight of pianists, was one of the first to give concerts in Germany. Throughout the war Cor-

The Kommandantur, on the Place de l'Opéra, contained the offices of the Kommandant von Gross-Paris, and virtually every Parisian had to apply there for requisite permits or other routine business.

tot's prestige lent glamour to many a Franco-German social occasion in Paris and even Berlin, as did that of Germaine Lubin, the singer who at the Bayreuth festival of 1938 had been singled out for praise by Hitler himself. Speidel in his memoirs has recorded how she and Max Lorenz sang in the Paris production of *Tristan and Isolde* on Wagner's birthday, May 22, 1941, with Winifred Wagner, the composer's English-born daughter-in-law, attending a party afterward (when Speidel was posted to the East in April 1942, Germaine Lubin sang Schubert songs for his farewell). The conductor of that *Tristan* was Herbert von Karajan, who was frequently in Paris during the war. So were other German musicians, like Wilhelm Kempff, Eugen Jochum, and Willem Mengelberg, the latter giving popular Beethoven recitals. Clemens Krauss inaugurated concerts for workers in the Paris factories of Gnôme-et-Rhone, the giant steel and engineering company. Wilhelm Furtwängler, however, refused to come to Paris, remarking that he wished to be invited to conduct thanks to his talent alone, and not the army's presence.

The Laboratoire Curie at the Collège de France had not been touched, and its famous head, Frédéric Joliot-Curie, returned to Paris on August 9 to resume work; he also ran the Institut du Radium. Before the war Joliot-Curie had been an anti-Fascist, but there was nothing he could do to prevent reaching an agreement that German researchers would be engaged under him. A colleague, Professor Paul Langevin, also a fellow traveler and anti-Fascist before the war, was among the first Frenchmen to be arrested, on October 30. Langevin was held for a little over a month and released partly because of Joliot-Curie's intervention; he finished the war in Switzerland. Joliot-Curie was cut off from the mainstream of nuclear research which was taking place in America, but all the same he was able to teach and experiment. By 1942, he had joined the Front National, which was run by the Communist party, and he was to stay in Paris until its liberation.

Julien Cain, curator of the Bibliothèque Nationale, was among the first to be victimized as a Jew. He was replaced by Bernard Faÿ, a Catholic and an author who specialized in attacking Freemasonry. Someone else to be sacked was Jacques Copeau, chief administrator of the Comédie Française. Among actors who worked in the company throughout the war were Marie Bell, Mary Marquet, Madeleine Renaud, and Jean-Louis Barrault, and the latter's interpretation of Corneille's *Le Cid* may have had some connection with Copeau's downfall. Several people wanted this prestigious job, among them Michel Bourdet. Léautaud recorded the infighting. "When Bourdet had his bicycle accident, which was serious, he asked Copeau (a producer along with Jouvet, Dullin, and Baty) to stand in for him until his recovery. When, just lately, he returned to take up where he had left off, Copeau answered him, 'Ah, no, I'm here and I'm staying.' Bourdet learned that in World War I Copeau and his sons had made a number of rather anti-German speeches in America, where they had been sent for propaganda. So he procured quotations of these speeches in American papers, as well as accounts of the speeches, and went to show the lot to the Germans. They insisted upon the immediate departure of Copeau. Bourdet started again in his post as administrator. But then the Vichy government no longer wanted him and nominated the illustrious Jean-Louis Vaudoyer instead"— that "illustrious" being sarcastic, for Léautaud considered the new man a nonentity. Still in the limelight were Mistinguett and Edwige Feuillère, Alice Cocéa, and the distinguished old actress Cécile Sorel. Edith Piaf found it convenient and safe in wartime to rent the top floor of a brothel for herself. Generous to the point of folly, she earned up to twenty thousand francs for a night's performance—the equivalent of an office worker's annual salary, according to Le Boterf. In the closing year of the

The former premises of W. H. Smith in the rue de Rivoli were converted into a German bookshop.

occupation, she helped to launch a newcomer to the music hall, Yves Montand. Maurice Chevalier lived mostly outside Paris but came in for singing engagements, in particular on Radio-Paris, for which he was heavily paid (but he had to pay more heavily still after the war).

Wives and widows of famous men provided continuity, like Madame la Maréchale Juin, Madame Poincaré, and Madame Courteline, widow of the playwright, excluded because she was Jewish from watching a rehearsal of one of her husband's plays at the Comédie Française. There was also Madame Edmond Drumont—as the leading French anti-Semite of his day and persecutor of Dreyfus, Drumont, long since dead, had come into his own posthumously and was now claimed as a major influence from the previous generation. Sylvia Beach, friend of James Joyce and owner of a famous bookshop, and Samuel Beckett on his Irish passport, and Le Corbusier, the planner of the house as a machine-for-living, were variously to be found in wartime Paris. Adding curious cosmopolitan touches were a handful of American Fascists such as John Hemming Fry, a good number of White Russians, not only Lifar but the dancers Ludmilla Tcherina and Gontcharova, and Polish émigrés, and Swiss, and from time to time the deranged English Nazi John Amery, who was to murder his French wife and end on the gallows in London, as well as assorted Algerian and Moroccan nationalists who were pro-German like Sidi Ben Thami. Enough semblance of the prewar structure and the prewar personalities, then, had survived for the game of Who's In, Who's Out, in society, the arts, and the sciences, and so to produce that appearance for which the Germans were striving, of a Paris as civilized as ever, but happier, purified, the showpiece of the new order.

Caviar was still to be purchased at Petrossian's. Hermès, Cartier, Boucheron, the luxury shops of the Faubourg Saint-Honoré, maintained standards not to be matched anywhere in occupied Europe. Dealers in pictures, books, furniture, indeed antiques of all kinds, enjoyed a boom. The leading auction house, the Salle Drouot, had never known such affluence, mostly due to speculators anxious to turn ill-gotten cash into something of lasting value. The sale of the Viau collection on December 11, 1942, realized a record 47 million francs, including 5 million for Cézanne's *Montagne Sainte-Geneviève,* sold to a German. Paris's best-known brothel, One Two Two, its name deriving from its address at 122, rue de Provence, was placed out of bounds to the occupation forces by the German authorities. The madam of the establishment, Fabienne Jamet, has recounted in her autobiography (naturally titled *One Two Two*) the high jinks of keeping her girls and her clients satisfied, providing them with the unlimited food and champagne to which they had been accustomed. She and her husband succeeded, raking through the black market and the underworld with which they had close ties. Her book is a study in joyful name-dropping. "I can say I have never been so happy," was her final verdict on the occupation.

Fouquet's, Lapérouse, the Marquise de Sévigné, the Tour d'Argent, Le Grand Véfour—these celebrated places remained exactly what they had always been. Maxim's, outwardly the same as ever, had been taken over by Horcher, the famous Berlin restaurateur. Night after night prominent or visiting Germans, Goering above all, and their French friends were shown to their tables by the old headwaiter Albert (his surname was Blaser) with a courtesy for which he was held accountable after the war.

In *La Vie parisienne sous l'occupation,* Hervé le Boterf has this description of the pleasures and perils of eating out: "One could have one's fill at the Berkeley, Chez Laurent, at the Pavillon de l'Elysée, at the Pré Catalan, at Claridge's, Ciros' in the rue Daunou, Chez Carrère, whose rooms were booked by Sacha Guitry for a New Year's supper party among friends. President Laval thought that lunch at the Café de Paris was of a high enough standard, for he invited there . . . a number of personalities who, quite exceptionally—was it not snobbery?—had to produce bread coupons. On the Place Gaillon, Drouant maintained its reputation, besides serving meals to the jury of the Goncourt Prize. The clientele was mainly French. Chez Pierre, opposite, was on the contrary favored by Germans. Nobody was in two minds whether or not Barnagaud, the *patron* of Prunier in the rue Duphot, was a Gaullist. His wife, it was said, had remained in London. In any event, while continuing to serve fish as before, Barnagaud kept an eye on his customers' security. He welcomed people wanted by the German police. . . . Any collaborator worthy of the name canvassed for admission to the Cercle Européen, that superclub on the Champs-Elysées, managed by Edouard Chaux, who had created the Lido, and which René Lefèvre compared to a 'sumptuous rubbish bin' because every profiteer could be found tucking in there. . . . In the Catalan, rue des Grands-Augustins, juicy chateaubriand steaks were grilled to perfection, and there Léon-Paul Fargue had one of his last outings before his stroke. At Picasso's table were sometimes grouped Eluard, Desnos, Braque, Leiris, Sartre, Auric, Simone de Beauvoir, and Albert Camus. . . . At the Niger, rue de la Fidelité, the *patronne* was a splendid African lady who had had her skin whitened, and at the Casita, rue de Washington, foie gras canapés washed down with champagne could still be procured." As usual, it was a question of knowing the right addresses and connections, and of course having enough money.

Comfortable social habits of the kind did not apply to official Paris, now so reduced that it was scarcely recognizable for what it had been. Not only were the majority of the personalities of the Third Republic absent but its expansive prewar style was defunct. The Ministry of Finance and the Banque de France continued in Paris as before, but the other ministries were now in Vichy and maintained only delegations in the former capital. Laval, at the Hotel Matignon, was a law unto himself. To all intents and purposes France had been absorbed into the German continental scheme, and Hitler, satisfied with strategic outlines, was content now to leave administrative details to the Wehrmacht.

After the armistice, the entire occupied zone was subdivided into regions, with regional offices, and placed under military government. This structure was intended to last as long as it might be required. Those stopgaps, Generals von Studnitz and von Briesen, were replaced by a Militärbefehlshaber in Frankreich, or military governor in France, General Alfred von Streccius at first. Streccius was over sixty-five and had been recalled from the reserves. For many years he had been a military adviser in China. Hidebound, with a Junker mentality, he was no friend of the French. In order to accommodate the military governor, his adjutants, and his staff, the Hotel Raphael was requisitioned. In addition, the military governor took over a private house known as the Palais Rose, on the avenue Foch. It had been built by the Marquis Boni de Castellane, but then belonged to Mrs. Florence Gould, to whom had come a share of one of the greatest of American fortunes. In the Vallée de la Chevreuse, twenty kilometers outside Paris, an old abbey had been taken over to provide a weekend retreat for the military governor.

The Majestic Hotel, off the avenue Kléber, had been requisitioned for headquarters. Sentries stood at the entrance. No Frenchman was allowed in without a pass. The hotel bedrooms had been converted for the ever-growing number of officials—eventually about 1,100. The Militärbefehlshaber had under him a military staff (Colonel Hans Speidel as chief of staff) and a Verwaltungsstab, or administrative staff, with Dr. Jonathan Schmid as its permanent head, carying the rank of minister. Schmid was not in the best of health, but was a somewhat stronger figure than his bureaucratic colorlessness might suggest. The Verwaltungsstab was comprised of two main sections, the first of which was for economic affairs, and headed by Dr. Elmar Michel, assigned from the appropriate Reich Ministry. When Schmid became too ill to continue at the end of 1941, Michel succeeded him. Michel was responsible for subordinating the French economy to the German war effort. After the war, he was tried before a Paris court, where his acquittal was taken to absolve the Verwaltungsstab as a whole. The second Verwaltungsstab section coordinated all branches dealing with civilian matters, from agriculture and transport to justice and the police. On August 1, 1940, Dr. Werner Best was appointed its head.

Members of the various Majestic sections were almost all selected for technical competence, having been drafted from ministries in Berlin. A high proportion were lawyers. Conservative and nationalist in outlook, they were pleased and proud to have France at their disposal, but their ethics as well as their skills had been shaped in pre-Hitler Germany, so that military government was not interpreted in the Majestic as a pretext for party methods. The odd man out in this milieu was Best, and his failure to assert himself in the early months of the occupation was not the least of the military government's achievements. Best possessed the zeal and fanaticism required for Nazi promotion to the top. At the age of eleven, he claimed, he had

Overleaf: **A party visiting the Louvre, amused by one of its most celebrated sculptures,** *The Hermaphrodite.*

31

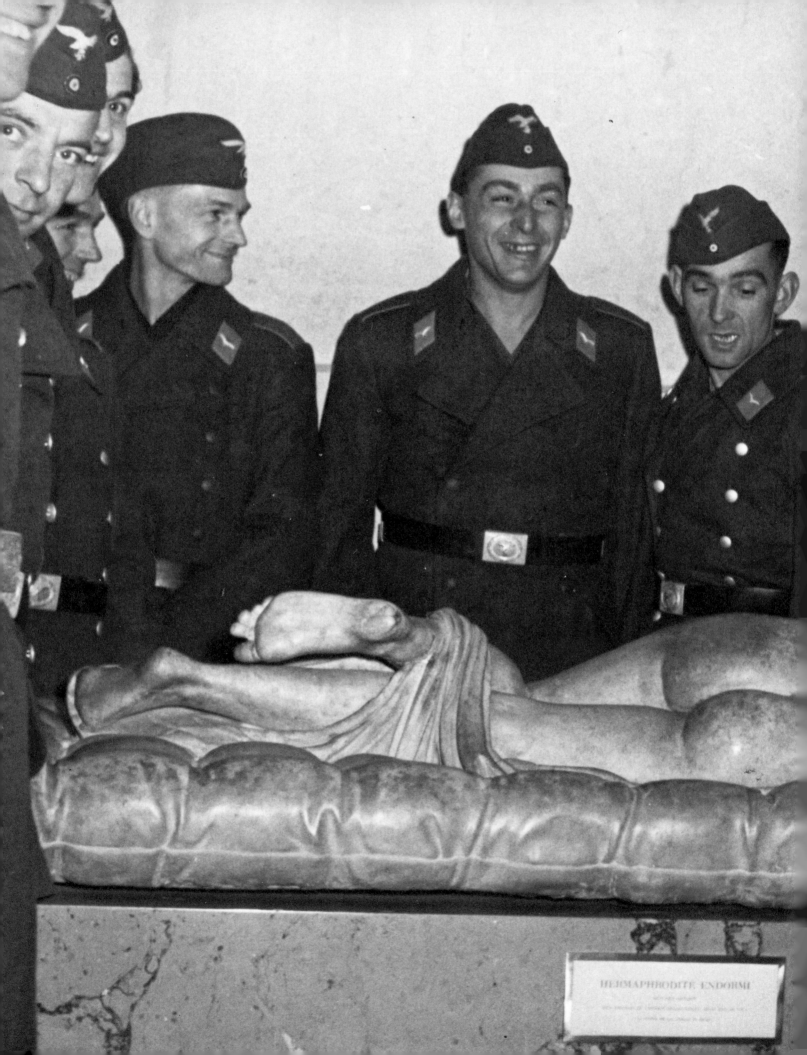

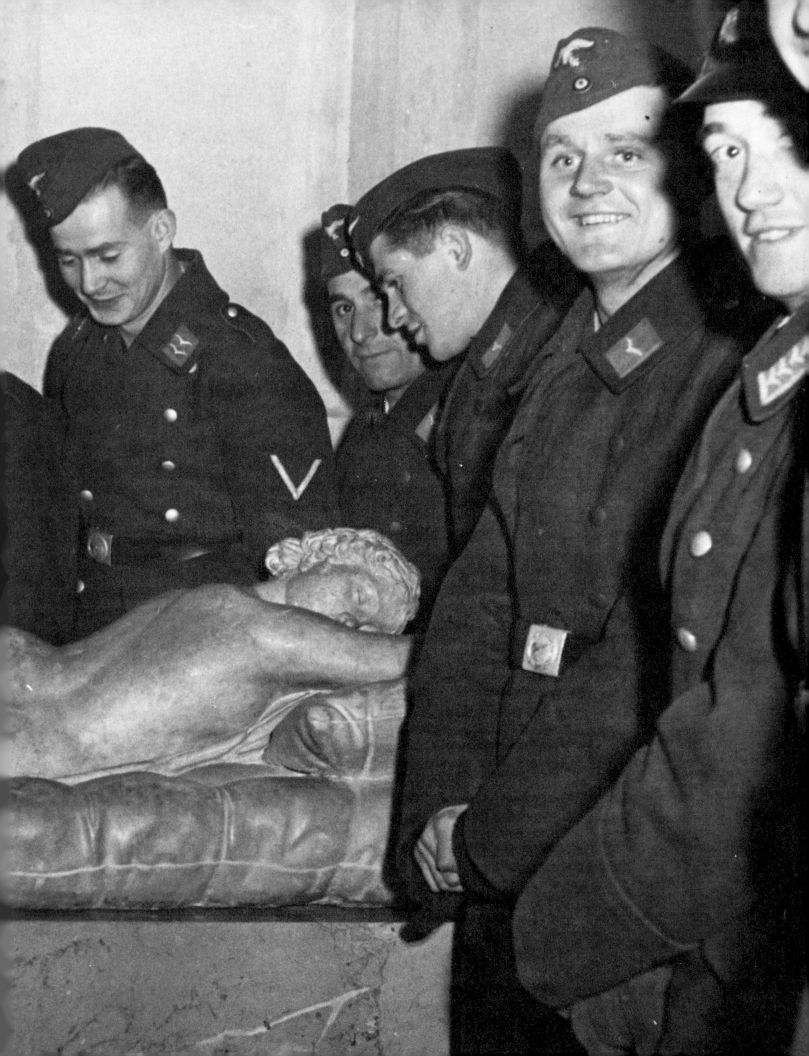

begun his struggle against the French, who were then occupying his native Rhineland. In 1931 he had participated in the so-called Boxheimer incident, which purported to be a Nazi-inspired coup but in fact was a display of the underhand means the Nazis were prepared to use in order to achieve their ends. Swiftly Best rose in the ranks of the Gestapo to become an SS *Brigadeführer.* In the Polish campaign he brought up the rear with the SS, and after the war he was to stand accused of the murder of tens of thousands of Jews during that autumn of 1939. For reasons which are obscure, he fell out with his immediate superior, Reinhard Heydrich, and was fobbed off with the Paris posting.

To Best, as he puts it in his memoirs (which remain unpublished), General Streccius seemed "preoccupied with ancient Chinese wisdom on the lines of Taoism—inaction, as a result, was preferable to action." Dr. Schmid displayed "through and through the most irenical powers of toleration and passivity." In the autumn of 1940, Streccius was replaced by General Otto von Stülpnagel, at whom the frustrated Best threw epithets like nervous, ambitious, persnickety, narrow-minded. Only with Speidel could he strike up "a real confidential relationship." Meanwhile his opposite number, Jean-Pierre Ingrand, the Paris delegate from the Vichy Ministry of the Interior, aided by his interpreter Dr. Wilhelm, seemed to him "a wonderful jurist in the French style." Best also dealt with Vichy ministers or delegates such as Jean Bichelonne, François Lehideux, Jacques Barnaud, and Jacques Benoist-Méchin, from whom arose no complaints about his administrative decisions and practices.

Paris itself and the departments of the Seine, Seine-et-Marne, and Seine-et-Oise were subjected to separate local administration, under the responsibility of the Kommandant von Gross-Paris, or commanding officer of Greater Paris, The Chambre des Députés was taken over, decked with swastikas, and converted into offices for the Kommandant. Across its front was stretched a banner: *"Deutschland siegt an allen Fronten"* (Germany is victorious on all fronts). More sentries at the door, more ceremonial duties. Modeled on the system at the Majestic, here too was a division between a military staff and a Verwaltungsstab, whose head, from June 16, 1940, until the spring of 1941, was General Harald Turner (he was posted to Yugoslavia and killed there by partisans). On the Place de l'Opéra was the Kommandantur, a large building designated by a huge white billboard with Gothic lettering on it. French civilians came here to transact whatever routine business might concern the Germans or required some special authorization.

Though in fact Gross-Paris was simply one of the regions subordinated to the Militärbefehlshaber, the arrangement nonetheless recognized the symbolic importance of the city. The Kommandant played a prominent role in public life; he was in evidence at the races, a figurehead in his box at the opera or at receptions and parties. Until August 1, 1940, General Alfred von Vollard-Bockelburg held the post. He was replaced by General Ernst von Schaumburg, a veteran of the old school, his hair close-cropped, in every respect a Prussian officer as traditionally conceived. According to his secretary, Ilse Grose, he was known as "Rock of Bronze" to his staff. "Old Shatterhand" was another of his nicknames, cribbed from the Wild West novels of Karl May. The Kommandant lived at 24, avenue Raphael, in the villa belonging to the perfume manufacturer François Coty. This had the advantage of being in the Bois de Boulogne, where Schaumburg was to be seen out riding punctually at seven o'clock every morning. The garrison troops which came under his command usually numbered about 25,000, including sappers, engineers, and other specialists. In 1943 a false report was spread by the Communists that Schaumburg had been assassinated by a grenade thrown at his car. This continues to be propagated in Communist literature, and spreads sometimes into more scholarly books. No such attack happened. Because of his age, Schaumburg was duly pensioned off in 1943, and he died after the war in his hometown in northern Germany.

One German general looked very much like another to the average Parisian, who was no expert at distinguishing badges of rank such as the width of the red stripe on Wehrmacht trousers, or the telltale lapels and collars and braid on jackets. To add to confusion, the commander of the Wehrmacht armies in the West had headquarters at Saint-Germain-en-Laye. Scattered around Paris were specialized Wehrmacht delegations such as an arms control commission under Colonel von Horn, a Rüstungskommando, or weaponry unit, under Colonel Elsässer, and General Max Thoenisen's mission to coordinate the production in France of mechanized vehicles.

Each and every Nazi minister or leader in Berlin felt obliged to have his or his ministry's interests represented in Paris. A microcosm of the Reich was thereby created; all sorts of domestic pressures and quarrels were reflected at long distance in a Paris setting, and the powers of the military government inevitably challenged and infringed. Viewed in the perspective of the Wehrmacht and the Majestic Hotel, the history of the occupation is the history of these inter-Nazi disputes for primacy and power. Bormann had a sinister shadowy figure, von Hummel, to look into whatever concerned the Nazi party or Hitler personally. Goebbels had his delegate, Dr. Berndt. General Friedrich-Carl Hanesse of the Luftwaffe, Goering's man, was sumptuously installed in the Rothschild house on the avenue Marigny. The Luftwaffe headquarters were in the Palais Luxembourg, and Goering also kept a private suite there. The Kriegsmarine had occupied all the installations of the Ministère de la Marine, including the naval ministry itself on the Place de la Concorde. Both Luftwaffe and Kriegsmarine maintained their own armed units of several thousand men, elite troops, imbued with Nazism to a greater extent than the Wehrmacht. Ordinary soldiers in Paris, either in transit or on leave, had at their disposal a *Soldatenheim,* literally a soldiers' home; the most prominent of these were on the Place Clichy and the Carrefour Medicis. For airmen, there were lodgings, a *Fliegerunterkunft,* on the Champs-Elysées, and for Luftwaffe officers a *Haus der Flieger* nearby in the rue du Faubourg Saint-Honoré. A number of French cinemas and theaters were converted into *Soldatenkinos,* reserved exclusively for occupation troops and showing only German films or entertainments. All over Paris were *lokale,* or army canteens, mostly in former restaurants, from which the French were banned unless provided with German permits. On the Place de la Sorbonne a German bookshop was started. Near it was a similar venture, the Rive Gauche bookshop, this one Franco-German; it was managed by Henri Bardèche and had the monopoly of selling books to the French prisoners of war. On the boulevard Saint-Germain was the Librairie Italienne.

Three hospitals were requisitioned for the German army. Some prisons, like the Santé and Fresnes, had German and French sections under separate jurisdiction, while others—the Cherche-Midi, Romainville, the Fort de Vincennes, with the Mont Valérian execution grounds—were reserved for exclusive German use. The central post office in the rue du Louvre was under control of the German authorities, who also took in hand cable and telegraphic traffic in the main exchange at the rue des Archives, acquiring unlimited possibilities for supervision, though it seems that not more than a few hundred telephones were tapped.

The historic center of Paris, in the grip of so much German activity, had its appearance transformed correspondingly. Along the Champs-Elysées were Radio-Paris and Radio-City, in the former Normandy Cinéma, both broadcasting stations now collaborationist. *"Radio-Paris ment, Radio-Paris est allemand"* (Radio-Paris is lying, Radio-Paris is German) ran the Gaullist slogan over the BBC from London. This was a reference to the leading broadcaster, Jean Hérold-Paquis, whose refrain was that England, like Carthage, had to be destroyed. He and his colleague Jean Azéma, who later joined the Waffen SS, could truthfully claim a national following. At 31 and 33, avenue des Champs-Elysées, in the old Marignan Cinéma, was the Organisation Todt, which commissioned whatever construction works the German army needed, subcontracting with French firms as well as directly recruiting a work force. Half a million French workers were paid above-average wages by the Organisation Todt to build fortifications along the whole coastline, submarine pens, bridges, bunkers, landing strips, communication centers. None of these workers were accused of collaboration afterward, though theirs was among the most significant of all French contributions to the German war effort. Some offices were generally familiar to Parisians—for instance one in the rue Galilée, where all sorts of *laissez-passer* were issued—but others were more discreet, like the Reich national bank, or Reichskreditkasse, on the boulevard des Capucines, which handled the 400 million francs a day paid through Dr. Hans Hemmen's armistice commission. In the rue Pillet-Will was the Devisenschutzkommando, controlling the circulation of foreign currency and gold. A German military tribunal sat permanently at 53, rue Saint-Dominique, later transferring to 11, rue Boissy-d'Anglas. All over Paris, finally, and no secret at all, were the multiple branches of the German police services, the SS, the SD or Sicherheitsdienst, the Gestapo, and the Geheime Feldpolizei or military police. These services came together under one roof at 11, rue des Saussaies, which was consequently considered "Gestapo headquarters" by the average Parisian. Previously this had been the Sûreté Nationale, and its archives were intact.

The senior personnel of this comprehensive network, wishing to live up to their stations, often decided not to be crowded into some hotel but instead expanded into a house left empty by absent owners, probably English or Jewish. Neuilly was a favorite spot, although the grander apartments in the center would also do. Some officials preferred the richer suburbs, like Garches and Marly. Wherever they were, they kept open house, entertaining in the style to which they considered Paris was accustomed. Dress uniforms. Soldier-servants in white gloves. Silver, expensive linen, the best food and wines, plenty of French guests to be impressed, and especially French women to balance the numbers. If tensions were to be discerned at these occasions, they were caused by the need to guard prerogatives among the many competing and overlapping services of the administration. Paradoxical as it may seem, waste of manpower and resources was integral to the system. Early in 1943, General Walter von Unruh arrived in Paris with a brief to rationalize duplication in the occupied territories; Unruh had promised Hitler that two army corps would be released from Paris for active service, and he did indeed draft tens of thousands of men to Russia, earning himself the nickname "Heldenklau" (the Clawer of Heroes). For all their enjoyment of the good things of Paris, the occupation officials from top to bottom knew that shifts of power in Berlin, or sudden whims of the führer or the party, might put an end to this most comfortable of wartime billets.

Of all the German institutions, only the embassy in the rue de Lille predated the war, although between August 1939 and June 1940 it had been closed down. Now its position was anomalous, for military government on the face of it excluded conventional diplomacy. The embassy, however, was the preserve of Foreign Minister von Ribbentrop, and he was no less determined than his colleagues and rivals to protect his interests. He nominated as his representative Otto Abetz, at first with the task merely of liaising with the Militärbefehlshaber in the Majestic Hotel. Although effectively German ambassador in Paris, Abetz was not accredited as such until late in 1940. By then it had become obvious that the complex styles and tones of Paris required more careful management than the simplicities of Vichy.

Abetz was a good choice to orchestrate a Franco-German entente. First of all he himself believed in it and had since his youth. Out of conviction he had joined the Deutsch-Französisch Gesellschaft, also known as the Comité France-Allemagne, which aimed at friendship between the two countries, although it was in fact a Nazi front organization typical of the period. Abetz was a teacher of art by profession. He had spent a good deal of time in France, he liked the country, and he spoke the language well. Among his many French friends was the salon journalist Jean Luchaire. One of Luchaire's secretaries was Suzanne de Bruyker, whom Abetz had married. Not long before the war Abetz had been enrolled by Ribbentrop into the foreign ministry section dealing with France, and in 1939 he was in Paris for purposes which have never quite been elucidated. In July he was accused of espionage and deported amid public outcry. To send Abetz back eleven months later in an important post had a symmetry which pleased Hitler, though he could never bring himself to overcome a suspicion that Suzanne Abetz was working up a pro-French bias in her husband. Twice, from December 1942 to the following November, and from March to May 1944, Abetz was in fact recalled by Hitler, whose complaints were groundless. Though Abetz had a mind of his own, and offered recommendations, he served Nazi policy faithfully.

In 1940 Abetz was thirty-seven, handsome if a little coarse, and confident of himself as a man with a mission. His initial brief from Ribbentrop was to assure "political control of the press, radio, and propaganda in the occupied zone and as far as possible to extend this influence to public opinion in the nonoccupied zone." The first minister in the embassy was Rudolf Schleier, who had been a prisoner of the French in World War I and whose hard-line Nazism had a spirit of revenge about it. The political section was placed under Dr. Ernst Achenbach, who had been on the embassy staff before the war and had good social connections.

To help Abetz inaugurate the embassy, two men with special expertise were temporarily recruited, Dr. Friedrich Sieburg and Professor Friedrich Grimm. Sieburg, then in his sixties, was a journalist in the public eye, on the staff of the *Frankfurter Zeitung*. A book of his about France with the tongue-in-cheek title *Wie Gott in Frankreich*, or in its French translation *Dieu est-il français*, had given him a reputation as a critic who meant well. Grimm, a lawyer and a member of the Reichstag, had for years been writing on Franco-German relations, and the argumentative tone of his innumerable articles and pamphlets did not conceal bile, and even hate. One book of his, *Hitler et la France*, written palpably to deceive in the appeasement years before the war, had an introduction by Ribbentrop. Grimm was a die-hard Nazi of long standing. To enlarge the German presence, Ribbentrop also sponsored the Deutsche Institut, to which he appointed Dr. Karl Epting. In prewar Paris Epting had run an office coordinating academic exchanges. He spoke excellent French.

Such, then, were the associates whom Abetz gathered in Berlin on June 14. They flew off that very day, with an overnight stop in the Ardennes. When they drove into Paris the next morning, Abetz was impressed that workers in what he knew were Communist districts turned out to wave at him and his party—the Russian-German Pact, as he saw for himself, had brilliantly disarmed opposition at a stroke. Grimm, in his memoirs *Mit Offenem Visier*, has also left a description of entering the city and reaching its deserted center. "Slowly we turned into the rue de Lille and arrived at the old building of the German embassy. Herr Grabowsky, who had remained there as the embassy's sole employee, and to whom the building's supervision had been entrusted, rushed out to meet us: '*Mein Gott,* where have you come from?' We reclaimed possession and settled ourselves in under the roof in the private quarters of the former ambassador." Losing no time, Grimm set off to find a friend, the mayor of Versailles, who told him that if their joint advice had been heeded, war would have been avoided. Next Grimm was off for more of the same kind of conversation with a former minister and appeaser, Eugène Frot, and to an acquaintance called Maurice Ribardière, who invited him to lunch with Pierre Laval. The politics of the occupation had begun.

At the end of that first week, the embassy was not yet shipshape for its first function, a lunch on the day the armistice was signed. One of the guests was Georges Oltramare, really called Charles Dieudonné, a Swiss (though in fact a paid agent of the Germans, as his trial after the war would reveal). "The armchairs in the salon had dust-sheets on. In the midst of packing cases and half-opened trunks, meals were being improvised in the cozy spirit of a family *pension,*" Oltramare wrote in his book, *Les Souvenirs nous vengent.* "There was the solid Schleier, a rich trader from Hamburg, Councillor Achenbach, thin, blond but balding, suave voiced but always alert, Dr. Feilh, his eyes bright and full of malice behind gold-rimmed spectacles." Out they all drove to Compiègne for the drama, and Abetz was to confide in Oltramare, "I have been receiving parliamentarians, municipal councillors, *préfets,* magistrates. Out of fifty of these dignitaries, forty-nine have asked me for special permissions of one sort or another, or for gasoline coupons—and the fiftieth spoke of France."

Very shortly, cards were engraved (in a French shop) with the words *"Botschafter Otto Abetz und Frau Abetz geben sich die Ehre zum Déjeuner einzuladen. . . ."* At these lunches the best etiquette would be observed: King Otto I, as Céline called him, knew how these things were done. Moreover, Abetz and his wife entertained at weekends in the beautiful eighteenth-century house at Chantilly which was put at their disposal by the French government (just as after 1945 it was lent to Duff Cooper, the new British ambassador). Some Parisians may have refused invitations to the embassy, but if so, they have left no authenticated record of having done so. The embassy became the forum par excellence where French and Germans could meet. Abetz's influence on Parisian life was all the more pervasive because the military governor had no alternative but to leave clear the social and political fields. The rue de Lille and the Majestic Hotel were therefore soon polarized.

The Deutsche Institut was in the rue Talleyrand, in the former Polish chancellory, also known as the Hotel Sagan. Epting complemented Abetz in the position he won for himself in Paris, though he was a somewhat unbending and donnish man. The German Youth Movements, in which romantic nationalism was soon clouded into Nazism, had influenced him. To promote collaboration, he edited a pompous bilingual journal, *Deutschland-Frankreich Revue.* In 1943 he published a collection of his essays, *Frankreich in Widerspruch,* mainly trite reflections on French writers like Robert Brasillach and Henry de Montherlant and Pierre Drieu la Rochelle. In Céline, whom he praised immoderately, he found a pretext for some anti-Semitic observations of his own.

The Institut offered German language courses which proved popular—thousands of students enrolled. (The main competition here came from the Berlitz School, whose advertisements in the collaborationist papers throughout the war left no doubt about the advantages of being able to speak German. But then all teachers of German were in demand. Among the classified ads in *L'Oeuvre* on December 19, 1940, is one, quite typical, for a teacher of German, "Aryan and if possible of German origins.") Other programs were quickly organized too; for instance, by October 25, 1940, Dr. Gross was already lecturing on the social organization of the Reich, followed the next day by Dr. Funke on German poetry. Visiting pianists like Walter Gieseking or Wilhelm Kempff were seized upon for a choice concert. Sometimes there was not much subtlety about Institut activities. To show the meaning of collaboration, a series of lectures on "Germany and Eastern Europe throughout the centuries" was held on April 22, 1943, and the occasion typified how French and German speakers could be made to appear as though in a common cause: Professor Seraphim talking on the economics of the occupied territories, Professor Aubin on their demography, Professor Herbert Schrade on the interaction of the German spirit with local cultures. "Germany took to those parts the stamp of European genius, and its mission there has been profoundly civilizing," wrote Gaston Denizot, reviewing these lectures in *La Gerbe,* just in case the point had been missed that France too was supposed to be in the process of being civilized by that self-same European genius.

Epting's assistants included Karl-Heinz Bremer, a minor writer whose blond good looks caused tremors in the homosexual milieu of Paris. Bremer had been lecturer in German at the Ecole Normale before the war. From 1941 he organized French writers to go on propaganda tours in Germany, and when he was eventually transferred to Russia, and killed there, his obituaries were fulsome. "You will always arise for us like a young Siegfried conquering evil spells," was a characteristic phrase, coined by Brasillach, who seems to have had feelings akin to hero worship for Bremer. Bremer was replaced by Professor Georg Rabuse, an Austrian literary critic who coedited a poetry anthology during the occupation.

Serge Lifar, himself a habitué of the Institut (and of the embassy too) wrote in his memoirs that among the mass of intellectuals and artists and socialites to be found there were Count Metternich, the military government's art expert, the playwright Giraudoux, and Comte Etienne de Beaumont, whose own house "was wide open for Franco-German intellectual contacts which were much encouraged by Marie-Laure de Noailles, Marie-Louise Bousquet, Antoinette Duchesse d'Harcourt at the head of the writers, and Georges Auric as the leading musician. Their special darlings were Friedrich Sieburg and Herbert von Karajan."

Admiration for the Germans made such people rather more close-knit and full of mutual congratulation than smart sets usually are; they could be quite sure that going to parties was also setting a political example; they felt themselves purposeful, contemporary, and in the limelight; or at least thrilled to be tempting providence. A spirited account of these upper reaches of Paris collaboration has been written in a memoir, *Pariser Begegnungen,* by Epting's wife, Alice, who was Swiss. She took her duties as the Institut's hostess seriously. For instance, when the Schiller Theater company from Berlin, under its director Heinrich George, gave a performance at the Comédie Française of Schiller's *Kabale und Liebe,* Alice Epting found herself arranging much of the detail: she had to escort the actress Gisela Uhlen to a Paris hairdresser, who "made her look enchanting," and she held a reception after the performance. *Signal,* the fortnightly illustrated magazine put out by Goebbels's ministry of propaganda, published photographs of this occasion in April 1941 showing groups of guests including Abetz and Schleier, Speidel and Serge Lifar, Gisela Uhlen and her colleagues Else Peterson and Heinrich George. Or again, another big night of the Institut's was an open-air concert given by a German orchestra under Hans von Benda in the gardens of the Palais Royale to commemorate the 150th anniver-

Mealtime in a kindergarten.

Looking after oneself at Les Halles market.

sary of Mozart's death. Or there was a dress show for Alice Epting to arrange at the Institut with Lucien Lelong for the French, and Benno von Arendt, Hitler's favorite designer, for the Germans. She herself had evening clothes made by Henry à la Pensée and laughed at herself for sporting those period hats, which she called "a shrub of artistic flowers or a small floral arrangement in the most varied forms and colors worn somewhere in the area of the left eye."

To the Institut came Jean-Louis Barrault and his wife Madeleine Renaud, Jacques Hébertôt, who ran the Hébertôt Theater, the producer Gaston Baty, Arno Breker and his Greek wife Mimina, Cocteau and Céline, Lucien Daudet, Alfred Cortot, the artists Charles Despiau and Paul Belmondo (father of Jean-Paul Belmondo, the actor), Professor Ernest Fourneau of the Institut Pasteur, and Alexis Carrel, the natural philosopher who had returned from New York in 1941 to launch his "Institut de l'homme" in what had been the offices of the Carnegie Foundation on the boulevard Saint-Germain—in short, not to enter the Institut's orbit was altogether exceptional. At the liberation, Alice Epting remarks pointedly, some personalities "whose names had become world-famous" wished that they had not been so forthcoming. When Sacha Guitry, for instance, a good guest as well as a good host to her, denied contacts of the kind, she wrote, "We Germans, who know better, willingly forgive these little circumstantial lies, for we honor the man of the theater." Even her butler Pierre had to answer for his behavior, putting on white gloves and a tailcoat, delighted to exchange compliments with Friedrich Sieburg, and providing the necessary food for parties through his "pals" in the black market.

At his trial after the liberation, Brasillach, accused of being a German propagandist by virtue of frequenting the Institut, answered that charity prevented him from mentioning everyone he had met there. But "the only time in my life when I met M. Gallimard, today the eminent publisher, was in the German Institute. I can say that everyone who mattered went there. M. Duhamel [laughter in court], I saw him at the German Institute. . . . I lunched with Jean Giraudoux at the German Institute and I don't think Jean Giraudoux was a traitor, celebrated as he is today by resistance papers, practically like a martyr. . . . I believe one could go to the German Institute like an ambassador to a foreign country."

Alice Epting and Suzanne Abetz shared a bosom friend, Nicole Bordeaux, at whose house in the rue de la Boétie were to be found "diplomats, industrialists, writers, actors, painters, sculptors, officers, and many of the young." A consumptive, Nicole Bordeaux had not the health to survive her arrest at the liberation. Alice Epting simply referred to another close friend as Girouette, meaning weathercock. "She was very eager to share our German-French way of thinking. She never missed a single reunion of Germans and French. She owned a very beautiful, large house in the avenue Charles-Floquet. . . . For someone French, she spoke fluent German, which enabled her to be associated with the Deutsche Institut as a language teacher. She did not let the matter rest there but hit on the idea of translating German books into French. . . . Madame Girouette also gave cocktail parties for German and French personalities. She had the knack of receiving and making the most of it . . . at the time she campaigned within her circle for true German-French understanding." Shortly before the Germans had to evacuate Paris, Madame Girouette left for the south of France. She returned a changed woman. Meeting her in the street at the eleventh hour, one of her former German friends (Alice Epting herself, no doubt, though she does not say so) asked, "Don't you recognize me anymore, Madame Girouette?" To hear the retort, "For the time being, things are different, everything's altered, and now I'm in the resistance."

42

Finally, since June 14, other Germans had installed themselves and their institutions in an altogether more clandestine manner. Colonel Rudolph, for instance, of the Abwehr or military intelligence, with Major Leyerer and Major Waag, nephew of Admiral Wilhelm Canaris (who was the head of the Abwehr in Berlin), took over the Hotel Lutétia. Fifty officers and men, with twenty women assistants, were to operate intelligence services there. Their first task was to appropriate files in the Ministry of War and in the Sûreté Nationale, at 11, rue des Saussaies, where in the future each branch of German intelligence and police was to share in a centralized bureau.

An undercover detachment of twenty more men had driven to the Hotel du Louvre on June 14. They had worn uniforms of the military police, but had been in unmarked cars. They were in fact from the Sicherheitsdienst (SD) and the Gestapo, twin branches of Himmler's Reichssicherheitshauptamt, or RSHA (the French were never to bother with departmental niceties, but used the label Gestapo to cover the whole lot). Whichever branch they were affiliated to, these were the instruments chosen to give physical expression to the political pressure and will of the Nazi party.

The leader of the small advance Sicherheitsdienst squad was SS Standartenführer Helmut Knochen. Though his name (meaning "bones") sounds odd in German, Knochen came from a respectable family. Only thirty, he was rather too dark in looks for Himmler's racial preferences, but tall and presentable. He passed as an intellectual. He had studied literature and been awarded a doctorate in the University of Madgeburg, his hometown. He spoke English and French. Instead of teaching, he had entered journalism, writing for the official news agency, Deutsches Nachrichten Büro (DNB), which continued to provide him with a front once he had joined the party and the SD. The Paris Exhibition of 1937 had been a useful pretext for him to reconnoiter the city at leisure. Shortly after the outbreak of war, he had distinguished himself in the kidnapping of two gullible English intelligence officers over the Dutch border, an exploit which drew the attention of the head of the SD, Reinhard Heydrich, and Knochen was rewarded with the Paris post.

SS Sturmbannführer Herbert Hagen had driven into Paris with Knochen as his assistant. A would-be academic and journalist too, he had the career advantage of friendship with Adolf Eichmann, who was in charge of the RSHA department dealing with policy toward the Jews. Hagen had traveled to Palestine with Eichmann in 1937, and he considered himself an anti-Jewish specialist on the strength of it.

Knochen and Hagen and the SD detachment moved from the Hotel du Louvre into the Hotel Scribe, with offices at 57, boulevard Lannes, and eventually headquarters at 72, avenue Foch. Nearby, at 82 and 84, avenue Foch, were additional premises, and by the end of a long and highly successful implantation over a two-year period, the SD and Gestapo had branches and substations throughout the city, with armed guards, garages, fleets of black cars, thousands of French informers at all levels of society, and the privilege of doing what they pleased. To complain back to Berlin about them was in effect to complain against the party. The Militärbefehlshaber and the Majestic had panoply, Abetz and the embassy had cachet, but Knochen and the party had power.

3 From the Camp of the Conquered into the Camp of the Conquerors

Collaboration, as an expression in daily usage, arrived with the Germans, although it acquired specific political currency only after Pétain and Hitler held their meeting at Montoire on October 24, 1940. Photographs of the two men shaking hands were published everywhere. "It is with honor," Pétain declared, "and in order to maintain French unity, a unity which has lasted ten centuries, and in the framework of the constructive activity of the new European order, that today I am embarking on the path of collaboration." What was good enough for Pétain was good enough for the man in the street. What else was constructive activity in the new European order if not growing crops that might feed Germans, or producing goods for the German economy? With or without troubled consciences and national susceptibilities, life had to go on as best it could—and that, Pétain was to argue at his trial after the war, had been the sum of his policy.

Besides, he was in Vichy, and by October he had been overtaken by the activity of his vice-president, Laval, in Paris. There, as every Parisian already knew, collaboration was the Laval-Abetz friendship. Brought together by such contacts as Professor Grimm, the two men had hit it off. In the German embassy Laval could be heard declaring that he had "saved the nation." Inwardly he was convinced that "the only way to moderate the Germans is to buy their goodwill, to play, besides, the carpet dealer." Not only did Abetz happen to like Laval personally, but he realized his extreme good fortune that any interlocutor at all had turned up on his doorstep, let alone a bargain hunter of this stripe. First impressions lasted. Abetz was to defend Laval through thick and thin.

Knowing that business would detain him in Vichy for much of the time, Laval needed a permanent representative in Paris. For the purpose he summoned Fernand de Brinon. Born in 1885, the son of a marquis, de Brinon was a right-wing journalist who between the wars had devoted himself to the proposition that Hitler was a man of peace. Active in the Comité France-Allemagne, he had been the first Frenchman granted an interview with Hitler. On receiving Laval's telephone call, de Brinon hurried to Paris, and in his memoirs he described how he found Abetz, Schleier, and Grimm at the embassy. "The renewal of contact was moving. Abetz did not conceal how painful the situation was: the führer was very aroused, and likely to be brought around to other feelings only with difficulty. He told me that the *policy of sacrifice* which was about to be imposed could only be put into practice by people like myself...." In the event, de Brinon was officially instructed by Pétain "to study all matters relating to the renewal of relations with Germany," and by the end of the year he had been granted the title of delegate—*"délégué général du gouvernement français dans les territoires occupées."* In the absence of Laval from Paris, Vichy business could therefore be transacted through de Brinon. The bizarre effect was to have a French ambassador to the Germans in Paris, and de Brinon gloried in his title of *"Excellence."* Conversely, the Germans had contrived through this delegation to have Vichy imported into Paris.

After the Montoire meeting, de Brinon explained in his memoirs, "in Paris, crowds of Frenchmen volunteered to do the dirty work for the Germans. Someone named Boitel, whom the Préfecture de Police put up with as a liaison to the German departments, and someone named Capgras denounced me as a friend of the Jews and an agent of the Intelligence Service. . . . Little by little it was necessary to get to know the right leaders, to explain, and carry weight as decent Frenchmen among decent Germans." His own role, he said, was to be the shock absorber between French and Germans, and he even managed to look the part; insignificant in stature, he was a head smaller than the German officers he moved among. In 1941 he requisitioned the house in the rue Rudé belonging to the Princesse de Faucigny-Lucinge (neé Ephrussi) on the pretext that he was actually saving it from requisition by Himmler in person. Madame de Brinon (neé Lisette Franck) was Jewish and lived most of the time in the country, since a divorce was not considered appropriate under the circumstances. Lunching in the rue Rudé in October 1941, the writer Ernst Jünger noted in his diary how de Brinon mocked *"youpins"* (a pejorative term for Jews) in front of his wife, Speidel (who was the guest of honor), and Sacha Guitry. Next to Jünger was the film star Arletty, who, he observed, was equally triggered off to laughter and gaiety by the word "cuckold."

More an ambitious busybody than anything else, de Brinon shared with Laval the instinct to compromise, to bow to superior force, and therefore he accepted shocks rather than giving them: a creature of the shadows, Céline called him. Collaboration, or that policy of sacrifice which Abetz had evoked so insinuatingly, could not have been feasible otherwise. What Laval had constructed via de Brinon and his delegation was the instrument whereby he and his like in Paris could tell Vichy what had to be done. To ensure this instrument's effectiveness, the Germans had only to render services in return, to grant permissions or exemptions to those who had proved themselves worthy of receiving favors, or who were perhaps sufficiently well placed to be able to demand them. Parisians felt, so wrote Pierre Audiat in *Paris pendant la guerre,* that the only means of gaining access to the Nazis was through de Brinon. The delegation, whose offices were in the Hotel Matignon, "was assailed by every sort of request, from some in search of privileges or gifts at the disposal of the Germans, and from others put into a panic by some desperate or even hopeless plight. This was an excellent vantage point to harness people, to measure appetites, sound out consciences, learn each supplicant's weaknesses and secrets, to exercise finally pressures and blackmail."

The element of deception masked German policy: an impression was created that the French were actually in charge of their own affairs. Had the Germans given orders directly to the population, hostility and even resistance would certainly have been provoked. Moreover, it was quite out of the question for Germany to provide the manpower necessary to run even the occupied zone, and therefore the French administration had to be used in its entirety. The only practical solution for the Germans was to turn the French into the instruments of their own coercion. Therefore Frenchmen who could be manipulated by the Germans had to be interposed between themselves and the mass of the citizens. This was Laval's and de Brinon's function; this was Vichy's great service to the German cause. The cunning lay in the fact that the Lavals and de Brinons and collaborators who lent themselves to this could argue that they were preserving French institutions and the French way of life. Otherwise, they maintained, the Germans would be free to administer a system of military government at will, as in Holland, Belgium, or Poland. The argument was self-seeking, to be sure, and, granted how thinly German resources were already stretched, defeatist in the extreme, though in the last analysis it is impossible to be sure what the consequences of a truly nationalist French response would have been. A real policy of sacrifice, perhaps.

As it was, the difficulties arose when the Germans became dissatisfied with some aspect of the French performance. Then, instead of correcting it themselves, they sent for Laval and de Brinon and their kind, who had to use their offices for their true purpose of bringing about whatever was demanded by the Germans. So in the logic of the collaborationist position were concession and surrender. So much so, indeed, that no collaborator could shield himself from the accusation of aiding the Germans to win the war, thereby consummating the defeat of democratic and republican France.

To resign—so ran the argument of prominent officials like the *préfet* Achille Magny, Roger Langeron, or Pierre Taittinger, the president of the Conseil Municipal who was running the Paris administration at the Hôtel de Ville—was unprofitable, since someone out-and-out pro-German could always be found as a substitute, and besides, all influence on events would be lost. Yet nothing could be done without prior liaison with the Militärbefehlshaber or Kommandantur. At every level French policy was controlled by a German with powers of veto and compulsion. To remain in office was by definition to be compromised. Later, men who had stayed at their posts were to claim that overtly they had been collaborating with the Germans, while covertly they had been in touch with resistance groups, to whom they were passing on information. Exceptional bravery and duplicity would be required for such behavior, of which there were indeed instances among ordinary people—firemen, doctors, one or two men doing business with the German army—but almost none in the higher echelons of the civil service.

The loyalty of the police was indispensable to the Germans. No doubt it was also comforting to Parisians that the *flic* in his familiar blue uniform was still on the beat. "How could it conceivably have happened," General A. Martin of the French Gendarmerie was to ask rhetorically after the war, "that the Gendarmerie of the Paris region, comprising a legion of Gendarmes, three legions of the mobile Garde Républicaine, a legion of the Garde Républicaine of Paris, with a special tank unit at Satory, under the command of a general . . . could continue its existence, intact, from June 14, 1940, the day of the occupation of Paris, until August 25, 1944, the day of liberation?" Unquestioning obedience had been instilled into these policemen, who all together usually outnumbered the entire German garrison. Resignations, defections, or lack of cooperation would have seriously impeded German control of Paris, perhaps even the maintenance of law and order.

Adrien Dansette, author of a standard work, *Histoire de la libération de Paris,* wrote that by August 1944 three separate resistance groupings among the Paris police numbered fifteen hundred, a thousand, and two hundred adherents respectively, or about 10 percent of the total police force. No source is given for these figures, which seem unduly high. A glimpse of the atmosphere within the Préfecture is to be found in *Cinq ans de patience,* the diary of Maurice Toesca, a civil servant with literary inclinations who was transferred to the *préfet*'s staff in September 1942. On arrival, he invited a police sergeant, Auguste Ransant, to assist him. He was already acquainted with the man, but he began by sounding him out. "I am anxious to know who can be relied on in the Direction, as well as those who are doubtful, of whom we must be suspicious. Answer: it is better to be suspicious of everybody. . . . No secrets with me about his position: he is a Gaullist, inscribed since October 1940 on the registers in London. He asks for my support in this respect, should 'anything happen.' I give him my word. Blanket approval equally for the papers and fake identity cards which he was to have made by those in charge of identity cards. I insist that he is serious in everything he undertakes: a fake card must be more real than a real one. . . . He promises to act with the necessary skill." Toesca depicts himself bending the rules to extend Picasso's permit to live in Paris; coping with an appeal from the Imprimerie Nationale on behalf of a printer arrested by the Germans; rescuing the publisher Gaston Gallimard and his nephew from being sent to work in Germany. Had this been the rule, not the exception, Vichy and its policies would have been little more than a phantom.

Traditionally the Paris police was a cohesive unit all of its own, detached from the Police Nationale, which came under the Ministry of the Interior. The *préfet* himself was not a police appointment, but a bureaucrat. The Préfecture de Police, known to those who worked there as the "Maison," possessed all the usual police branches and services and had powers of arrest. Representatives of the Militärbefehlshaber and the SD moved into the building at once and issued instructions. Early in 1941 Langeron was dismissed and for a while held in custody; far from being proud of it, he lobbied Vichy to have his job back. His successors, Admiral François-Marie-Alphonse Bard, René Bousquet, and Amédée Bussière, occupied the most awkward position in Paris, morally and politically, though in practice none found it too hard to run with the hare and hunt with the hounds.

For purposes of regimentation, a docile press was almost as essential as a loyal police force. Varied and vigorous newspapers had always been a significant feature in Paris, an intellectual stimulus as well as a standing challenge in the political arena. At the moment of the exodus, papers had ceased publication, and several of the best, such as *Le Temps* and *Le Figaro* and *Paris-Match,* did not intend to return to Paris, because publication in the unoccupied zone offered an alternative. Well aware that the vacuum created by the absence of a press could not be sustained, the Germans had assembled in advance their own suitable journalists and specialists, who were among the first troops entering the city. Before the war Hauptmann von Grote, for example, had been director of the Paris office of the Deutsches Nachrichten Büro, the DNB, or official German news agency. On June 14 he drove straight to the premises in the Place de la Bourse of the main French news agency, Havas. This hitherto independent private agency was then restructured as the Agence Française d'Information de Presse (or AFIP); under another German specialist, Sonderführer Hermes, it put out news and features which had been carefully doctored. Yet another former DNB correspondent, Sonderführer Weber, moved into the offices of *Paris-Soir,* the mass-circulation paper belonging to Jean Prouvost. The entire staff had fled, with one exception, Jean Schiessle, left behind as janitor. Schiessle had no proper editorial experience but nonetheless was ordered by Weber to set about starting up the paper again. Weber assisted by contacting French journalists, weeding out some, appointing others as he pleased. Power seems to have gone to Weber's head, and he was dismissed—only to resurface in the black market.

Early improvisations and initiatives were rapidly brought under the umbrella of the military government. The Propaganda Abteilung (department) was one of the major sections of the Militärbefehlshaber's staff, exercising censorship, influencing the appointment of French journalists and editors, indeed in absolute control of public opinion for the whole country. The Propaganda Abteilung came within Best's responsibilities, though its actual head was Major Heinz Schmidtke, who had the signal disadvantage of not speaking French. His assistant was Graf Schönfeld.

So important a section was bound to be subjected to bureaucratic interference, not only locally but from Berlin, with consequent shuffling and reshuffling. The Propaganda Abteilung was subdivided into *Staffeln* (staffs), one for each of the country's regions, the most important obviously for Paris. Other *Staffeln* existed within the

Abteilung to supervise censorship and to control the theater, broadcasting, films, the arts, the publication of books, and last but not least, the allocation of paper. The Propaganda Abteilung offices were at 52, avenue des Champs-Elysées, spread over several floors to accommodate so many branches. Any Frenchman earning his living in the arts or the press had to pass through these offices, where he could be judged on performance, and his degree of independence measured out accordingly.

To maximize confusion, there was Abetz's brief to control the press; the embassy accordingly developed a press department and a press attaché, Hans Schwendemann. Another field opened up for the duplication of services. The Propaganda Abteilung had no alternative but to issue bulletins and directives from Goebbels's Ministry of Propaganda, whereas the embassy was following the Foreign Ministry line. On Tuesdays and Thursdays, therefore, journalists found themselves receiving briefings at 52, avenue des Champs-Elysées, but on Wednesdays they were at the embassy. Protracted rowing between Abetz and Schmidtke followed, exactly reflecting the long-drawn and venomous feuding between Ribbentrop and Goebbels, which was a fact of life in Berlin. In the end the embassy had the better of it, but not before French journalists had been able to win more room for maneuver than might otherwise have been the case.

For the benefit of the Germans in the occupation, the Ministry of Propaganda published a weekly, the *Pariser Zeitung.* The offices of *L'Intransigeant,* a prewar anti-German paper, were taken over for the purposes, and the costs were demanded by Dr. Hemmen as part of the armistice agreement. The *Pariser Zeitung* contained official German handouts, but also reviews of the arts of a reasonable standard, as well as uncommitted fiction. No doubt the paper's purpose was to make the Germans feel that they had settled comfortably into Paris. Restaurants and nightclubs were written up and advertised. Announcements of where to go and what to see served as a guide: for instance, "The evening concert of the Kommandant von Gross-Paris will be on October 23 from 10 to 11 o'clock in Notre-Dame Cathedral. Bach, Haydn. Lucia Rach-Strassburg (contralto) and the regimental band of the Luftwaffe. Conductor Kurt Rienecker. At the organ Heinz Boger. Entrance free." French businesses paid for classified ads of this kind: "Upholstery materials, Silks, Percale, Curtains et cetera from Jeanne Bary, 83, rue La Boétie." The *Pariser Zeitung* also ran a French-language section with free-lance contributions from the pro-German small fry, Maître René Picard, R. Jullien-Courtine, Henry Coston, with occasionally more unusual personalities such as two anti-British Iraqis, Said Khoury and Habibi Rahman. *Signal,* another promotion of the Ministry of Propaganda, was released throughout the world in many languages including French, and was in fact widely bought for the quality of its color photography.

Temperament and opportunity played a determining part in what was to prove a crucial sphere of collaboration. On June 15 a broadsheet appeared with the title *La Victoire.* Its editor, Gustave Hervé, did not intend this to be interpreted as an anti-French jibe, declaring himself to be "with Hitler in his heart, with the man, with the German patriot." *Le Tempête* was a comparable sheet subsidized briefly but expensively by the embassy on behalf of Maurice Delaunay, who had one alias as François-Henry Promethée and another as Le Maître de Feu (The Master of Fire). He was a provincial Nietzsche dotty enough to write in alexandrines. Neither venture survived.

Le Matin, one of the leading dailies, as well as one which had not disappeared in the exodus, reappeared as early as June 17. The paper had been encouraged by the *préfet de police,* Langeron, who believed that the press would contribute to sta-

Selling official Nazi papers, in this case the *Völkischer Beobachter* on the Place de la Concorde in 1941.

bility and published a letter in *Le Matin* to say so. The paper's first editor was Jean Luchaire; his successor Jacques Ménard took to signing letters with *"Heil Hitler."* The proprietor, Maurice Bunau-Varilla, a very rich elderly South American, sympathized with Hitler's Germany, and at his funeral during the course of the war one German at least, Schwendemann of the embassy, was seen to weep. Bunau-Varilla, in the style of a press baron, brought Germans and French together in his house. In his dining room were not only a set of Raphael tapestries but on the table small French and German silk flags, according to Breker, a frequent guest.

Luchaire is said to have been the very first man in Paris contacted by Abetz. Luchaire, after all, was the close friend to whom Abetz had applied for the hand of his wife Suzanne. Before the war Luchaire and his paper *Notre Temps* had been receiving hidden subsidies from the Quai d'Orsay. Now he had only to continue the habit through the German embassy.

One of Luchaire's daughters, Corinne, was a minor film star, and in her memoirs, *Ma drôle de vie,* she drops names of friends like Rex Harrison, Count Ciano, and Aly Khan. Growing up, she had been amused to observe Abetz flirting with Suzanne de Bruyker. Now she called at the embassy with her father. "He told me that he had accepted the editorship in chief of *Le Matin* and he explained that Abetz had become ambassador and was in constant touch. He told me how very interesting it all was and how he was going to have a lot of work, in liaison with the new ambassador. I do not know why, this revelation gave me an uneasy feeling."

Luchaire's frame of mind at the time is revealed in a letter that he wrote on July 25 to the well-known journalist Jacques Chabannes, offering him the editorship of a proposed new paper. "I am back in Paris after having contacted Pierre Laval. I am sure you know that Otto [Abetz] is German ambassador. He will be in residence in Paris, not Vichy. The old friendship between him and me will explain a good deal. What is certain is that as *Le Temps* has fled to Clermont, I shall be starting up a big evening paper in Paris. . . . One must press on, my dear Jacques; one can't turn back in melancholy to a past that has been scrapped. We are young—we should not mourn but build." The consequences were that Luchaire was promoted from *Le Matin* and started publishing his *Les Nouveaux Temps* on November 1. The most influential (and best-written) of collaborationist papers, it became more and more doctrinal as the Nazi situation demanded and, needless to say, inflexibly supported its sponsors, Abetz and Laval.

A lot of work, in Corinne Luchaire's expression, did indeed come her father's way. He had his finger in many pies: in the German-promoted AFIP news agency; in a French-German newspaper holding company managed by a dubious figure with the name of Gérard Hibbelen, whose nationality was uncertain; as head of the Press Corporation set up to provide a corporate structure for the entire press. That he had personal charm is certified by Simone Kaminker, later to become the actress Simone Signoret, who had been a school friend of Corinne Luchaire's. Thanks to this friendship, at the age of nineteen she became the secretary at *Les Nouveaux Temps* between September 1940 and June 1941. Her job consisted of such errands for Luchaire as buying flowers for the German actress Zarah Leander on her way through Paris, and taking calls from Achenbach and Abetz or his wife. The office was luxurious, with a couch in it, Simone Signoret wrote in her memoir, *Nostalgia Isn't What It Used to Be,* and Luchaire received many people there. "I watched a whole raft of ladies pass rapidly through that padded doorway during the winter of 1940; some because their husbands were prisoners and they wanted them back (one even returned with her husband a few weeks later to say thank you), and others because they needed a quick permit for some commercial enterprise. Occasionally there were men and women who were so nervous before they went through the door that I knew their affairs would not be discussed on the big couch. . . . I saw very few of these same people do anything at all for Luchaire when he was condemned to a death he probably deserved. The only appeal for mercy filed at his trial was the one I forced my father to send when he came back in 1945."

To Luchaire, journalism was the best of facilities. He lived extravagantly; he was to be seen in the best restaurants with wads of notes. A business trip to Belgium at a time when food was scarce yielded him nine hundred francs' worth of meat, six liters of cream, fifty eggs, and twenty kilos of butter: he had short-term priorities, believing only in doing himself a good turn. As in the comparable case of de Brinon, the sudden access to power, coupled with self-indulgence, was covered over with a veneer of "New Europe" ideology.

La Révolution Nationale was another paper to receive secret subsidies from Laval, in this instance engineered by its editor Jean Fontenoy, an adventurous journalist and a born conspirator, who was also among the first callers at the embassy. Once a war correspondent in China, he had published two books about his experiences. He had fought in the Finnish campaign. To complete a saga which might come straight from a Malraux novel, his wife Madeleine was a well-known aviator, and when she died, he succumbed to drugs and despair, volunteered for the Waffen SS, and died fighting in the closing days of the war, a short distance from Hitler's bunker.

Fontenoy's paper was right-wing. Laval had once been a socialist, and he persuaded Abetz that if another organ existed to stress the social aspects of National Socialism, the left, and in particular the Communists, might rally to it. *La France au Travail,* a daily, was launched on German money. Its first editor was Oltramare, whose account recaptured how the Laval-Abetz empire-building proceeded. "The embassy dreamed up a plan to start a daily aimed at the trade unions and the working class. The lawyer, Picard, was given the task of recruiting among the Moscow brethren. Picard, a rancid and lugubrious cynic, who suspected blackmail, pederasty, and filth everywhere, beat up the most disappointing game with cries of triumph. 'I have stolen a march on Juliette Goublet! I'll have Maître Berthon! We'll lay lands on a cousin of Maurice Thorez!' Van der Brooke, half-crazed, a renegade from Marxism and more agitated than agitating, had hit on the title *La France au Travail.* Accompanied by the illiterate Houssard, he rigged up a dummy to flabbergast anyone. He was fired, but time was flying. How is a paper fixed up within a week? The first number was supposed to carry a June 30 dateline. Four days were dissipated in chat and on June 28, Friedrich Sieburg and Dr. Feilh proposed that I run *La France au Travail,* which had a printing press but no program. What next? I had forty-eight hours. On the boulevards I ran into Daniel Perret and hired him as editorial assistant. I set up my office in the premises of *L'Humanité,* rue Montmartre, where unrecognized geniuses, intellectuals on the dole, gossip penny-a-liners, hacks, came to solicit me, their copy clutched in hot hands."

Unlucky as Maître Picard and Oltramare might appear, hundreds of journalists were available to write for the collaborationist press out of conviction, wishing to express admiration for Hitler's Germany as well as deep-rooted anti-English sentiments. A number of prewar titles, *Paris-Soir, Le Petit Parisien,* and *L'Illustration,* were reshaped to suit the Propaganda Abteilung by men like Claude Jeantet, Henri Lèbre, Henri Béraud, Horace de Carbuccia (of *Gringoire,* now published in the unoccupied zone), Jacques de Lesdain, Robert de Beauplan—men who had enough reputation to attract readers.

Alphonse de Chateaubriant was certainly sincere in the inspiration for his paper *La Gerbe.* A country gentleman and minor novelist, he had visited Germany in 1936, met Hitler at Berchtesgaden, and retained afterward a quasi-mystical, if not crackpot, vision of Nazism. He was capable of writing sentences like: "And if Hitler has one hand to salute with, one hand to stretch out to the masses in his familiar style, his other hand, invisible, is in ceaseless embrace with the hand of Him whose name is God." White-bearded, with a heavy walking stick for his limp, at his side his mistress Madame Gabrielle Castelot (mother of the historian André Castelot, himself the drama critic of *La Gerbe*), Chateaubriant fitted some hoary notion of a sage; even quite hard-headed men like Dr. Epting believed in his greatness. Goebbels knew better, however, for when he received a letter in September 1943 in which Chateaubriant described the difficulties of being a collaborator, he commented candidly in his diary, "Chateaubriant is proceeding from the wrong assumption that the führer intends to do something special on behalf of France. That is not the case."

In its opening issue, on July 10, 1940, *La Gerbe* published Chateaubriant's interview with Pétain, to explain how collaboration would be "a network of complementary activities." It would not be long before Chateaubriant slipped into the further fantasy—all in his own messianic prose—that France and Germany were virtually

A selection of Nazi and collaborationist newspapers for sale at a kiosk on the Etoile. Note *La Gerbe,* on the lowest level, at the right.

one and the same. Still, *La Gerbe* had as contributors the collaborationist stars, Abel Bonnard, the Vichy minister of education, Cardinal Beaudrillart, Bernard Faÿ, Robert Valléry-Radot, Jacques Chardonne, Ramon Fernandez, the novelist of Argentinian origins, Sacha Guitry, the publisher Bernard Grasset, and Friedrich Sieburg. In its columns appeared fiction by Montherlant, Marcel Aymé, and Paul Morand, among others.

Its rival as an outlet for intellectuals was supposed to be *Aujourd'hui,* conceived by Abetz as a means of keeping the Paris literary marketplace bright and fresh. Henri Jeanson, its editor, was assured that he could pick his team freely and even promise them immunity from censorship—an illusion in the circumstances, for the first number, on September 10, 1940, was delayed a month thanks to a row with the censor. Few journalists were more in the limelight than Jeanson. Before the war he had resigned from *Le Canard Enchaîné* because of its Communist sympathies; he had written the script for the film *Pépé le Moko.* His pacifism sounded like teasing, but when he wrote an article in August 1939, "No, *mon Daladier,* we won't go to your war," he was sentenced to three years in prison. He was released on the eve of the German entry into Paris. To approach someone with this record was a clever calculation on the part of Abetz. Jeanson sought out his friends, the poet Robert Desnos, Marcel Aymé, Jean Anouilh, Jean Galtier-Boissière (who had chosen to close *Crapouillot,* the satirical weekly which he had edited), Guérin the cartoonist, and Marcel Carné, three years later the director of the famous film *Les Enfants du Paradis.* It was too good to last. After six weeks he was ordered to write an editorial committing himself to collaboration and was dismissed for refusing to do so. His successor, Georges Suarez, had written anti-German books before the war, but now recanted, switched tack, and brought *Aujourd'hui* to heel, suffering for it the fate of being the first intellectual tried and shot after the liberation.

Back at the Santé prison, as Jeanson told the story in his entertaining memoirs *70 Ans d'adolescence,* the jailer said to him, "What, you again?" Jeanson was to serve a further spell in 1942 because of a paragraph published by Alain Laubreaux. This was a reminder—as good as a denunciation—that Jeanson had once written an article in defense of Herschel Grynszpan, the teenager who in 1938 had shot dead a counselor at the German embassy in Paris in retaliation against ill treatment of Jews and his own father in particular.

Publications specializing in topics such as sports, car racing, or women's romance were allowed to continue as before. Otherwise Parisian papers shared the same format. The first page would lead off with a signed article, commissioned from within the circle of reliable and prominent collaborators, which was intended to be a guide to right thinking on the subject of the moment. German bulletins or dispatches filled out the remainder of the space. The turnover page contained a cartoon, almost without exception political, and below it "Echos," or "the talk of the town." In the form of short paragraphs, snippets, or even one-liners, these were potentially highly dangerous, because so easily exploited by anyone with a grievance. Regular features on pages three and four covered books, films, and plays, with a cooking column and a women's section. Reportage was more or less impossible as the war drew out. A good deal of space was occupied by serialized fiction, by writers like Drieu la Rochelle, Georges Simenon, Jean Anouilh, Marcel Aymé, André Thérive—indeed nearly every writer still active. Most had no alternative if they were to make a living. Jean Guéhenno was virtually alone among established authors in deciding not to publish at all as long as the occupation lasted; he could pay for this attitude by teaching at a lycée. Galtier-Boissière, after the brief *Aujourd'hui* experiment, also refused to publish; he sold secondhand books to make ends meet. Even known anti-Nazis were driven to seek publication for one reason or another. Sartre, who claimed that the line ought to be drawn at the collaborationist press, in fact wrote books and plays and the odd literary article for publication. *L'Etre et le néant,* the disquisition on German philosophy which was the basis of his professional reputation, was published in 1943 with the German censor's stamp of approval. Nothing that Sartre wrote in it about Heidegger or Husserl gave grounds for anything except official satisfaction.

Where opinion making and the press were concerned, collaborationists versus noncollaborationists was the latest of the many politico-literary realignments which have proverbially made Paris salons and cafés so enthrallingly contentious to those warring on the way in or out. Pierre Drieu la Rochelle brought a lengthy intrigue to a head when he dispossessed Jean Paulhan—hitherto kingmaker supreme in the realm of literary Paris—and in December 1940 took over the editorship of the prestigious magazine *Nouvelle Revue Française* (Abetz is credited with a crack that the Vatican, the Communist party, the Prussian general staff, and the *NRF* were the main forces in Europe). Drieu, who had coveted the job, did what he could to ensure the *NRF*'s standing, encouraging talent for its own sake, launching some contributors whom he knew to be Gaullists and even Communists. Malraux and Mauriac remained friends of his, in spite of political polarization. Galtier-Boissière warned

him in October 1940 that one day he would be shot. "What about you?" asked Drieu, to receive the answer: "Only by mistake." Incidentally the running preoccupation of who would be shooting whom, and in what circumstances, is particularly exemplified by Galtier-Boissière, who had the habit in public of roaring out "Have him shot!" at the mention of a name, any name, whether of Laval or de Gaulle or their respective supporters. Similarly in the French Revolution, groups of like-minded victims had been assembled for the guillotine by the public prosecutor, as though in a party game.

In Drieu the period's contradictions clashed head-on. His first wife had been Jewish, he lived off her money after divorcing, and he was vicious in his anti-Semitism. He had spent some time in England and become something of an Oxford aesthete, dressing like an undergraduate of the twenties. Yet he joined the Fascist party, the PPF, in 1938, and he could utter puerilities about its leader such as "Doriot is big and strong. Everything about him breathes health and plenitude: the abundant hair, his powerful shoulders." Before the war he had also met Abetz and visited Germany, where he had been wonderstruck by the Nuremberg rallies. Among the first to hasten around to Abetz in the embassy, he bombarded him with proposals for a united French Fascist party; he volunteered for collaborationist jobs and was always willing to furnish yet one more pro-German article. He knew everybody, he dined out, yet he remained the solitary artist, living alone. His last mistress was the very social wife of the car manufacturer Louis Renault (who was later accused of collaboration and died in prison after the war). "I am a Fascist," Drieu explained, "because I have taken the measure of Europe's progressive decadence. The only way I have seen to contain and measure this decadence is through fascism, and besides, not banking on the political resources of England any more than of France, and reproving the incursion into our continent of foreign powers like Russia and America, I have seen no alternative to the genius of Hitler and Hitlerism."

In October 1941, Drieu, Jouhandeau, Fernandez, Abel Bonnard, Chardonne, André Fraigneau, and Robert Brasillach toured Germany as an official delegation. Jouhandeau and Fraigneau in particular never quite lost a native skepticism. Jouhandeau, in Bonn, for instance, noted in his diary, *Journal sous l'occupation*, "For whom and for why am I here? Because since I first could read, understand, and feel, I have loved Germany, its philosophers and musicians, and thought that humanity had most to gain by our entente with her. In 1940 I closely observed what happened and it is not to be denied, except in bad faith, that the victorious Germans might have treated us worse." Yet it was in Germany, he concluded, that he felt most French. Drieu was similarly influenced. At any rate, he seems to have realized that the blitzkrieg against Russia was faltering already and that Germany might lose the war after all. His melancholy attraction to disaster got the better of his intelligence, so he continued to flounder in mistakes which he felt were past repenting. He spent 1942 writing his best novel, *L'Homme à cheval,* around the myth of dictatorship, and from then on he defied reality to prove his world picture wrong.

Maurice Chevalier entering the metro. He sang on the German-controlled Radio-Paris.

Such contributors to the quality papers as Drieu at least put the case for collaboration and Fascism with all the seriousness at their command. At quite a different level was the gutter press, which consisted of papers put out by the various Fascist parties without any aims other than propaganda and the browbeating of rivals. Even among these paid organs, *Au Pilori* stood out for its ignominy. Based on the German precedent of *Der Stürmer, Au Pilori* catered to anti-Semites. Its editor for the first part of the occupation was Jean Lestandi; he was succeeded by Jean Drault. The paper's offices were at 55, avenue George V, which *Au Pilori* delighted in renaming avenue Edouard Drumont. Besides Drault, who was over eighty, Urban Gohier and Lucien Pemjean were also octogenarians suddenly brought back into the public eye because they had forgotten none of their nineteenth-century racism and hatred. *Au Pilori* set itself with a will to defame and denounce Jews, staking out position as an unofficial police organ. Financially the paper prospered through high sales, but almost certainly some funding came from Knochen and the party, whose work it was so effectively doing.

Au Pilori carried little news as such. Exhortatory articles took up most of the space, under a title which as a rule made the text superfluous. On November 8, 1942, for example, the paper's political editor, Maurice de Séré, published an article under the heading "The Jewish question must be resolved immediately by the arrest and deportation of *all* Jews without exception." Or again, Henri Labroue's article of December 2, 1943, was headlined: "The Jewish people has placed itself outside the moral laws." Labroue, a provincial schoolteacher and author of *Voltaire anti-sémite,* had become professor of the history of Judaism at the Sorbonne, a chair specially created for him, probably on Laval's initiative. The paper also carried review columns, of which the most twisted was "L'Art Kasher," devoted to painting under the signature "Mosdyc." Its unsigned "Echos" were called "Micro et Confessions."

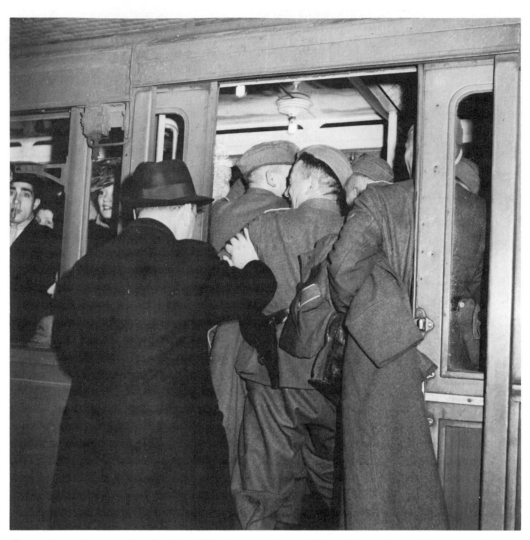

Rush hour in the metro, 1943.

Sometimes it was simply that "the lavatories at Saint-Germain-en-Laye station are disgusting," but usually the finger was pointed at somebody, who might be a humble grocer living on the avenue Niel whom Fascists were recommended to beat up or, more often than not, a Jew. In most cases, the authorities took the tip, if they had not colluded in it to begin with. That the paper received French government backing in some degree is shown by the advertisement which almost always appeared in it for the Loterie Nationale, in the form of a cartoon—drawn, incidentally, by Peynet, who was later well known for his cartoons of innocent lovers on park benches.

In a lengthy letter to *Au Pilori* on September 10, 1942, Céline wrote: "I have always encouraged defamation, I love it. The most solid stakes and the shortest ropes have always been knocked up that way, I find, absolutely of their own accord." Céline was very much at home in *Au Pilori*. What someone like Drieu was to the more thoughtful collaborator, pro-German because afraid of the Russians, Céline was to the man in the street, someone who instinctively liked *Au Pilori* for pandering to his fear and hate.

Céline must have been about the only person in Paris so besotted with apocalypse and death that the defeat of France and the occupation fell short of his expectations. Under his real name of Louis Destouches, he had been a cavalryman decorated for bravery in World War I. Then he had roamed the world before qualifying as a doctor, a fact of which he was proud. His early novels depict atrocity as com-

56

At the platform of the metro, Gare Saint-Lazare.

monplace and evil as banality. To him, what the Germans were doing everywhere in Europe confirmed that his views were not an aberration, but that nihilism had become the rule, as he had always said it would. Living with his wife and his cat in the rue Girardon, in Montmartre, he was outwardly a bohemian, inwardly a crazed executioner. Writing, to him, was vituperation and vilification. *Les Beaux Draps,* published in 1941, was his contribution to understanding contemporary events; it was dedicated to *"La corde des pendus,"* the hangman's rope, and there was no doubting the pleasure he took in the prospect of mass gallows. "An act of good faith, out in the clear, on paper!" he wrote to *La Gerbe* on February 18, 1941. "Are the Jews responsible for this war, or not? Let us have the answer down black on white, you acrobatic scribblers." The German writer Ernst Jünger ran into Céline on December 7, 1941, at the Deutsche Institut: "Large, bony, robust, a little cloddish, but alert in discussion or rather monologue. Turned in on himself, he has the staring look of a maniac, a look shining as though from the depths of some hole. . . . He said how surprised he was, in fact stupefied, that we soldiers are not shooting, hanging, exterminating the Jews—he is stupefied that anyone with a bayonet would not be using it all the time. 'If the Bolsheviks were in Paris, they'd show you how to set about it, they'd show you how to purge a population, district by district, house by house. If I had a bayonet, I'd know my business.'"

To Alice Epting, at her dinner table in the Institut, Céline on another occasion

In Les Halles, a wholesaler on a day when coupons for butter were redeemable.

said, "Don't you agree with me, Madame Epting, am I not right to say that if things go on this way, one fine day the Jews will be dancing on our graves?" Although he was an asset to the Germans, Céline had to be handled with care. In February 1944 he was dining at the embassy with his friend the painter Gen Paul, Déat, and Benoist-Méchin, when he let out his bitterness in front of Abetz. Hitler was dead, Céline said, and a false Jewish Hitler was impersonating him to pave the way for a Jewish victory. Gen Paul was then obliged by Céline to imitate this pseudo-Hitler until Abetz diplomatically had Céline driven home to the rue Girardon.

In Céline's position of being in the gutter press but not of it was the weekly *Je Suis Partout,* every bit as splenetic as *Au Pilori,* but with literary pretensions. *Je Suis Partout* also conceived collaboration to be the simple acknowledgment that Hitler knew best and Germany could do no wrong. But unlike *Au Pilori,* the fascist tone of *Je Suis Partout* was not because of the Germans, but in spite of them. Since 1930 it had been the mouthpiece of the extreme right. Its roots were in Action Française, whose doctrines of monarchy, anti-Semitism, and xenophobia had been brewed together by Charles Maurras. Living in the Vichy zone, an old man thundering away as ever, Maurras was perfectly suited to the present except in the one vital respect that he could not overcome a lifelong aversion to Germany. The prewar staff of *Je Suis Partout,* originally Maurrasians, had slowly come to see in Hitler the dictator

Left: **Youngsters distributing milk as part of the *secours nationale,* or relief program.**

Overleaf: **The dining room of the Hotel Prince de Galles in the avenue Georges V, requisitioned for the Luftwaffe.**

they aspired to for France. Some—Robert Brasillach, Lucien Rebatet, Georges Blond—joined up when the war broke out. Others were pacifist or defeatist, like Alain Laubreaux, who told Rebatet on September 3, 1939, "The only hope left for France is a short and disastrous war."

While the Germans were fulfilling this hope of Laubreaux's, the government cracked down on the *Je Suis Partout* contributors, searching their houses, summoning Brasillach back from the army to be cross-examined, and finally arresting Laubreaux and the paper's editor in chief, Charles Lesca. Both were interned in Gurs, a concentration camp then full of Jewish refugees, mostly from Germany. *Je Suis Partout* put out an issue dated June 7, 1940, and was then suspended.

Lesca, age fifty-three, was a rich Argentinian. Laubreaux came from French New Guinea and had been a radical journalist in Toulouse. Gurs was soon cleared out by the Germans; the Jews there were returned to Germany and later deported for extermination in the East, while Lesca and Laubreaux were released to Paris. There they met up with Georges Blond, who had been with the French navy in England but had elected not to stay there under de Gaulle (after the war he became a naval historian). Gradually the team came together again, and on Lesca's money *Je Suis Partout* could reappear. One of its first stories was entitled *"Quand Israel se venge,"* Lesca's own ignominious account of his recent experiences. Henri Poulain

wrote book reviews; Dorsay (real name, Pierre Villette) was the political commentator. Ralph Soupault's cartoons had a violent anti-Semitism all their own, even by the standards of *Der Stürmer*. One leading reporter and editorialist and smear expert was Pierre-Antoine Cousteau (brother of Commander Jacques Cousteau, the deep-sea diver), who claimed to have been fighting the war in "the Lévy company." Having visited America, where his father lived, in 1943 he published a book, *L'Amérique juive*. Alain Laubreaux was responsible for the paper's "Echos," or assorted denunciations and police tip-offs.

Brasillach, briefly a prisoner of war, was recalled to Paris and assumed the paper's editorship early in 1941. Gawky, stunted-looking, pallid, owlish in spectacles, he was a caricature of the bookish intellectual. Born in 1909, he had been at the Ecole Normale. A precocious literary critic for *Action Française,* he too had been overwhelmed by the Nazi rallies of Nuremberg and finally converted to Fascism by a visit to Léon Degrelle, leader of the Belgium Fascists or Rexists. Undoubtedly intelligent and a gifted writer, Brasillach seemed incapable of fulfillment, even to his friends. In his longing for a totalitarian regime and France's simultaneous integration into the German Reich can be caught an emotional urge incapable of finding less abstract outlets. He hated Vichy for sitting on the fence. In the summer of 1943, he and de Brinon and Claude Jeantet toured the eastern front and left a description of the site of Katyn, where the Russians had earlier murdered thousands of Polish officers. Summing himself up in an article in February 1944, he said, "It seems to me that the German genius and I had an affair. I shall never forget it. Whether one likes it or not, we lived together. Whatever their outlook, during these years the French have all more or less been to bed with Germany, and whatever quarrels there were, the memory is sweet."

What the *Je Suis Partout* team had in common was an anarchic relish for violence. Had there been no violence, they would have had to find it elsewhere. They dramatized themselves with the belief that their victory would be absolute—the difference with Céline was only that he visualized life itself as absolute and glorified defeat. Longing to kill, these people were also gambling with their own lives, and the tension of it makes *Je Suis Partout* sickening. All of them, all the time, wrote paragraphs like this one of Brasillach's on May 30, 1942: "Conviction has to be expressed. If a policeman explains to you (and we have seen such a thing at Puteaux) that you will be shot as a hostage by the Germans unless you stick to the studs when crossing the street, warn him that you are taking his number and he will be put on the rack for it. If some swine utters quips about the head of state or sob-stuff about the Jews, prevent him from opening his mouth. If a little town-hall clerk kicks up a fuss, grab him by the tie. You will soon see how you and a few brave activists put paid to all the faint-hearts and traitors."

Brasillach was literary enough to publish Jean Anouilh, Marcel Aymé, Jean de la Varende, René Barjavel, Michel Mohrt, and André Thérive, whose reputations could endorse the politically committed portions of the paper. That the paper swung behind it a considerable part of public opinion, and educated public opinion at that, is not in doubt. In his history of the paper, entitled *Je Suis Partout 1930–1944,* the historian Pierre-Marie Dioudonnat gives circulation figures rising from 100,000 in 1941 to an astonishing 300,000 by the end of the war—a success story unmatched at the time.

To the Germans, *Je Suis Partout*—akin to Céline—was a double-edged weapon. Its contributors, they realized, were abler than Nazi apologists elsewhere, and this was all the more valued because French. But more was being asked of the

Germans than the Germans could perform, and they were on their guard, not sure that their function was really to save the French from themselves. Of all the *Je Suis Partout* team, Lucien Rebatet looked most undeviatingly to the German model for salvation. Exaggeratedly wild in language and style, he set a standard for others. Like Brasillach, a close friend, he had an interest in the cinema and had started before the war to write the paper's film criticism under the pseudonym François Vinneuil. Once a bohemian, he had been a drinking companion of Modigliani. In 1938 he had edited a special anti-Semitic issue of *Je Suis Partout*. He too had been galvanized by touring Hitler's Germany, seeing in it what he wished France to become. Nazism for him converted all manner of public and private inadequacies and failures into strengths. During the phony war, he had been recruited into the Deuxième Bureau, or secret service, and the futility and inconsequence of this experience provoked him to the fiercest slapstick. He saw what had happened to him as symbolizing everything that had gone wrong. The French had lost, he preached, because they were exhausted, decadent, ridiculous, overrun by Jews and Bolsheviks, and he determined to tell them so in a memoir. This book, with the meaningful title *Les Décombres* (The Ruins), had a more sensational impact than any other during the whole occupation. On publication day, October 3, 1942, Rebatet spent the afternoon signing 1,500 copies for buyers in the Rive Gauche bookshop, and in spite of paper rationing, Denoel, the publisher, finally sold 250,000 copies.

The more scornful Rebatet could be about his compatriots, the more he exulted in their being taken by the scruff of the neck by the Germans. Hitler, he promised, would show them, and it was the gleefulness contained in the prospect that touched a profound collaborationist nerve and accounted for the success of *Les Décombres*. "What extraordinary and commanding language! What verve!" Brasillach wrote in his review of a book he could not praise enough. This was certainly true, but literary qualities could not hide how narrow was the range of ideas put forward. "Hate unto Death!" was Rebatet's program for national revival. He declared, "I have never had a single drop of democratic blood in my veins." Everyone on the *Je Suis Partout* team conceived sentiments of the sort to be patriotic, and Rebatet differed from them only in that he expressed with more memorable savagery the self-punishment at the center of the ensuing identification with Nazism.

There remained the Communists. Like the *Je Suis Partout* people, they had experienced the prewar years as a struggle of absolutely opposed ideologies. But the bedrock similarity of the totalitarian systems of Communism and Fascism had been revealed in the *coup de théâtre* of the Russian-German Pact of August 1939. Overnight Nazism ceased to be the enemy. The Communist party discovered that Hitler was completely absolved in whatever he did, and that only French and English capitalists stood to gain from the war. "Down with the imperialist war" was the slogan coined to fudge this peculiar piece of reasoning. Instructions were issued to party members to sabotage the French war effort, and some actually did so. Within a month of the Pact, the French government reacted by dissolving the party. Under the impact of events, thousands of members, including intellectuals and parliamentary deputies and even Marcel Gitton of the Central Committee, resigned in utter moral confusion.

The party was further demoralized when its leader, Maurice Thorez, abruptly defected from the French army, slipped into Belgium, and was smuggled off to Moscow for the duration of the war under the alias of Comrade Ivanov. Of the leaders remaining behind, Jacques Duclos became the senior, temporarily installed in Brussels, because through the Comintern network there he could liaise directly with Moscow. Under him, Maurice Tréand, nicknamed *"le gros,"* was responsible for party cadres and security. On June 14, 1940, Tréand made his way through the advancing German army into Paris, with orders from Duclos to start up the party paper *L'Humanité.* It is no exaggeration, then, to state that Muscovite elements among the Communists were the first and most wholehearted collaborators.

Some disagreed with the party line and favored going underground instead; of these the most prominent was Charles Tillon, a member of the Central Committee. In his memoirs, *On chantait rouge,* which are in stark contrast to the mass of material designed to lie about the party's role at the time, he has recorded how Tréand had received the green light from the Soviet embassy in Paris. So on June 19, Tréand, with another party stalwart, Denise Girollin, and an interpreter, Schrott, arrived at 12, boulevard de la Madeleine, then already the office of the ubiquitous Sonderführer Weber, to ask for permission to publish. As Tréand explained it to Tillon, "We and our interpreter were received by the press service of the Germans. The Fritzes asked us to explain in writing our position, and how far our propaganda would go." A text was prepared by Duclos to the effect that *L'Humanité* would be restricted to denouncing agents of British imperialism for wanting to drag French colonies into the war, and so forth. The German counterproposal was that *L'Humanité* change its title to *La France au Travail,* but no objection was made in principle. By June 22 the printers at the Dangan press had received fifty thousand francs for advance payment and volunteer sellers were ready. But with the copy for the first new issue on them, Tréand and Girollin were picked up at the Saint-Martin metro station by French police for infringing the decree banning the party and its activities. They were released on the twenty-fifth, Tillon writes, by order of the German military administration—which, with perfect symmetry, was simultaneously releasing the Fascists Lesca and Laubreaux.

A second attempt to obtain authorization for *L'Humanité* came to nothing, but the Germans tolerated the paper when it nonetheless appeared clandestinely. Well they might. On July 14, *L'Humanité* wrote, "It is particularly comforting, in these times of misfortune, to see numerous Paris workers striking up friendliness with German soldiers. . . . Bravo, comrades, continue, even though it may not please some bourgeois as stupid as they are mischievous." An article by Duclos was headed "Franco-German Fraternity." By September, the Communist slogan was "The French people demand, Thorez in power! Long live the party of peace." These unconditional demands for immediate peace between Germany and France continued unabated for another nine months; not even the Vichy regime had abdicated to the Germans to that extent.

The consequences were that Communists obediently allowed themselves to come out into the open, fraternizing as Stalin dictated. Tillon has described how Fernand Grenier, another Central Committee member (destined to leave the country and become the party agent with de Gaulle), returned to Saint-Denis and went about reorganizing cadres in full view of the Germans. Grenier was briefly arrested on October 5, 1940. During that month a German report showed how the wind was beginning to blow: "To stop increasing Communist party propaganda in Paris, the Paris police will take preventive measures and intern all party activists known in Paris." On October 21, the *préfet de police* Langeron confirmed developments: "The Paris police is collaborating loyally with the occupying authorities. It has arrested 871 militants in a few weeks." In Tillon's opinion, the Germans had deliberately sprung a trap, allowing the party to be reconstituted only to be better able to foreclose on it. Had the Germans in fact cooperated more fully, they would have pushed the

Jacques Doriot (right), leader of the PPF, with his assistant Simon Sabiani, saluting at the Arc de Triomphe, August 8, 1943.

party's hypocrisy to its limit and also been in a stronger position when the clampdown finally came after Hitler's attack on Russia on June 22, 1941. Overnight, again without warning, policy switched and prewar enmity was reinstated. Enough Communists still survived at large to prove to the Germans that it had been a mistake not to capitalize to the greatest possible degree upon the fraternity offered by Duclos.

Some of those who had quit the party after the Pact turned their backs on politics for good. But many thousands instinctively homed in on the leading Fascist party, the Parti Populaire Français, or PPF. In Germany, Communists by the million had been similarly reborn as Nazis. No doubt some French Communists resented the trick Stalin had played upon them, but more than that, the PPF offered them continuity; a comparable organization and comparable tactics; and doctrines of class consciousness and the greater good of the collective. In the ranks of the collaborators, Communists-turned-Fascists made a huge impact. For a start, they were disciplined. They were ready to sacrifice themselves for the cause. Among them were influential men. Henri Barbe had almost become leader of the Communist party. Paul Marion had been on the Central Committee and head of the Marxist college at Bobigny, to end up as a Vichy minister and president of the French Waffen SS. Among Communist deputies to Parliament who joined the PPF were André Parsal, Marcel Capron, Jean-Marie Clamamus, and Marcel Brout. Especially in working-class districts, numerous mayors made the switch, like Fernand Soupé, mayor of Montreuil, also formerly on the Central Committee, and Marcel Marshal, mayor of Saint-Denis, and Albert Richard, mayor of Pierrefitte. Well-known Communist organizers—Jules Teulade, Lozeray, Mathurin Boloré, Pierre Célor—joined the PPF. Journalists once on *L'Humanité* could continue publishing in the identical accusatory tone of voice in the collaborationist press, for instance, Maurice Lebrun or Camille Fégy (pseudonym Jean Meillonnas) editing *La Gerbe,* or the anti-Semitic cartoonist Ralph Soupault and the no less anti-Semitic Albert Clément.

Jacques Doriot, leader of the PPF, was an example to them all. The son of a blacksmith, and himself a metalworker, he had unimpeachable proletarian credentials. He had been only twenty-two when in 1920 he had incited the Jeunesses Socialistes in Saint-Denis to affiliate to the Communist International. Home base for him was in Saint-Denis, and this most proletarian of Paris suburbs treated him as its favorite native son for as long as his career lasted. Through his work in Communist youth movements, he visited Moscow, lectured in Russia, and by the mid-twenties was backing Stalin against Trotsky. In 1927, Doriot was on a delegation to Chiang Kai-shek's Kuomintang, with the object of ensuring that Stalin's policies were applied in the Far East. As an up-and-coming Comintern man, he secured his base at Saint-Denis, becoming its deputy. He might well have supplanted Thorez for leadership of the party, and his break with Communism seems to have had personal motivations. Losing the power struggle against Thorez, he was unwilling to knuckle under and was excluded from the party in June 1934. Ambition was Doriot's governing characteristic. Eighteen months later, his own PPF took off, and the Communist party then had a rival privy to its inner secrets and cabals. Doriot's Fascism consisted of everything he had learned from Communism, turned inside out.

At the outset, PPF membership was working class and Paris-based, spreading slowly through the rest of the country. Estimates vary, but eventually Paris probably had 100,000 members. At the PPF Congress of May 1941 were 10,000 delegates, of whom 2,700 came from Paris and the surrounding region. It was undoubtedly the mass movement with the greatest Fascist potential. Intellectuals joined, but they were mostly right-wing in temperament, or merely disaffected, like Drieu, Bertrand de Jouvenal, Alfred Fabre-Luce, or Ramon Fernandez. PPF policy in the years leading to the war had been muddled. A nationalist because an anti-Communist, Doriot could not advocate appeasement of Hitler, but he nevertheless accepted a subsidy from Mussolini. After the 1940 collapse, he too ended up in Vichy, among those aspiring to the pickings.

The secretary of the PPF, Victor Barthélemy, met up with Doriot there and learned how he summed up the situation: "France must pass from the camp of the conquered into the camp of the conquerors." Soon Doriot was established back in Paris, where Jean Fontenoy arranged for him to have an interview with Abetz. Doriot's fundamental hope to strike back at Soviet Communism could not be harnessed while the Russian-German Pact lasted. Abetz thought Doriot too crude. Doriot thought Abetz too smooth, and reported back to Barthélemy, "Abetz is no friend of ours. He will never be. It's the third time I've seen him and I am under the impression that we shall not be seeing each other much more." Once again, the Germans were being invited to do more than they wanted to; to place France in the camp of the conquered had been the fruits of the war so far. In this light, Doriot had to be restricted to Fascist propagandizing and party-building. By October 19, the PPF paper *Le Cri du Peuple* was being published in Paris. According to Schleier, debriefed after the war, the paper was receiving a subsidy from the embassy of 250,000 francs a month. On its masthead was the paper's rallying cry, "To work, its due, its entire due. To capital, its due, nothing but its due."

The party offices were off the rue de Rivoli in the rue des Pyramides, with a subbranch in the rue Volnay. In the sixteenth arrondissement, two large buildings were used as barracks for the men whom Barthélemy calls "the guards for various party functions"; in fact they were uniformed storm troopers who stewarded meetings and now and again took to the streets in demonstrations on the Nazi model. From the German point of view, a Fascist party which adopted proven German methods was best kept in reserve. Hitler never installed in power a fellow Fascist if there was an alternative, on the logical grounds that someone else's National Socialism might successfully challenge his. But if Laval proved unsatisfactory, then he could always be replaced by Doriot and the PPF. This threat to promote Doriot worked wonders in keeping Laval at heel. Meanwhile Doriot could do little but chafe and declare, with more ardor than he actually felt, how much he admired Pétain.

In the Paris game of divide-and-rule, the Germans had other choices besides Laval and Doriot. Marcel Déat, like Laval, had been a Socialist minister. Appeasement of Hitler in his case had developed into outright pacifism. In May 1939 he had published an article declaring that he would not go to war if Danzig was at stake. Déat, six years older than Doriot, was a very different personality, reserved and superior, the son of a schoolmaster and himself pedagogical in manner, small in everything except self-righteousness. Although he could work up a crowd, he was devoid of Doriot's magnetism. At Vichy he too had hoped for a job, was frustrated, and concluded once and for all that the French were in no position ever to reverse the German victory. He too would make for the camp of the conquerors, and like Doriot, he hastened to Paris. An article of his, on July 5, stated, "In the full spirit of the armistice convention, the French and German governments must be in constant touch and coordinate their actions. Material necessity imposes collaboration."

Georges Albertini (his pseudonym was Claude Varennes) was to be the secretary of Déat's party, the Rassemblement National Populaire, or RNP, and he has described in his book *Le Destin de Marcel Déat* how Laval and Luchaire introduced Déat to Abetz and Achenbach, but how in the end the one member of the embassy with whom Déat felt tied was Dr. Grosse, also a former Socialist, with an interest in trade unions. Subsidized to the same extent as the PPF, the RNP had its paper, *L'Oeuvre,* in which Déat published an article every day of the week—more than a thousand articles throughout the occupation. Every Sunday he sat at his typewriter and wrote the weekly quota straight out. In its opening issue, on September 21, *L'Oeuvre* celebrated the German occupation as "a festival in history."

Eight months later the paper was claiming half a million members for the RNP, but a tenth of this inflated figure was probably nearer the truth. The party had a synthetic quality, perhaps reflecting the fact that it existed only thanks to the occupation. In style of saluting, in its uniform and badges, and with its paramilitary squads for parades and party functions, the RNP favored Fascist trappings more or less identical to the PPF's. Déat's most consistent proposal was to form a single party of all collaborators, though this would have brought to a head his rivalry with Doriot for leadership and driven the partyless Laval into limbo. Nothing came of it except lip service. Déat too had no choice but to wait for German favors, and he hoped to force these by constantly attacking Vichy for its lack of pro-Nazi spirit. Meanwhile, he used *L'Oeuvre* to flatter Laval, and probably received funds for him too.

Déat's associates were nonentities, though for most of the RNP's first year— until October 1941 in fact—Eugène Deloncle was in the party. The word "condottiere" seems to arise naturally where Deloncle is concerned. In the thirties he had launched a not very secret anti-Communist society, known as the Cagoule, with an enrollment, he claimed, of twelve thousand men, five thousand of them in Paris. Arms were acquired abroad, and Deloncle soon landed up in prison, to be freed at the start of the war. Regrouping his Cagoulards, he looked about for an opening. The German historian Dieter Wolf summarized the disarray that someone like this could generate: "Deloncle had already looked into the possibility of a joint political action with Doriot. During the summer of 1940 he had met with the PPF chief several times at Vichy. The objectives which he was seeking remain obscure. By the autumn of 1940 he had already won over to the idea of collaboration a part of the former Cagoule and founded a party, the Mouvement Social Révolutionnaire. Apparently at this period he was already in touch with the Propaganda Staffel and the Paris headquarters of the SS. A telegram of Abetz's contains this precious clue: 'Through the Cagoulards of Deloncle, the proposition was advanced to us at the time [i.e., the summer of 1940] to authorize a march on Vichy or to allow a coup d'état to be organized under our auspices in the unoccupied zone!'"

Contacts with the SS led to a subsidy and gave Deloncle a little leeway as he veered between throwing his lot in with Déat or with Doriot. All three, with varying degrees of fantasy, dreamed of putsches, marches, a single totalitarian party under their control, and death to their enemies. To throw in their lot with the Germans, who were after all their conquerors, caused none of them the least hesitation or scruple. Treason was an accusation they reserved for Gaullists, and had anyone accused them of it, they would have given the identical answer: Germany had won, Communism had to be resisted at all costs, democracy was bankrupt, France including Vichy had no future except insofar as allowed one by Germany. Their anger and scorn were directed in particular toward the silent majority who were *attentiste*—in other words who preferred to wait and see what would happen before committing themselves to either the Nazi bloc or the democratic Allies.

Doriot, Déat, and to a lesser extent Deloncle, with their regular meetings in the Salle Wagram or the Salle Pleyel, their marches and their speechifyings, made the Paris headlines, but they were not alone in letting imagination race behind Nazi victory. A number of other men who in ordinary circumstances would have been the kind of nuisance which democracy must bear were enabled by the collapse of institutions to emerge as would-be dictators. The occupation created the stage upon which to act out what were more often than not solitary dramas of self-importance, nihilism, and paranoia. Without the Nazis, few would have heard of someone like Jean Boissel, who wanted to create a Racist International. The Front Franc which he formed in 1940 with the help of an ex-Communist called Emile Nédélec was nothing but a group of frantic anti-Semites. Boissel's links to Germany were through Julius Streicher, and when the latter was disgraced by the party for corruption, Boissel sank too.

Marcel Bucard of the Franciste party.

Pierre Costantini, founder and chief of his own splinter group, the Ligue Française, took it upon himself to declare war against England. Hérold-Paquis, the broadcaster, sketched in his memoirs a scene which told all: "As I looked at this fellow whose credit never quite ran out on him, I was reminded of the terrible sentence of the German Beumelburg, in his office one day in the rue des Saussaies when I was introducing to him the painter Beltran-Massès, saying about Pierre Costantini, who had just had his visiting card sent in, 'Excuse me for a minute, it won't take long, today's his payday!'"

This money went into a paper, *L'Appel,* which matched *Au Pilori* for abuse and invective. So Costantini, or his aide the Marquis Xavier de Magellan, earned a seat on public platforms, access to a microphone, and a pat on the shoulder from the PPF, with which his Ligue was loosely affiliated.

Pierre Clémenti had a party and a paper. So did Marcel Bucard, whose publicity photograph carried the caption: "The man who never made a mistake." His Francisme was indistinguishable in rhetoric or styling from any other group, yet the few thousand Francistes specialized in disrupting the meetings of rival collaborationists. Opposing stewards frequently finished in hospital or even prison. Yet no overriding factor decided why a person joined one group rather than another. It was a matter of luck, of friends, or of neighborhood. To the Germans, the greater the variety, the better. In the spectrum of collaboration were Communists, Socialists, liberals, radicals, Social Democrats, conservatives, and extremists and racists of all kind: something for everyone. A parody of prewar democracy had been constructed, in which it was still possible to pin labels of left-wing and right-wing on those who held identical attitudes to Germany, the one thing which counted. Proliferation induced the misleading sense that French politics were still as vital and effervescent as ever. Personalities clashed, lobbies formed, meetings were held, hands were raised, French public opinion took note, and the Germans had manipulated it all.

An indication that under the surface might exist a French national spirit in distress occurred on November 11, the day commemorating the end of World War I. Students in one or two lycées, and at the university, had been protesting at the sight of uniformed Germans among them. Then Professor Langevin was arrested, and rumors of demonstrations spread. On the morning of the eleventh, wreaths were laid at various spots, including the Tomb of the Unknown Soldier. By the afternoon the Germans were dispersing anyone on the streets. Although the Gaullist radio in London took pride in announcing that some demonstrators had been shot dead, this was not so. For once the official pronouncement was correct: "As a result of the incidents on November 11, 123 arrests were made, among them 90 school pupils and 14 students. Four people have been lightly hurt, none killed." Abetz drew the correct conclusion in his report to Berlin that the Gaullists were a very small minority.

Paris under occupation remained more tranquil than it had ever been in the years of peace, and nothing comparable to this one and only demonstration happened until the approach of the liberation in August 1944. Its one true victim was a civil engineer, Jacques Bonsergent, who had had nothing to do with the demonstration. In Paris for the wedding of a friend, he had the misfortune to be jostled on the pavement near the Gare Saint-Lazare by a party of drunken soldiers. Perhaps he struck one, but it appears more likely that he had been separating his friends from the Germans. Arrested, he was sentenced to death for "an act of violence against a member of the German army." No doubt his execution on December 23 was an exemplary warning to potential Gaullists or subversives. Stülpnagel, the Militärbefehlshaber, was responsible for this decision, which was proof positive of the way he mistook harshness for strength, a consistent failing of his, and in the end his undoing. Nothing so severe was justified. In the first six months of the occupation, Parisians had watched their city being occupied, and their police and their politics and their press being reconditioned, and they had reacted with absolute docility. Whether out of demoralization or prudence, or approval, they had adapted to conditions. Nothing had taken place that can be called resistance. One or two tracts had been printed, but their sentiments were literary and their distribution marginal. A few friends employed in the Musée de l'Homme were arranging reunions among themselves, but they were academic and Communists, mainly Jews, several of them onetime refugees already, without means of enlisting wide support and anyhow under observation by German agents. Otherwise, little more serious than random clipping of telephone wires, switching of railway points, or drunken brawling in bars filled out the monthly reports back to Berlin.

At the public level a ceremony had been planned to reward the French for their collaboration and to symbolize for them the new Franco-German reconciliation of 1940: the body of Napoleon's only son, the Duke of Reichstadt, was to be exhumed from the imperial vault in Vienna and laid alongside his father in Les Invalides. Hitler much approved the gesture. December 16 was the date fixed for the solemnities. An official ode was commissioned from Maurice Rostand. The coffin was brought to Paris by armored train, laid upon a gun carriage, and escorted by French and German soldiers to the courtyard of Les Invalides at midnight. That night was cold, it was snowing, and the arrangements were delayed. Those invited to be present, important and elderly for the most part, regretted that they were standing frozen out of doors in the small hours. A solemn and sinister occasion, thought Sacha Guitry.

Lucien Rebatet was standing next to Doriot, who explained vividly what had gone wrong with what he called "the romantic gesture of the führer." The fine, dignified ceremony had been impeccably staged, in Rebatet's opinion, "but went off half-cock because the Marshal should have been present, but the previous evening he had lent himself to a reactionary pro-English plot and had had Pierre Laval arrested." Rebatet continued, "I was flabbergasted. Montoire could go and jump in the lake; the German response might very well be brutal and could compromise four months of difficult negotiating. . . . But to my great surprise Doriot was rejoicing: 'We're well rid of that pimp Laval. Now we can roll our sleeves up.' Then he swiveled his spectacles on to Marcel Déat, all by himself under a flaming torch, dressed in black, an ironic smile fixed on his face. 'There's someone else to put under lock and key. That little swine over there. Luckily it won't be long now.'"

Doriot, for all his boastfulness to Rebatet, took the precaution of sleeping away from home for the next few nights. (Not that this was unusual: during the war he kept a mistress in Paris and had a child by her.) For indeed, without warning, Pétain had fired Laval and for good measure ordered his arrest and that of Marcel Déat.

Quite what impulses Pétain had acted upon have not been satisfactorily explained. Pique partly, plus contempt for Laval, plus mistrust of his deputy's blatant personal scheming in Paris. *L'Oeuvre* maintained that fascism could never be realized through Vichy, and Pétain may have thought that this put Déat in the same boat as Laval. Perhaps he believed he was asserting his independence. The outcome had less to do with high politics than comic opera. Abetz himself hastened to Vichy, had Laval freed, dined with him in a restaurant in full view of everyone, and returned with him to Paris in Achenbach's car. Déat was simultaneously released on Abetz's say-so.

For a short stretch, Laval was to be succeeded by an old parliamentarian, Pierre-Etienne Flandin, and then by Admiral Jean Darlan. To the latter, Hitler was blunt about the Pétain-Laval tussle, saying that whether Laval was in office or not was a matter of indifference to him. What counted was whether France would adopt a hostile stance—in that case no goodwill could be expected on his part. Abetz was disappointed by the storm in the collaborationist teacup and worked assiduously to restore Laval, whom he judged indispensable. In practice the Nazi administration was already implanted strongly enough to survive ups and downs of this kind.

One way or another, the Germans in Paris could congratulate themselves on having so much to celebrate at the end of 1940. They could not know that this was also their heyday. One of the season's balls, in fancy dress, was held at the Château de Bouffemont, owned by Baron Johnny Empain, chairman of the metro. Corinne Luchaire went dressed as a Hungarian dancer, and among the many happy Germans dancing she noticed Dr. Franz Albrecht Medicus, who was then on General Turner's staff in the Palais Bourbon and destined to succeed Dr. Best in 1942. For the big New Year's Eve reception at the embassy, she wore a full white dress and thought it "very virginal." Suzanne Abetz, she saw, "was receiving the countless guests *à la française* . . . dressed in a rather striking manner, loaded with heavy jewels which had just been bought and to her mind marked her way up in the world." Corinne Luchaire met Fernand de Brinon and Schleier, whose way of raising a lady's hand to his lips, she thought, was awkward and disagreeable. Also Rahn, "so well mannered that he had received a good hundred invitations to luncheons or dinners." Lights were ablaze, in spite of the curfew. "The buffet was groaning. Champagne flowed. The German officers, the airmen especially, in their best gala costumes, did the honors, busy as bees circling around, and none of them was restricted to speaking his own language. . . . The senior ranking officer was General Hanesse, in a white frock coat, his chest blazing with medals. . . . Here was Tout-Paris in the sphere of literature, the arts, politics, the theater."

4 The Spread of Terror

Rudolf Breitscheid and Rudolf Hilferding had been in the German government in the days of the Weimar Republic, before Hitler seized power, whereupon they fled to France for safety. In the exodus of June 1940, both had left Paris for the Vichy zone, where they completed formalities to embark for America. Pressure was immediately exerted on the Vichy government to hand over men like these, as well as the many thousand more obscure German émigrés who had been detained in camps as a precaution during hostilities. Avowed political opponents of the Reich, whether Marxists (like Hilferding) or Social Democrats (like Breitscheid), were on wanted lists, and in Paris it was relatively easy to round them up without delay. In the Vichy zone, a so-called Kuhnt Commission, which was nothing but the SS, was permitted to check on internees in the camps and deport whom it liked back to Germany, thereby settling prewar scores once and for all.

On the night of February 8, 1941, Breitscheid and Hilferding were arrested by French policemen wearing ordinary clothes. Both politicians—and their wives—suspected that some trickery was up, but they received categoric assurances that this was not so. Nevertheless both men were handed over to SS Hauptsturmführer Georg Geissler, who—armistice or not—had offices in Vichy, although he seems to have been the official police representative there only after 1942. Breitscheid and Hilferding, without their wives, were then driven from Vichy to the Paris prison of La Santé. Hilferding committed suicide there and was buried in the Père Lachaise cemetery. Breitscheid was deported to Buchenwald, where he was killed on August 28, 1944, in an air raid along with other eminent prisoners including Princess Mafalda, daughter of the King of Italy, and Michelin, the tire manufacturer.

Herschel Grynszpan was similarly hunted down. He had been in prison, pending trial for shooting and killing a counselor at the German embassy. Evacuated ahead of the German army, he found himself free in the chaos, only to be arrested again by the Vichy government. Professor Friedrich Grimm intervened, for he took a particular interest in the case, having been retained for the prosecution. To Grimm, it was clear that Grynszpan would never have killed a German official as an act of vengeance: some wider conspiracy must have had a hand in it. Grynszpan's files at first were missing, and the French official who was responsible was threatened with execution. The files were recovered, and Grimm continued his attack until Vichy handed Grynszpan over. In 1942 Grimm published a pamphlet, *Der Grünspan Prozess,* intended to prepare public opinion for a new version of the Dreyfus trial, which in fact never happened.

Tragic cases like these exposed the utter fiction of Vichy's independence. Conniving with the Nazis, indeed facilitating their aims, the Vichy government hoped to bank up goodwill by washing its hands of anyone who was not French, although until that moment the right of political refugees to claim asylum in France had been one of the country's traditional contributions to the liberties of Man. Anticipating that the Germans would make racial or doctrinal demands, Vichy took the decision to surrender to them in advance.

A decree was passed on August 13, 1940, outlawing secret societies, which in effect meant Freemasonry. In an attempt to ward off the blow, a few days earlier Arthur Groussier, president of the Grand Orient (in other words, the leading Freemason), had sent Pétain a letter announcing the voluntary dissolution of Masonic organizations. Later Groussier was to give this account of what happened to him: "I returned home. A search had taken place. The day after I was back, I reported to the Kommandantur at Enghien . . . then they came to find me. One day I saw seven German officers sitting around my table, and I had a long conversation with them. They found my house rather humble. The first thing I heard was 'Is this your château?' I was supposed to be rich, like most Grand Masters in Europe . . . they saw at home how I organized a simple life by myself. . . . My feeling was that I was responsible for the fate of Masons. Lists of Masons were in their possession, and no act of mine was to serve as a pretext for treating Masons as they treated Jews. . . . One day a police commissioner who was driving me into Paris to appear before a German inquiry told me that he and his services were being criticized for not uncovering the ultrasecret cells of Freemasonry, and he added, 'I begin to think that the reason for this is that there are none.' I answered, 'Obviously. If there had been any, you would have found them.'"

Freemasonry had been depicted in France as an occult power, anticlerical, demonically bent on subverting family life and virtue ever since the Revolution. Some critics thought this rather exaggerated but nonetheless believed the Masons to be an old-boy network of industrialists and bankers. What the Germans actually found was a clublike organization that did charitable works, held luncheons and meetings, and commanded limited loyalty among members. The Masonic habit of stylizing members on paper as FF ∴ imparted a mysterious accusatory air when incorporated before somebody's name in the collaborationist press.

To deal with anti-Masonic investigation, the Canadian embassy in the avenue Foch was requisitioned and Dr. Pfannstiel of the SS installed there as director of a Service for Secret Societies. Through him, with the approval of Pétain and Abetz, corresponding French services were set up at 16, rue Cadet, in the confiscated headquarters of the Freemasons. Bernard Faÿ was installed there as "delegate of the French government to liquidate Masonic lodges." Another organization, for archival purposes, was the Centre d'Action Maçonnique, under Henry Coston, with offices in another expropriated Masonic building in the rue Puteaux. A special police force, recruited from Fascist elements, was at the disposal of the anti-Masonic services. Lists were established of Freemasons who by profession were bureaucrats or soldiers, and these lists, with addresses, were published in alphabetical sections in *Au Pilori*. Among his other contributions to the same paper, Coston was to publish an article tracing the links of Admiral Darlan (via his father) to Freemasonry.

At the beginning of October 1940, an anti-Masonic exhibition opened at the Petit Palais. Jacques de Lesdain reviewed it in *L'Illustration*. "Visitors filing through the Petit Palais now know that if they were not receiving in life the due rewards of their work, it was because other men, united by what they imagined was a secret and hermetic knot, shared out the best and most lucrative jobs without having staked claims to them through personal merit or skill. On the floor of the Petit Palais Freemasonry lies in its death throes."

In his diary André Thérive was less high-flown about his visit to the exhibition. "Interiors of the lodges, initiation rites, triangles, skulls, liturgical ornaments and

Voici le genre de Manifestations Artistiques qui accueillaient le visiteur à la GRANDE LOGE DE FRANCE (Rue Puteaux)

Pictures taken from Masonic lodges.

vestments, assorted accessories (among them the money box and collection bag, as in all cults). Also a diagram denouncing all the Freemasons in history, from which it appears that 96 percent of Great Men belonged to the Three-Dot Brethren. Brochures were selling for forty sous, and everybody is hopeful of finding in them the name of some friend or colleague." Always observant, Thérive that same month spotted an exhibition of another kind in a public lavatory whose walls were scribbled with proposals for appointments in the German language, along with graffiti like *"Heil männliche Liebe,"* or "Long Live Homosexuality."

Out of a 1939 membership of 50,000, 6,000 were harassed one way or another by anti-Masonic measures. According to Pierre Chevallier, who has written the official history of Freemasonry in France, 989 Masons were deported, of whom 545 died in concentration camps or were executed; however, the same authority leaves open the question whether or not responsibility for this total lies exclusively with the anti-Freemason services. Pétain himself had certainly set a tone with a much-publicized remark, "A Jew cannot help being what he is, but to be a Freemason is a choice." As the climate of suspicion widened, thousands of anonymous denunciations poured in. Abetz, Rahn, and Achenbach were variously rumored to be Masons, and Achenbach probably had Jewish grandparents too, or so Rebatet decided with his usual witch-hunting flair.

The anti-Masonic exhibition which opened in the Petit Palais in October 1940.

CORDONS, TABLIERS
DE LA
FRANC-MAÇONNERIE
ANGLAISE
TROUVES CHEZ LE
F∴ ROTSCHILD
A PARIS
LA HAUTE BANQUE
JUIVE EST MAÇONNIQUE

These allegedly English Masonic emblems are said to have been found in Paris at Rothschilds (which has been misspelled).

Toward Jews in general, Pétain felt indifference tinged with distaste, an attitude typical of army officers like himself in the aftermath of the Dreyfus trial. Laval probably had no special bias one way or another until he perceived that German racial dogma had presented him with a bargaining counter. If the Germans wanted the Jews so badly, in other words, they could have them, but at the price of conceding something he might want. In Vichy there was no discussion about the morality of handing over to the Germans people earmarked for persecution. It was a matter of expediency. Once again Vichy hoped to curry favor by taking the initiative and passing decrees against Jews before the Germans asked such measures of them. By the autumn of 1940 a commission had been appointed to purge from public life anyone who had recently acquired French citizenship (its vice-president, André Mornet, was to be transformed after the liberation as attorney general into a ferocious purger of collaborators, assisting at Laval's trial and execution), and Jews had been banned from the liberal professions and the administration.

In Paris, the embassy and the party (or the SD) hoped to create the impression that anti-Jewish measures were demanded by the ordinary Frenchman on the street. In the weeks following the armistice, Langeron was complaining in his diary about groups of Fascist youths paid to harass Jews in public. On July 18 he wrote, "For the time being anti-Semitic propaganda is specializing in blockading the entrances of

A model at the anti-Masonic exhibition, bearing the description: "Brother to the 33rd degree in the Grand Orient of France."

Jewish shops. Young people place themselves before the doorway and forbid customers to enter until the police arrive and clear free passage." *Au Pilori* treated these scuffles as the opening of a campaign and in August started running a series of articles on the theme: "The Jews must pay for the war or die."

At a meeting between Abetz and Best and members of the Verwaltungsstab on August 17, it was decided to examine ways to limit the residence of Jews in the occupied zone, and whether their property might be seized. The result was the decree of September 27 forbidding Jews in the Vichy zone to return to the occupied zone. Jews were also compelled to carry specially marked identity cards and, if they were shopkeepers, to stick up in the window a rectangular yellow and black poster announcing "Jewish business."

On the day after this decree, the so-called Otto list was announced. The Propaganda Abteilung had suggested to the French publishing houses that they voluntarily purge their lists. None refused. In an act without precedent French publishers were therefore collectively consenting to impose censorship on themselves. More than two thousand works by 842 authors were withdrawn. German émigrés like Stefan Zweig and Emil Ludwig, along with Freud and Einstein, were featured on the list, with French nationalists, English writers, and Jews, against whom this measure was primarily aimed. One or two were wrongly labeled Jewish, like Blaise Cendrars, who

The floor show at Shéhérazade.

The cloakroom at Shéhérazade, one of the Germans' favorite nightclubs.

French cancan at the Moulin Rouge.

The drum majorettes opening the Cirque Medrano.

The Moulin de la Galette in Montmartre.

"Gay Paris" or "Paris bei Nacht," in the Moulin Rouge.

The strong man at the Moulin de la Galette, at which Germans only were permitted.

managed to have himself struck off the list. *Mein Kampf* was also a prohibited book, on the interesting grounds that the French had better not know what Hitler had written about them.

The end of September also marked the arrival of SS Hauptsturmführer Theo Dannecker. Only twenty-seven years old, he belonged to the branch of the RSHA which specialized in the Jewish question, and therefore he reported back to his superior in Berlin, Adolf Eichmann, and so directly to Heydrich and Himmler. Dannecker appropriated offices at 31, avenue Foch, and in 11, rue des Saussaies.

To begin with, Dannecker followed the estimates of Heydrich and Himmler that there were more than 800,000 Jews in France—an exaggeration by a factor of three or four—and that their eradication would be troublesome. At no time did Dannecker's anti-Jewish section muster more than a score of men, far too few for their task unless the help of the French authorities and police at all levels could be taken for granted. This was the case. In response to Dannecker, a new administrative section to deal with the Jewish question was set up within the Préfecture de Police. Commissaire de Police François headed a staff of sixty, but had at his disposal all police and *gendarmerie* resources as well. A census was the first step, and Dannecker was gratified that this was carried out without a hitch. Throughout October, Jews were obliged to register in alphabetical order at police stations, where they provided details of their domicile, nationality, and profession. Henri Bergson complied with the statement: "Academic. Philosopher. Nobel Prize winner. Jew." (Bergson died soon afterward, on January 4, 1941, and only three days later Rebatet was writing in *Je Suis Partout* that Bergson "had so often furnished some sort of alibi for the very worst of Jews that it would have been better if he had never had the right to write or to teach in French.") Known as the "Tullard dossiers," after André Tullard, the police official in charge of them, the files thus accumulated were always at the disposition of the Germans and were the indispensable tool of what was to follow.

The Jews remaining in Paris were in the great majority working class. A good many were either recent immigrants from countries subjected to Nazism or first-generation French citizens whose nationality was open to question. Within the community, it was believed as a matter of instinct that safety lay in obeying the law. To the German administration the danger was that the Jews might become suspicious, panic, and turn to resistance with unforeseeable consequences. If they received orders from within the Jewish community, therefore, their fears might be allayed, and to this end Dannecker created an umbrella organization, the Union Générale des Israélites en France, or UGIF. Its leaders had to do what they were told, for the purposes of cajoling or even deceiving the Jewish masses, and several chose suicide or in the end insisted on being deported along with their families.

The political implications of anti-Jewish measures extended far beyond the realm of Dannecker and the party. Every week, therefore, a committee met to coordinate policy between Dannecker, the embassy, and the military administration. Abetz or Schleier often represented the embassy, or else Achenbach or Karl-Theo Zeitschel, who acted as permanent liaison between embassy and party. Within the military administration, Dr. Michel's economic staff now developed a further section to deal with the Jewish question. Its head, Dr. Blanke, proved equivocal, imparted information to the French resistance, but was detected and executed by the Gestapo in 1944.

A circular from Dr. Michel to all *Feldkommandanturs* demonstrates the official approach in the opening stage of the occupation. "Two points of view are decisive in the action against Jews in the sphere of the economy. First, it is necessary to ensure that the elimination of Jews will also persist after the occupation. Then beyond that, on the German side an apparatus cannot be constructed which will measure up to the large number of Jewish enterprises. These two considerations have led us to bring the French authorities in on the elimination of the Jews. This is a way to have French services sharing the responsibility, and we have at our disposition the French administrative machine. In conformity with this, we will proceed in the first instance to nominate provisional French managers, unless major German interests are at stake. The object is, in principle, to replace Jews by Frenchmen, so that in this way the French population can participate equally in the economic elimination of the Jews, and so avoid creating the impression that Germans alone wish to take the place of Jews."

It remained only to extend the underlying idea by creating some French body which would take responsibility for anti-Jewish policy in general. French anti-Semitism could be harnessed for the purpose, and at the weekly coordination committee the Commissariat Générale aux Questions Juives, or CGQJ, took shape. Among those suggested to run it were Léon de Poncin, Georges Batault, Bernard Faÿ, Vacher de la Pouge (who was *préfet* at Montpellier), Darquier de Pellepoix, Professor George Montandon, Bucard, Boissel, Clémenti, the journalist Jean de la Hire, and Comte Armand de Puy-Ségur, until Xavier Vallat was finally selected.

Vallat had been severely wounded in World War I, losing an eye. His inspiration lay in Action Française; he had been an extreme right-wing parliamentary deputy. His anti-Jewish prejudices dated to the Dreyfus trial, but he never quite overcame nationalistic reservations about the Germans. He appointed Colonel de Jarnieu to run the CGQJ offices in the Place des Petits-Pères, and while keeping his own gentlemanly hands clean, he employed under him men who did not scruple to enrich themselves by blackmail and the sale of certificates of Aryanization. At his postwar trial, Vallat called his sponsor Dannecker "a frenzied Nazi who went into trances as soon as the word Jew was uttered." For himself, he claimed that what he did to keep Jews out of social and economic life was so moderate that he could hardly be accused of discrimination. In fact, he never quite trusted the Vichy government, his actual paymaster, not to cover its tracks at that stage of the war by disowning him and his activity.

Not that Vichy was squeamish when it came to taking advantage of the new racism. In October 1940 the Contrôle des Administrations Provisoires was created, nominally under the French Ministry of Industrial Production, to liaise with the military administration over the sequestration of Jewish businesses and factories. Its first director, Fournier, had been governor of the Banque de France. His successor, Regelsberger, an Alsatian, an inspector from the Banque de France, but now entitled Director of Economic Aryanization, was to draw up lists of Jews to be arrested and dispatched to concentration camps so that their property could be made available. Twenty-one thousand businesses were transferred to French (and sometimes German) profiteers, from huge concerns to small workshops, factories and warehouses, freeholds, restaurants, shareholdings in private companies, anything which hitherto had belonged to a Jew. The only calculation that mattered was that the former owners should never return to claim what was theirs, and this prompted every kind of denunciation and accusation. Dr. Joseph Billig, author of the definitive history of the CGQJ, concluded, "As executor of the policy of Vichy, and in the occupied zone serving the policy of the occupying authorities, the CGQJ was the instrument par excellence of collaboration."

In a report dated February 22, 1941, Dannecker stated with confidence, "The

Jews were forbidden to use public telephones—one measure among many designed to isolate them from other Parisians.

French inspectors formed and instructed in collaboration with our section for Jewish affairs today constitute an elite body, as well as training cadres for Frenchmen to be drafted in the future to the anti-Jewish police. In the occupied zone, our section has acquired total influence over the anti-Jewish police." A policy of spoliation on a national scale, it was realized, required special policing beyond what Commissaire François could provide. Acting once again through the Préfecture de Police, Dannecker occupied the offices in the rue de Téhéran of an American-Jewish welfare organization, The Joint. There he installed what another historian, Claude Lévy, has called "a Franco-German police agglomeration."

Two aides of Dannecker's, Limpert and Busch, both SS men, recruited French inspectors and interpreters. In November 1941, Pierre Pucheu, the Vichy minister of the interior, transformed this rue de Téhéran staff into the Police aux Questions Juives, the PQJ or anti-Jewish police, under another Alsatian *commissaire de police,* Schwebelin. Further premises were acquired at 8, rue Greffuhle. Some inspectors were seconded from the Préfecture to the PQJ; others were placed under Knochen in the avenue Foch. This anti-Jewish police ranked with the anti-Masonic squad under Jean Marquès-Rivière, and what were eventually called the Brigades Speciales to deal with Communists and the resistance. Between Commissaire François's section

84

A Montmartre restaurant
distributed soap on Sundays
to down-and-outs, one of
whom is wearing the yellow
star imposed on Jews.

at the Préfecture and Schwebelin's PQJ were ramifications and bureaucratic dupli-
cations complicated by encroachments from other police agencies and intelligence
branches.

The PQJ, permeated by Fascists and anti-Semites, was soon involved in extor-
tion and blackmail, and Schwebelin had to be dismissed. In 1942, when Vallat himself was replaced by the far more fanatical Darquier de Pellepoix, the PQJ was
strengthened and centralized under its new chief, Commissaire Permilleux. According to Claude Lévy's figures, the PQJ altogether was to arrest 35,000 Jews, compared
to the 20,000 arrested by Commissaire François and his men in the Préfecture.

Pithiviers and Beaune-la-Rolande were camps installed deep in the countryside
by the prewar French government for aliens and refugees or anyone else considered
undesirable on account of politics or nationality. At Compiègne, only a few kilometers from the railway carriage where the armistice had been signed, was a similar
camp, known as Royal-Lieu. These facilities were taken over complete by the Germans, but for Paris—where the census showed many Jews to be living—a more convenient site was needed. One was found at Drancy, next to Le Bourget airport as well
as Drancy–Le Bourget railway station. The new concentration camp consisted of a
housing project not quite completed before the war. In the summer of 1941 the

perimeter of this estate was surrounded with barbed wire and watchtowers. Drancy remained in full view of many neighboring working-class apartments and had nothing secret about it.

Camp regulations were drawn up by Dannecker but signed by Admiral Bard, then the *préfet de police* and the *général de gendarmerie* of Paris. Bard and the Préfecture designated the French officials who ran Drancy; their offices and living quarters were in high-rise buildings around the prisoners' block, a large U-shaped building of four stories with an inner courtyard whose dimensions were 200 by 40 meters. Arrangements for plumbing and sanitation had never been completed. There were no furnishings.

Georges Wellers, one of the first and longest-surviving inmates of the camp, in his book *De Drancy à Auschwitz,* left a description of the first camp commandant, Laurent, with Dannecker. "Laurent with his limp runs out to greet the German and shakes his hand for a long time, backbone bent and face illuminated with affection." Wellers found this former furniture salesman and convinced anti-Semite to be "evil," and Laurent was dismissed when two of his inspectors, Thibaudet and Körpreich, were convicted of stealing from the prisoners at their mercy. His successor, Commissaire de Police Guibert, was more correct in his behavior, in Wellers's opinion. In order to maintain contact with the French administration of the camp, Dannecker sent his twenty-year-old assistant, Ernst Heinrichsohn, for daily visits.

Finally, to maximize the impression that racism was spreading everywhere through the spontaneous agency of the French themselves, Dannecker used Gestapo funds to launch an Institut des Questions Juives. Independent of the CGQJ, this Institut had the task of propagating anti-Semitism and generally creating a climate in which German racial persecution seemed in line with public opinion. Even Laval said that the Institut had the role of a glorified police informer. At its head was Capitaine Paul Sézille. He was in the mold of Darquier de Pellepoix, whose right-hand man he had been in a prewar anti-Semitic group called Rassemblement Anti-Juif. Nothing was too trivial to escape his notice, whereupon he would write a memorandum to Dannecker on behalf of the Institut. On June 8, 1942, for instance, he wrote complaining that Jewish children in schools, notably in the Lycée Condorcet, "which had always been a Jewish lycée," and in the lycée Jules Ferry, had not yet been separated out. French porters, furthermore, had been observed carrying luggage for Jews. Jews, he added, should be forbidden "to use French labor and in particular to have their shoes polished in kiosks installed at stations or on the streets, manned by Aryans."

The Institut was at 21, rue La Boétie. A specimen lecture program—actually in the second week of June 1943—ran like this: "Tuesday at 5 o'clock: Ethno-Raciology by Professor Montandon. Tuesday at 6 o'clock: Genetics and Eugenics by Professor Montandon. Wednesday at 5 o'clock: Social Genealogy by M. Bernardini. Wednesday at 6 o'clock: Judeocracy by M. Laville. Friday at 6:30: Ethno-Racial Philosophy by M. Villemain. Saturday at 3 o'clock: History of Judaism by M. Jean Héritier." Other habitual speakers and promoters of Nazi racism included René Gérard, Dr. Louis Querrioux, who was a friend of Céline's and specialized in attacking Jewish doctors, and Jean Boissel.

Under the Institut's patronage came offshoots, like Les Amis de l'Institut, of whom there were four thousand in the Paris region, and the Association of Anti-Jewish Journalists, whose president was Jacques Ménard. An attempt to link Jews and Freemasons was made through the Commission d'Etudes Judéo-Maçonnique. Its president was Gueydan de Roussel, who seems to have spent his time giving or attending receptions. As reported in L'Appel, on November 5, 1942, he threw a typical lunch party in honor of the bilingual publication *Weltkampf,* devoted to the Jewish question in France. His guests included Dr. Brethauer of the Einsatz Rosenberg, Dr. Fegers of the Deutsche Institut, Dr. Biederbick and Dr. Klassen of the embassy, together with Céline and his friend the painter Gen Paul, Costantini, Jacques Ménard, Robert Denoel the publisher, and Paul Riche. Professor Montandon eulogized the Deutsche Institut's late assistant, Bremer, recently killed in Russia. And Bernardini, billed as "a great specialist in Jewish onomastic studies," brought proceedings to a close with a demand for "ethnic control." The same men went around and around in a whirlpool: pamphleteering, eating together, pocketing their subsidies, and reproaching the Germans only with being too lenient and dilatory in their racism.

As intimidation built up, even those who had nothing to fear on the Jewish score found that discretion was the better part of valor, while anyone with Jewish ancestry, especially if it was hidden or remote, was liable to be exposed and persecuted at any moment. Nobody could be sure what the dangers of malice or a well-placed smear might prove to be. The singer Charles Trenet had to defend himself from the charge that his surname was an anagram of Netter. Serge Lifar's name, if spelled backwards, it was cunningly worked out, had the Jewish sound of Rafil. In his memoirs Lifar described what happened when he was summoned to the rue des Saussaies, where a German officer informed him that he had been denounced as a Jew and he had to show proof of Aryanization. "I felt bewildered, helpless, and in my confusion I made an attempt to produce the physical proof of a bodily integrity which would be appreciated by the German racists." Whereupon the officer accused him of insulting the German army, as well as protecting the Jewish Marie-Laure de Noailles's house and staging Jewish ballets. Surnames beginning *Bar-* or *Ben-* were automatically assumed to have an origin in Hebrew, and a genuine Fascist—and Corsican as well—like Victor Barthélemy was irked at having to defend himself. A music-hall star like Aimé Simon-Girard had to prove that the first part of her double-barreled name was not Jewish. In *La France au Travail* Sacha Guitry was declared to be really called Gutmann, grandson of a peddler of glasses. He cleared himself. "In provincial town halls I have been gathering papers which attest to my origins. I have thus learned who my forebears were. Not a single Jew, but, to make things foursquare, three generals, a canon, and two bishops." The Grand Rabbi penned a supplementary letter regretting the fact that so talented a man was not Jewish.

Arthur Honegger also had to clear himself, although a Swiss citizen and a willing member of a delegation of musicians to Germany. Music by Jewish composers was banned, although nothing could prevent Offenbach's "Cancan" from being played a few hundred times a night in cabarets. A patron called Judas Colonna, who had sponsored annual concerts of classical music, proved to have been Jewish, and the concerts were suspended. His adopted daughter published a letter in the press to explain that kinship had been wholly involuntary on her part.

The theater named after the famous actress Sarah Bernhardt had to become the Théâtre de la Cité. Streets named in honor of Jews had to be rechristened. Coco Aslan, whose photograph appeared in public among a group of Jewish actors, had his lawyers attest that he was Armenian. Lissac, the well-known opticians, put a sign in the window, "Lissac is not Isaac." The Café Dupont, in the Quartier Latin, advertised "Forbidden to dogs and Jews." *Au Pilori* published articles about aristocratic families, some of whose members had married Jews, and received letters of repudiation, as from Comte Bruno de Franclier, who wrote in to say that "a Jewish marriage would be the greatest dishonor." A descendant of the Montmorencys wrote about his historic family, "At no moment could any of these direct ancestors be suspected of the least Jewish taint whatsoever."

5 Spoils of War

n his memoirs Werner Best cracked a sarcastic joke about an important organization, JEIP—Jeder Einmal in Paris (Everybody Once in Paris), meaning that each and every high-ranking German could think of no better way of filling in a spare moment than by making a trip to Paris. With the direction of the war swinging toward the Mediterranean and North Africa, France became a province well away from battle zones. Safe and quiet, Paris kept its wine-women-and-song cachet, all the attractions which the Germans traditionally had called *"Paris bei Nacht."* More than a hundred nightclubs advertised in the German language for German customers. Outside restaurants and brothels, on billboards everywhere, signs in German enticed the soldiers. The occupation had hardly begun when André Thérive was writing in his diary, "At the Casino de Paris 90 percent of the public is German. A potbellied officer, though not without some distinction, promenades his lady dressed like a floozy by some facetious couturier who must have persuaded her that this is really fashionable in Paris. Up in the gallery some French louts, unfortunately, are very ugly and common and noisy." A few days later he had a similar experience. "We are a party of three Frenchmen at the Folies-Bergère, and one of the three is the doctor on call (who is a Jew) and all around are fifteen hundred German soldiers brought in by bus. . . . The sight of sixty naked women under fairy-like lighting seems to fill them with doleful stupor." The longer the war lasted, the more desirable Paris was as a posting. Comfortable trains with sleeping cars rolled in from other capitals dependent on the Reich, or incorporated into it: Warsaw, Budapest, Athens, Vienna, Belgrade. The image was fixed of Paris as pleasure ground, treasure house—Babylon, as Hitler called it.

Goebbels first visited Paris in July 1940, as usual taking his cue from Hitler but staying longer to inspect the monuments. When he was shown around the Opéra by Lifar (who tells the story), he was given a Hitler salute by a Frenchman called Dupont, whom he answered with an insult. Goebbels was never convinced that French collaborators could be sincere; he suspected that Pétain was playing a waiting game and judged Laval unsympathetic. Though he came to think quite well of Abetz, an aside in his diaries gives insight into the contempt he felt for Franco-German efforts. "A tapped telephone disclosed that the wife of our Ambassador Abetz has been expressing herself very irresponsibly to some French politicians. Well, she is a Frenchwoman." Goebbels issued orders for a catalog to be drawn up of all works of art that a victorious Germany could claim. Further, on November 28, 1940, Goebbels's ministry was to send a memorandum to Abetz: "The result of our victorious struggle should be to smash French predominance in cultural propaganda, in Europe, and in the world. After having taken possession of Paris, the center of French cultural propaganda, it is possible now to give this propaganda the blow to finish it off, whereas assistance given to it, or tolerance shown, would be a crime against the nation."

On the day upon which this memorandum was issued, Alfred Rosenberg, the philosopher of the Nazi party, happened to be making a speech in the Palais Bourbon. His theme was "the settling of accounts with the ideas of 1789." *Le Matin* subsequently published the text, in which the French could read that their genius lay largely in producing prophets of racism like Joseph de Gobineau. "Whatever opinion the French may formulate about their great defeat of 1940," Rosenberg declared, "they will, if they are honest, one day admit that the German army defeated the French army, but simultaneously Germany freed the French people from those parasites which they were no longer in a position to be rid of by their own methods."

But beyond preaching that racism was the determinant of history, Rosenberg had a further mission in Paris, authorized by Hitler in person, and for which he had established a special staff, the Einsatzstab Rosenberg. Ostensibly this was to collect Jewish and Masonic books and documents for a Nazi superuniversity to be erected after the war; in practice it was a looting agency. Anything which could be defined as politically or culturally significant might be prey, for instance the novelist Turgenev's library, on the pretext that its curator was a Freemason. The Einsatzstab Rosenberg had headquarters at 54, avenue d'Iéna, whose Jewish owner had escaped abroad, and four other branches as well as four warehouses, one of them the Levitan department store in the Faubourg Saint-Martin. Running the staff was Baron Kurt von Behr, a prewar cosmopolitan who spoke good French and whose cynicism appeared enhanced by the hard shine of a glass eye.

At the same time, Hitler had issued separate instructions to Abetz, on June 30, 1940, "to take into custody all objects of art, whether state-owned or in private Jewish hands." This was not expropriation "but a transfer to our safekeeping, as a security for eventual peace negotiations." Abetz decided that as much art as possible ought to be secured in the embassy, and hundreds of packing cases were crammed in until lack of space became intolerable. The cases were then removed to the Jeu de Paume. Museum pieces had been seized, as well as assorted Rothschild collections and the stock of dealers like Seligmann, Wildenstein, Alphonse Kann, Rosenberg, and Bernheim.

Abetz was disposed to take the easy solution and order packers to send the lot to Germany and sell off in the trade what was not desirable. But the military administration had a say in the matter. Its Kunstschutz Abteilung, the department for the protection of art, argued that Hitler's instructions meant the preservation intact of these collections in France. Graf Franz Wolff Metternich, head of the department and a professional museum curator, maintained this principle until he was dismissed in the summer of 1942 (after the war he was awarded a decoration by the French government, the only German in the entire administration to be so honored). Metternich's superior, Best, who had been approached on the subject by Alfred Rosenberg, saw no reason to oppose the appropriation of nonstate property. Art, Best decided, should be seized "as though it were enemy munitions or comestibles." Moreover, other members of the Kunstschutz Abteilung, such as Dr. Hermann Bunjes, also an SS Obersturmführer, went behind Metternich's back, so that in practice Metternich was far from successful. In particular Bunjes was briefed to acquire arthistory books for the Deutsche Institut, whose head, Dr. Epting, was soon complaining to Abetz, "The difficulties which have arisen are exclusively based upon the personal conduct of Count Metternich."

There was eventual agreement by everyone, including Goebbels, that works of art should not be transferred out of France before a peace settlement, but this proved unenforceable. The vested interests opposing Metternich were too great. The embassy retained whatever it fancied; so did Ribbentrop and the Foreign Office. The Spanish embassy took in charge a silver bowl by Cellini, and in other embassies prospects of trading were aroused.

With Goebbels and Rosenberg laying claim to works of art, Goering was not one to stand aside. Paris was his special stamping ground during the war. He regularly stayed either in rooms converted to his use in the Palais Luxembourg or with General Hanesse. He and his wife Edda were seen by Serge Lifar shopping in the most expensive places, "Lanvin, Lelong, Boucheron, Rochas, Pomba, Dior, Trémollet, Cartier, Hermès." He relished the luxuries and cuisine unavailable elsewhere. Entering select restaurants or hotels, he liked to be attentively applauded, imagining that the white *Reichsmarschall* uniform he had designed, complete with jewels and decorations, made some sort of imperial figurehead out of him. Dealers were asked to reserve their best pieces for him, but compulsory acquisition from French collections was to him a way of using his position for self-enrichment without suffering the least scruple. Works of art originating in Germany, or which might be considered "Germanic," ought in his view to have been repatriated without more ado. Bunjes was one of the team rootling through France and French treasures on Goering's behalf. Aware of what the embassy had accumulated in the Jeu de Paume, Goering was eager for first pick.

A French curator, Rose Valland, whose book *Le Front de l'Art* is the most comprehensive account of this massive spoliation, was among those who had to receive him: "Goering in civilian clothes, a long overcoat and a trilby hat pulled well down on his forehead, quite different from how he had been expected, made his entry accompanied by his own art consultant, Walter Andreas Hofer, and specialists from the Einsatzstab and from the Luftwaffe." November 3 was devoted to Goering's selection, and the day was not long enough: the works of art in the Jeu de Paume had to be displayed to him again on November 5.

Robert Scholtz, head of Rosenberg's Einsatzstab in Berlin, hurried to Paris to head Goering off. The result was a letter to Rosenberg in which Goering defended skimming off the best things for himself. "I would like to draw your attention to the fact that I have been able to obtain valuable cultural objects from Jewish owners. I had them procured for me in their hiding places, which were very difficult to find. I had them unearthed a good while ago, through bribery and corruption and the use of French detectives and criminal agents. This activity still continues for the time being, as well as the activity of my authorized investigators into foreign exchange and searching of safe-deposits in banks. In both these cases the results will be notified to your staff, whose duty will then be to seize these articles and transport them. I consider cooperation between your staff and General Turner's office in Paris to be excellent and corresponding to the utmost to my intentions."

On February 4, 1941, Goering was again in Paris, conferring with the Einsatzstab and with Medicus, General Turner's chief of administration. On March 9, 11, and 14 he returned to the Jeu de Paume—that year he made a total of ten visits there. In a letter to General Turner, Bunjes noted that Goering "wished to cut through matters complicated by the legalists in the Majestic." During a stormy interview, Metternich finally had his objections met with a phrase wholly typical of Goering, "The highest jurist in the state is me." As a result of these February and March forays, Goering had what he wanted from the Rothschild and Seligmann and Wildenstein collections, fifty-three pictures in all, including one each by Goya, Rembrandt, Teniers, Rubens, Boucher, and Frans Hals. At the same time fifteen cases tactfully reserved for Hitler were dispatched straight to Munich.

Collections which had been placed for safekeeping in French museums could not in fact be protected. During 1942 Goering sequestered for his country house Karinhall, among other items, twenty-five pictures from the David-Weil collection and fifty from the Jacques Stern collection, laying hands on ten canvases by Renoir, ten by Degas, two Manets, three Sisleys, four Cézannes, and five Van Goghs. In a speech

An artist in Montmartre, 1943.

on August 6, 1942, to Reich commissioners summoned to Berlin for a conference on supplies, Goering put on record his attitude toward the occupation. "France could have quite another agricultural yield altogether if *messieurs les paysans* were compelled to work harder. Besides, the French population is so stuffed with food that it's a scandal. . . . I shout myself hoarse that I consider, when all's said and done, that occupied France is a conquered country. In old days things were simpler, there was plundering, whoever conquered a country could do what he liked with its wealth. Now they do things more humanely. For my part I go plundering. . . . Collaboration, it's only Monsieur Abetz who does it, not me! The collaboration of *Messieurs les Français* I see in only one light: let them deliver whatever they can until they can't deliver any more: if they do so voluntarily I'll say I'm collaborating; if they stuff their mouths all the same, then they aren't collaborating. The French must realize what's what. You'll object that there's Laval's foreign policy. Monsieur Laval pacifies Monsieur Abetz and I'm willing to allow Monsieur Laval the right to go into a Maxim's forbidden other Frenchmen. As for them, they've got to learn their lesson right now. Their cheek is unimaginable."

Toward the end of the occupation Robert Scholtz drew up an inventory of 21,903 works of art looted through the Einsatzstab Rosenberg, whether for Goering or whomever. The list was admitted to be incomplete, perhaps by as much as a third again. The following items were specified, however, somewhat swelling the inventory's total.

10,890	pictures and drawings
684	miniatures, incunabula, and manuscripts
583	statues, figurines
2,477	signed pieces of furniture
583	tapestries and carpets
5,825	objets d'art, bronzes, and porcelain
1,286	Far Eastern and archaeological pieces
259	classical art

Among the Goering entourage was a press photographer, Eitel Lange, whose book *Der Reichsmarschall im Kriege* contains a vivid portrayal of one of these Paris art raids. "We were all aware what the Reichsmarschall was up to during these two days. Together with General Hanesse, the Luftwaffe commanding officer in Paris, and his adjutant Hauptmann Drews, he was 'shopping.' Hanesse was the smooth, obliging, deft type of officer, who spared nothing when it came to 'shopping' for the Reichsmarschall. They drove around the art galleries, the antique dealers, the little boutiques, the perfume shops, and bought. Herr Hofer, who personally handled the buying of pictures for Goering, had spent weeks beforehand in Paris seeking out suitable objects. The Reichsmarschall then had to inspect them in person. Everything pleased him, he seemed like a naïve child who wanted to have everything he saw. . . . He seized on everything, and had everything shown him, so long as it was large in shape and looked rather bombastic: altar cloths, Gobelins, jewelry. First and foremost, however, came pictures. He bought them ceaselessly, in bulk. . . . On the evening before our departure from Paris, I saw that two large freight cars had been attached to the train. And I saw how they had been loaded with the purchases of these two days. The neighboring platforms were firmly barricaded off. It made me very thoughtful that these two gigantic freight cars had been crammed full of booty. A huge wooden crucifix could only just be shoved in."

Huge-scale systematic pillaging of art was not only a matter of rolling stock at the Gare de l'Est or the Gare d'Austerlitz. Zeitschel, the Jewish affairs attaché at the embassy, sent a memorandum to Abetz, dated August 11, 1941, about a sale of thirty canvases remaining in the embassy. These ought to be auctioned while a decent price was obtainable, Zeitschel argued, before the Einsatzstab flooded the market with *entarte Kunst,* or "degenerate art." For some, there were profits to be made on the side; for others, there was ideology to enforce. The Rosenberg staff was not averse to selling off in lots works by artists who were not Jewish and passed doctrinal tests, but were not considered meritorious, for example Bonnard, Vuillard, Matisse, Braque, Dufy. Jewish family portraits, however, were carefully weeded out and kept in three requisitioned rooms in the Louvre. There they were eventually slashed to ribbons by the members of the Einsatzstab themselves, in what Rose Valland calls "this strange massacre."

Works that were dismissed as unfit for sale were also stacked up in the Louvre. Military trucks brought them to the Jeu de Paume, and in the garden within the courtyard there, a bonfire was lit on May 27, 1943. Similar scenes had happened in Germany. Between five and six hundred pictures by Masson, Miro, Picabia (whose daughter Jeannine was in a resistance network with which Samuel Beckett had contact), Suzanne Valadon, Klee, Max Ernst, Picasso, Kisling (the man himself, a Jew, had been denounced by the model he so delighted in painting), Léger, La Fresnaye, and Mané-Katz (to quote Rose Valland's partial list) were burned to ashes, the smoke dissipating into dusk and the blackout.

Rationing was introduced in September 1940. Cards were issued in local town halls. The cards comprised "tickets"—the English word was borrowed, while in England the French word "coupon" was used—which were valid for specific foodstuffs. Shoppers registered at the neighboring butcher, greengrocer, and dairy in the hopes of regular supplies. Age and occupation regulated each person's entitlement. Category A was adults between twenty-one and seventy, with Category T for those classified as workers. Farmhands were Category C, and those above seventy were Category V. Babies were Category E, and children from three to twenty-one graded as J1, J2, or J3. Babies accordingly received less bread than the old, but the old received no milk. At first, an adult in Paris had 350 grams of bread a day, a weekly 350 grams of meat, and a monthly 500 grams of sugar, 300 grams of coffee, and 140 grams of cheese. Rice, noodles, soap, and fats were rationed next. Within three months, Parisians had passed from plenty to penury.

Benoit-Guyod, just retiring as an officer in the Garde Mobile, a section of the Paris police, commented in his diary for October 30, 1940, "For the second time since settling into Paris, I have received the family's ration cards. This operation is carried out in the rue Choiseuil, near the Bon Marché, in the playground of a primary school, with the help of temporary staff. There, like everyone else, you have to form a line, even several successive lines, as a result of which you obtain a clutch of bits of colored paper. Snipping them out during the coming month will permit you not to die of hunger. The daily rate of each person's ration is absolutely inadequate. However did it come to be fixed? A mystery." He supposed that the state had requisitioned too little for its requirements, and too many foodstuffs escaped its control. "Would it not have been better," he wondered, "to fix the daily rate at twice its present level, with a clause for revising it if necessary? What's happening instead looks as if it's been arranged to make quick fortunes for anyone with foodstuffs and illicit customers."

"Ils nous prennent tout" (They're swiping everything): the sentence had the force of folklore about it. How else were empty shops to be explained? And in fact between half and three-quarters of the entire French produce—from crops to cattle and wine—was siphoned off to Germany. In March 1941 pastries could no longer be sold. Fish, chocolate, tobacco, textiles, and wine (one liter a week for each adult) were then added to the ration cards. Only seasonal fruits and vegetables escaped. A new diet had to be endured, and new tastes too, like herb infusions, ersatz coffee, skimmed milk, saccharine derivatives, turnips (*rutabagas* in French, fed to cattle exclusively before the war). Babies supposedly received an adequate number of calories, but every other category officially had a calorie deficit. Deficiency diseases flourished. The average height of children growing up between 1935 and 1944 sank by seven centimeters for boys, eleven for girls. A generation was to suffer from poor teeth.

Had Parisians been obliged to subsist on their tickets, widespread hunger would have resulted. For those on a salary of under three thousand francs a month, community restaurants were started, and these "Rescoes" offered a government-subsidized three-course meal for a few francs. Up to 270,000 people enjoyed these meals daily. A majority of the population had relatives or friends in the country who could send parcels or from whom food could be fetched. In these cases, rationing laws were being infringed, and there was a risk that an officious policeman might intervene. What was called the Système D, for Do-It-Yourself, applied to everyone. A doctor would examine a plumber and be paid with the chicken that the plumber had earned cleaning the drains of someone with poultry in the backyard. Almost nothing was too cheap for barter. In the place Maubert was a recognized exchange for cigarette butts, even though they consisted of a blend called "national tobacco" (which included a good proportion of herbs and dried grasses). Rabbits and hens were reared in many apartments. Window boxes and roofs were used to grow vegetables. In April 1943 open spaces, including the historic esplanade of Les Invalides, the Luxembourg Gardens, and the Tuileries Gardens, were plowed up by cart horses and planted out with potatoes, carrots, and beans. According to contemporary statistics, 71 percent of an average Parisian budget went for food.

By the autumn of 1940, shop windows like these had disappeared. *"Ils nous prennent tout"* ("They're swiping everything") became the current grumble.

Memoirs and diaries of the period are preoccupied with how to eat. Arriving in Paris for his job at the Préfecture de Police, and therefore a privileged person, Maurice Toesca on July 14, 1942, described how he had dug up the lawn in front of his new house: "I sowed and planted out tomatoes, cabbages, and several rows of French beans." Léautaud, who liked smoking and had pets to look after, complained almost every day in his diary about having too little to eat; by the tenth of each month, he usually found, he had used up his entire bread ration. In contrast, Fabienne Jamet's *One Two Two* is full of gloating about how well she and the girls in her brothel ate and drank, thanks to their underworld contacts.

A fifteen-year-old girl, Micheline Bood, in her diary *Les Années doubles,* recorded menus which she prepared in March 1941. The family was comfortably off; her mother was away on a visit to the country.

Saturday	Midday: beans, two slices of sausage, cheese
	Evening: soup, chestnuts, demi-sel cheese
Sunday	Midday: bean salad and boiled beef, a dessert I made up (with chestnuts)
	Evening: soup, beans, jam
Monday	Midday: an egg each, vermicelli, jam
	Evening: beans, bean soup, jam
Tuesday	Midday: beans, two eggs, vanilla
	Evening: pancakes, an egg for Papa, jam
Wednesday	Midday: vermicelli, pâté without tickets, jam
	Evening: pancakes, noodles, demi-sel cheese

Micheline Bood complained of being hungry too, so she stole a pot of jam and hid it in the school library where she could have surreptitious spoonfuls.

Otherwise there was the black market for those who could afford it. This too was risky, since the black market existed through German connivance. Rahn, the embassy counselor, had a conversation with the Paris *préfet de police,* who told him that whenever he arrested a black marketeer, the man slipped away, to leave him holding on to a German uniform. *Je Suis Partout* and *Au Pilori* campaigned against the black market, because it was seen as an obstacle, as well as a standing reproach, to collaboration. On Radio-Paris, the star commentator, Jean Hérold-Paquis, made it one of his main themes.

L'Oeuvre described how matters stood on September 10, 1941. "Nothing has been settled about how to feed Paris. No doubt everyone would agree that the time

A favorable exchange rate, as well as post-armistice payments by the Vichy government, facilitated German purchasing at all levels.

A butcher's announcement about who was entitled to meat rations, and when.

has come when something must be done. . . . The sight of the black market spreading everywhere, with impunity, is enough to spark off those with the slowest temper. . . . Nobody can be expected to put up with the fact that indispensable vegetables are swept off the board and only the minority who can pay through the nose enjoys them. People of average means are in fact deprived, and those same people receive no parcels and have not the wherewithal to take the time to go and eat in Normandy or Brittany. . . . On the open markets in Paris, potatoes are practically unfindable. But the black market manages to infiltrate enormous quantities for restaurants or customers willing to pay eight or nine francs a kilo. How is it possible to bring in these quantities? Is it because supervision at railway stations or the main thoroughfares is inadequate? Are they all effectively aiding and abetting each other? Facts are facts. It is obvious that when restaurants are allowed to charge thirty-five or even fifty francs, not including wine, for a meal consisting of soup, eggs, some vegetables, and cheese, then some restaurants can afford to pay the top prices for vegetables, offer four or even five francs for an egg, and still make a handsome profit."

Not only collaborators felt like this. Almost each time Galtier-Boissière dined out, the flagrant injustice of the experience provoked another burst of angry irony in his diaries. On February 13, 1941, he was invited to a fashionable restaurant on the *quais*. "The room was crowded. Sitting at the bar, Léon-Paul Fargue, a cigarette stuck between his tortoiselike lips, was waiting for a table. An enormous Fritz, who, it seems, was Lieutenant Weber, Führer of the Franco-German press, was treating his friends to champagne. No restrictions: forbidden beefsteaks were hidden under fried eggs. A nouveau-riche clientele. The finest wines flowing. Fat cats are on top in the New Order. With cash, plenty of cash, one can always stuff one's face as much as one likes, while housewives stand in line for hours in the snow for turnips." Luxury restaurants frequented by the Germans, he noted, were allowed to serve meat openly, on payment of a special 10 percent levy to the Secours Nationale. At the Tour d'Argent, Galtier-Boissière recorded, on May 2, 1941, *canard Frédéric* cost fifty-five francs a head, as did *asperges sauce hollandaise.*

A year later, on July 4, 1942, Ernst Jünger also happened to dine at the Tour d'Argent. He looked down from the first-floor window at the Seine below, where weeping willows were reflected in the silvery darkness. "One has the impression that people at tables up there, eating soles and the famous duck, are watching at their feet, with diabolic satisfaction, like gargoyles, the gray ocean of rooftops under which jostle the starving masses. In times like these, to eat well and to eat a lot gives a feeling of power."

André de Fouquières, a somewhat precious figure at the best of times, partly a gossip writer and partly the Emily Post of prewar Paris, wrote an article in the 1942 edition of *L'Annuaire général du spectacle en France* containing social hints which would not have been publishable in any other European capital that year. "The soup tureen is more often than not an ornament because soup nowadays is served by the butler. The same does not hold for fish and meat, which are presented on silver dishes to the master of the house. It is also in good taste—at least it shows imagination— to lay the table with whatever is both decorative and necessary, silver sugar castors, saltcellars, mustard pots, the usual little accessories which give the cuisine its savors and piquancy. It is right and proper, of course, to change plates with each course; some hostesses are more stingy and have them changed only after the fish."

Those who have enough to eat, and those who do not, are on either side of a social divide which in all times and all places is beyond bridging. Jean Bourgoint was by no means one of the starving masses; he had been the model for the young boy in

Stamps were bought and sold every Thursday in the Champs-Elysées.

Cocteau's *Les Enfants terribles,* and then he became a drug addict. After the war, he entered a religious order as Frère Pascal and worked with lepers in the Cameroons, where he died. What he described about his mother, in a letter to a friend in the middle of 1943, was quite the opposite of any feelings of power in those dining in the Tour d'Argent. "You cannot imagine the courage with which she has faced events. I can even say that her character has been rejuvenated: it's amazing. She always used to live with such a fear of the future, but now I hardly recognize her. It never strikes her to inquire if something is too expensive: quite simply, either it can be bought or it can't. . . . Maman has adapted so well to spartan times and the thinnest of leek soups that I make a point of invariably hiding my surprise when she tells me what we are having. Morning and evening, soup reigns supreme. Then we have a large dish of carrots, or some noodles, or boiled sausage (black market) because the margarine lasts only for the first few days of the month. Finally, bread and butter, which is exquisite. Maman has moved heaven and earth to get a double ration of butter, and she prefers to put it on the table. For breakfast, lime tea. . . . But wine, the wine we do not have, is our great deprivation, our true sorrow, our deepest regret. We would gladly put up with beer, even this Nazi beer, but remember that you can get it in the cafés only during licensing hours."

In theory, rationing should have worked out more equitably, for wages and prices were fixed, and there were hundreds of inspectors to enforce the economic

97

laws. But shortages, aggravated by German demands, could not fail to inflate prices. The repercussions on ordinary people have been portrayed in Jean Dutourd's novel *Au bon beurre,* subtitled, "Ten Years in the Life of a Dairyman." Dutourd relied on wit and restraint to point out how rationing had made losers of everybody except shopkeepers. His couple, Julie and Charles-Hubert Poissonard, are not the least disconcerted by the occupation. They invest to the hilt in stocks of food and drinks, buying short and selling long, on the time-honored principles. They and their daughter gorge themselves in the kitchen where nobody can see. More selfish and greedy than wicked, they nonetheless trample on everyone in the neighborhood; they tell their customers that if they do not like tightening their belts, then they had no business losing the war in the first place; they water the milk; they write a letter to "Monsieur le Général de la Commandature de l'Opéra" denouncing an escaped prisoner of war, who is the son of a good customer. To the Poissonards, the local *Soldatenheim* is the *Soldaténème,* just as they talk about Hitler's book, *Mène Camphre,* and the *Jestapo.* Hans—"Ans" to them—is a kindly German soldier who has his uses providing goods from German stores. Making a colossal fortune, the Poissonards buy a country house, marry their daughter into the aristocracy, and of course pass themselves off in the resistance when the moment comes. This really means bundling poor "Ans" off to be dealt with by the crowd at the end of the street. Poissonard heroism, in Dutourd's view, was the general rule—and the devil take the hindmost.

The winter of 1940–1941 was long and severe and snowbound. A skiing contest was even held at the porte Saint-Cloud on January 5, 1941. Fuel too was rationed. Heating oil became unobtainable, coal supplies dwindled uncertainly, and even kerosene, used more and more for cooking, was scarce. Parisians were not to be warm in winter until the war was over. Cold, chapped skin, and chilblains were sometimes harder to bear than hunger. *L'Illustration* gave the overall picture. "Today, for people with time on their hands, the best solution is to stay in bed wearing a pair of fur gloves, a polo-necked sweater, even the kind of nightcap the smart designers are already proposing. Those who must get up for their work should count up to three, then bravely plunge out into a room like a freezing swimming pool. . . . Sunday is the critical day: the children are shivering at home and a café is no solution to the problem; the Sunday stroll which used to end in a cinema or a museum now leads nowhere except a bench deep down in the metro, in the warm bosom of the earth. A few churches which had heating until not long ago were also a good objective. . . . Some make for hospitals, or botanical greenhouses and the monkey house of the zoo. Others find nowhere better than the lobbies of banks. . . ."

Colette, the novelist, echoed this advice in a little book, *Paris de ma fenêtre.* "Economy and hygiene unite to sum up my message: Go to bed. The countryside is far away; the days are short. You are lucky enough—or frustrated enough—to sleep by yourself? Go to bed. Get the Saturday, or Sunday, meal over and done with, and the household chores finished, and go to bed with a hot-water bottle for your feet. . . ." Colette also recommended wearing gold jewelry as a heat conductor; she even put in a word for *la tarte au rutabagas* and recommended turnip juice as a remedy against wrinkles.

Adversity put varying complexions into social life. Between shivering and starving on the one hand, and showing the maximum resourcefulness on the other, were a whole range of possible social attitudes. What was to be done about sharing? Or invitations? Poor relations? What if German acquaintances or contacts offered meals, weekends in the country, presents of steak or coffee or cognac? Was it a moral

Only 7,000 cars were licensed in Paris, and the feldgendarmerie supervised traffic and permits.

necessity to have nothing to do with them, and never mind the deprivations? Day-to-day conduct had to be carefully weighed.

"The friend who is expecting you to dinner has gone without, that very morning, to save the ticket which enables him to give you a treat, and you are doing him the honor in your turn of crossing a dark city. The diet does not cut appetites, and around the table there is a fresh-air good humor. . . . A certain art of living subsists, and even a hint of luxury can be contained around frugal tables in frozen apartments."

Alfred Fabre-Luce, the author of these observations (in the volumes of his *Journal de la France 1939–44,* published at the time and praised by Cousteau in *Je Suis Partout* as "perhaps the best overall study we have of the convulsions of conquered France"), caught the drama of the occupation in such details. "The streets fill with automata," he reported; "frail shoulders are bowed down under the burden of parcels and suitcases; old men ride secondhand bicycles, their bodies rigid, their expression anxious, their hands gripping the handlebars as though they were accomplishing a heroic performance. Those who have no leverage whatsoever and have nothing to barter with must learn to be humble in the extreme. When one has to spend several hours in line, filling in forms, getting the paperwork together, signing that one is not Jewish, one does not recover one's self-respect any too quickly."

Two telltale signs gave away the elite: he spotted that they were able to wash

High heels of wood in the latest fashion.

and refused to discuss food or heating. All the same, a limit had been reached when the Comtesse Greffuhle, celebrated original of Proust's Duchesse de Guermantes, was to be seen wrapped in a fur coat and huddled over a stove in her salon. "But there is still a ruined *Faubourg* [i.e., smart set] which is proud to be so short-tempered. . . . Forced to walk, they find it inelegant to drive. (Anyone with a car is under suspicion of having dealings with the enemy.) . . . They draw up lists of whom to proscribe. Their meetings are like war councils and smell of witch hunting. They get the same pleasure that children do when speaking double Dutch in the attic to mystify the grown-ups (the grown-ups are the Germans). Around the tea table, on which is a pudding sent by a British prisoner, they tap the letter V in Morse code with their finger on the cups." In the black market, according to Fabre-Luce, the right address was not enough. "The seller must be seduced by procuring for him goods he does not have. Whoever wants tobacco brings a chicken, and whoever wants a bag of raisins trades a cheese. This oblique traffic in every case implies a trip into the country. Trains are now called after vegetables. One says the *train des haricots* or the *train des patates.* Right by the entrance of the metro, the barrier onto the station has already been shut and the train stormed by the black-market squads: two to three thousand men, yesterday unemployed, have been recruited by some racketeer."

Sacha Guitry managed to obtain a special coal allocation, and he had a car, and he was most certainly suspected of having dealings with the enemy for it. By November 1940 only seven thousand private cars were licensed in Paris, the remainder—several hundred thousand—having been seized by the Germans or laid up in garages for the duration. The license, or SP (for Service Public), was issued in the Préfecture de Police in an office specially set up for the purpose under Hauptmann Fein. The usual Franco-German mixed bureaucracy ensured that those who knew how to pull strings, or were bona-fide collaborators, had priority, along with doctors, midwives, the fire brigade, and such night workers as bakers. Charles Braibant, sitting outside a café on October 26, 1943, observed, "As silent as the country! Out of curiosity, I am counting vehicles crossing the square between twenty past twelve and half past: three cars, one motorbike, a fiacre. On the Place de la Bourse, at an hour when normally Paris would have been bustling, hustling, all alive!" On Sundays only Germans were allowed to drive cars.

Gasoline shortages promoted a curious novelty, the *voiture à gazogène,* or a natural-gas-propelled car. A French company, the Société Imbert, marketed this German invention. Luchaire's *Les Nouveaux Temps* reported on December 15, 1940, that collaboration had taken a step forward with "the constitution of a Franco-German company for manufacturing and distributing gas-propelled vehicles. Under the auspices of Dr. Spengler, five hundred Imbert gas-propelled vehicles have been imported from the Reich and handed to M. Berthelot, secretary of state for public transport." A car or van could be enlarged and adjusted at the rear to fit an ungainly natural-gas cylinder several feet tall. A few hundred buses were also converted to gas. The principal disadvantage was that a cyclinder was exhausted after about 40 kilometers, and refills were available at limited depots.

People became accustomed to bicycling. In the opening three months of the occupation, as the facts of life sank in, 22,000 bicycles were stolen. By 1944 there were 2 million bicycles in Paris, virtually one for every able-bodied person. Of these, 850,000 were new, and they cost almost as much as a prewar car. Out of the bicycle developed the velo-taxi, really only a pedal-powered rickshaw, for hire at stations or on call in the streets. As a rule a velo-taxi could accommodate two passengers in its little trailer. Fares were high. Maurice Chevalier was photographed riding in one

Opposite: **Making do with alternative means of transport.**

Leaving the metro, in 1944, with sacks and supplies probably acquired in the countryside.

with the boxer Georges Charpentier for some publicity stunt, while in other surviving photographs young couples can be seen leaving for their honeymoon. In each instance there is an air of embarrassment about exploiting this odd form of human labor. Horse-drawn cabs and fiacres did better, but hay was hardly easier to supply than fuel.

Crucial to the good order of the city, the metro remained the efficient service it had always been. Although a few stations were closed, throughout the occupation the metro enabled the population to report for work and adhere to normal routines. Virtually the whole of Paris traveled on the underground, to judge by the number of tickets sold every day; sales rose from 2.2 million in December 1940 to 3.5 million in 1942 and higher still as the war lengthened. In addition German soldiers were allowed to travel free. Sometimes the proximity of jackbooted officers or men with rifles and kit bags provoked outbursts which would not have occurred in the light of day. *Rauchen verboten,* the German no-smoking signs in the carriage, were occasionally disfigured to read *Race Verte,* or Green Race, in reference to the color of Wehrmacht uniforms—this form of defiance was much like chalking V for Victory on walls, or tearing down official posters.

A velo-taxi out to the races at Auteuil.

The last trains ran at eleven o'clock and carried home pell-mell entertainers, concert pianists, actors and their audiences, anyone on an evening out. Those too late for the last train had to spend the night wherever they might be. Either the French police or German patrols took curfew breakers into custody in the local police stations. The last-minute rush was described by Edmond Dubois, a Swiss journalist in Paris, for his Geneva newspaper. "People no longer invite you to dinner around half past eight. No, they are more time-conscious: 'Be here at eight sharp. To catch your last train, you'll have to leave at ten fifty, so let's make sure we have time to talk.' Theaters and shows drop the curtain at half past ten, and if something crops up to delay it by a few minutes, it is not uncommon to hear the commissionaire shouting at the throng in the cloakrooms, 'Anyone who has to change trains on the metro must hurry up! People with through trains can please stand aside. Let's hurry, it's already twelve minutes to eleven!'"

In the circumstances everybody walked more than before, and the repair of shoes therefore became critical. Leather was more or less unobtainable; the German military purchasing organization had cornered the supply of hides. Leather substitutes were uncomfortable, flimsy, and not waterproof. Necessity again proved the mother of invention. By 1943, 24 million pairs of wooden shoes had been sold in France; they were distinct from clogs because of their cleverly articulated soles. Hairdressing salons were ordered to recover hair clippings for forwarding to a slipper manufacturer.

Exaggerated high heels, even if fashioned out of wood, in a way challenged the present. So did the wearing of fantastic hats, either huge and floral or little pillboxes with black lace veils or turbans like Arletty's in *Les Enfants du Paradis,* as well as the divided skirts and padded shoulders then in vogue. Not for nothing did a Paquin perfume advertise that a single drop contained all the magic of the rue de la Paix in the good old days. Reporting the summer fashion collections of 1942, the magazine *Comoedia* had a touch of nationalism. "Each material, each design, each color, represents a victory for French ingenuity, a success for Parisian taste." Style, in any medium, was itself counter to totalitarianism.

To the generation just reaching maturity, to be *"zazou"* was an alternative to the adult either-or choice of collaboration or resistance. *Zazous* lived in an ambiguous zone in which they could appear either as striking a blow for style and individuality or else chillingly unconcerned with anything except showing themselves off. *Zazou,* as a slang word, had a couldn't-care-less ring to it, but no hard and fast meaning. To be *zazou* was to be "in," one of the gang, paying tribute at second hand to jazz-age Hollywood, whose films were no longer imported and whose music was interpreted, secondhand again, by such players as Alex Combelle and his "swing" band, Django Reinhardt, and Jonny Hess. The *zazous* sat about in their favorite spots, like Ledoyen on the Champs-Elysées, or the Colisée Café, or the Select Bar. It was *de rigueur* to wear dark glasses and to raise a mannered forefinger in the air. As early as December 19, 1940, these stylized reactions appeared when a jazz festival was organized in the Salle Gaveau by Charles Delaunay of the Hot Club de France and proved a wild success.

"Around the tables, they can be easily recognized," a journalist wrote in *L'Illustration* in March 1942. "The men wear a huge jacket which thumps their thighs, tight drainpipe trousers and unpolished shoes, and a tie of linen or thick wool, and as if that were not enough to distinguish them from other Parisians, they cannot find anything better than oil to rub into their locks, which are too long and fall onto soft collars kept in place in front by a pin. This rig is usually finished off with an anorak which they do not like removing, even when it is soaked through. They are really themselves only under the rain: obeying one of their cherished rites, they love to drag their feet through puddles, exposing to the downpour their greasy matted hair. As for the women, under the skin of some animal they conceal sweaters and a short pleated skirt; their shoulders are emphatically too square, in contrast to the men who 'wear' theirs drooping; their long hair curls down over the neck; their stockings are stripy, their shoes flat and heavy; they are armed with large umbrellas which remain closed whatever the weather."

Abel Bonnard, the pro-German Vichy minister of education (himself a homosexual, or *tapette,* which prompted student circles to coin the pun "Gestapette" about him), called *zazous* "jokers in bad faith, incapable of being either lighthearted or serious . . . the last remains of an individualist society." PPF youth squads made a practice of waylaying them, beating them up, and shaving those greasy heads. The popular singer Jonny Hess had helped to launch this youth cult, and in a postwar interview (in *Les Zazous,* a book by Jean-Claude Loiseau) he claimed that there was more to it than dropping out. "*Zazous* came out of the blue. I must have coined the word on stage one day. . . . *Zazou, swing,* were spontaneous, a way of showing the occupiers what we thought of them. I wore long hair and dark glasses. The collabo press insulted us. We were tickled pink. . . . My secretary and I imitated the newsreels, music as well as commentary, the speaker's solemn tones. . . . Sometimes I'd sing in cabarets where the Germans were—in ordinary clothes, not in uniform. I speak fluent German: I was born in German-speaking Switzerland. I could hear them saying in between songs, 'That fellow ought to be inside.' . . . In Paris, during the daytime, I'd circulate in a velo-taxi. Sometimes it amused me to take the place of the 'chauffeur' on the bicycle. Passersby would recognize me. Whether on the Champs-Elysées or at the Opéra, they'd call out from the pavements, 'Well, Jonny, *toujours swing?*' Things like that. Clusters would gather and the police would break them up. . . . In the Paramount cinema, they came on two occasions, little groups of twenty who called me 'a *judéo-gaulliste.*' Contemporary slogans, what?"

The *zazous* and their *swing* were in the tradition of the Quartier Latin, where the children of the rich and the bohemians had always met to entertain one another. Had there been no war, they might have carried on the same. But as it was, their clothes and trappings were obtainable only on the black market, and therefore to be themselves meant having the savoir-faire to dispense with dreary tickets and live within an extended Système D all its own.

Austerity can be a spur to civic spirit, but what destroyed it instead in Paris was the inequality with which austerity was distributed. In effect the poor and the badly connected and the virtuous had to suffer irremediable drops in living standards, as well as endure the sight of the well-to-do and the cunning prospering in their tens of thousands. The painter Derain put his finger on the free-for-all spirit prevailing, "Parisians despise the poor, but hate the rich." In the circumstances, to behave more righteously than one's neighbor was to be a fool, which is why the Poissonard mentality was so widespread, with its grudges and greeds and denunciations. Even Cardinal Suhard was to be found justifying "modest operations outside the law" because of their bearing on the necessities of life.

How was an individual or a family to decide when "modest operations" overstepped the mark and became gross, indecent? "It was no small hardship having to throw our moral scruples to the winds and settle down to a dishonest way of life, in

A shoemaker's shop, with the notice that no more orders can be taken for the moment.

full view of the children and in contradiction to all we were striving to teach them," wrote Janet Teissier Du Cros in her memoirs *Divided Loyalties*. She was the daughter of Sir Herbert Grierson, professor of literature at Edinburgh, and her husband, François, was a scientist posted from Vichy to the Paris ministry of Ponts et Chaussées, or public works department, to plan the Paris-Lille autoroute. Between November 1942 and May 1944, they lived in the rue du Cloître Notre-Dame, with a view of the cathedral; upright and decent people driven by circumstances to little deceits and so to shifts of conscience. Coffee substitutes, tea made from apple skins, drinks called Banania and Phoscao for the children went only so far; counterfeit bread coupons and food smuggled in from the countryside were acceptable; it was when the maid Lucie scratched out the signature on the ration card at the fishmonger's and so a second ration was dishonestly obtained that some kind of a limit had been reached, and Lucie had to go.

Much of what Janet Teissier recorded was helpless, abandoned: two Indochinese students, for instance, gazing at a bowl of rice displayed in a grocer's shop in the boulevard Saint Germain; an underfed baby in a go-cart; the interior of Notre-Dame one cold January day when she attended a Bach concert, while icy wind blew through the canvas that had replaced the stained-glass windows and a tall German officer fixed her suddenly with his pale, cold, inhuman eyes.

Yet for some undefinable reason degradation could stop, sometimes even in public. "I was standing in an interminable queue in front of a stall where there were cabbages for sale. The weather was cold and damp, and the long queue of weary people moved very slowly forward. As the mother of three children, I had a priority card which meant that I queued to the right instead of to the left of the cabbages, and that we moved forward a little faster than the others. Suddenly a little old woman with the yellow star on her thin black coat came humbly up and stood hesitating on the edge of the pavement. Jews were not allowed to stand in queues. What they were supposed to do I never discovered. But the moment the people in the queue saw her they signed to her to join us. Secretly and rapidly, as in a game of hunt-the-slipper, she was passed up until she stood at the head of the queue. I am glad to say that not one voice was raised in protest, that the policeman standing near turned his head away, and that she got her cabbage before any of us."

In such times of apathy and moral confusion, the insidious argument runs (to undermine those who are weak or wavering), are not all means of looking after oneself permissible? Maurice Sachs certainly thought so, and his example reveals in an extreme form how easy and gradual, but remorseless, the descent into hell can be. A gifted and intelligent man in his late thirties, he was at home in Cocteau-Proust aestheticism and aspired to write a masterpiece himself. In *La Chasse à courre* he described his return to Paris in 1940. "Photographs of Pétain were multiplying. Collaboration with Germany was generally accepted as a paying proposition: people still believed that the English would rapidly be beaten and the French from 1940 onwards certainly only reasoned (if reasoning it can be called) with short-term interests in mind. . . . The black market was at full blast. And what should I do except take part in the black market? I saw some friends. Excepting a few grand ladies, officers, priests and scholars, scientists or academics, was anyone not doing black market?

"On the telephone:

"'*Allo, chéri*, listen. I've got three tons of sugar at sixty francs a kilo.'
"'And I've got a hundred liters of oil.'

Opposite: **A shoe shop with all the right models, 1942.**

106

By the end of the war, a bicycle cost almost as much as a new car had before the war.

The elegant woman of 1941.

Choupinette, known to friends as Choup, a model from Schiaparelli, at Longchamps races, July 1941.

"'*Allo,* old boy, I need five tons of copper. No nonsense, it's for the Germans.'

"'You wouldn't need rice?'

"'Could do . . . how much?'

"'*Allo*, how are you, *cher monsieur*? Would you have any clue about narrow-gauge railway engines and a hundred kilometers of track? If you could manage the procuring, I'd see you had a truckload of Belgian tobacco as profit.'

"'Ah, I've nothing in that line, *mon cher* . . . I've just had a proposition for *cognac d'origine,* in transit, with special permits. And hams too.'

"'Forgive me, I'm hanging up. I think I've got a crossed line and I'm being tapped. Let's meet this evening instead at Fouquet's.'"

Sachs dealt in gold and jewelry. "Some days I sold three or four hundred thousand francs' worth of louis d'or and dollars, with fifty thousand gold francs for breaking up. A Russian smelter in the rue Montmartre made for me little tablets in eighteen-carat gold, in the shape of visiting cards, which I sold to those who were crossing the frontiers . . . the louis was rising in value (starting at less than a thousand francs in 1940, it reached seven thousand francs in 1942)." As a precaution Sachs asked a collaborator who was his friend to introduce him to the Deutsche Institut, where he was invited to contribute to Epting's *Cahiers Franco-Allemand* so long as he steered clear of politics. But a German named Hauptmann Hayden-Linden in the theater

110

"The Magician Agnes" presents her new creations utilizing new German fabrics, October 1941. Behind the model, to the right, sits Frau Abetz, wife of the German ambassador.

section of the Propaganda Abteilung forbade any works of his to be performed on stage. Then a Major Neubauer entered his life, speaking perfect French and English, wearing riding breeches, driving a Hispano-Suiza, and sending chocolates to the Gestapo, for which he was clearly working. A homosexual, Sachs frequented the Select Bar on the Champs-Elysées, crossed the paths of the *zazous,* gigolos, the underworld. As a Jew himself, he had adopted a young Jewish orphan called Karl Heinz, but he grew bored with him and palmed him off on the Quakers.

By 1942, Sachs had decided that someone with so many strikes against him had better make a break for it. Where could he be safer than in Germany? Under his mother's name of Ettinghausen, which sounded less Jewish, he volunteered for work there. Once in Hamburg, absolutely unfitted for a factory, he drifted into the role of police informer. One compromise always led to another, but the price for saving his skin was rising. By the time the Germans arrested him, as they were bound to, he was past reprieve. At the end of the war, when the prison wardens ran away, the other Frenchmen in the prison lynched Sachs in his cell; the abandoned Alsatian guard dogs gnawed what was left of his corpse. Little or nothing morally distinguished Sachs from these vindictive fellow prisoners. From trivial beginnings, Sachs's drama had proceeded involuntarily to its horrible climax. It had been a matter of will, of survival. Unlike the Poissonards and their kind, he had been too ingenuous, perhaps too head-in-the-air, to get right the timing upon which life and death hinged.

7 A Change of Direction

The situation, according to Henry de Montherlant, that master of equivocal language, was *sans peur et sans espoir*—without fear or hope. In February 1941, Paul Léautaud was worrying out more nuances than that: "France's interest lies in collaboration, entente, agreement with Germany. An English victory, which would not prevent the reorganization of Europe, would bring us back all our long-lost scoundrels." A few weeks later, the next stage of the argument struck him. "What would be funny, in the event of the English carrying the day, would be the sight of everybody appointed by the Germans being chucked out. They would have to yield their jobs to their predecessors or others of the same stripe, who had been evicted to make way for them. In that case it would be just as comic to see how anti-Germans from before the defeat, who under the occupation became pro-German and anti-English—in the style of Jacques Boulenger—would switch back to being anti-German and pro-English, and who can tell, even philo-Semite." Among the French, above all in the working class, Léautaud went on, there was "a disposition to wait and see, with hope, with patient resignation, with a secret silent mockery toward the Germans. This state of mind is condensed in the indifference they show toward the presence of Germans; they pay not the least attention when passing them in the street. There is a void between their docility and our insubordination, our mockery and their seriousness, our 'esprit' and their 'thick-headedness,' our taste and their vulgarity."

On the political horizon, in the spring of 1941, no prospect could be detected that the occupation would end. Who could believe in England's eventual recovery when the weeks brought news like the Wehrmacht campaigns in Greece and Yugoslavia? The high-water mark of Nazi success was reached thanks to developments in the Middle East. During the month of April, Rashid Ali led an uprising against the British in Iraq and appealed to Hitler for help. Had Rashid Ali succeeded, Egypt and Palestine, and indeed the entire British position from the Mediterranean down to the Persian Gulf, might have foundered. But Rashid Ali could be reinforced only through Vichy-controlled Syria. Admiral Darlan, Flandin's more amenable successor as prime minister, at once consented. Rudolf Rahn (under the pseudonym of Renoir), the embassy troubleshooter, was dispatched to Syria, where he quickly arranged for French armaments to be released for use against the British and for air bases to become available. In his memoirs, *Ruheloses Leben,* he has described the goodwill he found among the French in Syria.

Darlan and his advisers, including Benoist-Méchin and Abetz, then set off for a meeting with Hitler at Berchtesgaden. Hitler, they found, was immersed in preparations for the forthcoming attack on Russia and temporarily set back by the flight of his deputy, Rudolf Hess, to Scotland. But Hitler was prepared to repay the Vichy government for its help to Rahn and the German endeavors in Syria and Iraq. The occupation costs would be diminished by a quarter, the French navy increased, some prisoners of war released, and the onerous controls at the demarcation line relaxed. For the last time in the war, in fact, France had something to offer the Germans; collaboration therefore had the elements of a deal about it.

These terms were ratified in a document known as the Paris Protocols, signed at the end of May in the German embassy. That the Protocols were signed in Paris implied that Vichy was somehow being stood off, or at least that military matters, not politics, were the issue. French and English soldiers, allies only twelve months previously, were now fighting one another. In fact, Rashid Ali was quickly overthrown; he fled to Berlin. Syria was then conquered by an Anglo-Gaullist force. In the light of the Franco-German military cooperation envisaged by the Paris Protocols, it is legitimate to speculate what would have been the outcome had Hitler at any time between June 1940 and June 1941 offered Vichy genuine inducements for a *renversement des alliances*. Behind these Protocols lay Hitler's lost opportunity to have France as his ally.

At any rate, that spring in Paris was a Franco-German honeymoon. All sorts of reasons were elaborated by all sorts of people for joining the Nazi bandwagon; there was no alternative, for one thing, and there was advantage in it, for another. In the Salle Gaveau, on April 24—to give one example of such thinking—Henri Clerc, a well-known commentator, gave a speech which he later had published as a pamphlet by Fernand Sorlot, one of the newcomers doing well out of collaboration. Clerc posited that the French economy could not survive an English victory. Since French exports were not competitive, collaboration with Germany remained the only answer—the two main continental economies would have to fuse. He quoted a German authority in support. "One of the Reich's most eminent theorists, Professor von Dietze, declared in a recent lecture in Paris, 'The working community must not be forged in the interest of such and such a European country on its own, but exclusively for a Europe well organized as an entity, comprising as many countries as possible, united by a true spirit of collaboration.'" Jacques Dubois, an economist, and Dr. Karlheinz Gerstner, economic counselor at the embassy, both agreed with Clerc, concluding that only Germany could take up the slack in the French economy. Even an intellectual as cautious as Alfred Fabre-Luce reacted to the apparent permanence of Nazi rule; he was planning his *Anthologie de la Nouvelle Ordre* (for publication the following year), with extracts from Hitler, Rosenberg, Wagner, Sorel, and Gobineau, to familiarize the public with what in the future would have to serve for political philosophy.

A sense of defeat crept into the diaries of someone as independent minded as Jean Guéhenno. Take his description of the first Sunday in May: "We dawdled in the Bois, along the Champs-Elysées, on the pedestrian crossings, among crowds as obedient as cattle. Nothing on the roads except now and then a Mercedes, its windows sparkling, as it bears along some square-heads. On the lake in the Bois, whole flotillas of Germans were massed. We lined up at the office to hire a boat. But the occupying authority was claiming priority for leisure and pleasure too, so that only two or three couples of French lovers had their patience rewarded at long last. The occupying authority thought that this was the Spree. They had removed their jackets and were snoozing stretched out in the bottom of the boats, a boot dangling out on either side. Gramophones blared out 'O Tannenbaum.' . . . From the other shore, those under occupation had to resign themselves to this magnificent scene of repose. Near me, a little girl asked her father if it could be her turn to climb into a boat. 'Yes,' he replied, 'when there's no more of that music.'"

A German writer named Werner Bökenkamp was lecturing on May 2 at the Deutsche Institut on "Nietzsche and the Critique of Modern Man." At Les Ambassadeurs, on May 8, a vast charity gala brought together the whole of smart Paris on behalf of prisoners of war. Eighteen different brands of champagne were there for the comparing. That week Ernst Jünger enjoyed the sunshine on the terrace of the

Brasserie Lorraine, in the Place des Ternes. In World War I, Jünger had received the Pour le Mérite, Germany's highest decoration for bravery, and now he had been recalled as a captain in the infantry. A novel of his, *Marmorklippen,* had established his reputation as a romantic, a nationalist. In June 1940 he had brought up the rear, marching through France with his regiment, an experience which he described in a diary published straightaway under the title *Gärten und Strassen,* or *Routes et jardins,* in its French translation. Its freedom from anything like chauvinism or Nazism, indeed its almost unnatural detachment, captivated a wide range of French readers. In his middle forties, handsome, a collector of rare books, interested in plants and zoology and beautiful women, Jünger was also on friendly terms with the senior officers who mattered in the Majestic; he could choose among whom to move. In the diary which he continued to keep throughout the occupation—with interruptions for leave, and for one long trip to the Caucasus—he combined his contacts and his cool intelligence to produce a record of his doings which is also a work of art, its power deriving from the certainty that Nazism had to be destroyed but much of civilization would also be destroyed in the process.

On May 3, Jünger dined at a favorite restaurant of the Germans, the Rôtisserie de la Reine Pédauque, before returning to his quarters at Vincennes to read the letters of the grand dukes to Czar Nicholas. On May 7 he was again at the Brasserie, for a cup of tea and some sandwiches. The Jardin des Plantes, the church in the rue Duphot with its fig tree, the Bastille, caught his fancy on a long walk. On May 11 he heard that there had been disorders in the Place de la Concorde, but he did not specify their nature. Six days later, near the Madeleine, he bought some presents for a lady friend and entered a shop kept by a black man to ask for rum.

Like any interested visitor, in short, except for a few duties. He and his company had to mount guard at the Hotel Continental on May 20. "Beforehand, muster on the avenue Wagram. I had them carry out the arms drill we had been practicing for a month; then I led a march at the Tomb of the Unknown Soldier. We also passed the Statue of Clémenceau, who, to give him his due, had foreseen all this. I gave him a slight nod, as between augurs. That night, on duty, we had to deal with forty cases, mostly soldiers either drunk or absent without leave and the girls they had picked up. Health inspection. From Montmartre came a little eighteen-year-old prostitute who stood to attention like a soldier." She was in such high spirits that Jünger asked her to sit down, and she then chattered away "like a canary." Once the guard was dismounted, he was free to dine at Prunier's with Graf Clemens von Podewils, a war correspondent, Lieutenant Horst Grüninger, who was Speidel's adjutant, and Höll, an officer with artistic pretensions. The party then moved to the Ritz, where Speidel joined them late at night. Grüninger was to tell Jünger that this rhythm in Paris would keep him and his work up to the mark far better than more normal habits.

At the end of May, Jünger found himself detailed as officer in charge of a firing squad. A deserter had to be executed. "I thought at first of reporting sick; but that seemed too facile a way of getting out of it. . . . I must admit that an uppermost sense of curiosity finally carried the day." Nine months previously, this noncommissioned officer had quit his unit, disappearing into the capital, where a Frenchwoman sheltered him. He had circulated in civilian clothes or in the uniform of a naval officer and had been busy with all sorts of commercial deals. Becoming too self-confident, he made his mistress jealous and then started beating her up. In revenge, she denounced him to the police, who handed him over to the German authorities.

"I went with the judge to the chosen spot: a little copse near Robinson. In a clearing stood the oak, its trunk torn to shreds by previous executions. The marks came at two levels: up above, one for bullets at the head; lower down, another for bullets at the heart. Right in the bark's entrails, among the tiny fibers, a few bluebottles were asleep, and these made my feelings concrete at the moment of inspecting the place: it has something of a slaughterhouse about it.... The man faces the military judge, who is at my side; he has, I see, his arms handcuffed behind him. He is wearing gray trousers, of good-quality material, a gray silk shirt with unbuttoned field denims over his shoulders. He holds himself straight: well built, with features and an expression attractive to women. The sentence is read. The condemned man listens with the greatest attention, but somehow I have the impression that he does not hear the text.... I remember that I have to ask him if he wants his eyes bandaged. The priest accepts on his behalf, while wardens tie him up with white rope to the oak. In a half-whisper the priest asks him a few more questions, and I hear him answer 'Yes.' Then he kisses the little silver cross put before him, while the doctor pins to his shirt, above the heart, a piece of red cardboard the size of a playing card.... Then come the orders, and at that moment I regain a conscience. I want to look away but force myself not to, and I seize that split second when, in a salvo, five little black holes appear in the cardboard, like falling drops of dew. Shot, the man is still upright against the tree: his expression one of incredible surprise."

"It's a long way to Rome." A poster aimed at undermining the idea of German defeat in Italy.

Such severe discipline was exceptional at the time. The Franco-German harmony of the Paris Protocols was reflected privately and publicly. At the Grand Palais, Jacques de Lesdain mounted a large exhibition, "La France Européene" with the theme "For a strong France in a united Europe." An ex-diplomat, he had traveled in Tibet and Mongolia, and his current wife, his third, was German. Blowing his own trumpet in *L'Illustration,* de Lesdain wrote, "How can France contribute to the world, and to Europe in particular? By developing its agriculture to the maximum. Under the regime which lately collapsed, the farmer had to stand by passively while every sector of agriculture was ravaged. Nobody realized how he had been bound hand and foot in this state of affairs and thrown on the mercy of international speculators of the type of Louis-Louis Dreyfus. A group of Jews had only to put pressure on France for their fellow citizens to be reduced to dying of hunger, their hands stretched out in supplication." For centuries, nobody in France had in fact known hunger until this moment.

A Richard Wagner exhibition opened in Meudon, where the composer had stayed a hundred years earlier while writing *The Flying Dutchman.* Léautaud and Marie Dormoy, the lady who devoted much of her time to caring for him, were invited there by Charles Léger, curator of the Meudon museum. "Many German officers and their womenfolk. Ambassador Abetz arrived, Ambassador de Brinon, more officers, Professors Epting and Bremer, many inhabitants of Meudon and people from Paris. Charles Léger made a speech of thanks to the German authorities, and the two ambassadors spoke afterward. On two large tables, decorated with flowers, were bottles of champagne and glasses, which the servants filled. Drinks all around. I drank nothing, for fear of making a fool of myself, since I am no longer used to it."

At the Salle de la Mutualité—a favorite place of his—Doriot on May 25 proposed to a large PPF rally: "The interest of Germany is to obtain the adherence of France. The interest of France is to give this adherence, an adherence to the New Order." Beyond that, he wanted agrarian reform and radical policies, by which he meant uniting "revolutionaries." De Gaulle, he said, would only usher in a "Judeo-Marxist social revolution."

At the first congress of the RNP on June 14, Deloncle also called for the same type of "revolution" as Doriot, though when he boasted, "We have a tough hide and hard fists and any attempt on us, from wherever, will be punished with exemplary violence," he seemed to be aiming at rival Fascist challengers as much as at anyone else. In the middle of June, Déat was writing in *L'Oeuvre* that German and Russian interests were so closely bound together that the possibility of a conflict was nothing but a BBC-Gaullist rumor. Guéhenno and a friend had received an invitation to attend the RNP meeting. "In the Salle Wagram there were five or six thousand people, not one a worker. The huge mass was composed of white-collar employees, shopkeepers, would-be intellectuals." Déat, Guéhenno concluded, wanted quite simply to be the leader and "would do it in German if he can't in French: he will be führer if that's to be the language of the new Europe."

The Communist party spoke in an identical idiom of collaboration. In April 1941 the party devised new Popular Committees for Those Demobilized 1939–1940 and issued on their behalf a sentimental appeal hardly different from Doriot's or Déat's.

> To spare our cities their destruction,
> To halt the destruction of French territory,
> To obtain the liberation of all prisoners,
> Sign immediately peace between France and Germany.

A Communist manifesto in May of that year recommended not only the traditional friendship with the Soviet Union but also "the establishment of fraternal relations between the French and the German people in memory of the action taken by the Communists and the French people against the Treaty of Versailles, against the occupation of the Ruhr basin, and against the mutual oppression of peoples."

A senior Vichy official, Pierre Nicolle, spent a week in Paris between June 13 and 22, 1941, but the only unease he noticed was at a basic bodily level. "Parisians are famished; their visible physical deficiencies have the clearest repercussions on morale. In the occupied zone, and Paris above all, people have ceased to use their reason; their digestive tube constitutes their main daily preoccupation. It is painful to state an impression that within families, divisions are on the increase."

Probably not a dozen men in Paris had wind of the turning point which had been reached. On Saturday June 21, Fabre-Luce met one of them, Friedrich Sieburg, dining at the house of François d'Harcourt. Sieburg was distracted, he found, as though hiding something, and his parting words were: "Don't forget to listen to the wireless tomorrow morning." Here was one of those weekend nights, Fabre-Luce went on to comment, during which lazy statesmen are nowhere to be contacted, lazy soldiers are boozing, and Nazi chiefs are unleashing immense operations.

In the wake of the attack on Russia, Hitler's ultimate blitzkrieg, collaboration immediately ceased to have the one dimension of acquiescence in force majeure. German favors no longer had to be begged; they could be earned. Doriot might have his wish to move into the camp of the conquerors. In his element at last, Doriot was interviewed in *La Gerbe* and said, "Until now, the war was between the National Socialist revolution and Anglo-Communism plutocracy. Today the war goes beyond that and is now a war against that specially degrading form of society which is bolshevism." His *Le Cri du Peuple* carried headlines, "Soviet blackmail is over." If Soviet Communism was to be destroyed, then Hitler offered a cause, a historic mission. It was possible now to present a case that collaboration was honorable, patriotic, no less than the defense of Western civilization. Graf Westrick, a counselor at the embassy, summoned to a conference in the Majestic all the leading political collaborationists, Déat, Deloncle, Costantini, Clémenti—Doriot was away speechifying around the country—and the idea of the Légion des Volontaires Français took shape.

The LVF was to be akin to the International Brigade in the Spanish civil war. Its sponsors included prominent collaborators such as Alphonse de Chateaubriant, the industrialist Gabriel Cognacq, Abel Hermant of the Académie Française, Chanoine Tricot, the vice-rector of the Institut Catholique, Professor Georges Claude, a distinguished scientist, and Cardinal Beaudrillart, who called the LVF "the best sons of France." Pétain approved the reassignment of regular army officers to the LVF and declared, "On the eve of your forthcoming battles, I am happy to know that you have not forgotten that a portion of our military honor rests with you." One hundred and seventy-three recruiting offices were opened, many of them in former Jewish-owned shops. Volunteers had the inducement of good pay, extra rations, leave centers, and guaranteed welfare for their families. Jean Guéhenno, out for a walk on Bastille Day, July 14, saw that this was still not enough. "In the boulevard des Italiens, the crowd had gathered around the magnificently empty recruiting offices of the anti-Communist legion, whereupon someone shouted out: 'Line up. Get into line, line up now.' Loud laughter burst out."

Among those who enrolled were a Prince de Polignac and Frédéric Pompidou (uncle of the future French president) and Monseigneur Jean Lupé de Mayol, the LVF chaplain, a veteran who loved the association of spiritual values and gunfire. Like many, he wore his Iron Cross alongside French decorations. Doriot enlisted in the LVF, held the rank of lieutenant, and won himself an Iron Cross. No doubt he had intended to set an example, but he did his political standing in Paris more harm than good by absenting himself on the eastern front for a total of eighteen months.

An inspection of the first contingent to leave for the East was held on August 28, at barracks near Versailles. Paul Colette, a young volunteer, stepped out of the ranks and fired point-blank at Laval and Déat, who were among the guests of honor. Both survived their wounds. Colette was accused of being a Communist, but in fact had a right-wing background, and Laval and Déat remained convinced that Fascist rivals had arranged the attempted assassination. Deloncle was the prime suspect. The corpse of one of his secretaries, a Madame Masse, was fished out of the Seine; she was murdered, so it was put about, because she had intended to warn Laval and Déat.

Militarily speaking, the LVF distinguished itself. It might have done better still had Hitler permitted more than a token gesture. He limited its numbers to 15,000 and insisted that the men should wear German uniforms as well as swear an oath of loyalty to him. The LVF proved hardly more than a mechanism for converting a Frenchman into a German soldier. According to the embassy, 10,788 volunteers had come forward by May 1943, of which 6,429 had passed the stringent physical tests and been accepted. On July 19, 1943, the LVF had its one and only parade in Paris, and on September 1, 1944, it was incorporated, along with all other Frenchmen in German units, into the larger French Waffen SS division.

Fascists were not alone in having their ideas clarified and simplified by Hitler's attack on Russia. "Russia's entry into the war," as Simone de Beauvoir put it—quaintly, considering the enormity of the measures taken by Stalin to believe in Hitler's good faith and therefore not to enter the war—"in the most tragic way removed all doubt concerning the position of the Communists." Much lost ground would have to be made up. The party leadership had no answer to the charge that its complicity in the alliance with Germany had alienated members and prevented resistance except of a sporadic personal kind. The leadership, faithful to Moscow at any price, had been resisted in vain by a few "nationalist" intellectuals like Charles Tillon, Gabriel Péri, Georges Politzer, and Jacques Decour. In reply to Alfred Rosenberg's public lecture in November 1940, Politzer had written a tract to stress that the German New Order was a euphemism for Nazi supremacy, but to him too the English and the Gaullists were "imperialists." Critics have pointed out that what Politzer most minded was the replacement of class by race as a determinant of history. At any rate, Politzer, like Decour and Péri, paid for his beliefs before a firing squad.

As for the organized resistance, Charles Tillon has said in his memoirs, "The Paris region did not contain fifty combatants capable of using any weapons at all in the spring of 1941. . . . I had contacts established among old veterans from Spain, like Carré, and Pierre Georges, who was called Fredo at that time and who was to become Fabien, in order to train our best instructors." In August 1941 he arranged for publication of the first issue of a paper, *France d'Abord,* printed by Maurice Gleize at his press in the rue des Cloys; it called for armed struggle, however ill-prepared for it the party might be. Charles Tillon became head of the Communist Francs-Tireurs et Partisans, the FTP, which by 1943, he says (almost certainly exaggerating), had 25,000 in the occupied zone. To illustrate the handicaps and lack of preparation which had to be overcome, he quotes Gilbert Brustlein, one of his most daring lieutenants, saying, "It's one thing to derail a train or leave a bomb somewhere, but it's quite something else to attack a Nazi in the middle of Paris with old firearms that jam."

On August 13, 1941, at the porte Saint-Denis and the porte Saint-Martin, fighting broke out between demonstrators and the French and German police. Those arrested were Communists, and on the nineteenth two of them were executed, "the Jew Szmul Tyszelman, the aforesaid Henry Gautherot," in the words of the German poster announcing the event. Two days later a German naval cadet by the name of Moser was shot down in the metro station of Barbès-Rochechouart by a young Communist, in fact Tillon's agent Fabien, who was soon to assume the rank of colonel in the FTP. On August 29 in Paris the Germans then executed a naval officer, Comte Jean d'Estiennes d'Orves, and two others who were among the first agents sent from London by de Gaulle. Almost immediately, they had been treacherously denounced to the Abwehr by their radio operator. At more or less the same moment, then, competing campaigns had been opened by Gaullists abroad and resistants at home; the parallelism was to mark all anti-German endeavors to the end. With this rivalry as a point of departure, resistance in France was turned in upon itself. On the one hand were Communists and any who were prepared to compromise with Communists, and on the other hand were those who insisted on their independence with the argument that no cause could justify alliance with Communists. Each broad group suspected the other of being concerned primarily with preparing its postwar supremacy, by armed methods if need be. The split was beyond resolution. Energies which might have been turned against the German troops were dissipated in factionalism.

To the military administration in the Majestic, the threat was twofold: the harmony between French and Germans might be disrupted, and law and order among the French might break down. The murder of Moser, as the historian Robert Aron says, had an insurrectional aspect about it: "Killing was taking place outside the laws of war; judging was taking place outside the customary rules of justice." The Germans reacted with disproportionate violence. Hitler demanded merciless reprisals in the hope that further resistance would be stopped in its tracks. The day after Moser's death, Ingrand, delegate of the Ministry of the Interior in Paris, was summoned to

Doriot, in the course of a ninety-minute speech at an anti-Bolshevik rally held on August 8, 1943, at the Vélodrome d'Hiver.

the Majestic and informed that the German High Command had ordered the selection of a hundred hostages, half of whom were to be shot at once and their bodies exposed in the Place de la Concorde (no such thing was ever done, in fact). However, nobody would be shot if the French took it upon themselves to sentence and execute six men "legally," in other words after an appearance before some sort of tribunal. Meanwhile General Schaumburg, as Kommandant von Gross-Paris, put out an announcement. "Beginning on August 23, all Frenchmen taken into custody, either by the German authorities in France or on orders originating with them, will be regarded as hostages. Should any further criminal action occur, hostages will be shot in a number corresponding to the seriousness of that action." In the future, German posters from the Kommandantur, in red or gold with black borders, announcing death lists were to be a regular feature on the streets. "The nightmare is beginning," commented *La Gerbe.* For sure enough, on September 16, Hauptmann Scheben was shot dead in the boulevard de Strasbourg, and his funeral service, at the Madeleine, was attended by the dignitaries who ordered the execution of twelve hostages in consequence. Terrorism and reprisal were launched in a vicious circle.

"Not all Parisians approved the gesture of killing someone unidentified," wrote Pierre Audiat, a journalist, in his *Paris pendant la guerre,* published in 1945 when the experience was still fresh. "It was by no means clear how the elimination of a German soldier whose opinions were unknown and who was there only in obedience to military discipline might bring succor to the allies or influence the outcome of the war. Had some truly heroic gesture been at stake, then the murderer should have fulfilled his patriotism by being right out in the open." Benoit-Guyod, first and foremost a patriot, entered in his diary for August 23: "The news of the assassination has been received everywhere with reprobation. Enemy soldiers on their own never show the least hostility toward Parisians, and until now scuffles have been very rare indeed. Besides, what we are now presented with is not a hand-to-hand fight but the cowardly assassination from behind of a defenseless man. So odious is the deed that it arouses spontaneous indignation, made more complex from a feeling that the killer, with the advantage of picking his time and place, has every hope of escaping, leaving behind innocent witnesses who are in great danger of being suspected instead of him."

Léautaud had this to say on September 19: "One or two more German soldiers have apparently been killed. This morning the papers have a decree from the general commanding Paris and the department of the Seine. It is forbidden to be out of doors from nine at night to five in the morning. Restaurants, cafés, cinemas, are shut at eight o'clock. Anyone in breach of these regulations will be held hostage. This is to last until Tuesday next, at noon. Not too terrible, it has to be admitted. The decree is accompanied by an Appeal to the Population from the same general. This Appeal is beyond reproach. No anger. Nothing brutal. An appeal to good sense. Not a word out of place. The truth is: these attacks have nothing to do with patriotism; they are murders, pure and simple. Unfortunately it is to be feared that the disorders will continue. Then we shall see what they bring down on us." Besides, there were the usual preoccupations. When *La Semaine,* on September 11, stated, "We are not used to such a tempo in events in Paris," the reference was to the return from holidays in Nice of stars like Maurice Chevalier, Vivianne Romance, Cécile Sorel, Tino Rossi, and René Lefèvre.

Attacks against individual Germans, the Communists argued, might serve to divert resources which the Wehrmacht could use elsewhere, as well as expressing solidarity with Soviet Russia at a crucial hour. It was also calculated that the severity of the German reprisals could only alienate the French population. The Germans, as

The departure to the Russian front on June 18, 1942, of 1,000 volunteers in the LVF. Left to right (all in civilian clothes): General A. Pinsard, Otto Abetz, Graf Westrick (counselor at the embassy).

a matter of policy, were to be goaded into harming their own interests by as much violent overreaction as possible. Collaboration, in the circumstances, would seem less like participation in the New Order than befriending the enemy, and therefore treason. To show what traitors could expect, the Communists gunned down the former party secretary Marcel Gitton, who had been privy to innermost Comintern secrets before defecting to the PPF. The murder by the PPF of Marx-Dormoy, a former minister of the interior and opponent of Doriot's, kept accounts level. From the beginning, French resistance against the Germans also encompassed the war of the French among themselves.

A German source (Oscar Reile of the Abwehr in his book *Geheime Westfront*) itemized incidents which the authorities in Paris had to deal with at the end of 1941.

22 November	Hand grenade thrown into a Wehrmacht canteen.
26 November	Attack with revolver and bomb on a sentry post.
28 November	Rue Championnat. Grenade attack on a military traffic post. 2 soldiers and a Frenchman killed, 7 wounded.
2 December	Boulevard Magenta. Army doctor Kerscher wounded by pistol shot.
"	Boulevard Auguste Blanqui. Bomb attack on RNP offices.
5 December	Rue de la Seine, Major Friese wounded by two pistol shots.
"	Boulevard Malsherbes. Attempted assassination of an MSR leader.

121

A French noncommissioned officer leading another contingent of French volunteers for the Waffen SS out of the barracks at Clignancourt.

Members of the LVF leaving for the East on January 29, 1943. "Death to the Jews" has been chalked on the carriage door.

6 December	Boulevard Péreire. Lt. Rohl wounded by a pistol shot.
7 December	Rue de la Convention. Attack on a Wehrmacht canteen.
8 December	Rue des Maronites. Attempted shooting of a French policeman.
25 December	Rue des Maronites. Second attempt on French policeman.
26 December	Boulevard Montparnasse. Hand grenade attack on a Geheimfeldpolizei man.
7 January 1942	French policeman, posted in front of a Wehrmacht garage, shot dead.
18 January	Fireman Kremer severely wounded by a revolver, Port Maillot.
20 January	Field Post assistant Pepler wounded.
5 February	Avenue Suffren. A soldier and a Frenchman wounded in bomb attack on a Wehrmacht canteen.
8 March	Dynamite charge set off at anti-Bolshevik exhibition.
22 March	A sailor, Hugel, wounded by revolver firing.
"	A German civilian, Spiegler, shot in the stomach at Villacoublay.
8 April	Avenue de Versailles. Corporal Schweitzer severely wounded.
20 April	Corporal Rohland severely wounded at metro Molitor, later dying.

Incidents like these were not in themselves drastic, but they were regular, and Stülpnagel had the duty to protect the men under his command. His instinct was to crack down hard, and in this he had the support of his staff. The outrages against Germans, he declared, were "perpetrated by men in the pay of the Anglo-Saxons, the Jews, and the Bolsheviks." He fined the Jewish community a billion francs. He sanctioned the shooting of hostages and announced that "a large number of criminal Judeo-Bolshevik elements will be deported for forced labor in the East." But he had the intelligence to realize how harsh measures played into the hands of the resistance. More usually than not, hostages were entirely innocent victims, rounded up at hazard, curfew breakers perhaps, and in no way connected with the anti-German activities for which they had to pay with their lives. Public opinion was bound to turn against the Germans for their series of arbitrary injustices. Yet Stülpnagel could hardly allow attacks on his men to be dealt with by the French police, and passed over in silence by the Majestic, without being accused of weakness.

While Stülpnagel was hesitating and changing his mind, Knochen and the SD in Paris were in no doubt about inflicting collective punishments. Then a murky act of sabotage brought about a decisive confrontation between Stülpnagel and the party. In the course of the night of October 2, explosive charges destroyed six synagogues, and a seventh, where the fuse had failed, was blown up the next day "for safety reasons." One of Knochen's men, Obersturmführer Hans Sommer, had provided the dynamite and the transport to a small flying squad, who were all members of Deloncle's MSR. By means of this plot, Knochen aimed to furnish evidence that the French really did resent Jews of their own accord. (In much the same way, the Kristallnacht pogrom of November 1938 in Germany had been manipulated by the Nazis to look like a national uprising against the native Jewish community.)

Knochen explained to Stülpnagel that this was "nothing but Jewish business," but Stülpnagel already knew this to be untrue; he had in his possession an Abwehr report detailing the role of the SD. Sommer was questioned by a member of the military administration, but Knochen himself declined to take part in any such proceedings, instead sending his deputy Kurt Lischka (who had also been responsible for arranging details of the Kristallnacht pogrom). Sommer was recalled to Germany, but Knochen and Lischka had Himmler's protection and could not be touched.

Although the destruction of the synagogues had failed as an anti-Semitic device, Knochen perceived in its aftermath the chance to maneuver Stülpnagel's downfall and appropriate for the SD the authority of the Militärbefehlshaber. For several weeks, the SD and the Majestic fought for supremacy by means of secret cables to their sponsors in Berlin, respectively Himmler and Heydrich, and the Wehrmacht High Command. It was a foregone conclusion. The Wehrmacht High Command needed only the pretext for caving in and found it in January 1942 when Stülpnagel expressed his newfound objections to executing hostages. The reaction, from General Keitel especially, was that Stülpnagel had lost his nerve and had to be retired.

The most vivid account of Stülpnagel at his sorriest comes from Ernst Jünger, who had been invited by him to a farewell tea in the Palais Talleyrand on February 23. "In him, delicacy, grace, suppleness, are oddly mixed, suggesting a ballet master, with features like a wooden *guignol,* melancholy and maniacal. He had sent for me about the question of hostages, because he is most concerned that the record in the future should be accurate. Besides, the question is the only one which has to do with his departure. Seen from the outside, he displays the grand proconsular power of someone in his position, and there is no way of learning the secret history of the quarrels and intrigues within the palace walls. The story is filled out with the struggle against the embassy and the Nazi party in France, the latter slowly gaining ground, without the Army High Command lending its support to the general. On Speidel's instructions, I have been tracing the ins and outs of this struggle in the secret archives." Stülpnagel, he further relates, told him of the human aspect first: "Visibly these things have worked on his nerves and profoundly shaken him." The campaign in Russia was taking an unexpected turn, and Stülpnagel considered that Germany's tactical interests lay in securing its empire with the minimum of force. Reproaches of weakness hurt his old-soldier pride, but the fact was that those isolated revolver shots and grenades were unleashing hatred and rivalry which he had been unable to dominate.

His successor was his cousin, also a general, Heinrich von Stülpnagel, transferred from the Wiesbaden Armistice Commission. The coincidence of surname and rank meant that only Parisians in the know were aware of a change. Heinrich von Stülpnagel was fifty-six when he assumed the office of Militärbefehlshaber on February 27, 1942. He was lightly redheaded, and therefore known as "the red Stülpnagel." The well-placed Jünger spent the evening of March 10 with him, and they discussed *Marmorklippen,* Jünger's famous novel, turning afterward to botany, and then the history of Byzantium, which was a hobby of Stülpnagel's. "Contrary to his cousin and predecessor, he has a light touch, no doubt about it," Jünger decided, "as well as that regal manner fitting to someone in his position." Slender and stylish, he acquired the nickname of the "Nutcracker King."

This introverted Prussian-army intellectual was not to regain the prestige that the Militärbefehlshaber once enjoyed. His heart was not in Hitlerism. French collaborators were becoming more extreme than he or the majority of his staff were. At a meeting in the Vélodrome d'Hiver, on February 1, 1942, Doriot spoke to a PPF crowd of fifty thousand, according to his party's estimate; thirty thousand, according to the Propaganda Abteilung. André Thérive, in the audience, witnessed how the crowd roared in turn for Hitler, Pétain, and Rommel. Even Abel Bonnard with his exquisite voice aroused thunderous applause. The other side of the coin was that all over Paris people now had friends or acquaintances who were being arrested. Galtier-Boissière's diary is all of a sudden a record of rising drama.

January 10, 1942. Claude Blanchard has been arrested by the Gestapo, then released after a night spent in the police station and an interrogation in the avenue Foch.

February 25. Michel has just informed me of the arrest of his delightful niece Marie-Claude, daughter of Lucille Vogel and widow of Vaillant-Couturier.

March 20. Jean Dumaine was arrested just as he was climbing into the express to Monte Carlo with a Jew whom he was getting through into the free zone. A large sum of money was confiscated from him, as well as the stamps which he used for faking forged passports for his friends. His secretary Thérèse brought us the news. At the Gestapo she was confronted by him, because she had lent him her own *Ausweis.*

May 1. Lacan the Egyptologist, the Orientalist Pelliot, and a dozen of their colleagues at the Collège de France and the Académie des Sciences have been thrown into Fresnes prison for a few days. It is thought that the police found their names on a list of those helping an underground paper. Lacan tells me that they were able to keep up with the news by asking for lavatory paper, and the wardens cut up the daily newspaper.

The worsening grind of the war in the East had social and political repercussions which further diminished the Militärbefehlshaber's powers. Manpower shortages led the Germans to import whatever labor was available anywhere in the New Europe. Already on November 19, 1941, Dr. Michel had been to the Gare du Nord in order to congratulate the one hundred thousandth worker volunteering for a job in Germany. The man, a truck driver, had been presented with a travel kit and a watch. But volunteers on the scale required for total mobilization were not forthcoming. If other methods of recruiting, including compulsion, were to be used, a wholly amenable collaborator would be required as prime minister. Prompted by Ribbentrop and Abetz, Hitler turned again to Laval, who replaced Darlan on April 18. Two months later, Laval deliberately wrote into a broadcast the sentence which fixed him more firmly than anything else in the public mind. "I desire the victory of Germany, because, without it, bolshevism will establish itself everywhere." Laval's first important measure was the *Relève,* a scheme whereby anyone who volunteered for work in Germany would secure the release of three prisoners of war. Managers were ordered to provide lists of men available, and everyone was assured, in the usual collaborationist argument, that work in Germany not only brought individual benefit but would earn France its just rewards.

The return of Laval marked the moment when the New Order unremittingly caught up with France. The Militärbefehlshaber in his monthly report for April–May 1942 had no illusions. "The majority of the French population persists yet further in its apparently unshakable lethargy. Their morale is low. German-French cooperation is rejected, and in the occupying power is seen the cause of all restraint on them, indeed the general distressed condition of France." From the point of view of the military administration in Paris, grappling with the terrorism-reprisal cycle, the appointment in mid-February 1942 of a Höherer SS und Polizeiführer was more significant than any change in the French government. This special SS title had been devised by Himmler in order to group police and security functions in occupied territories under one man, who was responsible to the party, not to the army. Hitler needed no persuading that this was the most effective way of disregarding Geneva Conventions or any other codes regulating the conduct of war. The title had a sinister ring, not lost on Abetz with his warnings about a "policy of sacrifice," nor on Laval, who was always conjuring up the "Polandization" of France.

General Karl Oberg was forty-five when he arrived in Paris as Höherer SS und Polizeiführer at the beginning of May 1942. Born in Hamburg, he had been a small businessman and fruit importer before joining the SS in 1931. His wartime reputation for savage repression had been made in Poland. Physically, he was a tubby caricature of Himmler, shortsighted, his hair cropped to the skull. He spoke little or no French. Knochen now became his deputy, while Lischka had special responsibility for supervising the deportation of Jews until the end of 1943, when he returned to Berlin.

Heydrich, head of the SD, personally introduced Oberg to Paris. First he assembled the SD and Gestapo personnel to inform them of the decision, taken earlier that February at the Wannsee Conference by the leaders of the SS and the SD, to kill all Jews everywhere. He explained plans and programs in detail. Next a conference was held in the Ritz, on May 5, between Heydrich, Oberg, and René Bousquet, who three weeks previously had been appointed by Laval *secrétaire général* of the police, Georges Hilaire, the *secrétaire général* at the Ministry of the Interior, de Brinon, and Darquier de Pellepoix, on his very first day as the new head of the Commissariat aux Questions Juives. In order to suppress resistance and deport Jews for the "Final Solution," Heydrich demanded that the French police forces should be subordinated directly to Oberg. A precedent for such a step existed in Belgium.

In the account which he left of the meeting, de Brinon explained that Bousquet had very rapidly made himself popular with the Germans as a man of action and decision. "Heydrich must have had some sort of soft spot for Bousquet, who appeared to him full of goodwill, affirming his wish to collaborate with the German authorities in order to struggle against Communism. Bousquet professed, in words at least, a great admiration for the courage of the SS. . . . Bousquet sketched a program to combat terrorism. Patriotically he pointed out that the French administration was anxious to be independent, and he proposed that arrests in this sphere should be made by the French police, and the delinquents subjected to our jurisdiction." Heydrich and Oberg agreed not to insist on the bureaucratic formalization of their superiority.

The grouping of all German police services under Oberg marked the victory of the party over the military administration, in other words the army. From now on, although the French police alone were capable of carrying out arrests on the scale required, questions of policy concerning hostages, reprisals, executions, and mopping-up operations in the countryside were dealt with exclusively by Oberg. To be deprived of the "Gruppe Polizei" was too much for Best, who resigned from the staff of the Majestic, considering himself once more done in by Heydrich and, as he says in his memoirs, "ready for a nonmilitary job." When Heydrich was killed by Czech partisans a few weeks later, Best recovered and obtained promotion to run the occupation of Denmark.

Heinrich von Stülpnagel seems to have been relieved by having so much unpleasant responsibility removed; he and Oberg had served in the same regiment in World War I and remained on affable terms. The relationship between the two has been described by de Brinon in his memoirs. Stülpnagel, wrote de Brinon, "affirmed in whatever he said an absolute indifference to anything political, and he liked to consider that there were no problems of that kind between France and Germany. The occupation regime was the one and only issue. Very courteous, although brutal by nature, he hardly ever left his office, and he displayed the greatest detachment toward the excesses committed by General Oberg and his services, excesses which he did not care for but had to let happen. He appeared not to have heard about the embassy, and never went there, shutting himself up in the Majestic with his chief of staff, Colonel Kassel [de Brinon's slip for Kossman], Speidel's successor and a man who kept to himself."

Under his command Oberg had a total SD and Gestapo strength of about 2,400. As he reported to Himmler, he could carry out whatever repression was deemed suit-

Death sentences in red with black borders were put up in the street by the German authorities.

able, on the condition that he was sent reinforcements. By that stage of the war, not more than half a dozen men could be spared, and in the absence of SD specialists, Oberg had to rely on French assistance. "Polandization" was not a practical possibility. French collaborators taking reprisals against fellow Frenchmen were likely to swing public opinion emphatically toward resistance. So Oberg in his turn reached much the same conclusions as the disgraced Stülpnagel. As security worsened, paradoxically, the Majestic even began to press for radical reprisals which the Höherer SS und Polizeiführer judged unprofitable.

Hans Umbreit, in his comprehensive study *Der Militärbefehlshaber in Frankreich,* has summarized Oberg's opposition to shooting hostages. "Since he could point to a close and relatively successful cooperation with the French police, and since as a member of the SS he was above all accusations of weakness, he seldom needed to order the execution of hostages, now known as *Sühnepersonen* [or 'expiators,' referring to Oberg's decision that everyone in a family would be held responsible for the action of a single member]." Umbreit gives the figure of 254 hostages or *Sühnepersonen* shot under Oberg's dispensation between May 1942 and the liberation. Abetz in his memoirs provides the same figure, adding that before Oberg's arrival 498 hostages had already been shot. To place this in perspective, Abetz also states that between January and September 1943 there were 534 assassinations in the whole of France, of which 281 involved German soldiers, 79 were French policemen, and 174 were collaborators. Robert Aron quotes Father Stock, the German chaplain at Fresnes prison, to the effect that between 1,500 and 1,700 men in Paris alone were put before the firing squads. Rousseau and Céré, authors of *Chronologie du conflit mondial 1935–1945* (a book published in 1945 and therefore soon after events), write that during the entire occupation of France the Germans executed or massacred in reprisal a total of 1,845. Jacques Delarue, however, in his *Histoire de la Gestapo,* claims that 29,600 men were shot in France, 11,000 of them in the Paris region alone, but he gives no source for these inordinately high estimates, which would have involved the shooting of an average of 25 people a day throughout the occupation, which certainly did not happen.

In the occupied zone, the Front National and the FTP represented the Communists and fellow travelers who had initiated resistance and suffered the greatest losses accordingly. The Vichy government connived to make sure that hostages taken by the Germans were Communist activists if possible. Four other networks, known as Ceux de la Libération, Ceux de la Résistance, Libération Nord, and L'Organisation Civile et Militaire, recruited among Social Democrats and Gaullist sympathizers. In the Vichy zone, three more principal groupings emerged: Franc-Tireur, Libération-Sud, and Combat, under Henri Frenay, which was the largest and best-organized, implanted by 1943 throughout the country. As numbers increased in these loose structures, the debate began in earnest: should striking at Germans have priority over politics, or, on the contrary, did ultimate social and political objectives for postwar France have to be coordinated before anything else? The Communists knew very well what kind of society they were aiming at, and the clarity of their long-term revolutionary ends alarmed many who otherwise approved of their means of armed struggle against the occupation. Often hesitant and less disciplined, the democratic movements had to divert energies in order to match the Communist challenge.

Time had been required to enlarge the determination of particular individuals no longer to accept apathetically the German presence. Like-minded friends could certainly meet and hold discussions, but how were they to transform intentions into activities? Who would prove loyal, no matter what pressures were applied? Who might inform, or had been planted by the SD or the Abwehr? How were weapons to be acquired, or safe houses? Marie Granet, a French historian who has made this thorny subject her own, has this to say about organizational difficulties: "People knew each other very little and not at all well; they were ready to see in other groups, not friends working for a common purpose, but rivals disposed to poach adherents. A movement tended to form a kind of family, or 'clan,' shut-in, jealous: identical dangers and hopes were shared, there was solidarity in that, but also suspicion of intentions, even lies, on the part of others. The head of a movement said: *my* agents, *my* assistants, *my* movement, with proprietary feelings. Instead of that cooperation which ought to have been so logical and natural, there was mistrust and strife." Such personality-based fragmentation was like a mocking reflection of the opposing collaborationist parties.

The plight was worsened by lack of hard information about de Gaulle. Nobody could be quite sure what he stood for, whether he genuinely supported the former Republican institutions or was perhaps an undemocratic military adventurer. De Gaulle and his Free French did after all rely on the BBC for a hearing; they could not dispense with British help and arms—indeed they could reach France only by means of British aircraft or submarines. A number of Frenchmen were in British pay and in British uniforms—were they then comparable to the LVF in German uniforms? Early Gaullist attempts to land men like d'Estiennes d'Orves in France had all failed, and at the end of 1941 one man alone, Gilbert Renault alias Colonel Rémy, represented the Free French within the borders of France. Rather than utter praise which might be premature, and later regretted, the Communists were silent about the role of de Gaulle until 1943.

In fact de Gaulle had criticized individual attacks against German soldiers because of the reprisals they engendered, and this was taken as condemnation of Communist tactics. Policy, de Gaulle declared in a famous broadcast in the summer of 1942, meant driving out the Germans. "Everyone has the sacred duty to do everything he can to help liberate the country by crushing the invader." He was politician enough to add, "The French people are not only uniting for victory, they are preparing for a revolution." Gaullism, like Communism, crystallized resistance around popular discontent with shortages of supplies, rising prices, and the personal disruptions of the *Relève*. Finally, the prospect of German defeat became more and more likely, and by 1943 virtually certain. The huge passive majority was then in a position to decide safely on which side it would be preferable to finish.

Uncertain of Allied support, holding off the Communists and other challengers, discouraged by the indifference of the masses, de Gaulle nonetheless managed to assert his primacy over the resistance in France. Not the least part of his achievement was to weld out of the disparate resistance elements a central body, the Conseil National de la Résistance, or CNR. To bring this about, he sent Jean Moulin as undercover political representative into France. "The unification of the French resistance is the work of Jean Moulin," René Hostache stated unequivocally in his history of the CNR. Moulin had been a *préfet,* with a left-wing reputation. He had escaped from the Vichy zone to Portugal, making his way from there to England. On the first day of January 1942, he was parachuted back into France, where he contacted the leaders of the various networks, some of whom he had come to supplant or at least to subordinate, thus arousing all manner of suspicions. Moulin went to Paris. Eighteen months later, on May 27, 1943, the reward for his efforts of persuasion was the

Overleaf: **Laval (at the microphone, with Rudolf Schleier the second figure to his right, and Jean Luchaire the third figure to his left) greeting the first train of prisoners returning from Germany, on August 11, 1942.**

The Fort de Vincennes. The steps of this tower gave access to the ditches in which hostages were put before firing squads.

Execution posts.

Marks left by the hands of prisoners in their agony.

first meeting of the CNR under his presidency. Fourteen members representing their eight respective movements gathered in a private house, 48, rue du Four. Less than a month later, Moulin was arrested near Lyons, taken to the Paris Gestapo head-quarters at 84, avenue Foch, and tortured to death. He revealed nothing in the ordeal.

The CNR continued to act as a transmission for de Gaulle's orders. Maquis operations were out in the deep countryside. For all its revolutionary fame, Paris was disadvantaged by the concentration of German services, and resistance there scarcely rose above the hit-and-run level. A demonstration on May 31, 1942, in the rue de Buci led to the death of two policemen and the wounding of three others. Apparently housewives had been protesting against food shortages, but actually the incident had been set up by the Communist party. Nothing like it had been seen in Paris since the student protest in November 1940. Several of the organizers were arrested, and three were executed. On September 27, 1943, Dr. Julius Ritter, who had been in charge of the Paris office of the Sauckel Organization, running the *Relève,* was killed on the corner of the rue des Reservoirs by three FTP men. Shortly afterward, files of men about to be drafted to Germany as forced labor were burned in a daring exploit.

"You have only to look in the metro, keep your ears open, listen to them dis-cussing nothing but food, young boys and girls, jostling, laughing, cuddling and kiss-

134

ing, in their hundreds, in the cinemas of the avenue d'Orléans, in order to see for yourself what kind of rubbish is needed, and I mean needed, by the general public. Nothing is going on as far as they are concerned, and they are too stupid and too ignorant to take an interest in anything that has a political or European aspect. You can understand a writer continuing to write as though times were normal, but this crowd of employees, shopkeepers, workmen, with their petty distractions, seem interested only in themselves—they eat, they put in a day's work, they sleep, and there's nothing more to it." The sour Léautaud may have rightly caught the mood for the end of 1942. But by the end of 1943, Benoit-Guyod could encounter something new and different: "Met young B, former schoolfriend of my son at Melun. He is a member of a clandestine resistance formation and is living in Paris under a false name. Once a Socialist, he has joined a predominantly Catholic group and for the time being is busy with the dangerous job of printing propaganda tracts, as well as false ration cards for those like him who are on the run. He has all his equipment in an attic, near the Bon Marché. But what indiscretion to be spilling such secrets to me in the course of conversation."

Not more than a handful of people committed themselves to the hardships of clandestinity with a false identity in an attic. If the general public, so despised by Léautaud, did not go beyond *attentisme* and the evening broadcasts of the London *Bibici,* it was for fear of General Oberg and the men in black unmarked cars. During Oberg's first twelve months as Höherer SS und Polizeiführer, the German army everywhere retreated: Stalingrad was followed by reverses in the Western Desert, the Anglo-American invasion of North Africa, the collapse of Italy as a partner in the Axis. Only in France did the Germans appear to be extending their rule, occupying the Vichy zone in November 1942. From then on, Petain and the Vichy administration were directly subordinate to the German military authorities and could not claim otherwise. In one perspective, Nazi defeat became a real likelihood; in another perspective, Allied victory was approaching slowly but surely. The more that might be asked of the French in the changing balance of power, the greater the threat of repression. According to de Brinon, 1943 was the year of the SS.

The Palais Berlitz on the boulevard des Italiens was the site of an anti-Jewish exhibition which opened on September 5, 1941, when, by coincidence, the first acts of armed resistance were linking Jews and Communists in a manner gratifying to Nazi propaganda. Huge posters, drawn by René Périn, showed a demonic ghoul of a figure digging fingernails into the globe, labeled in red "Le Juif et la France." The initiative for the exhibition, as Abetz reported in a cable to Berlin, came from his own counselor, Dr. Zeitschel, with the collaboration of the SD, but "in the eyes of the public, the Institut Français des Questions Juives directed by the Commissaire Générale des Affaires Juives is responsible." Four months later, Sézille on behalf of the Institut wrote to Vallat at the CGQJ that the exhibition "had registered a paid attendance of 500,000, which, with free or half-rate entrances, represents close to a million visitors altogether. Besides, I was able to take the temperature of public opinion in sixty-four meetings which I addressed personally. In addition to these meetings, four speakers a week during every single week of the four months in which the exhibition was open discussed the Jewish question before a large and attentive audience, made up of the man-on-the-street sometimes to the number of seven thousand." C. F. Duguet, one of Sézille's four speakers, lectured on up-to-the-minute themes like "Napoleon: Victim of the Jews and the English" and "Bolshevism at the Order of Jewry." Incidentally, a painting by Dali, in a section supposed to illustrate the iniquities of Jewish art, had to be withdrawn when the Spanish consul general, Bernardo Rolland, wrote in to explain that the artist was not Jewish.

No doubt this exhibition had appeared to Knochen as an ideal screen to the burning of the synagogues. To have taken the synagogue issue up in the first place had exposed Stülpnagel to the charge of being soft on the Jews, and no doubt too that was why he fined the community and ordered the arrest of a thousand Jews, with several well-known men among them, as a reprisal for resistance activities. Interned at Drancy, these Jews were at the mercy of Lischka, Dannecker, and the SD—a clear example of how the party obtained what it wanted from the army. In any case, in accordance with the decision just taken at the Wannsee Conference that every Jew everywhere was to be exterminated methodically, Eichmann, in charge of the logistics of this so-called Final Solution, cabled Lischka on February 26 to deport as a preliminary the thousand Jews already arrested on Stülpnagel's orders. Lieutenant General Kohl, in charge of rail transport in occupied France, set to work—according to Dannecker, Kohl was "an uncompromising adversary of Jews, who approved a hundred percent the final solution of the Jewish question whose objective is the elimination to the last remnants of this enemy."

The first transport left for Auschwitz on March 27, 1942. Georges Wellers had been among the thousand arrested the previous December and was not to be deported himself until 1944. He has depicted how the column of prisoners made their way from Drancy to the nearby railway station "in front of numerous local people who stood watching in silence, somber, preoccupied, but discreetly making gestures of encouragement and sympathy. The deportees, particularly thin, their complexion earth-colored, and their gait tottering, had a shattering effect on the crowd. Nobody was yet used to such sights. . . . Near the station, people had gathered, and by a

On August 27, 1943, the LVF celebrated its second anniversary with a service at Saint-Louis des Invalides. Left to right: Fernand de Brinon, General Heinrich von Stülpnagel, General Karl Oberg.

miracle there were many wives who had made their way out from Paris, having heard on the grapevine of this departure. The Germans prevented them from approaching the ranks, and last farewells were at a distance." Half of these deportees were French Jews, making an immediate mockery of Vichy's claims to be saving its citizens.

Means more effective than exhibitions and the instigated burning of synagogues had to be devised in order to divide Jews from the rest of the population. The risk was that anyone upset or angered by what was about to happen might take to resistance. On May 29, 1942, nonetheless, Jews were ordered to wear a six-pointed yellow star, as in Germany and Poland. This star, the width of a man's palm, was embroidered with the word "Juif" and had to be worn on the left side of the jacket or overcoat, in the region of the heart. Textile coupons had to be traded in exchange. A couple of dozen arrests were made of men and women who expressed solidarity by sewing on the star although they were not Jewish, or ridiculing it with some other word, for instance "Français" or "Goy," the Yiddish for Gentile.

In *Je Suis Partout,* Rebatet reacted at once. "Only last month I was remarking in this journal how pleased I was to have seen in Germany the first Jews marked by their yellow seal. It will be a much keener joy to see this star in our Paris streets where as little as three years ago this execrable race was treading us underfoot." Brasillach was disagreeably surprised by the number of yellow stars he spotted; he had no idea, he said, how many Jews he had been living among. Critics or fainthearts were told in an editorial in *Je Suis Partout*: "The yellow star may make some Catholics shudder but . . . it renews the most strictly Christian tradition." Every Paris paper approved. *Paris-Midi,* for example, wrote on June 8: "The abundance of Jews on the Paris pavements has opened the eyes of the most blind." The same issue resorted to the obvious next step of singling out offenders. "Marcel Hirsch so-called Hutin, former editor in chief of *L'Echo de Paris,* was arrested on Friday evening for refusing to wear the Jewish emblem." A new area of denunciation was available for "Echos," as in this example, from *L'Appel:* "Some Jews left without hope of returning; others are returning without shame. In the Select, one of the large cafés on the Champs-Elysées, the horrid little *youtre* [a pejorative term for Jew] of a filmmaker, Wengeroff, has recently reappeared, making no secret of what he is. Today, when people are amazed by his presence, he tells them, with an effrontery all the more astonishing because he is not wearing a star, that he is a pure Aryan—but alas has no proof because his papers are lost, so his story goes. Is there no more room in the concentration camp at Drancy?"

June 8 happened to be a day when Ernst Jünger had lunched at Maxim's with the novelist Paul Morand, who was about to be posted as French ambassador in Bucharest on account of his pro-German opinions. The two had talked with admiration about Richard Hughes's novel *A High Wind in Jamaica.* Afterward, wrote Jünger, "In the rue Royale I encountered for the first time in my life the yellow star, worn by three young girls who passed close by me, arms linked. These insignia were distributed yesterday. . . . in the afternoon I saw the star again far more frequently. I consider that this is a date which will leave a deep mark, at the personal level too. A sight like this cannot but provoke a reaction. I was immediately ashamed to be in uniform." On June 14, Léautaud, who admitted to disliking Jews, put down in his diary the news he had heard of a twelve-year-old in the Alésia-Orléans neighborhood jumping out of the window to his death as a result of having to wear the yellow star.

Dérogations—the French for "exceptions"—were possible. Pétain put forward a short list of his Jewish acquaintances exempted from wearing the star, headed by the Marquise de Chasseloup-Laubat and the Comtesse d'Araman. Certificates of

The entrance of the anti-Semitic exhibition "Le Juif et la France" at the Palais Berlitz in
September 1941.

Aryanization, of the kind issued or illicitly purchased from the CGQJ, came to have the power of life or death. Certain categories of "economically useful" Jews were granted an *Ausweis* to continue trades given priority by the Wehrmacht, such as cobblers or furriers making clothing for the Russian winter. Blank certificates might be stolen or forged. Those who claimed to be Bulgarian or Iranian, or even more exotically Shiite or Uzbek or anything defying simple categorization, were sent to an institute run by Professor Montandon, to submit to what was known as an "Ethno-Racial Test."

Since the majority of Jews were not conscious of having done anything wrong, they obeyed this law along with all the others and sewed on their stars. Class distinctions, as much as temperament, governed some to accept their lot, others to bluff things out. Simone de Beauvoir saw how the rebellious or the bohemian by nature had an advantage. "Optimism remained so obstinately rooted in French heads that a certain number of Jews, particularly small folk without adequate resources, naïvely supposed that by observing the regulations they would escape the worst of what was happening. In fact, few of those identifiable by the yellow star survived. Others, equally ingenuous, thought they could flout all the decrees with impunity. I never saw anyone wearing a star in Montparnasse or Saint-Germain-des-Prés. Neither Sonia nor the pretty Czech girl nor Bella nor any of their friends changed their way of life in the slightest degree, even when from July 15 they were forbidden to enter any public building, such as restaurants, cinemas, or libraries. They still turned up at the Flore and chattered away until closing time." Henri Jeanson, who liked gestures, tells the story of how one day he ran into the minor dramatist Pierre Wolff wearing his star and smoking a cigar while out riding down the Champs-Elysées in a fiacre. Wolff explained, "Believe me, my dear fellow, this is not the moment to hide one's light under a bushel."

Délation—the French for "denouncing"—was the other side of the coin. Tens of thousands of letters poured into the German offices and the anti-Jewish police, fattening the files, leading to inquiries. This example was anonymous, like most: "Since you are taking care of Jews, and if your campaign is not just a vain word, then have a look at the kind of life led by the girl M.A., formerly a dancer, now living at 31, boulevard de Strasbourg, not wearing a star. This person, for whom being Jewish is not enough, debauches the husbands of proper Frenchmen, and you may well have an idea what she is living off. Defend women against Jewishness— that will be your best publicity, and you will return a French husband to his wife."

"J'irai le dire à la Kommandantur" (I will go and tell the Kommandantur about it) had been the title of an article by Robert Desnos in *Aujourd'hui* as early as September 1940. To stop the widespread habit of anonymous denunciation, Desnos had appealed to "the sense of dignity." In February 1941 Guéhenno met a friend, Monod, "who told me that the occupying authorities had just arrested a teacher of German at the Lycée Jansen de Sailly because of denunciation through a pupil. The occupying authorities apparently pay a hundred francs for each denunciation."

On August 13, 1942, *Au Pilori* was giving advice about procedure. "Numerous readers ask us to which organization they should address themselves in order to point out the occult activities or frauds of the Jews. It is sufficient to post a letter or a simple signed note to the Haut-Commissariat aux Questions Juives, or failing that, to the offices of our paper for onward transmission." One such letter (quoted by Claude Lévy in *La Grande Rafle du Vél d'Hiv*) that arrived at the Commissariat was written on Ministry of the Interior notepaper: "I have the honor to draw to your attention, for whatever useful purposes it may serve, that an apartment at 57 *bis,* boulevard Rochechouart, belonging to the Jew Gresalmer, contains very fine furniture. [Signature illegible]" *Au Pilori* led the incitement. For instance, "Nathan, at 9, rue Méchain, Paris, has a former Jewish owner whose house is close to the workshop. In the gardens Jewish receptions are held right under the noses of underfed workers. Besides, recently the former Jewish owner has had twenty-six wooden cases made; 50 centimeters by 50, they have been filled with who knows what and sent off who knows where." In its very last issue, on August 9, 1944, *Au Pilori* was still at it: "The Jewess Marie Kahn celebrated Sabbath with a dinner whose suave odors perfumed the whole district, revealing food unknown to those on rations. Among the guests, we hear, was M. Taittinger, Président du Conseil Municipal, and André de Fouquières, a habitué of the Kahn salon. Will they kindly deny it?"

Informers created the climate of intimidation, and intimidation was an indispensable component of the smooth functioning of Drancy. Everybody in Paris knew what was happening; yet there was neither spontaneous nor organized protest of any kind.

Once the first transport from Drancy had set the precedent, Eichmann himself arrived in Paris, at the end of June 1942, to discuss with Dannecker "the objective of deporting all French Jews as soon as possible. Pressure needs to be put on Vichy and the pace of deportations accelerated to three transports a week." The immediate outcome of this visit was a briefing at the SD offices in the avenue Foch on July 7. Dannecker and his assistant Heinrichsohn met with Darquier de Pellepoix and representatives of the French police services, including Jean Leguay and André Tullard, keeper of the census files. No Germans were to be in evidence for the huge roundup planned at this stage of genocide. Eight hundred and eighty-eight teams of French police were constituted and allotted among five arrondissements, with a reserve of four hundred PPF youths. Fifty buses were requisitioned from the Compagnie des Transports, those familiar old green and white buses so much a part of Paris. From Tullard's files 27,388 names were selected.

Once concerted, the operation was launched on the night of July 16, and it lasted well into the next day. Its scale immediately earned it the name "La Grande Rafle," The Great Raid. The five arrondissements were sealed off. Whole parts of the city were dislocated. Some advance warnings had leaked out, spreading by word of mouth through the Jewish community, with the result that almost half of those on the lists had left home and escaped arrest.

One who survived was Madame Rado, and her testimony is quoted in Claude Lévy's book *La Grande Rafle du Vél d'Hiv.* "I had taken a pram for my littlest child. On top I had piled up a few things and some saucepans, because I had supposed that the children would need to have something prepared. We went out of the house, rue du Faubourg Saint-Antoine, at Japy, me pushing the pram and the four children holding on to me tightly, frightened and ashamed of being led away by policemen. On our clothes we were wearing the yellow star. People stared at us. I don't know what they were thinking. Their expressions were empty, apparently indifferent. Place Voltaire, there was a small crowd. A woman started shouting, 'Well done! Well done! They can all go to hell.' She was the only one to shout at us. The children huddled against me. We were passing in front of the crowd and a man turned to this woman, saying, 'After them, it'll be us. Poor people.' The woman left, downcast. The policeman hurried us along."

The buses drove those arrested to the Vélodrome d'Hiver, an indoor sports arena with grandstands. Its capacity was insufficient for the 15,000 people now incarcerated there. Meals were not served; sanitary arrangements collapsed. According to the eminent Paris doctor, Professor Pierre Abrami, 106 people committed suicide and 24 more died, including 2 pregnant women, during the eight uninterrupted days of this atrocity. Then those incarcerated were transferred in cattle trucks to Pithiviers, Beaune-la-Rolande, and finally Drancy.

All these Jews were foreign refugees and either stateless or naturalized French. Often their children had been born in France, and the Vichy government therefore faced a dilemma: if foreigners in France could be so disposed of at the will of another state, what about French-born citizens? What precedent did that establish? The Vichy perception that French Jews might be saved for the time being by the sacrifice of foreign Jews cut across and contradicted the reality of the situation: the Germans had no intention of sparing any Jews, no matter what their national origins. French-born Jewish children were supposed to be exempt from the mass arrests of July 16, but families preferred to stay together. Enforced separation of parents and children in the camps led to harrowing scenes, about which the police themselves complained.

Laval intervened. His attitude to French-born children had been clarified at the planning stage in a telegram from Dannecker to Eichmann. "President Laval has proposed, in the case of deporting Jewish families from the nonoccupied zone, to include as well children under sixteen years of age. The question of Jewish children in the occupied zone is of no interest to him."

On July 17, with the Grande Rafle still in progress, another Franco-German conference took place, which Dr. Joseph Billig has summarized: "Bousquet, *secrétaire général* for the Police Nationale, working in perfect harmony with Laval and Leguay, his representative in the occupied zone, intervened very vigorously in the question of the Jewish children at Drancy. The minutes of the conference of July 17 were written by Heinz Roethke, and Leguay as well as the representatives of the Préfecture de Police and Darquier had been present. The representatives of the French police expressed the wish several times to see the children also deported to the Reich." Although Laval could present this in a quasi-humanitarian light, as the desire to keep families united, in fact he had specifically asked the Germans what the fate of these people would be; he had received a truthful answer: they were not being sent to labor camps or settlements, he well knew, but to their death. Since all the Germans involved had been briefed in detail about the Final Solution by Heydrich, it is impossible to credit the ignorance claimed after the war by the senior French officials and policemen who worked alongside them day after day in close cooperation and partnership.

So it was that through late July and August, four thousand children, already orphans, some only a few months old and none above the age of twelve, were accumulated at Drancy. Georges Wellers, retained in the camp administration, witnessed the scene. "They were dumped from buses in the middle of the courtyard, as though they were tiny beasts . . . the majority of the gendarmes did not hide sincere emotions at such a sight, nor their disgust at the work they were made to do." Nonetheless, not one gendarme refused to carry out the assignment. Many children were too young to know their names and were entered as question marks on the train lists. They were in a constant state of panic; they were often screaming. Nobody could comfort them, nobody could tell them what their destination was, and they invented among themselves a name for the fearful place for which they were bound: "Pitchipoi." The word lingered in Drancy long after the children had been killed in Auschwitz. "We knew that the London radio carried tales of horror and gas chambers and other methods of exterminating Jews," wrote Wellers, "but nobody could really believe it."

A Red Cross helper, Annette Monod, posted this last letter from a seven-year-old: "*Madame la concierge*. I am writing to you because I have nobody else. Last week Papa was deported. Mama has been deported. I have lost my purse. I have nothing left." Annette Monod was present at the children's departure. "The gendarmes tried to have a roll call. But children and names did not correspond. Rosenthal, Biegelmann, Radetski—it all meant nothing to them. They did not understand what was wanted of them, and several even wandered away from the group. That was how a little boy approached a gendarme, to play with the whistle hanging at his belt: a little girl made off to a small bank on which a few flowers were growing, and she picked some to make a bunch. The gendarmes did not know what to do. Then the order came to escort the children to the railway station nearby, without insisting on the roll call. The thing that mattered was to reach the right number overall. The place where we were was only about 200 meters from the station. But the distance was made no shorter for these tots by their awkward bundles. That was when I saw a gendarme carry the miserable package of a wisp of a boy of four or five, for him to be better able to walk. But a warrant officer objected, bawling out the gendarme on the grounds that a Frenchman in uniform does not carry the baggage of a Jew. Crestfallen, the gendarme gave the child back his package. I followed the column, my heart aching, unable to turn my back on these little children who had been in my care for a few weeks. I could hardly restrain my tears, and I must say that many gendarmes also did not hide their feelings. When we reached the departure platform, I noticed that a German sentry, standing on a passageway above the station, had us covered with his machine gun. Getting onto the train then took place with an anxiety which had suddenly turned feverish. The freight cars had no foot boards, and many of the children were too small to step up. The bigger ones climbed in first and then helped pull in the smaller ones. The gendarmes lent a hand, taking the youngest, still babies in arms, and passing them up to those already inside, among whom were a few women, indeed the few who were breast-feeding. Whereupon the children gave way to fear. They did not want to leave and began to sob, calling on the social workers and even the gendarmes to help them. I remember little Jacquet, aged five and especially endearing. Begging for my help, he called out, 'I want to get down, I want to see the lady again, I don't want to do pipi here, I want the lady to help me down to do pipi. . . .' The door of the wagon was closed and padlocked, but he still stuck his hand out through a crack between two planks; his fingers moved; he continued to cry out, 'I don't want to do pipi here, I want the lady to help me to do pipi. . . .' The warrant officer whom I have mentioned gave that hand a blow."

"Yesterday," wrote Ernst Jünger in his diary on the day after the Grande Rafle, "a large number of Jews were arrested here in order to be deported—first of all the parents were separated from their children, so that their crying could be heard in the streets. Not for a single moment can I forget how I am surrounded by wretched people, human beings in the depth of torment."

Claude Mauriac, son of the novelist, had the experience of encountering the buses, the gendarmes, and their prisoners. "Many of the vehicles were filled only with children looking amazed and sad. I had it confirmed that during the roundup this morning, families were broken in order to be scattered to the four winds of unhappiness. It is shaming to be here, heartsick, a silent bystander at these ignominious sights. In the evening I met Georges Izard on the terrace of the Deux-Magots. Jean-Louis Vaudoyer looked in, thinner and depressed. Despiau was sitting behind us. At the next door table, the odious Brasillach, overweight and wan, the very picture of treason and crime, was holding forth calmly to a friend. Ramon Fernandez went past without greeting him. Then came a poor forgotten Jewish family, with a kid of seven, on their chests the blazon of the yellow star. Georges Izard was discussing the latest news of the war, which was none too good. It is said that Laval might be replaced by Doriot: 'There's nothing for it except to put up with the misfortunes of others and of oneself with as much fortitude as possible,' Georges Izard was saying. 'For oneself, the worst must be anticipated, but one must carry on as if life will continue normally and peacefully in respect of work and hope. . . .' So then off I went to dine in the rue du Dragon with Janine, toward whom, after a couple of days of being apart, I felt a real tenderness. Life continues."

Three days later Claude Mauriac was at the station seeing his mother off to the house in the country where she and François Mauriac spent the war. "A long goods train was ringed with police in impressive strength, and at the narrow openings of the cattle trucks were pressed the white faces of children. That is what I saw yesterday morning, at the Gare d'Austerlitz. . . . Maman was shattered by the sight. Our parting was put under a shadow by it. All day I was haunted by this shaming vision."

These operations in Paris were considered insufficiently speedy and efficacious by the RSHA in Berlin, and Eichmann exerted pressure to accelerate the rate of deportation. Office wrangling resulted in the transfer of Dannecker to Bulgaria, and his replacement at the end of July 1942 by Heinz Roethke. From then until the liberation, regular transports from Drancy ferried a thousand people at a time to their death. Just a year later, for the first time a German was appointed camp commandant of Drancy, reflecting the priority given to the Final Solution among war aims. Hauptsturmführer Alois Brünner came fresh from murdering the eighty thousand Jews of Salonika. As seen by Georges Wellers, Brünner "was small, badly built, puny, with a look that gave away nothing, but wicked little eyes. His monotonous voice hardly ever rose. Perfidious, pitiless, a liar, he was unmoved by the dignified attitudes of his victims, their uprightness and good faith. In contrast he cynically exploited human weaknesses and had no scruples about resorting to the most blatant blackmail, in other words, deportation, to achieve his ends. . . . He hit people rarely and without savagery but ostensibly affected physical repugnance of Jews." His assistants, Bruckler and Weisel and Koepler, were sadists. According to Wellers, the appointment of these Germans in the final year of the occupation to replace the French hitherto in charge of Drancy arose from disputes between Roethke and Brünner.

Procedure at Drancy did not vary. The inmates slept on straw. They were starved, exposed to disease, and brutalized. Then the moment came when their names were put on a list to be deported. One morning at dawn, it was their turn to be searched one final time, robbed of remaining possessions, and marched to the station. Their names are known, because the complete transport lists—all eighty-five of them—have been reconstituted by Serge Klarsfeld in his monumental *Le Mémorial de la déportation des Juifs de France*. Occasionally a fate stands out: on Transport Number 5, for instance, the name of Adolf Ziffer, born in Belsetz in Poland in 1904, a painter, living in Paris at 5, rue de Burentin, married with one child, was ruled through by the Germans, with the marginal comment, "Shot attempting to escape."

As established from these lists, 75,721 Jews were deported, though Klarsfeld explains that this "must be considered the minimum number." Deportations from some parts of the occupied zone, and of individual Jewish resistants, remain uncertainly quantified. As nearly as can be determined, one-third were French Jews, two-thirds were foreign Jews. All told, some 3,000 survived. The homes and property which the Jews were obliged to abandon were taken over by the Einsatzstab Rosenberg, in an organized act of looting known as Action M. Everything portable was to be transferred to the East for the benefit of Germans colonizing their new Slav *Lebensraum*. Reporting on July 31, 1944, on the results of Action M, von Behr wrote, "69,619 Jewish dwellings, of which 38,000 are in Paris, have been emptied of everything in daily or ornamental use."

The number of non-Jewish Frenchmen and Frenchwomen deported to Auschwitz, Klarsfeld appends, was 2,825, though he does not specify how many more were sent to Buchenwald, Mauthausen, and Ravensbrück, where as a rule political prisoners, Communists, and members of the resistance ended up. How many there were is a matter of contention. A French government source, the *Journal Official* of February 24, 1962, provides a total of 49,135 deportees and 27,917 internees, figures which apparently are supposed to include Jews, which, if so, certainly invalidates them. On the German side, the historian Hans Umbreit asserts that approximately 100,000 Frenchmen were deported on political grounds, in other words excluding Jews but including 5,000 (he says) who were the so-called *Nacht und Nebel* hostages, held responsible for an act of resistance committed by some member of their family.

Once all ideas of voluntary labor and the *Relève* had been converted into a compulsory scheme known as the Service de Travail Obligatoire, upwards of a million Frenchmen were sent to work in Germany, in what might be called a form of civilian deportation. Nor should it be overlooked that 2 million French prisoners of war spent five years in German camps. In the end, there must have been very few French people without some close family member away in Germany or on the run to escape going there for one reason or another. To cross frontiers illegally was hazardous, and few succeeded; some who did were then handed back by Spain or Switzerland. But the internal movement ran from north to south, for even after the whole of France was occupied, the Vichy zone still had fewer German garrisons and more inaccessible countryside. Those for whom no *dérogation* or *Ausweis* was forthcoming could hope to shelter under some alias in a town where they might pass unknown, or on a farm out of sight.

This ferment of lists and trains and unknown destinations had another side to it: intercession. Arbitrary cruelty and injustice and death began with the Germans and might be stopped by them—Vichy always justified collaboration as the one means of mitigating French chaos and losses. In individual cases it was possible to appeal to the local Kommandantur, and beyond that to the *préfet* for help, in which case the requisite file might be forwarded to the Paris office of Fernand de Brinon for any appropriate demand for leniency or reprieve. The better-connected someone was, the more chance that his arrest might contain the element of a deal. What could he or those pulling strings for him offer in the event of his release? To be on the safe side, it was as well for a Jew or a member of the resistance to cultivate the friendship of some powerful collaborator, just as the latter might insure himself by plucking a few well-chosen victims out of the Franco-German police machinery. In his memoirs, written just before he faced the firing squad, de Brinon declared that his reward for his collaboration was that he saved thousands of French lives, which begs the question why those lives had been endangered in the first place. Begs the question too whether it was morally right for a Frenchman to integrate himself into the machinery of the occupying enemy. If approaches through French channels failed, then the Germans and their services were there, for those willing and able to try.

Much cleverer than de Brinon, Sacha Guitry put forward the same point of view with passionate indignation in his memoirs, *Quatre ans d'occupation*. He had done a short stint in prison after the liberation and saw himself as having been abominably treated by his compatriots. He did not deny his wartime privileges, but held that they had been his due; he had been manifesting the artistic and spiritual values which made France everything it was and everything that Germany was not. "From 1940 onward, it seemed to me right that the Germans met head-on the formal maintenance of the intellectual prestige of the French nation in the face of the adversary and adversity. They had to understand at once that their illusions were pointless and French culture was so strong and coherent, even in its diversity, that orders or external influences were wide of the mark." In the light of his intentions, he thought, "the only reproach which can truthfully be made against me is that I remained civilized."

Much of his spare time, in his account of it, was spent turning to advantage his high-level German connection, interceding on behalf of people only too happy and indeed anxious to call on him for help, like Colette's Jewish husband Maurice Goudeket, or Madame la Maréchale Juin, or Clémenceau's son Michel. On October 12, 1943, he heard that Tristan Bernard and his wife had been taken to Drancy. Tristan Bernard was his old friend, a writer, and his rival in wit—but a Jew. Guitry telephoned the film star Arletty, who shared his opinions about the Germans, and together they hastened to the embassy. "While I was making my way toward M. Schleier, he was chatting with M. Friedrich Sieburg, the noted German author. I happened to meet Alfred Cortot, and I implored him to join with me.... The next morning I received a telephone call from M. Schleier to announce that he had kept his promise and that M. and Madame Tristan Bernard were now at the Rothschild Hospital." Guitry visited them and was profusely thanked. The Bernards survived the war, a fact which justified to Guitry any number of meetings and parties at the embassy or anywhere else, and he could not feel that the cold contempt proffered to him by Tristan Bernard's son was merited.

Max Jacob, the surrealist poet, also Jewish, was arrested in February 1944. On the way to Drancy he managed to write, and have delivered, a letter to Cocteau. "I am writing this in a train, profiting from the tolerance of our guards. We shall soon be at Drancy. That is all I have to say. Sacha, when he was told about my sister, said, 'If it were Max himself I could do something.' Well, this time it is myself. *Je t'embrasse.*" Cocteau, Sacha Guitry, and others drafted and signed a petition to Abetz, but it was already too late. Old and frail, Max Jacob died in Drancy. The dilemma remained: had those men compromised their moral stature by being in a position to write such a petition, or were such considerations irrelevant when someone's life was at stake?

Did the Germans set up this cat-and-mouse game in order to humiliate those playing it, or was it in the nature of a totalitarian regime? Robert and Yuki Desnos were at the center of the chic artistic set who before the war wrote and painted and danced at Le Boeuf sur le Toit, like the poet Jacques Prévert, and Marie-Laure de Noailles, Foujita, Picasso, Galtier-Boissière, Ghita Luchaire (sister of Jean), Marcel and Juliette Achard, and Mimina, the Greek model who married Arno Breker. The longer the war lasted, the more Desnos objected to the Germans, but he continued as a journalist and poet all the same. "On February 22, 1944, at 9:25 in the morning, three Gestapo agents rang," Yuki Desnos has written. "They had just arrested the poet André Verdet. Warned a few minutes earlier, thanks to a telephone call from a friend, Madame Grenier, on the staff of the paper *Aujourd'hui,* where they had stopped off first, Robert had time to escape, but he wanted to save Alain Brieux." (Brieux was a young man on the run from compulsory labor service in Germany.)

Yuki Desnos had determination. The film producer Roland Tual advised her that in a small street off the Champs-Elysées there was a lawyer who was apparently an Alsatian and knew his way through the Gestapo. In fact he wore a German uniform; his bejeweled secretary boded no good either. Yuki Desnos shuttled between the SD offices in the rue des Saussaies where she importuned a Hauptmann Uttemann (probably she meant Hüttemann), and Fresnes prison to deliver parcels, until finally she learned from a director of the Red Cross, the Comte de Gramont, that her husband was at Royal-Lieu camp, near Compiègne, with the number 29,803.

The editor of *Aujourd'hui,* Georges Suarez, continued to pay her Robert Desnos's salary. Raymond de Cardonne, who ran an art gallery in the rue des Beaux-Arts, introduced her to Gerhard Heller, the German censor. Dr. Schmitz of the Red Cross told her to talk to Dr. Heinrich Illers of the SD in the avenue Foch, but she was thrown out when she called there. Another friend, Julia Marcus, ex-dancer of the Berlin Opera, impersonated the secretary of Suarez and telephoned the authorities to beg for Desnos's freedom. Yuki then went to Compiègne to tackle two German officers billeted on the wife of a French general, and they sent her on to Possekel, commandant of Royal-Lieu. She picked up the rumor that Alain Laubreaux had informed Dr. Illers that Desnos was a Communist and despised the Germans. So finally she was one of a number of other wives who saw their husbands for one last glimpse as they were marched out of Royal-Lieu camp to Compiègne station—in his case, never to come back. He had been included on the transport lists like humbler men of whom nobody had heard, and for whom nobody perhaps had interceded.

Wondering after the liberation (in *Les Confidences de Yuki*) what more could have been done, Yuki Desnos concluded, "I was led to defend Georges Suarez, whom they shot all the same; it had all been rigged beforehand. Women had their heads shaved before my eyes and I could do nothing to protect them. People had become very wicked. . . . The first time I heard the word 'resistant' was in a little bar in the rue Cujas which I used to frequent because the man sold *pastis* and cigarettes under the counter. Only black marketeers and wheeler-dealers went there, not bad fellows, but ready to serve anyone and anything. One of the more sympathetic of them proudly showed me his brand-new card and said, 'I'm in the clear; I've worked my passage as a member of the resistance.'" Places like Drancy and Royal-Lieu, Yuki Desnos had found, just like places where women had their heads shaved, were simply where other people suffered misfortune.

9 Underground

By 1941, eight purchasing agencies had already been established in Paris to help the Wehrmacht or other German services remedy the shortfall of raw materials. One of them, Das Deutsche Beschaffungsamt in Frankreich (German Procurement Staff in France), had existed since June 1940 and might have been living on another planet, as Fritz Molden put it in his book *Exploding Star*. At the age of eighteen, Molden had arrived in Paris in November 1942, fresh from a penal battalion in Russia, and had reported to the Palais d'Eiffel in order to take up his posting to this staff. In the entrance hall officers in tailor-made uniforms and fashionable ladies passed by "with such languid grace that it was almost like watching a film. Parcels were delivered; bunches of flowers were borne by orderlies to the upper floors." Baron Riki von Posch-Pastor, the thoughtful friend who had found him a posting as a staff interpreter, explained, "We make ourselves pretty comfortable here, you know." Molden was billeted in the Hotel Wagram on the avenue de Wagram. The job was "to buy essential articles and goods on the black market in both occupied and unoccupied France," essential goods ranging from naval guns and ball bearings to caviar. He acquired a little Simca, although "on weekends it was inadvisable for a member of the Procurement Staff to go joyriding in a private car with French number plates." With a girl he knew, Ulli Rüdt von Collenberg, and a few like-minded friends, he "wandered about Paris, just as any young people would if given the chance of exploring the city. We talked of books and art, went to plays, visited museums and art galleries, and sat for hours in the cafés of the Champs-Elysées. . . . I doubt if I ever enjoyed anything so much in my youth as those three or four months in Paris."

The Procurement Staff was quite open and aboveboard, compared to some of its competitors, the most prominent of which was the Bureau Otto (Otto was the code name for the agency's head, Hermann Brandl, of the Abwehr, the official military intelligence). The Bureau Otto had offices in the Square du Bois de Boulogne and branches throughout the country. Using funds from the overall occupation costs furnished by Vichy, the Bureau Otto bought metals and leather and foodstuffs for onward dispatch to Germany. The price of leather was fixed by Vichy at nine francs a kilo; dealers paid fifteen francs for it, sold it on at thirty, and the Germans finally paid seventy francs a kilo. Between the first purchase by a Frenchman and the last price paid by the Bureau Otto, copper rose from fifteen francs a kilo to eighty-five, and lead from six to twenty-seven francs.

As the situation worsened, the Bureau Otto and similar agencies paid higher and higher prices for an increasing range of items, including jewelry and wines and clothing that had nothing to do with the war effort. With materials and produce vanishing from the open market, the Germans needed more and more informers to track down hidden stocks—"auxiliary police," as they were called in advertisements openly placed in the papers. Originally six thousand Frenchmen had volunteered for this work, but by the end of the war, five or perhaps even ten times as many had offered their services. The cornering of supplies and the deliberate inflating of prices for the benefit of selected profiteers were what the Jews as a race stood accused of, but the truth was that these were exactly the practices of the Germans in occupation.

The informers and small-time traders and crooks who swarmed around the German purchasing agencies received cash payments. The Bureau Otto alone spent hundreds of millions of francs. No *Ausweis* or other documentation was demanded; no record of transactions was kept. Later some of the profiteers thought fit to argue that they had only been reclaiming by their methods French money extorted by the Germans, and therefore that patriotism had motivated them, not personal gain. But huge tax-free fortunes had been amassed, and so many business reputations were at stake that this aspect of the occupation was afterward deliberately allowed to lie untouched in its own murkiness.

One profiteer alone, Michel Szkolnikoff, had salted away an estimated two billion francs in hotels and real estate. He drove a Rolls-Royce, and Hélène, the woman he lived with, was reputed to have ordered a new dress every day from the fashion houses. Their lavishness was a byword in Paris. Szkolnikoff had under contract scores of industrialists and suppliers, mostly of textiles, whose goods he sold on to the SS. Such was the scale that it has been suggested that the SS purchasing agency had found in Szkolnikoff a perfect front. At any rate, he was murdered in mysterious circumstances in Spain before he could be called to account. Joseph Ioanovici had a similar career. A scrap-metal merchant, he made millions out of the Bureau Otto and hoped to cover his tracks by contacting the resistance. Ioanovici escaped relatively lightly as a result, and his accomplices and suppliers were never unmasked. Szkolnikoff and Ioanovici were without principles of any kind, but both were foreign-born Jews liable at any moment to be deported to Auschwitz; they therefore hoped to save their skins by compacting with the Germans.

A construction firm like Sainrapt & Brice claimed after the war that unless it had dismissed its work force and gone into voluntary liquidation, there would have been no realistic alternative to building fortifications for the German army. The argument was considered valid; the firm was allowed to retain war profits of 360 million francs. German purchasing agencies were theoretically no different in commissioning French employees, but in practice they acquired a hold over those who approached them and could compromise them further by a judicious mixture of bribes and threats. If someone was ready to sell supplies illicitly, what stopped him from selling his compatriots? Desire for money imperceptibly shaded into treason.

At his trial after the war, Hermann Bickler, an officer of the Abwehr in Paris, declared, "We needed 32,000 native Frenchmen to cover the country, and we had these agents." The real number was probably far higher. These men were *"Gestapistes français,"* or French Gestapo, a proportion of them given German registration numbers, uniforms, and arms (and not to be confused with the other 100,000 Frenchmen who volunteered for the Waffen SS, the LVF, the Organisation Todt, and regular units of the sort). Purchasing agencies like the Bureau Otto served as an ideal screen under which to extend activities into counterintelligence, tackling the resistance through the underworld of French agents and informers already on the payroll. Some had been enlisted before the occupation. The Belgian Georges Delfanne, alias Christian Masuy, had contacted the Abwehr in January 1940 and perhaps earlier. He was permitted to run his own purchasing agency, partly in order to finance his gang of several dozen, partly in order to enrich himself. In one of his premises, 101, avenue Henri-Martin, he and his men brought in anyone they suspected of Communism or resistance. Masuy specialized in the torture of plunging a man into a cold water bath repeatedly until the drowning point was reached. Frédéric Martin, known as Rudy de Mérode, had been a German agent since 1928. Also permitted to hide behind a purchasing agency, he tracked down bullion for the Germans, and the Ministry of Finance was to calculate that he and his gang, the so-called Neuilly Gestapo, had made themselves 900 million francs.

"The Gestapo of the rue Lauriston" was the most notorious of these German proxies, thanks to the personality of its leader, Henri Laffont, or Lafont. Born Henri Chamberlin, he had been a petty crook before the war. In May 1940 he was detained in a camp pending charges, but seems to have freed himself with German connivance. At the end of June he made his way to Paris, where he was attracted by the openings offered by the Abwehr. In the company of an Abwehr officer, he went around Fresnes prison in August 1940, hand-picking criminals whom he knew and who were then and there set free for him. Eventually well over a hundred men belonged to his gang, including his second-in-command Pierre Bonny, well known as a Paris senior inspector of police before the war, several other former policemen, a secret agent, Pierre Romain, the owner of a Pigalle nightclub, and assorted killers and thieves.

Ninety-three, rue Lauriston, near the Etoile, had been a private house on three floors. Laffont's office on the second floor was steel-lined. Above, the servants' rooms were converted into cells. A second building nearby, 3 *bis,* Place des Etats-Unis, was taken over from an absent American owner for more cells and torture facilities. Laffont drove a white Bentley; he lived with his mistress Anne-Marie Duflos in Neuilly but enjoyed seducing aristocratic women and, when possible, involving them in the rue Lauriston operations. His contacts included Laval and de Brinon (who did not repay the compliment, claiming in his memoirs that he had been "persecuted by the unswerving hatred of the hideous rue Lauriston gang, whose chief I constantly refused to meet, however much he insisted"). In typical gangster style, Laffont treated Masuy and Rudy de Mérode as rivals, but his particular enmity was reserved for the Corsican underworld that had thrown in its lot with the SS. Its leader, Carbone, was killed in 1943 in an unexplained train accident which may have been the work of Laffont on behalf of the Abwehr. Tip-offs to the Germans were usually more effective in disposing of someone than intergang killing. In her memoirs Fabienne Jamet has described the tensions and brawls when these assorted criminals happened to meet for a night out in her brothel, One Two Two.

Whimsically, as an exercise in power, Laffont might ask the Germans to release or reprieve somebody. At the postwar trial leading to his execution, he artlessly gave away his lack of conviction. "If the lads on the other side, the resistance, had made me some sort of an offer, I'd have taken it, no doubt about that. Only, there it is, at the time I never heard a thing about resistance, I never caught a whiff of it. I never knew there was such a thing." In fact he was officially licensed as a German policeman with the number 10474 R, and in 1941 he took German nationality. A warrant officer from the SD by the name of Hesse was permanently attached to the gang, whose members were issued German uniforms and officially taken on to the strength as the "Gruppe Hesse." Laffont and his men penetrated a Belgian resistance network as a result of which six hundred men were arrested and at least four more circuits besides, one of which, Défence de la France, Laffont claimed in 1943, had been eliminated wholesale.

It was more trouble than it was worth to flush out Maquisards, the bands (sometimes several hundred strong) who for one reason or another had chosen to live out somewhere wild and remote, although sometimes the Germans unleashed their French auxiliaries against them with devastating effect. Escape lines set up to rescue shot-down Allied airmen and smuggle them back home, mostly by way of the Pyrenees, were another minor nuisance. Spanish Communists and the Poles in exile had underground circuits to foster their own interests, and the Poles had a notable success

Above: On the steps of the Madeleine. Note the soldier to the left, with his rifle over his shoulder. This probably dates the picture to the second half of the war, for a sentry would not have been required earlier.

Overleaf: An afternoon in the summer of 1943. Le Colisée, on the Champs-Elysées, remained the fashionable restaurant it had been before the war. It also became notorious as a meeting place for black marketeers and swinging youth.

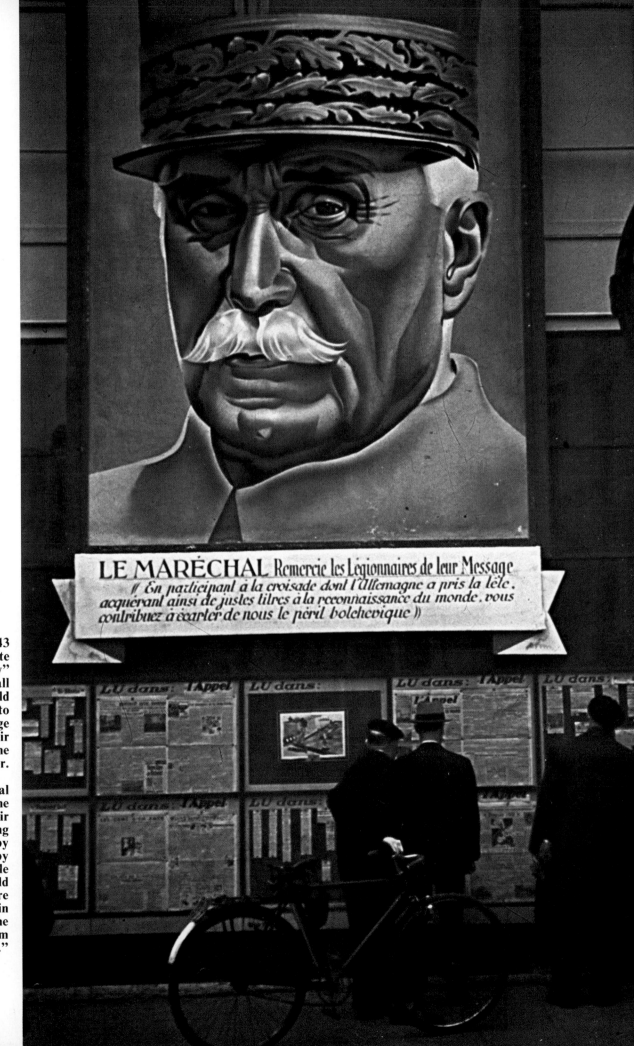

Left: A 1943 exhibition to promote the "European Unity" of the Reich. "If all the lads in the world were willing to put to sea, we would bridge the world with their craft," runs the poster.

Right: The Marshal thanks the Légionnaires for their message: "In joining the crusade led by Germany, thereby gaining the undeniable right to world gratitude, you are playing your part in warding off the Bolshevik peril from our land."

Bicyclists and horse-drawn cabs in Place de la Concorde.

A poster appealing for workers to go to Germany.

Blue-tinted glasses: an echo of the blackout.

A lady keeping her appointment, thanks to a velo-taxi.

The bus has been adapted to travel by gas propulsion.

The yellow star, worn by a Jewish woman, rue de Rivoli.

A velo-taxi waiting for customers outside Maxim's.

Drinks, a pipe, and a copy of the German-sponsored *Signal*.

Queueing for stockings: a lucky boutique near the Opéra.

Porters hauling a meat consignment at Les Halles.

The billboard for the anti-Bolshevik exhibition, 1943.

Eating cherries in the peaceful streets of Mesnilmontant.

Above: In the Flea Market, German soldiers could obtain goods long since unavailable at home. For them Paris was a posting unmatched in Europe.

Overleaf: Every day at noon, band playing and colors flying, the soldiers of the Kommandant von Gross-Paris's garrison marched ceremonially down the Champs-Elysées.

1944, and the soldiers are getting visibly younger.

A soldier at the zoo. Necks like his gave rise to Parisian mockery.

Right: Keeping up
with the times by
wearing trousers
in order to ride a
man's bicycle.

Far right: A copy
of *Signal* has
again crept into
this sunshine
scene.

Above: **Some traditional aspects of Paris were invulnerable to change, no matter who the occupier might be.**

Left: **German officers in their best uniforms, with a French woman, studying form at Auteuil races.**

The opera almost dwarfed by traffic signs for various branches and services of the German forces. Behind, on the Place de l'Opéra, was the Kommandantur, or offices of the Kommandant von Gross-Paris.

when, in November 1942, they smuggled through Paris a special courier from Warsaw, Jan Karski. He was a witness of the Warsaw ghetto and of Belzec extermination camp. Through him, authentic news of German policies in Eastern Europe reached British, American, and Jewish leaders. On his route out, he spent twelve days in Paris and was struck by the fraternization, and even servility, of the French toward the Germans. Such an attitude was unknown in the Poland which he had just left.

Of much greater concern to German counterintelligence were networks controlled by agents parachuted from London who might be preparing serious sabotage ahead of the invasion, which was becoming more and more likely after 1943. Special Operations Executive (SOE) had been set up by Churchill in July 1940 for purposes of subversion and sabotage in all countries under Nazi occupation. Its French section (F) was under British control with French subagents only as subordinates. The RF (for République Française) section, however, was manned almost exclusively by Frenchmen, though in British uniforms with British ranks. (It so happens that perhaps the most famous of all such SOE agents, Wing Commander Yeo-Thomas, alias "the White Rabbit," was one of the Englishmen in the RF section. A keen Gaullist, he arrived in Paris in 1943 with Pierre Brossolette, who later jumped to his death to avoid interrogation by the SD. His father lived in Paris, and when his son called on him with all due care, old Mr. Yeo-Thomas said to him, "What the bloody hell have you been doing for the last two years? You ought to have been here long ago.")

Professor M. R. D. Foot, author of the official history, *The SOE in France,* has written, "Inter-section jealousies within SOE were endemic; between F and RF sections they often raged with virulence. Each of these two sections was sure that its own men and methods were sound, while its rival's were not." A further source of annoyance was that it appeared to those in France who were running the daily hazards of life with the Germans that superior persons arrived from London to tell them what to do. SOE operations in France started sporadically from March 5, 1941, the date of the first parachute drop of an RF agent. F section followed in May, but by October almost all its agents had been arrested. The year 1942 had little better to show, and when in June 1943 Jean Moulin was arrested, as were some of his leading aides and SOE networks, the entire policy appeared prejudiced. Only with the Allied landing in June 1944 were SOE operations able to pay off, when some fifty circuits were in the field, though many of them recent. Sixteen hundred agents altogether were dropped, of whom a high proportion were killed or died in concentration camps. Ten thousand tons of supplies were also parachuted, a reasonable proportion of which the Germans missed. Professor Foot stresses that the French were enabled by SOE to have the impression that they were liberating themselves, which did wonders to their morale. The rewards, though, may well not be thought worthy of the bravery and self-sacrifice of the men and women involved.

Where Paris was concerned, the risks of being caught were extreme, so much so that not a single agent is known to have operated there with impunity for any length of time. The city did not lend itself to clandestine operations. Once a safe address or a cutout was detected, it became a "mousetrap," which the Germans had only to watch before rounding up everybody calling there. German detection of wireless transmission was good, and as a rule SOE wireless operators were lax in observing security precautions. But damage was mostly done by capturing an agent and turning him around by offering to spare his life and the lives of those he gave away. So it came about that German counterintelligence—in the person of Sturmbannführer Josef Kieffer of the SD in the avenue Foch, or Josef Goetz, the chief of his wireless section, or the Abwehr in the Hotel Lutétia—was frequently running whole circuits, even transmitting to London undetected, until the most advantageous moment came to foreclose on everybody. In this way agents were sometimes parachuted straight into the hands of waiting Germans. Some F section networks, like the one code-named Prosper (five hundred strong by the lowest estimates), were arrested more or less complete.

In August 1943, so successful had the SD and Abwehr been that British officers in the Paris field had either been arrested or recalled to London. The one exception was Noor Inayat Khan, whose epic story has been told in Jean Overton Fuller's *Madeleine,* the title being Noor's code name. A descendant of Tippoo Sultan and a Sufi saint, Noor had been born in the Kremlin in 1914 but brought up in Paris. A more unlikely SOE operator is hard to imagine, but she spoke fluent French and was determined. Once in Paris, she contacted old friends, as well as doomed Prosper connections like Professor Serge Balachowsky of the Institut Pasteur, Emile Henry Garry, a French army officer, and two directors of the Société Française Radio Electrique who nominally worked for the Germans, visited Germany, and even knew men like Kieffer socially, but actually were passing information to the resistance and London. Moving into an apartment on the boulevard Richard-Wallace in Neuilly, Noor was surrounded by German officers (she once asked one of them to help her with some piece of radio aerial which he mistook for a washing line). Deceived by the SD and arrested in the autumn in her turn, Noor was taken to 84, avenue Foch, and debriefed by Kieffer and a young Frenchman in his thirties, Pierre Cartaud, known as Peter, which he liked pronounced in a German accent. Jean Overton Fuller writes of Cartaud, "He had started in the resistance, but after he was captured had agreed, to save his life, to work for his captors. He did this with a fidelity which distinguished him from the common run of traitors . . . he lodged at avenue Foch and received a small salary; after the war he hoped to be allowed to become a German citizen." Noor, with an English officer and a French colonel also held in the avenue Foch, tried desperately to escape, she refused to cooperate with the SD, and she was sent in chains to Germany, to be executed at Dachau on September 12, 1944. In connection with the way that Noor had been exposed to the SD at a moment when the Prosper network was collapsing, Madame Balachowsky, herself a lucky survivor, later wrote to Jean Overton Fuller to express a view of SOE: "I believe in a total incompetence of the service."

If this is harsh, Professor Foot nonetheless concurs that fundamental mistakes arose from lack of security in wireless procedure and in the unsystematic training and accepting of agents. Once in the field, especially Paris, agents were vulnerable to the manipulation practiced by German counterintelligence through traitors and turncoats like Pierre Cartaud or the Laffont-Bonny gang, maximizing suspicion and hatred.

Pierre d'Harcourt, in *The Real Enemy,* has described his experience, which was only too characteristic. A Vichy army officer, in 1942 he was living near the Porte d'Orléans, looking for means to resist the occupation. A friend, Simoneau, had put him in touch with somebody belonging to another organization and told him that he would be the only person in his own Paris circuit in a position to filter through this stranger whatever information might be helpful. "This is how I met the woman known as La Chatte. I went to a restaurant in Paris, and soon she came up and got into conversation with me," wrote d'Harcourt. "La Chatte had a radio in Paris and was in direct contact with London. It may have been the very first link." La Chatte was succeeded by Felix, ostensibly an Austrian civilian working for Siemens, the huge electrical concern. On the grounds that he was disenchanted with Nazism, Felix claimed to have documents which he was prepared to hand over. After dining with Felix, d'Harcourt was going home by metro. "Ten yards along the dimly lit tunnel there was a sharp turning. As soon as I had walked around it, I found myself face to face with two men in black suits, wearing soft hats and with revolvers in their hands. One of them stepped up behind me and pushed the muzzle of his gun into my back. The other, with his gun pointed at me, went through my pockets with his free hand to make sure that I was unarmed. In bad French and in a low tone that I shall never forget, he said, 'Shut up! It's all over!'" D'Harcourt broke away, was shot, and landed in a hospital, where, to his despair, he was confronted by the people whom he had known in his brief "resistance activities." And so to Buchenwald.

La Chatte was Mathilde Carré, most notorious of double agents. Felix had been some disguised Abwehr man. This fraught and hermetic world was like a game of chess in one perspective, but in another like some secret society in which everybody knew what everybody else was up to, but could not say so. Equivocal figures, La Chatte for one, were actually flown over to London when they were known to be betraying people to the Germans. After the war, it was sometimes impossible to decide in court whether a man deserved a firing squad or a decoration. Nor was it always easy to accept that German evidence should finally settle the fate of a Frenchman.

Hugo Bleicher, also called "Colonel Henri," though in fact never a commissioned officer, seems to have been almost ubiquitous in Abwehr investigations, crossing the paths of many agents including Odette Sansom and Peter Churchill. In his memoirs Bleicher has left an account of how he turned around Roger Bardet, an undoubted traitor who gave away hundreds of former resistance colleagues. Bardet is quoted as saying, "Must I stay and rot in this cell till the end of the war, or must I be shot through the fault of others?" As though common sense alone dictated the conclusion, Bardet said, according to his interrogator, "Life is too short for that. I will make you an offer. Let me go free and I will work for you." In his *SOE in France* Professor Foot has the comment: "Undoubtedly Bardet kept to his part of the bargain; he was in and out of Bleicher's flat, carrying scraps and snippets of information about SOE." Whether his French colleagues at that point were traitors or dupes remains unclear. Bardet decided in May 1944 that the safest place to conceal himself from vengeance to come was in the resistance, which he rejoined. In fact he was not shot after the war.

In the cells of the avenue Foch, or in the Neuilly house of Sturmbannführer Carl Beumelburg, who was in charge of the RSHA section which could properly be called the Gestapo, or in the rue des Saussaies, men and women were incarcerated for months in a drama of alternating villainy and heroism. Edmond Dubois, the Swiss journalist who lived around the corner from the rue des Saussaies and observed the comings and goings, learned how to read the signs for himself day after day. "In front of the door of the building two Gestapo sentries are on duty. Their faces are blank, hostile, bestial. A line of civilians, clutching summons in their hands, stand a few meters from the entrance. Farther off, on the little square which opens to the rue Cambacérès, is another mass of civilians, also with summons, allowed to cross the pavement only to fill up the line opposite."

Anne Guéhenno, the writer's daughter and a member of the resistance, portrayed her routine in her autobiography, *L'Epreuve.* The dilemma for someone in her position was that orders could not be checked out, and might have been pointless or issued by someone unreliable, but nonetheless had be to obeyed without question. "There were two daily rendezvous for all of us who were in Paris, where we exchanged news of our mission, took orders, learned of setbacks. We took precautions going there; the places changed every three or four days. They were usually cafés full of young people where we would not be spotted, but in different districts. Sometimes around the Etoile we mixed in with a rich young set busy black-marketeering, and sometimes near the Bastille, at the Tambour or the Flambeau, we met among a weird and rather shady selection of people whom we tended to imitate . . . we drank an ersatz coffee or a bad apéritif on licensed days. Paul offered cigarettes all around. Sometimes we lunched together. On other days I went to my parents, who somehow managed to rustle up something from the cupboard to add to the turnips or Jerusalem artichokes which were all they would have had otherwise. At the evening rendezvous, missions were allocated for the next day. I would be off at dawn to Amiens or Le-Gault-Saint-Denis in the Beauce." A courier in good faith, meeting Lysanders landing from London, how was she to know that Paul—real name Henri Frager, an Alsatian—was in touch with Bleicher at the avenue Foch? "I met Cyprian two or three times in Paris, then in Lille, from where one day he was deported." Anne Guéhenno summarized what happened to these Paris associates of hers. "A handsome face is all I can recall of Luc . . . from one day to the next I stopped seeing him and never heard a thing, not even if he was still alive. Yvonne and Jean-Louis were in love and met between rendezvous if they could, until Yvonne was arrested and deported. They were the picture of the sort of love we were nostalgic for. Mic left for the same camp as Yvonne, and all I can see is her head thrown back, full of coquetry and laughter. Jacqueline, with her Florentine good looks, was deported too."

Christopher Burney was a young subaltern who was supposed to join a RF circuit under a French officer, Philippe de Vomécourt, which thanks to La Chatte had in fact been rounded up already. SOE therefore parachuted him unwittingly to certain capture, and it was remarkable that he was able to remain on the run for eleven weeks. Eventually he had to fill in a *fiche* as a guest in a hotel and the Germans picked him up, in August 1942. His first cell in the rue des Saussaies was "not unlike a saddle room without harness, with khaki blankets thrown across an iron cot." Later a prison van transferred him to Fresnes, to cell 449, where as the door slammed shut, he saw through the peephole "a cold blue eye, like slimy glass," watching him. "Footsteps were always coming to my door," he wrote in *Solitary Confinement,* a book which stands out in the literature of the period; "they passed, but not before they had asked the eternal questions. Did they handcuff you? Did they explain what would happen? Would it be short or long? . . . It seemed important only that I should be able to keep my knees straight at the critical moment." At last, a Tribunal, though there was nothing legal about it. In the rue des Saussaies, a major in the uniform of the Gestapo "came in again savagely, hitting and kicking and swelling with fury as I parried or avoided his blows. Then the big man came and held me from behind while the little one put a pair of rigid handcuffs on my wrists. Then the major attacked again, nastily now and without anger." Back in his Fresnes cell, Burney was greeted by his warden August, "*Aber du lieber Mann!* That was a Tribunal!" Holding out, he stayed in solitary confinement for eighteen months. "The summer shimmered gently on. As my patch of sky became misted with the heat there arose a new loudness in the air. Each day more and more aircraft came over, and the alarms, which sent the prison staff securing all the locks and taking refuge downstairs, grew longer and longer, until, on the fourteenth of July, there was what seemed to be a victory parade. Squadron after squadron flew across, and the whole prison was afire with excitement. I could hear the others singing the 'Marseillaise' all day long, and I became infected and sang too."

Early in 1944 he was deported, as everyone else in his predicament had been. "We were formed up and marched into buses, which took us to Compiègne during the afternoon. . . . We arrived at Compiègne near nightfall and were crowded together in a shed to spend the night there on the floor. The heaped and jostling bodies oppressed me, and the shouting and singing made me long for silence. But silence and privacy were gone; an episode was ended. Solitude, with its mysteries and adventures, had passed over me like a wave and washed back into the spreading ocean of the past, while the next sea, cold and clamorous, already mounted." He reached Buchenwald. On August 8, 1944, the rest of the captured British agents in Paris were taken on that same journey from Compiègne to Buchenwald—thirty-one men in all, as Yeo-Thomas remembers, and he was one of them, with at least four women. The women were shot in Ravensbrück. A few of the men, like Yeo-Thomas, escaped from Buchenwald, or like Christopher Burney managed to save their lives in a last-minute uprising, but the majority were hanged there while the war was coming to its close.

The Soviet Union, not interested like SOE in furthering the liberation of an ally, was engaged meanwhile in more classic espionage in Paris. Its principal spy was Leopold Trepper, one of the masters of his profession. In *The Great Game,* written years afterward when he was beyond Soviet reach, Trepper did not have to hide behind false modesty when recounting his achievements. Already in 1939, two Soviet officers, Mikael Makarov and Victor Sukulov, were established under false identities in Paris. Bringing Trepper in, they started as a front a business known as the Foreign Excellent Trenchcoat Company, with branches in Italy, Germany, France, Holland, and Japan. A few days after the German entry into Paris, Trepper was ordered to follow. "It was a heartbreaking spectacle," he wrote. Throughout the summer of 1940 he concentrated on forming his Parisian group. Hillel Katz and Leo Grossvogel were the hard-core, both one-time Jewish émigrés from Russia to Palestine, where as Communists they had been disillusioned with Zionist developments. On January 13, 1941, the Excellent Trenchcoat Company was transformed into Simex, a textile import-export house. Trepper, under the alias of Monsieur Jean Gilbert, made himself known to the Germans as a highly successful entrepreneur. The Simex staff included an interpreter called Vladimir Keller, who had to translate correspondence with German firms. Born in Russia, a longtime resident of Switzerland, Keller was convinced that he was working for a respectable commercial company and would answer the telephone with a "Heil Hitler."

Katz recruited a printer, Emmanuel Mignon. "We were not aware that Mignon was a member of a resistance group called La Famille Martin, whose objective was to keep an eye on businesses working for the Germans. Mignon, we later learned, informed a certain Charbonnier—who posed as a member of the resistance but was exposed and executed after the war as an agent of the Gestapo—that Simex was collaborating with the occupying forces." Simex moved into offices on the Champs-Elysées, opposite those of the Organisation Todt, one of its main clients. Trepper often ate at a Russian restaurant, Chez Kornilov, with the Organisation Todt people and their black-market contacts. A Madame Likhonin, a White Russian, actually an anti-Communist but out for herself, was trying to profiteer from the Organisation Todt; she became the Simex representative there. Better still, another White Russian, Baron Vassily de Maximovich, had been recruited by Dr. Hans Kuprian of the military administration on the grounds that he must be anti-Bolshevik, and a job had been found for him in the Majestic Hotel, no less. Kuprian's secretary, Anne-Margaret Hoffman-Schulz, fell in love with the baron, and when she went to work for Abetz, she passed over embassy documents. Anna Maximovich, a psychiatrist "six feet tall and built like a lumberjack," had as a patient Kaethe Volkmar, a secretary in the Sauckel Organization running the forced labor programs. Helping out, the Communist party furnished trusty militants, including Mira Sokol and Fernand Pauriol for wireless work, and a former German Communist called Johannes Wenzel who had had experience of underground work.

"Twice a week," Trepper explained, "I went to one of the twenty to twenty-five hideouts Leo had selected—usually a villa in the suburbs. Katz or Grossvogel, who had picked up in a series of rendezvous the intelligence gathered during recent days, would bring me this material. I sorted it and classified it; from this mass of information I wrote a brief, condensed report which I divided into four or five dispatches. This job required at least a day's work. A liaison agent then took charge of the material and passed it to a coder, usually Vera Ackermann, who would in turn pass it to the Sokols for radio transmission."

The big scoop came early, from Grossvogel, who had heard in advance from an Organisation Todt engineer named Ludwig Kainz of Hitler's invasion of Russia. Leakages of this importance alarmed the Germans, and a special unit, or Sonderkommando, was established to counteract what was christened "the Red Orchestra" or Rote Kapelle. In October 1942 this Sonderkommando arrived in Paris and moved into the fifth floor of the headquarters of the French Sûreté in the rue des Saussaies. Its head was Karl Giering, until he was replaced by Heinz Pannwitz, who had the tenacity and ability to attack the Red Orchestra. Several of the clandestine Soviet officers, including Sukulov, were turned around and became informers. Trepper was arrested, but a year or so afterward, while on an outing with his complaisant warden, he either escaped or more probably was allowed to escape. The Red Orchestra was shaken, and some of its members, like Fernand Pauriol, were executed, but it continued to transmit intelligence to Moscow. Peacetime proved more dangerous to the survivors than war. Trepper himself, flown back to Moscow in 1945, was arrested, imprisoned in a Gulag, and rehabilitated only to be persecuted again as a Jew, before being allowed to emigrate to Israel. That Stalin chose to ignore what he learned, at such cost to others, was no criticism of the Red Orchestra.

On Christmas day 1941, Raymond Ruffin reflected on his fellow worshipers at morning Mass with all the jaundice of the twelve-year-old that he was. As he recorded in his *Journal d'un J3,* "Just look at the German officers sprinkled around the congregation, taking refuge in humility, kneeling during the Sanctus without hesitating to wrinkle the creases in their beautiful uniforms, crossing themselves with devotion at the Blessing: how correct they are! So you see: we are much closer to these fervent Catholics than to the hideous Bolsheviks, the horrible Jews, the Anglo-Saxon criminals! The Marshal and Laval are right, and Cardinal Beaudrillart too: the New Order must be set up with a big effort all around, and what Jean Hérold-Paquis so elegantly calls 'the gangrenous member' must be cut off." Ruffin went on ironizing about how these righteous people liked to be observed dropping their alms in the box. "And when they have made this display of themselves, then with little shivers, coat collars turned up, out they all go back to their dining rooms heated on black-market coal, to tuck into nice courses brewed up out of the black market. So what? One must live!" With hindsight Ruffin adds the comment, "They were to continue to live cozily like that until August 1944, 'getting by all right.' And they would make a point of being present at the Paris Hôtel de Ville on August 15, 1944, to cheer General de Gaulle—our liberation, they'd claim—with a sigh of 'Ouf, liberation at last. But what a nightmare the occupation was. We won't be forgetting that in a hurry.'"

One fine Thursday in May the following year, he went from the suburbs with his friends Robert, Claude, Janine, and Jocelyne for an excursion into the country. There, suddenly, in the undergrowth, two booted legs were visible: a sleeping German, thought Claude; the corpse of a soldier, said Robert. They decided not to report it for fear of spoiling their outing.

Micheline Bood, a couple of years older than Ruffin, was another child offended by the lack of heroism in the older generation. Brought up properly in a good family, she had a schoolgirl crush on some English officers she had met in 1940, and her brother was with the Free French in England. In her diary, *Les Années doubles,* on June 5, 1941, she wrote, "It is terrible to say so but I have reached the point when I find the French no longer men: I am renouncing my country, I no longer want to be French! When you see now how one and all have become collaborationist and are licking the boots of the Germans out of fear and cowardice, even in my own family! I'm terribly sickened by this lousy country. Nobody has ever seen people so conquered as the French are, all the more because they don't know how long the conquerors will be here. Bernard, a cousin of mine who was always unbearable, saw a German film in a Champs-Elysées cinema. He didn't like the star and spat at her photo on the way out. A German saw him and insisted on an apology: he refused, was arrested, and was taken to Fresnes prison. Now here he is coming out of Fresnes, having turned into an out-and-out pro-German! His parents are very annoyed and are trying to get rid of him by having him packed off to England."

Micheline Bood used to go swimming in the Neptuna Pool, in Clichy, which was always frequented by Germans from the huge *Soldatenheim* opposite. The first time

Right: **A Franco-German encounter in Montmartre, at the famous Moulin de la Galette.**

Opposite: **Making friends on the Place du Trocadéro.**

she went, with her friend Yvette, she had been shocked to see several Germans skillfully and successfully flirting with scantily dressed French girls, only to chuck them into the water. Another of the French girls was sitting next to a stolid German. "She was talking into his ear and suddenly kissed him deeply on the mouth. The Boche looked a bit put off by that. So she did the same thing to another of them nearby. Behind the first one's back, she kissed someone else!" Monique, her closest friend, came to the pool too, like Yvette, during December 1941. "She told me today that Ludwig had kissed her yesterday evening, in the avenue Gabriel. It had to happen one day but really it's a lousy story. Monique is fifteen and it's really disgusting of her to let herself be kissed by this Boche who is an enemy in a conquered country. . . . It's a shame, but it's in her nature, absolutely, and there's nothing more to add. I don't know what to do."

But by the end of May 1942 Micheline Bood, Monique, Claudine, and Yvette were going out regularly with Germans. "He was all in white, like Lohengrin, in a white linen jacket, shining eagle emblem, knight commander of the Iron Cross, white cap and white gloves. . . . It was the first time that we went out with an officer and really marvelous: all the soldiers saluted, and the women, the *Blitzweiben* or little gray mice, scowled at us. Actually he's only a second lieutenant: he has hardly got his wings, but you might mistake him for Goering." As for Jacqueline Ducastel, she "is absolutely longing to leave home and go to Germany. To do that, she has decided to have a baby with Richard, the latest of her Germans. Naturally he thinks like her, but I get the impression that once she has her baby, he'll drop her."

Monique went to work as interpreter at the Kommandantur at Saint-Germain,

early in 1944, and she explained that every day the mail contained letters of denunciation which she did not dare throw into the wastepaper basket. Micheline Bood had been taking language lessons at the Deutsche Institut, and in March 1944 she made friends with Alice Ostermann, age twenty, the German secretary to a civil engineer working for the Luftwaffe. They larked about together. Without an *Ausweis,* Micheline was taken to dine at the Fliegerheim in the rue de l'Elysée. She found the restaurant dirty, its food greasy and tasteless. Micheline's mother allowed her to stay out as long as she was home by curfew. So on May 26, 1944, she dined at the Carlton with Alice Ostermann and Rudolf, a major, and two more officers. On to the Normandy Hotel, then the Commodore Bar on the boulevard Haussmann. "It gave me a glimpse of the famous Paris nightlife and women carousing with Germans. There was a pianist actually, and some very beautiful women and a lot of German officers. The atmosphere was distinguished rather than amusing. We had drunk champagne and all of a sudden the Wehrmachtsperre entered, that is to say a captain and some soldiers checking the papers of all civilians." Rudolf and the other Germans had to talk the Wehrmachtsperre out of ordering Micheline to have a medical inspection on the excuse that next morning she would instead have to be in school.

Contradictory emotions in these teen-age girls, as in more mature women, were mostly the result of sexuality. The risks they were running were too exciting to be suppressed. To have a good time thoughtlessly was also all that Corinne Luchaire wanted, to judge by her memoirs. After a brief marriage to a Frenchman named Guy de Voisins, she found herself fancy-free, escorted night after night to places like Shéhérazade, drinking champagne and watching the floor show with German officers. She borrowed Suzanne Abetz's box for concerts. One day an airman called Wolrad Gerlach fell in love with her, and she had a baby with him. Suzanne Abetz warned her, "You know, everything will be all right but nothing should be left to hazard. If it doesn't work out, you could quickly slip off to a hotel in the Black Forest, where you could be in peace. We've been thinking it out for a long while." Which eventually happened. Corinne Luchaire's baby daughter Brigitte was only one of 85,000 illegitimate children fathered by Germans with French women, according to the only figure available, which was issued by the Paris Immigration Services in October 1943, and therefore certainly well below the final total at the end of the occupation. Incidentally, in *Les Décombres* Rebatet remarked how collaborationism ought to have made better use of the goodwill of homosexuals toward Germans. Guéhenno thought so too, adding that homosexuals had reacted toward the German army the way prostitutes did in a country town when the local regiment marched in.

Related to sexuality in the Franco-German encounter—and equally promoting the life-must-go-on attitude—were the instinctive admiration, deference, and abasements which people feel toward those in power over them, even when, or especially when, that power has been forcibly acquired. Léon Werth, who published his *Journal 1940–44,* called this "the penetration of Hitlerism" and gave an example. "'Hitler is a saint,' was what Madeleine B. was telling me only a few weeks ago, although in October 1939 she had been eating Boches for breakfast in the 1914 manner. While she was introducing this new saint into her hagiography, her husband was earning a few millions dealing in metals with the Germans. Madeleine is unable to go through with an act of the most gross self-interest unless she first sublimates it. But she would have been a Hitlerian even if self-interest had not propelled her into it. The main ideas of the day penetrate her by osmosis."

Galtier-Boissière kept a *Dictionnaire des Girouettes,* or Directory of Weathervanes, to chart the way opinions veered according to how much power the Germans

160

had. In October 1941, dining out, he sat next to the brother of Amédée Leperche, "who displayed a flamboyant Hitlerism. Before the war, he had experienced the new Germany at first hand and been stimulated by its discipline, its urbanism and social reforms. 'But good heavens!' I told him, 'life isn't all swimming pools. There's also freedom of thought and speech.' I tried vainly to open his eyes to the horror of a police state, concentration camps, and racial persecutions. His answer was 'That's all brainwashing.' He is a thorough Nazi mystic. And when I declared that the Fritzes will be thrashed, he screamed with laughter. 'Oh, you literary types and artists, there's no point in arguing with you, you're all fantasists!'" A month later, Galtier-Boissière had another specimen entry for his Weathervane Directory. "In the *Biblio* Charles Fraval has just put out the following puff for his book *Révolution Communitaire*: In this work by a patriot proud to be a Frenchman in the author's own definition, Fraval examines the effects of the 'Révolution Communitaire' in all spheres, and he pinpoints what the France of tomorrow will be like. Fraval is the author of an ultradefeatist *Histoire de l'arrière 1914–18,* well documented as a matter of fact, and in 1937 he was the chief editor of an anarcho-Communist firebrand preaching preventive war against Hitler's Germany and a democratic crusade. Now he has fallen in step behind the Marshal. We've seen it all." Whatever would happen, Galtier-Boissière quoted the comedian René Lefèvre as saying, "if we could no longer have confidence in our traitors?"

"Criminals always revisit the scenes of their crime." An anti-English poster.

But where were lines to be drawn? At what point did polite manners or curiosity or plain indifference acquire moral shadings? The higher up the social scale a person was, the more compromising it was to be in the company of Germans, whatever the political opinions of those Germans might be. Maurice Toesca, confronted by a boyhood friend of his called Walter Heist, now a sergeant, suffered agonies in case the neighbors spotted them meeting and mistook him for an open collaborator. Yet Heist, short-sighted physically and defeatist mentally, did no more than tell him that Germany had lost the war. Louise de Vilmorin, on the other hand, a *salonnière* preciously suspended between society and the arts, was married to a Hungarian Count Palffy (later she became Romain Gary's wife, and the love of Malraux in his old age) and used to visit Hitler's Berlin, being so ardently pro-German that she earned herself the nickname of Lulu de Poméranie, the pun based on the French for a Pomeranian terrier. Florence Gould, French-born but married to an American, continued to give lunch parties every Thursday at which Germans of the stamp of Jünger and Gerhard Heller could meet the people they might have been lunching with in peacetime: Paul Morand, the Jouhandeaus, Léautaud, Giraudoux, Marie-Louise Bousquet. Publishers, his own translator, book dealers, Princess Murat, Benoist-Méchin, and Braque were among scores of Parisians in Jünger's daily life. On July 22, 1942, he chose to pay a call on Picasso and found the single blue-penciled word "Here" on the studio door. He heard Picasso say, "The two of us sitting here, as we are, could negotiate peace this afternoon. This very evening, everybody could light up." When Sacha Guitry asked after the war whether association with Jünger made someone guilty of collaboration, he was finding an anecdotal way of stating that life goes on. But at the time people did not think of themselves as having moral choices to make; they had careers and ambitions instead. Those who made life go on normally argued that anyhow nothing would have been served had the French denied social contacts to the Germans as long as the occupation lasted. To deaden Paris like that risked being more of a punishment to Parisians than to Germans; cutting off one's nose to spite one's face. Gaullists and resistants answered that business-as-usual attitudes played into the Germans' hands; fellowship toward them was undignified, misplaced, wrong.

Consider the Arno Breker exhibition that opened on May 1, 1942, at the Orangerie. Breker had been influenced by Rodin, and in the twenties had lived in Paris. His neoclassical idealizations of the human figure coincided with Hitler's preconceptions of great art, with the result that Breker became a kind of Reich sculptor in chief, an artist of the new heroic taste. His Orangerie exhibition was intended to show what heights a German artist was capable of, and by implication to glorify the society that produced him. At a press conference in the offices of the Propaganda Abteilung before the opening, Breker made a statement that gave away the underlying reality of the event. "As an old Parisian hand," he informed journalists, "I insist on being treated as if this exhibition were taking place in normal circumstances—that means in peacetime. This exhibition must not be considered as a sequel to the occupation, and I stand guarantee of anyone who might publish sincerely hostile criticism." Put more straightforwardly, hostile criticism of Breker was certain to be read as criticism of Germany, and land the critic at once in trouble. For a Frenchman to attend the exhibition became in itself a measure of approval of Nazi art and society, since in form it *was* a sequel of the occupation. Abetz, General Schaumburg, Gauleiter Sauckel, Oberg, and others from the administration attended the opening ceremony, at which Benoist-Méchin made a formal speech. The old sculptor Aristide Maillol (later murdered by the resistance) was present, as were Dunoyer de Segonzac, Cocteau, Derain and Vlaminck, Bonnard, Laval, and de Brinon, legitimizing the collaborationist aspect of the exhibition. Arletty was also there, and she caught a little of the atmosphere with a story (told in her memoirs) of some young man going about trying to work out a formula for propaganda on the similar initials for water closet and Winston Churchill.

A Kees Van Dongen retrospective exhibition opened at the Galerie Charpentier on November 4, 1942. At Breker's instigation, Van Dongen had been one of a number of painters on a guided tour of Germany the previous year. Abel Bonnard opened this exhibition, attended by the same collaborationist set. Yet Van Dongen was showing work dating back over fifty years to the nineteenth century. Was he to be blamed, and should he have to suffer, for living into times when art had become an outright extension of politics? He painted the way he had always done—in contrast, Breker had politicized his style on purpose, to suit the hour. Van Dongen, with or without his expedient pro-German attitude, would have had the honor of a retrospective exhibition in Paris, whereas Breker—crucial difference—had taken advantage of circumstances to organize a show on a scale that made him out to be of major importance. Whatever attention he might have received on intrinsic merit was bound to be inflated, and the temptation was too much for him to resist.

Work was not collaborationist by virtue of being produced during the occupation. To suspend working altogether was a moral choice too hard for anyone to take, and in any case not required, since it could be interpreted as a Nazi victory over the free spirit. The dilemma arose because creative work had to be submitted to German officials, and their granting or withholding of permission in effect controlled reputations. Performance thus had compromise built into it; no creative artist could be quite sure how much of his independence he might abandon until put before the test of having no public at all. What gave the cultural world of Paris its hectic wartime brilliance was the customary vanity of men whose drive to self-expression always compels them to live in the public eye, no matter the danger of doing so. Traditionally there had been salon ideologies, and for the time being Nazism was dominant among them. A man with his way to make fitted himself into the landscape or risked the

Opposite: **One of the characteristic statues at the exhibition of Arno Breker's work, which opened at the Orangerie on May 1, 1942.**

familiar perils of being an outcast. Illusions of ego were often more involved than considered choice. Here, in other words, were the same sort of impulses as those governing Corinne Luchaire, Micheline Bood, and the thousands of girls out flirting with soldiers—artists also did not care to stay at home, invisibly, missing their due rewards and flatteries. Life could go on; the Germans could be propositioned light-heartedly enough for self-respect still to seem intact. "The facts speak for themselves," Hervé le Boterf opens his book *La Vie Parisienne sous l'occupation*: "it would be fruitless to deny that during these four years of German occupation Paris continued to be a brightly lit spectacle and to spread its great artistic influence throughout the country."

The Propaganda Abteilung understood in any case how clumsy an instrument censorship was. The content of any work of art was less likely to carry a risk to security than the act of banning it. The greater the license allowed, the more the Germans could point to the complicity of French intellectuals and artists, just as they took satisfaction in their soldiers fraternizing with French women. Intellectual and artistic productivity, as widespread and stimulating as ever, surely proved that the French did not feel themselves oppressed? Gerhard Heller, the censor of literature, made a practice of passing virtually everything. Abetz was proud to record how "in spite of shortages, French publishers received substantial allocations of paper; from 1941 to 1944 the average annual production of purely literary, artistic, and scientific books was not inferior to what it had been in peacetime. In 1943, at the height of the war, French publishing led the world with 9,348 titles, ahead of America with 8,320 titles, Britain with 6,705, and Switzerland with 3,325."

Two hundred and twenty-five full-length feature films and four hundred documentaries and cartoons were put out by the French film industry during the occupation, overtaking production in Germany. A Comité d'Organisation du Cinéma gave the industry a corporate structure. To help finance production, however, and so to supervise content, the Germans set up a company, Continental Film, under Dr. Alfred Greven, another laissez-faire member of the Propaganda Abteilung. Thirty of the total number of films were financed by German money—and of course programs all contained newsreels shot exclusively by German teams. Studio difficulties and shortages notwithstanding, the cinema "experienced a particularly brilliant period in its history," in the words of le Boterf, who listed the new wave of directors to emerge: Henri-Georges Clouzot, Robert Bresson, Jacques Becker, Louis Daquin, André Cayatte, Claude Autant-Lara, Jean Delannoy. Giraudoux, Robert Desnos, Jacques Prévert, Pierre Benoit, Marcel Aymé, and Jean Anouilh wrote screenplays. As actors, Jean Marais, Michèle Alfa, Gisele Pascal, Serge Reggiani, Alain Cuny, Martine Carol, Danielle Darrieux, Danièle Delorme, Gérard Philipe, Maria Casares, Sophie Desmarets, and Daniel Gélin made their first marks.

Pontcarrel, Delannoy's film, a ripe historical romance, contained a line that was taken by audiences to refer to the present: "Under such a regime, sir, it is an honor to stand condemned!" Henri-Georges Clouzot's *Le Corbeau,* released in 1943, depicted a provincial town terrorized by an anonymous letter writer. Every cupboard is revealed to have its skeleton; love affairs and fatal diseases are exposed, and suicides follow; everybody accuses everyone else of sending the poison-pen denunciations. The film's comments on real life were as pertinent as could be. A scandal developed as people saw a mirror being held up in which to see themselves, so much so that after the war Clouzot had to appear before a tribunal, the *comité d'épuration* purging his profession, to answer charges of having served the Germans by showing the French as they really had been.

L'Eternel Retour, released in 1943, was also Cocteau's return to the cinema, in cooperation with Jean Delannoy. The story of Tristan and Isolde had been reworked, with Madeleine Sologne and Jean Marais in the roles. Sologne was made out to be a folkloric maiden, while Marais had dyed blond hair and a costume of tunic and boots, giving audiences the impression that here were two SS idealizations rather than legendary lovers. More or less simultaneously, Cocteau's new play, *La Machine à ecrire,* was staged at the Théâtre Hébertôt. Jean Marais again had the lead, and the homosexual aura of the play offended several critics, particularly Alain Laubreaux, who as usual said all that he thought, and more, in his *Je Suis Partout* column. One evening, coming out of a restaurant near the theater, Marais and Cocteau happened to meet Laubreaux on the pavement. Supposedly with a shout of "So much the worse for you!" the actor punched the critic's face. In spite of Cocteau's fears, no action was taken against him, his play, or Jean Marais. The incident merely proved that the entertainment value associated with Cocteau was constant, occupation or not.

Cocteau and Marais, in the apartment they shared in the Palais Royale, lived much as though the war was passing them by—at least in that respect, as the great majority would have wished to live too. "How will I get my opium?" was Cocteau's first priority, according to his biographer Francis Steegmuller. The answer was as usual, from someone friendly on the staff of a restaurant in the rue Royale, who was apparently tolerated as a supplier by the SD. *"Vive la paix honteuse"* (Long live the shameful peace) was a quip of Cocteau's which contained his aspirations. Running into him by chance one day in 1943, Jean Bourgoint wrote to a friend how Cocteau "obliged me to accompany him to the hairdresser. It was well worth my while taking the trouble: not only the sight which I had seen before of his hair done up in masses of tiny buns before being backcombed, but the German soldiers who were being cropped next to him or were waiting their turn in line, and whose faces were the picture of total amazement. Jean was holding forth in the style 'I couldn't agree with you more that except for the sculptor (Breker), who has been very useful to us, all of this lot are fit to go and jump into the lake.'" In an article in *Comoedia* Cocteau wrote an extended eulogy of Breker's exhibition. As late as 1944 he published poems composed in German, or so he said. What Cocteau had chosen to live in, Jünger decided, was a cozy little hell all his own.

"A few months ago a young man was arrested for theft from a bookshop. His name is Jean Genet," Maurice Toesca wrote in his diary on February 23, 1944. "After being kept in the Santé for rather a long time, he has been sentenced to eight months in prison. A most token punishment, considering he has been sent down twelve or thirteen times before. Cocteau gave a sensational character reference at the trial. 'You have before you,' he declared, 'the greatest poet of the century.' The Directeur de la Police Judiciaire (petty crime and burglary) does not see things in quite the same light. . . . Today I had remitted to Genet a block of blank paper for him to be able to write. The manuscript of his novel will be handed to the policeman in charge, who will give it to a typist sent to Genet by his friends." Five days later Genet communicated with Toesca, acknowledging what he owed Cocteau and the writer-doctor Henri Mondor as well. "Since our relationship is not that of a lay-about to a police bureaucrat, but as one poet to another, I know you would not be cruel enough to doubt me or mock my word. I am ill, and above all I want some place that is not prison in which I can write the completion of *Notre-Dame des fleurs.*" Taking up the case, Toesca nonetheless remained unsentimental enough to recognize manipulative skill when he saw it. Genet showered letters from prison onto people well

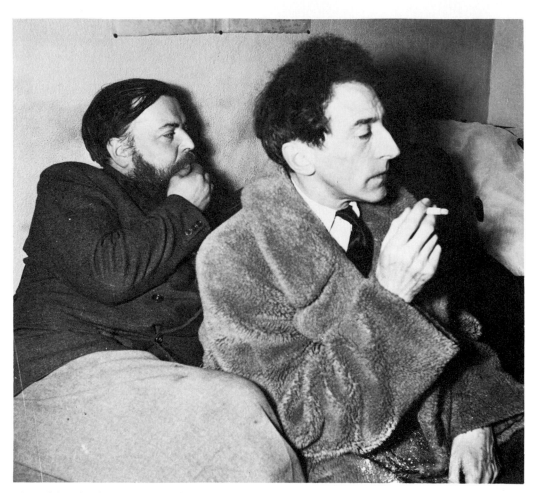

Jean Cocteau (right) and the designer Christian ("Baby") Bérard, before a rehearsal of Cocteau's play *Renaud et Armide*.

placed in the literary world, including Jouhandeau, for whom he had instructions: "You are a bit responsible for my situation. Send me a food parcel once a week." On March 2, 1944, Toesca took his seat at a performance of Rameau's opera buffa *Platée* in the Salle du Conservatoire, where the artistic establishment was present in force: Jean Paulhan, Professor Mondor, Jean Marais, and Cocteau "in the first row of the circle, posing without intending to pose," and Marcel Arland, with whom he could walk home discussing the bad influence of American fiction on Sartre. This soirée happened to be at the moment when convoy number 69 was being prepared at Drancy, consisting of 1,501 people, of whom 178 were under eighteen; all but 20 of the total were to be exterminated in Auschwitz.

Genet got what he wanted, as a result of immersing himself and everybody else within reach in his fantasies. *Notre-Dame des fleurs* actually qualified for the escapist genre of *"comédie sans tickets"* or comedy without coupons, in a phrase coined by Brasillach to describe the unreality of seeing plays which made a point of not referring to basic contemporary facts of the occupation like rationing. Reviewing Simenon's novels, Brasillach elaborated the obvious flight from reality. "How bizarre it is not to find circulating in his books truckloads of black marketeers or terrorists, not to hear passwords muttered in the backs of shops between brand-new millionaires, traders, forgers, the *Unterwelt* now seething so alarmingly."

Perhaps thanks to comedies without coupons, and the diversions they offered, the theater went from strength to strength. Box-office receipts in 1943 were 318 million francs, three times what they had been in 1938. Shakespeare, Ibsen, Synge, Shaw, Racine, Corneille, and Gerhart Hauptmann were staged and were sometimes interpreted in the perspective of current events. Since direct commentary could not hope to pass the censor, the present had to be coded through mythology or some text from the past, much as Cocteau had tried to do in *L'Eternel Retour*. Montherlant's *La Reine morte,* an adaptation of a sixteenth-century Spanish classic, centered upon a king who for reasons of state has his daughter-in-law killed. Stern conceptions of duty won over loose conceptions of revolt—a conflict not lost on audiences who responded warmly when the play opened at the Comédie-Française on December 9, 1942. Upset during rehearsals to hear of the Allied landings in North Africa, Montherlant had proposed to delay the play's production as a token of mourning. In his plays *Eurydice* and *Antigone* Anouilh also traded on familiar stories. Staged in modern garb, *Antigone* was a study of rebellion versus government. Anouilh's own ambiguous sympathies seemed to prefer public order, on the grounds that unjust rule is more bearable than no rule whatsoever. The events of 1944, when *Antigone* had its season of success, appeared to be arguing this proposition out in the open.

Of all the costume dramas, Paul Claudel's *Le Soulier de satin* was the most resounding. The Gothic poeticism of the play, the Catholic dogma so confidently displayed, seemed to belong to quite another age, and no doubt that was part of the appeal. The production's lavishness was also unmatched. Claudel had been persuaded to write the play for the Comédie-Française. Honegger was commissioned to write the musical accompaniment. Picasso is said to have turned down the offer to do the sets, refusing to have anything to do with the Catholic Claudel. The first performance was on November 26, 1943, but what with the inordinate length of the play and the inconvenience of curfew, the curtain had to rise at a quarter past one in the afternoon. Jean-Louis Barrault had devoted most of the previous year to preparing for this moment in which he starred. That winter, he says in his memoirs, there was no heating and they had to act in the cold, sometimes two degrees below freezing, so that he had to pinch his leading lady, Marie Bell, to prevent her from fainting. On the day, the whole of Paris, *le Tout-Paris,* turned out. "Claudel was in the second row. Just behind him was Valéry. Conductor, André Jolivet. The orchestra began tuning up. *Exactly* at the very second when the loudspeakers were supposed to say: 'In case of an air raid warning . . .' the sirens all over Paris began wailing. It was a genuine air raid warning. A jolly beginning. The audience rose to go to the shelters. But Claudel, already a bit hard of hearing, had not heard the sirens. He stood up, turned around, waved his arms, and shouted: 'No, no, stay where you are! Don't be alarmed—it's part of the show!' Valéry finally managed to convince him of the reality." Abel Bonnard slept through several hours of the play and afterward said how grateful he was that the satin slipper of the title did not have a pair. But there were fourteen curtain calls and evident enthusiasm from the German officers in the audience.

Jean-Paul Sartre had published his novel *La Nausée* before the war but had felt insistently drawn toward the theater, where his successes during the occupation were to mold the coming generation in his image. Traditionalists like Claudel, Giraudoux with *Sodome et Gomorrhe,* another hit of 1943, or even Montherlant were made to look antiquated in content and style by Sartre's particular brand of Marxism, Stalinist apologia, and existentialism. Sartre had been mobilized and then briefly captured in 1940, so that it was not until after the Easter holidays of 1941 that he returned to his profession, teaching philosophy at the fashionable Lycée Condorcet to the class that was preparing the entrance examination for the Ecole Normale, France's most prestigious institute of higher learning. He sought out those he knew shared his political-philosophical interests, and they used to forgather in Simone de

Beauvoir's room in the Hotel Mistral. "Cuzin, Desanti, three or four of their friends, Bost, Jean Pouillon, Merleau-Ponty, Sartre, and myself," according to Simone de Beauvoir in *La Force de l'age*. Among themselves, they circulated a news bulletin, with a view to preparing the future for "socialism and liberty," which was also the name Sartre gave to this clique of friends and former pupils. "Politically we found ourselves reduced to a condition of total impotence," Simone de Beauvoir admitted. At least they all knew each other well from old days, so that, unlike resistance groups who were militant or armed, they were spared the danger of being infiltrated by someone who might give them away.

Preoccupied with busy literary careers, "We used to have breakfast in the Café des Trois Mousquetaires, and sometimes I would work there, with a great hubbub of voices and rattling crockery all about me, loud enough to drown the radio, which was always turned on full blast. In the evening we would meet at the Flore, where you could now drink nothing but ersatz beer and coffee." Writers in the occupied zone, she explains, had tacitly formulated rules not to publish in journals or magazines there, nor to broadcast, though similar work in the Vichy zone was permissible. Nobody kept firmly to the rules. Sartre published his essay on Melville in *Comoedia,* a highbrow but nonetheless collaborationist monthly, and Simone de Beauvoir had her program on Radio-d'Etat. By the winter of 1942–1943, "We got into the habit of spending all our leisure time in the Flore. . . . I tried to arrive as soon as the doors were opened, in order to get the best and warmest table, right beside the stovepipe." At adjoining marble-topped tables were other regulars, celebrities mostly: Thierry Maulnier, the critic; Dominique Aury; the poets Jacques Audiberti and Jacques Prévert; Michel Leiris, the anthropologist, and his wife Zette; the sculptor Giacometti before he pushed off to Switzerland; Arthur Adamov, the playwright; Mouloudji, sponsored by Sartre; Picasso and Dora Marr, whom he was then living with; Jean Grenier, a philosopher who embarrassed Simone de Beauvoir by asking, "What about you, madame, are *you* an existentialist?" In the Café Flore, according to the novelist Boris Vian, what with the stove, the nearby metro station, and the absence of Germans, "people were cheerful and created the atmosphere of a club from which it would have been embarrassing to be left out. Once such feelings of embarrassment had been aroused, everybody wanted to be included."

At Christmas and Easter, Sartre and Simone de Beauvoir enjoyed holiday trips to the country, or else she went skiing by herself in the French Alps; in summer the two of them did bicycle tours of the south of France, on the first occasion calling on Malraux and Gide. The capacity for enjoyment, she explains, had not been spoiled. Gallimard the publisher had founded a new Prix de la Pléiade, with Sartre as one of the judges, and when on February 26, 1944, the prize was awarded for the first time, to one of his close friends, Mouloudji, "there was a very gay party." On March 18, 1944, followed another splurge, so incongruous in the circumstances that it had the quality of a landmark—a reading of Picasso's play *Le Désir attrapé par la queue.* Had Picasso not been the author, this most indifferent relic from surrealist days would have stayed in a bottom drawer.

"The reading took place about seven o'clock at night in the Leirises' drawing room. They had set out a few rows of chairs, but so many people turned up that a large proportion of the audience remained standing at the back, or in the anteroom." It was as good as a cultural parade: Braque, Jean-Louis Barrault, Jacques Lacan, the Freudian psychologist, Georges and Sylvia Bataille, Armand Salacrou and his wife, Henri Michaux, Raymond Queneau, Maria Casares, the actress; with Sartre, Camus, and de Beauvoir among those reading parts in the play. "A year before we would never have dreamed of gathering together like this and having a noisy, frivolous party that went on for hours." Until dawn, in fact. After this, what Michel Leiris referred to as "fiestas" were organized regularly until the end of the war. These were for the initiated, as Simone de Beauvoir explained: "We let rip on the food and drink. . . . We stayed our pangs of hunger with shameless zest. Casual lovemaking played a very small part in these revels. It was, primarily, drink which aided our break with the daily humdrum round: when it came to alcohol, we never held back, and none of us had any objections to getting drunk. . . . We constituted a sort of carnival. . . . Filled with the joy of living, I regained my old conviction that life both can and ought to be a real pleasure." Meanwhile she had once been out to Drancy to wave gaily through the wire around the perimeter at a young Jewish acquaintance; he had a few more weeks to live. Knowledge of the camps, Simone de Beauvoir drops in another of her ineffable asides, "was still very incomplete."

Sartre's first play, *Les Mouches,* was originally supposed to have been staged by Jean-Louis Barrault, but personal disagreements arose between the two of them; Charles Dullin did it instead, on June 2, 1943, at the Théâtre de la Cité (once the Sarah Bernhardt). Sartre had refurbished the classical story of the house of Atreus, to represent Orestes as that very Sartrean character, the justified murderer, conscienceless about killing the mother and stepfather who stood in the way of his cause. Liberty proved to be defined as the power of his will over everyone else's. Naturally the Propaganda Abteilung had no objection to this totalitarian concept, and it passed the censorship. Alfred Buesche, the German critic in the *Pariser Zeitung,* warmly recommended the play as "a theatrical event of the first order."

Huis Clos, Sartre's best-known play—one of whose lines, "Hell is other people," has entered the stock of tags current in the minds of people who may have no idea who the author is—was presented for the first time in the Théâtre du Vieux-Colombier, according to the play's published version. Simone de Beauvoir says that the production had been delayed by electricity shortages and the play finally "came before the critics and the public" on June 10, 1944. Two women and a man locked into each other's company without means of escape had an air of allegory, with the occupation just about to wind to its end in certain bloodshed. The cowardice and superficial pessimism with which the human condition was represented in the play appealed right around the political spectrum, in spite of one or two calls (by André Castelot, critic of *La Gerbe,* for instance) to ban it. Cocteau complimented Sartre and took the opportunity to go for a long walk with him down by the Seine, giving the advice that poets ought to be indifferent to the follies of war and politics— although airplanes flew overhead and searchlights were illuminating the sky that night. Brasillach reviewed the play, had reservations about art which he found "lucid and rotten," but decided in a judgment typical of the times that the play was cruel enough to be beautiful. The play was rumored to be anti-German but in so subtle a way that the Germans themselves had failed to perceive it, or so said Simone de Beauvoir. In any case the play had passed the censor, and so it came about that what are considered Sartre's masterpieces had seen the light of day with the swastika seal of approval set on them by the Propaganda Abteilung. Galtier-Boissière, it will be recalled, had preferred to sell secondhand books for a living rather than accept the indignity of submitting what he wrote to Nazi officialdom.

Albert Camus, Sartre's contemporary and friend until the ideological divide between them grew absolute, came to the Vichy zone from his native Algeria in the late summer of 1942. He was not quite thirty. In the hopes of tackling the consumption from which he was seriously suffering, he stayed in a village in the mountains.

A crater in front of the Sacré Coeur. The one and only visit to Paris by Pétain, on April 26, 1944, was occasioned by this raid.

The Sacré Coeur at Montmartre was damaged in an air raid on April 21, 1944.

By the time he wanted to rejoin his wife in Algeria, the means of making the journey no longer existed—the Allies had invaded North Africa and the Germans were in control of the whole of France. In January 1943, and again that June, he visited Paris, and he settled there in the autumn. He was an up-and-coming author. Drieu la Rochelle had offered to publish extracts of Camus's first novel, *L'Etranger,* and his essay *Le Mythe de Sisyphe* in the *NRF.* Camus resisted a breakthrough under such auspices, though he did allow Gallimard, publishers of the *NRF,* to bring out both works in book form. Marcel Arland at once wrote a favorable article about Camus in *Comoedia* on July 11, 1942. In *Cahiers de Sud,* a magazine published in Marseilles, Sartre followed suit in the February 1943 issue, saying, "*L'Etranger* is a classical work, a work of order, written about the absurd and against the absurd." The fact that on November 5, 1942, *Au Pilori* saw fit to comment on *L'Etranger* shows the impact on the public of Camus's assertion of the primacy of choice and individuality, however despairing the human condition might seem. "Lack of experience is soon perceived, though excused. For the story is not badly constructed, and at times reveals the author's true storytelling gifts. The hero leads a life without purpose, ideals, or nobility, exactly like many young men today who think no further than their tobacco, their cocktails, and their steak and chips."

Sartre and Camus met for the first time at the opening night of *Les Mouches.* By the autumn Camus had been incorporated into the Café Flore set and was a regular at the "fiestas." At the time, Sartre was joining the Comité Nationale d'Ecrivains (CNE), a self-elected body dominated by Communists and fellow travelers less interested in resistance than in drawing up lists of other writers and journalists whom they would proscribe and silence after the war. To Camus, these CNE methods closely resembled the totalitarianism he was fighting, and he was never to approve them. Meanwhile, covered by a job as a reader for Gallimard, he was engaged in more genuine resistance work, writing leaders for *Combat,* an underground paper founded in 1942 in Lyons by Henri Frenay on behalf of the network he ran under the same title. By October 1943, *Combat* had begun printing and distributing in Paris, and Camus, in the words of his biographer Herbert Lottman, was transformed from an interested but casual contact of the underground "into a committed activist, taking risks." False identity papers described him as Albert Mathé.

While Camus was thus preparing in secrecy for *Combat* to appear in post-liberation Paris, his first play, *Le Malentendu,* was staged at the Théâtre des Mathurins on June 24, 1944. The play's theme, that man must strive to be free even though freedom is illusory, sounded an appropriate *envoi* to the Germans, discouraging as the tone was. With eight final weeks of the occupation ahead, anyone with collaborationist ideas was bound to be provoked. One of the first-night critics hit out at this: "The public at the opening night didn't want us to forget the immortal vulgarity of which it is sometimes capable. Its sneering laughter followed many lines of *Le Malentendu.* Is it too much to ask of this public that it wait until the curtain is lowered before demonstrating?" Simone de Beauvoir found the play weak but consoled herself with the thought that hostile Fascist critics like Alain Laubreaux were almost certainly attending their last opening night. On July 2, just forty-one days before his paper closed for good, Albert Buesche was able to publish his reaction in the *Pariser Zeitung.* "More than any other play, *Le Malentendu* touches the heart of the evil which surrounds us, indeed man's whole spiritual and moral existence. It seems to affirm that man today cannot hope for a future unless he knows how to renew the very basis of his existence."

"When will peace arrive so that we can
give ourselves up to the pleasures of civil war?"
—*Brasillach.*

11 To Each His Own Laws

"We were returning with Robert Rey from dining near the Opéra," wrote Galtier-Boissière on March 3, 1942, "when the antiaircraft opened up violently, making the ground shake. Away to the west there was a terrific raid. The Pont Neuf was crowded with bystanders who watched the bombing as they would have done a firework display on July 14." This, the first massive air raid on Paris, was targeted on the Renault factory at Boulogne-Billancourt, where tanks were being built for the Wehrmacht. The bombing was inaccurate; some 500 people were killed and three times as many wounded. Next morning a cenotaph to the dead was erected in the Place de la Concorde, and a huge crowd, 300,000 strong, filed past. The leading collaborationist intellectuals signed a manifesto saying: "There is a distinction between occupation and extermination." Rebatet, who pointed out that the Renault workers had been fulfilling Wehrmacht orders without the least slacking, sneered, "The Hitlerian savages had not been able to foresee that the Royal Air Force might decide to kill Parisians in cold blood." If liberation was to be perceived as entailing civilian casualties on a huge scale, then an opening existed for inciting anti-Allied sentiment.

This did not materialize to any great extent. An informer in German pay summed up the public's attitude in a report to the military authorities. "There are still many French people who during the night of March 3 to 4 split hairs about the bombing and the military necessity of this aggression without growing indignant about the cruelty of the action. In general, if the pulse of public opinion is taken, indignation is not widespread enough. Besides, it was pointed out to us that Jews were doing the rounds of those who had been hit in order to explain to them that the aggression of which they were the victims had been necessary. It was, the Jews maintained, the only way to force the Germans out of Paris. None of those hit took the Jews to task, as they deserved."

Even on occasions when bombs fell so widely astray that racegoers on the Longchamps course were subjected in broad daylight to casualties, public opinion remained relatively unaffected. Benoit-Guyod, on September 25, 1943, went down the rue de Rivoli, and at the level of the Magasins du Louvre, "I noticed that these buildings had been damaged where a fire had started on the upper floors. This came from the crash of an English twin-engined bomber, shot down in flames the previous night by antiaircraft fire. I followed the crowd on to the rue Saint-Honoré. There, surrounded by a cordon of police, the remains of an enormous plane could be seen lying in the middle of the thoroughfare. . . . The public stared but made no comment at all." That same month in a personal odyssey without precedent, P. G. Wodehouse and his wife Ethel arrived in Paris, where they were to stay at the Bristol Hotel until the liberation. Taken from his house at Le Touquet in June 1940, Wodehouse had been interned in Poland, then released on grounds of old age, given the ill-starred chance to deliver some broadcasts, and sent on to Paris precisely to be safe from the bombing of Berlin, where otherwise he and his wife would have had to spend the winter.

Sirens became part of the background. American aircraft, it was thought, could be distinguished from British by their noise and by their unexpected flight patterns, from east to west. As in every capital at the time, familiarity bred contempt. Fabre-Luce described the scene after a heavy raid had damaged inner Paris on April 21, 1944. "The sky is alive with enormous stars, with multicolored tracers, signs of a human astrology none can yet decipher. Then, in the rattle of bombs, a big red blaze lights up around the Sacré Coeur. In the surrounding neighborhood, the houses shudder. To place a hand on the window-catch is like feeling a bird's heartbeat. Next day the inhabitants of Montmartre and Batignolles sleep out of doors, some on benches, others in metro stations or cinemas left open on purpose. At eleven o'clock, someone without a roof over his head settles down into the armchair which the last bon vivant has just quit. . . . Those making for open country are crammed into slow trains crossing an infernal landscape: rails upended like skis, engines one on top of the other in monstrous couplings. . . . After a few days of respite, Parisians come to believe in their immunity. On the boulevards or the Champs-Elysées, they gaze up as spectators at the dogfights over the suburbs . . . the sirens wail several times a day now. Then you see people all of a sudden change direction, shopkeepers slam their doors shut in customers' faces, theaters chase the audience out. But you never see anyone going into a shelter."

Bombing was a regular reminder of the trial of strength coming to a head. From the German standpoint, the impression had to be created that any turning of the tide in favor of the Allies served only to strengthen collaboration and Fascism. No demonstration of Fascism in Paris during the course of the war was comparable to the annual congress of the PPF which opened on November 4, 1942. At the time, the congress appeared to mark a peak of its kind, designed to muster adherents, to arouse faint-hearts, to sap the will of opponents. Eighty-eight organizations were represented by 7,198 delegates, of whom 1,556 were ex-Communists, 588 ex-Socialists, 1,007 from Colonel de la Rocque's prewar Croix de Feu, and 420 from Action Française. Underlining the occasion, the congress took for its theme how the PPF was to come to power. This question was debated at meetings in the Salle Pleyel and the Salle Wagram, the Palais de la Mutualité and the Gaumont-Palace cinema. In a speech lasting eight hours, Doriot recapitulated the party's position and prospects. He was supported on the platform by Deloncle, who had shifted his allegiance away from Déat's RNP. "It is impossible to know to what extent the leader of the PPF was acting on his own initiative," Dieter Wolf, the historian of the party, has commented, "or how far he was encouraged by the Germans. Abetz and the embassy were convinced that the SS and the propaganda sections were urging Doriot on in his plans."

The PPF members swaggering around the city in their uniforms suggested that a coup was in the offing. If so, it was overtaken by events, for on November 8 the Allies landed in French North Africa, and the immediate German riposte was to occupy the Vichy zone. That day Doriot had been billed to give the closing address to the congress in the Vélodrome d'Hiver, where only weeks before the Jews had been incarcerated. Laval decided not to allow Doriot to make this one last speech, and Abetz concurred. Disappointed PPF members and delegates milled in the streets, marched down the Champs-Elysées, and collected outside the party headquarters in the rue des Pyramides—twenty thousand strong, in some estimates. From the balcony of the headquarters, Doriot spoke to them impromptu. "Our North Africa can be saved only if we accept the intervention of the German army, navy, and air force.

Above: At a meeting on April 11, 1943, protesting Anglo-American bombing of Paris. Left to right: Alphonse de Chateaubriant, Marcel Déat, Paul Chack.

Overleaf: Miliciens swearing an oath of loyalty at a rally in the Vélodrome d'Hiver on April 11, 1943, in protest at Anglo-American bombing raids.

That may not please the powers that be. Then let's speak frankly. Let's have it out once and for all, that collaboration is rejected, but in that case let our troops not be sent in vain to their death." Writing after the war (under the pseudonym of Saint-Paulien, in his *Histoire de la collaboration*), Maurice-Yvan Sicard, who had been in charge of Doriot's press relations, described the atmosphere. Below him, the crowd, which he thought numbered fifteen thousand, was seething and "at times fearfully resembled rage itself. In the background, in the place des Pyramides, the inspiring statue of Joan of Arc foundered in the dusk and fog. We all felt our hearts tightening, as if with the presentiment that our North Africa was lost forever. We wondered whether to direct this crowd to the Place Beauvau, to Matignon (i.e., the offices of de Brinon and Laval respectively), the Préfecture of the Seine, and the police. Here was putsch, adventure, bloodshed." Doriot, however, put a stop to it. "A revolution against the Wehrmacht is not possible," he is quoted as saying. "We would get people killed for nothing. In a matter of hours the German army would crush us."

Coming out of the Colisée cinema at five o'clock that afternoon, Charles Braibant saw nothing of this supposed putsch, adventure, and bloodshed—he was a government archivist with Gaullist sympathies. "We found a large demonstration on the Champs-Elysées. The Doriotists were holding a manifestation. Lamentable! A few score toughs wearing all sorts of uniforms, some Prussian blue (a proper color in the circumstances), others sky blue. Half these poor creatures looked tubercular, the other half neurotic. Furtive, obstinate expressions. Nearly all must have been pederasts who missed their vocation. 'The police are against them,' a fellow next to me said, as he watched the Préfecture cars passing full of policemen. The sad groups tried shouting 'War with England.' The Boches can see for themselves the weakness, disorder, and worthlessness of this Doriotist movement on which they had been relying."

Doriot was in touch with the SS and the SD, and Dieter Wolf has also revealed how Oscar Reile of the Abwehr was paying 160,000 francs a month to Albert Beugras, one of the PPF leaders, to have access to party files and intelligence reports. Rumor of a putsch was leverage on Laval, who did risk losing control when the Allied landings coincided with the *"congrès au pouvoir."* What probably stayed Doriot's hand was the need to see Pétain's reaction. The rump French army in the Vichy zone might have fought—the fleet in Toulon was scuttled (and the famous Paris toy shop Le Nain Bleu consequently put in its window models of ships with the flags at half-mast). Some of Pétain's advisers were pressing him to break off relations with the Germans and wind up his regime by withdrawing to North Africa, but he never seriously considered such a course of action.

France was no longer divided into two zones by the demarcation line, and this reunification ameliorated the details of daily life. But by the same token, the Germans had extended military administration to the entire country, and they at once set about arresting resistants and Jews still at large in the former Vichy zone. Hitherto it had been plausible to argue that under the terms of the armistice, France had managed to retain a portion of her territory, and to ensure that her interests would be represented to some degree at a European peace treaty dictated by Hitler. Pétain's regime had been a policy of insurance in the event of ultimate German victory. A German defeat would not mean that this policy of insurance, taken out in a moment of cataclysm, had been misconceived, but after November 8 there was no longer justification for it. Logic dictated a new choice: the Pétain-Laval regime had either to reject the fait accompli which had destroyed the armistice conditions or to become an outright part of the German machinery of occupation, as it were the rod laid on the back of France.

Pétain and Laval had not wished for this fate, but they had neither the courage nor the foresight for anything except staying put supinely. So their choice, made by default, demoted them to becoming mere accomplices of the Germans: they condemned themselves to decline helplessly to the point when they were on a footing with other collaborator-Fascists. Why, Hitler reasoned, with Ribbentrop and Abetz assenting, should he run the risk of a headstrong Fascist regime when Pétain and Laval kept up appearances and were obediently responsive to pressures put upon them? The reality of public apathy, however, was recognized. In his monthly report for June 1943, the Militärbefehlshaber wrote, "The circle of those who stick to Germany and wish for a German victory has become very small indeed." So a man like Doriot, missing his chance for a putsch, could declare out-and-out Hitlerite aims more and more forcefully as the war drew out but still find himself unexpectedly superfluous, preempted by Vichy.

The disappearance of Vichy's raison d'être raised a question starkly: Was the war now so evidently lost to the Germans that each individual Frenchman ought to be doing something about it? That run-of-the-mill couple, the Poissonards, in Jean Dutourd's novel *Au bon beurre,* found their sentiments evolving in the direction of the new mainstream. "The year 1943, spent like the two previous years, in making money, marked a turning point in their existence and saw a deep change in their political attitude. German military reverses, and the first successes of the Allies which could no longer be ignored in spite of distorted news reports, and their tangle with the Fraud Squad, had altogether disposed them to a new outlook on current events. As sincerely as they could, they began to turn their attention toward the other camp, where across the seas democratic principles were upheld."

The few engaged Allied sympathizers increased accordingly in proportion to their likelihood of winning the day. The pro-Germans became die-hard. The polarization brought out into the open the conditions of civil war. Although only a few thousand formed up on either side on the barricade, their respective commitments were enough to temper and subdue the Poissonard masses. For the fury with which ideologically opposed Frenchmen went for each other outstripped any fury that had gone into attacking Germans. No doubt Vichy's self-perpetuation was a good deal to blame for this. Vichy provided the institutionalized focus for anti-Allied opinion; in simple terms, obliging a proportion of official France in the administration and army and police to be dumped on the losing side. Yet the public continued to imbue the figure of Pétain with deeply felt aspirations for continuity and legitimacy, as well as with nostalgia for the past and a longing that the present should be other than it was. So venerable and frail, he was a living symbol, if little else, and treated as such when he paid his one and only visit to Paris under occupation, on April 26, 1944. He had just had his eighty-eighth birthday. Huge crowds gathered and cheered him when he visited a hospital and attended Mass said by Cardinal Suhard in Notre-Dame and spoke from the balcony of the Hôtel de Ville. Although the policy he stood for had inexorably been proved wrong at that eleventh hour, the affection with which he was everywhere greeted was genuine. The masses recognized in him their own hope to be excused from any fighting that had to be done.

In the absence of real power, Vichy, as though a collaborationist group like any other, had need of its paramilitary formation, on whose activities a blind eye could be turned. The Service d'Ordre Légionnaire served the purpose. Founded in the spring of 1941, the SOL had originally been intended as an outlet for patriotism, and it had the usual Vichy flavor of flags and parades without much more content than muscularity. At its head was Joseph Darnand, born in 1897, one of the seven children of a railwayman. In both wars, he had served with conspicuous bravery and been much decorated. The old-soldier type, Darnand was anti-German by disposition, though willing to be impressed by the social policies of Nazism. Encouraged by Pétain, he soon came to visualize the SOL as a formation to be compared to the Brownshirts or the early SS, and the embryo of an authoritarian party in which he would take a political lead. His associates in the Vichy zone were Noel de Tissot, Jean Bassompierre, Max Knipping, and Marcel Gombert, men of simplistic outlook who pushed him increasingly into the anti-Communism which aligned the SOL with the Germans. By the summer of 1942, when Darnand paid his first visit to Germany, the SOL was thirty thousand strong. The November 8 landing in North Africa appeared to him as an attack on the French empire, and on November 19 he was heard broadcasting in the language of any collaborator. "You will never achieve your revolution if the baggage of the conquering Anglo-Americans brings back democracy, capitalism, and international Jewry."

Pétain approved. He wrote to Laval, "Indeed a few spectacular executions are better than riots and the breakdown of law and order." The SOL was transformed in January 1943 into the Milice, with Darnand as its *secrétaire général*. Laval consented for several reasons: he was acquiring storm troopers of his own, he was therefore able more effectively to ward off challengers like Doriot, Déat, and Bucard, and he was able to meet Oberg's demands to supplement the regular police. Darnand insisted that the first obligation of the Milice was the destruction of Communism, a euphemism which he and Oberg equally understood to mean all forces opposed to Nazism.

Fernand de Brinon described in his memoirs the conflict bound to arise between existing state institutions and a body like the Milice with attributes outside the law. "Oberg and Hagen acquired a considerable ascendency over Darnand, who had no trouble sweeping away Laval's influence as well as the feeble maneuvers of René de Chambrun [Laval's son-in-law]," he wrote. "Indeed in the note which he addressed to Laval through my good offices, General Oberg specified all the powers which he was preparing to extend to Darnand: total control of the police, the submission of the Préfecture de Police, responsibility for suppressing dissidence, a more energetic crackdown on terrorism, control of the economic police, the extension of the Milice, and eventually its installation in the occupied zone."

The Milice acquired a training school and a newspaper, *Combats* (not to be confused with *Combat,* the resistance paper and network under Henri Frenay). Its editor, Henri Charbonneau, was married to a niece of Darnand's. The paper borrowed staff from the PPF and from *Je Suis Partout*. Its high-pitched, not to say psychotic, tone was mitigated by outside contributions such as "Les Fanatiques," an essay by Colette in the issue of May 29, 1943, with illustrations by the cartoonist Peynet, which proved to be about the theater. The Milice was armed by the SD and the SS and trained alongside the LVF. Darnand accepted the honorary rank of *Obersturmführer* in the Waffen SS. Superficially he appeared to be just another Fascist warlord like Doriot and Déat, heading yet one more group expeditiously spawned under Nazism. The distinction was that when he entered the power play on his own, he had an arm of the state at his disposal.

The resistance responded to the new threat, and on April 24, 1943, Paul de Gassovski (an organizer in Marseilles) was the first *milicien* to be assassinated. The tempo of murder and reprisal rose through the rest of the year. Victor Barthélemy, secretary of the PPF, wrote of the attacks multiplying against party activists and offices. "On September 6, Jean David, secretary of the Evian branch, was killed. Manfredi, *secrétaire corporatif* in the Bouches-du-Rhône, fell on September 22. On

180

the twenty-seventh, it was the turn of Dr. Paul Guérin, *président des groupements corporatifs français*; on the twenty-ninth, Dr. Jolicoeur, *secrétaire fédéral* of the Marne, was killed. In the provinces charges were exploded in several of the party offices, and on September 9 a grenade was thrown into the offices of the eighteenth arrondissement, in the rue Lamarck, while a meeting was in progress; there was one death, Madame Brunet, and twenty wounded." In one of the last interviews he gave, at the beginning of August 1944, Doriot was quoted in *Je Suis Partout* as saying that to date six hundred PPF members had been killed. Other Fascist groups recorded much the same. In *Le Franciste*, for example, on July 14, 1943, "Our comrade Giguel, a shepherd, has been killed." On July 17, "Our comrade Dr. Zaepfel has been assassinated." On July 23, "A *franciste* woman has fallen, Micheline Fabre. . . ." Speaking at her funeral, Bucard promised "implacable and definitive justice." In an article on January 23, 1944, Bucard wrote, "If everything cracks up, the men from Moscow will be cutting off heads," and his last article, on May 28, 1944, was entitled "Revolution or Civil War? Regression Toward Animality."

When Ritter, Gauleiter Sauckel's representative, was shot dead in Paris at the end of September, Goebbels summed up: "We shall have to take extremely severe measures to make the French de Gaullist population understand there is a limit to German patience even in our present military situation." By way of revenge, fifty hostages were executed at Romainville, in the Paris outskirts. Ernst Jünger, who had been appalled when he tried to buy some stationery only to encounter the shopgirl's eyes pinpricked with hate, commented on September 12, "Hatred is growing uninterruptedly though it is dissimulated. A large number of people are receiving little model coffins through the post." (Charles Braibant, in his diary for September 7, 1943, noted a circumstantial piece of evidence: Dr. Heuyer, the eminent mental-health specialist, gave him the figures that the 38,000 people certified mad in 1938 had by then dwindled to 18,000. Alcohol restrictions were perhaps as responsible as politics. "Professor Debré and Drs. Heuyer and Pierre Bourgeois acknowledge the other side of the coin, that all sorts of derangements are swarming, the small change of lunacy, the obsessed, maniacs, etc." That month, too, he reported a conversation with Denise Clairouin, Graham Greene's translator, who was soon to be deported to her death. She had been told by a collaborationist editor with whom she was discussing the likely course of the war, "I couldn't care less. I'll spend six months in the country, I'll go fishing, and then I'll return to Paris and start writing propaganda for the English.")

"On October 17, I stopped off at Chantilly," wrote Fernand de Brinon, who had acquired a country house there in order to spend weekends close to Abetz. "The previous day I had been out shooting with Paul Néraud and I had brought home some partridges. That morning, with Marcel Boussac, I had watched his string of racehorses under training. Then we had galloped together along the Route des Lions. At two o'clock in the morning, I was awoken by a detonation." He escaped unharmed. Philippe Henriot, before the war a Catholic right-wing deputy, subsequently a Vichy journalist and *milicien,* in one of his popular broadcasts was lamenting on November 13, "Alas, it is no longer enough to speak of civil war; the truth is that the manhunting season is now open."

By November 23, 1943, the resistance had killed twenty-five *miliciens* and wounded twenty-seven more. The attacks for the most part occurred in the open, in places like restaurants or in the victims' houses. "La Milice en Deuil" was the heading of the column in *Combats* recording with expressions of revenge the funerals of dead *miliciens*. That November, too, *Combats* took to printing a front-page warning:

Thirty thousand members of various Fascist groups attended a meeting on December 19, 1943, at the Vélodrome d'Hiver on the theme "Europe United Against Bolshevism." Left to right: Marcel Déat, Professor Georges Claude, Philippe Henriot, Joseph Darnand, Jean Hérold-Paquis.

"*Miliciens,* point out hostages to your leaders . . . and you might even tip the word to the interested parties themselves." At the same time, Darnand, with his assistant Noel de Tissot, and Déat and Luchaire, drafted a plan for national revival which was presented to Hitler, Himmler, and Goebbels. In return for full cooperation with Germany, they asked to be allowed to exercise sovereignty in France. As a result Darnand was invited back to Berlin, where agreement was reached to regroup all paramilitary units, the Milice at the head, into the French division of the Waffen SS, each man under an oath of loyalty to Hitler. Recruiting offices for the so-called Ersatzkommando Frankreich des Waffen SS had been opened at 24, avenue Recteur-Poincaré. An enlisted man was paid six hundred francs a month. Posters with the slogan "La SS t'appelle" appeared all over Paris, and the usual mass rallies emphasized the crisis measures. At the Salle Wagram on December 12, Henri Lèbre, Ralph Soupault (the *Je Suis Partout* cartoonist who had first started drawing his favorite guillotines and gallows as a Communist in *L'Humanité*), Sicard, Coston, and Dr. Queyrat (a PPF intellectual) spoke. A week later, on the nineteenth, a huge reunion at the Vélodrome d'Hiver was held on the theme "Sommes-nous bolchevisés?" A banner across the stands read "Bolshevism = Massacre." Speakers included Henriot, Darnand, Hérold-Paquis, and Déat, all of whom proclaimed their Nazi faith. Guy Crouzet, in *La Gerbe* on December 16, wrote, "It is a question of recognizing who among us is the enemy, who among us must be eliminated, symbolically or otherwise. One part of the French, among those who believe themselves capable of reasoning, answers: The Germans. . . . Other French, no less patriotic, but more reflective and lucid, answer that the complex of Jewry, Masonry, and Bolshevism must be tamed." Tomorrow, he concluded, Darnand's men, "the best sons of France," would fight those whose hands they might once have shaken.

The moment had been reached when collaborators and Fascists had supplanted Pétain and his government in all but name. Pressure from Hitler at the end of the year brought Darnand into the government, with the post of *secrétaire général au maintien de l'ordre*—though he and the Milice were the principal disturbers of the law and order they were supposed to maintain. Déat and Henriot also became ministers. Thrust into the vacuum of political life, enraged by losses at the hands of the resistance, *miliciens* started taking initiatives. Butcher's work was to be answered with butcher's work. On December 2, 1943, Maurice Sarraut, owner of the newspaper *La Dépêche de Toulouse* and a prewar politician particularly hated by the right, was shot dead as he was returning home. The SD connived with the Milice in this murder, as also in the killing on January 10, 1944, of the eighty-four-year-old Victor Basch, formerly president of the Ligue des Droits de l'Homme, together with his seventy-nine-year-old wife.

Eugène Deloncle was murdered in accordance with the law that those who live by the sword perish by the sword. Probably because he had seen which way the wind was blowing, he had ceased to be on close terms with Knochen and the SD, though still supporting Doriot and the PPF. He paid a visit to Spain, after which it was rumored that he had been in touch with London and the Free French. Unlikely as this was, the SD held him for a brief interrogation. Then, on January 7, 1944, a squad of his former SD accomplices burst into his Paris apartment and shot him down, also wounding his son. His wife and an assistant, Jacques Corrèze, were then accused of the crime. Victor Barthélemy, who had been seeing Deloncle over the previous months, wrote in his memoirs, "It was claimed that the small SD squad was commanded by Spirito, a hit-man from the Marseilles underworld and well known in political circles. . . . Paul Carbone might have told me the truth, but he had just

The German film *The Adventures of Baron Münchhausen* at the Normandie Cinéma on the Champs-Elysées drew such a crowd on February 2, 1944, that the police were obliged to form it into separate lines.

Maupassant's *Bel Ami* filmed by Goebbels's Department of Propaganda and released in the
Cinéma Imperial, boulevard des Italiens, 1942–43.

died in December 1943 in a railway accident near Lyons." Perhaps the SD had decided to tidy away condottiere who had become counterproductive through personal excess, for Marcel Bucard was arrested in the course of the summer, caught red-handed in the holdup of a jeweler's shop. His bodyguard had opened fire and killed two policemen. Galtier-Boissière could not resist commenting in his diary that Bucard's downfall occurred when *franciste* posters on the walls of Paris proclaimed, "Follow the leader who has never yet made a mistake."

In the middle of January 1944, responding to Oberg's demands, the Milice moved up into what had been the occupied zone; it was as though Vichy was exercising a last and desperate revenge on Paris. Jean Hérold-Paquis on Radio-Paris welcomed them: "To bloody arguments they reply with a declaration of war. They are waging war against war, against that form of it which has no name but terrorism, against dishonorable men with dishonorable ambitions." The Milice's *délégué général* in the north was Max Knipping, an aviator from Marseilles, with some five thousand men under his command, perhaps a tenth of them stationed in Paris. Offices of the Milice were at 61, rue Monceau, in a house belonging to the Menier family, makers of France's best-known chocolates, as well as at 44, rue Le Peletier, in the old Communist party headquarters. The Milice also occupied the Auteuil synagogue and requisitioned hotels. The Lycée Louis-le-Grand served as a barracks and depot. Publicity was in the hands of Francis Bout de l'An, a professor of history, once a Socialist, with help from Claude Maubourget, a *Je Suis Partout* journalist.

Knipping himself left a description of his activities, in a document which remains unpublished but has been quoted by Jacques Delperrié de Bayac in his *Histoire de la Milice*. "Every week, on the Thursday," Knipping wrote, "a conference was held in the headquarters of General Oberg, at which were present three or four German officers and two or three representatives of the Maintien de l'Ordre. The object of this conference was to discuss orally the several questions which were pending, such as measures to be taken against the sabotage of electric cables, canals, or railway lines; close attention was paid to individuals and their cases. Each functionary had a file kept on him by the Germans. . . . According to information from the regional Kommandanturs, they were noted and classified as 'Gaullistes' or 'friends of the Germans.' Dr. Kuebler, who was in charge of this filing service, pointed out to me who ought to be promoted and who ought to be kept under surveillance, retired, or even arrested." Delperrié de Bayac added that other evidence existed to suggest that Knipping and the Milice themselves drew up the lists of suspects and submitted them to the Germans.

In Maurice Toesca's diary on February 12, 1944, Darnand's manner was recorded when he called on Bussière, the *préfet* of police. "M. Darnand explained, after a short speech from the *préfet,* that the position which he occupied was to be restricted to maintaining law and order: 'I insist on one thing only from the functionaries under my orders, that government instructions are obeyed. I want the government's authority to be effective. I do not ask functionaries to take a political stand, though I do myself, and that's my business, something distinct from the job in hand.'"

Laval declared to regional chiefs of the Milice that democracy was the antechamber of Bolshevism, and "I am in full agreement, in total agreement, with Darnand." He also justified the special tribunals which the Milice began holding as a device for summary executions by firing squad. According to Delperrié de Bayac, at least two hundred such death sentences were carried out. The Milice had acquired license to kill whom it judged fit, and on June 16, 1944, Jean Zay, minister of education in the Popular Front, was taken from the prison where he had spent the war and shot by the roadside. Zay was Jewish—Je vous Zay (a pun on "I hate you"), as Céline referred to him. Laval did not condone this brutality, if only because his own violent death became that much more imminent.

Philippe Henriot was then shot dead at dawn on June 28. He and his wife had been spending the night at the Ministry of Information in the rue Solférino, when members of the resistance tricked the concierge and made their way in. One of the men, who had a criminal record, was himself shot and killed in a holdup a fortnight later. Henriot's popularity was attested by the 400,000 people who filed past his bier over a period of four days. "The death of Henriot," commented Gertrude Stein, in her retreat with Alice B. Toklas at Culoz in the southwest, "has been an immense excitement, it is hard to make any one who has not lived with him realise how really tormented the population has been in its opinions and Henriot did perhaps more than anybody to turn Frenchman against Frenchman, he was a very able propagandist, he used the method not of a politician but of a churchman, he had that education . . . and he held the middle classes."

The vicious circle was widened with the murder of Georges Mandel ten days later, on July 8. With Reynaud, Mandel had embodied the will to resist in 1940. After the abortive Riom trials, he had been imprisoned in Germany but was returned by the SD in order to be used as a hostage now that the D-Day landings were a month old and the fall of Laval could be envisaged. On the morning of the eighth, Laval was telephoned by Knipping, to be informed that Mandel had spent the night in the Santé prison, but while being transferred elsewhere had been gunned down in the forest of Fontainebleau. It was another joint Milice-SD act. So too was the suppression of a revolt in the Santé on the night of July 14. The mutineers were exclusively prisoners in the sections reserved for long-term offenders. Political detainees, among whom Bucard happened to be classified, had not reacted. The men set fire to cells. On the morning of the fifteenth, Knipping and Bassompierre, together with SD officers, supervised the storming of the prison by *miliciens* from the Lycée Louis-le-Grand. Twenty-eight of the prisoners were put before a tribunal and executed then and there against the prison wall.

On August 6, Pétain, isolated in his Vichy hotel, reacted, although too late to be absolved from what he had condoned, or even to salvage honor. He wrote to Laval, "For some months, many reports have informed me of the Milice's sinister action. On separate occasions I have discussed this with you in the hope that improvement would result in the many activities of this political police. This has not been so. On the contrary. . . . Proofs of collusion between the Milice and the German police are daily provided. I have learned, sometimes from the highest departmental authorities, that French prisoners are denounced and handed over to the German police. I must stress the deplorable effect on the population, which might understand arrests carried out by the Germans themselves but can never condone the fact of Frenchmen delivering their own compatriots to the Gestapo and working in cooperation with them. . . . I cannot pass over in silence torture inflicted upon often innocent victims in places which, even in Vichy, are less like prisons of the French state than Bolshevik Chekas. Such is the tragic situation which it is my duty to point out to you."

Shown this letter by Laval, Darnand replied to Pétain: "In the course of these four years I have received compliments and congratulations from you. You encouraged me. And today, because the Americans stand at the gates of Paris, you start to tell me that I shall be the stain on the history of France? It is something which might have been thought of earlier."

"Nous ne sommes pas des dégonflés" (We are not deflated) was the slogan coined by Rebatet and taken up with the ferocity and illusion born of despair in circles where the possibility of German defeat could not be openly admitted. For how could someone back out of pro-German commitment without being accused of careerist expediency for having supported the Nazis when the going was good, and abandoning them now in an abject panic about saving his own skin? Colors had been nailed to the mast. To prove that he was not deflated, Rebatet published a leader in *Je Suis Partout* as late as July 28, 1944, in which he spoke of his admiration for Hitler: "a mortal in the grand mold . . . his is the honor before History for having liquidated democracy." In the same issue of the paper, Laubreaux wrote, "Napoleon said of his foreign minister Talleyrand that he was shit in a silk stocking. Now we have only the silk stocking." Laval took it personally and had Abetz suspend *Je Suis Partout*, though it reappeared once more, on August 16, carrying interviews with Doriot and Déat.

Small fry were able to make themselves scarce, sometimes adopting the cover of joining the resistance. The more intelligent, or the more famous, wondered whether sincerity would excuse the choice they had made, or the course of action which they would argue they had been compelled to follow. Throughout June 1944, Lifar was rehearsing his ballet *Chota Roustavelli*. "All Paris turned up at my rehearsals in the presence of Honegger, Charles Munch, Vuillermoz, Larionov, Roland Petit, Tcherepnina, Gontcharova, Felix de Lequerica (who had been appointed Spanish minister of foreign affairs), Nordling, and the critics," he wrote in his autobiography. Zeitschel, a contact of his, offered to fly him out in von Karajan's private plane, but he decided to stay, moving into Coco Chanel's house, with her butler Léon and her maid Germaine. Nevertheless, he received an intimation of what to expect when he attended a party on July 14 given by Marie-Laure de Noailles, who presented him with a copy of her new book, adding, "Well, Serge, how do you feel? Get ready to stand up for yourself."

The German takeover of the whole of France was the beginning of the end of Drieu, although his main reproach of the Nazis was that they had not been more proficient. In his diary he wrote, "The Germans are bloody idiots, and so am I. Raving, haughty, clumsy, dedicated idiots like me. They represent admirably what I wanted to be. I want only to die with them. I belong to a race, not a nation." He began to fantasize his death as a Roman, falling on his sword.

Brasillach, writing in *Je Suis Partout* on November 13, 1942, had judged the German move into the Vichy zone to be "rigorously necessary," but all the same, "the week which has just passed has been so rude a shock for aware Frenchmen that it seems inappropriate and difficult to keep one's head and take stock." He lacked the morbid self-renunciation of a Drieu, but he realized what lay ahead. Regret began to allay the denunciatory tone of his prose; he explained in conversation that he could no longer be a party to deceiving the young about Fascist prospects. To the dismay of his colleagues, Rebatet especially (who took him to be *dégonflé*), Brasillach broke with *Je Suis Partout*, resigning the editorship in the summer of 1943, just after he had returned from a journey to the eastern front. At his trial he was to explain what had prompted the split. "When the month of July 1943 arrived, discussions had been going on for at least a year between what might be called the two wings of *Je Suis Partout*. One was represented by me and two or three of my friends, supporting a policy of Franco-German collaboration but claiming first and foremost that this policy was a French policy. The others were . . . 'ultras.' They wanted to go further than Vichy, they wanted an extremely forward policy with Germany, and

A well-known *pâtisserie* in the rue de la Lune at the Porte Saint-Denis distributed ersatz cakes baked with flour substitutes in the closing stages of the occupation.

these 'ultras' in 1944 signed the famous declaration for a more active policy."

From September 1943 until August 1944, Brasillach contributed to *La Révolution Nationale,* then edited by Lucien Combelle, as well as writing a fortnightly article in *L'Echo de la France.* He ceased recommending for his enemies "the definitive and peaceful reconciliation of the coffin." He felt pro-German and French, he explained in a letter to the indignant Rebatet, but more French than National Socialist. What had been National Socialist about him, he seems to have believed, with his head firmly in the air, was a form of literary indulgence, easily absolved. That others would not treat it as such did not really sink in, though a realist like Jean Azéma of *Je Suis Partout* and Radio-Paris and the Waffen SS warned him one day in a café in the rue Richelieu: "The liberation will be a bloodbath. They will pardon every son of a bitch and black marketeer, but they will be merciless to journalists and idealists."

Most of the ultras were by one means or another in the pay of the Germans; all were compromised by what they had done to facilitate the German occupation against the interests of France and the French. The military authorities and the SD held them in a cleft stick: on the one hand backsliding collaborators could be directly deported, or even murdered without any questions asked, as in the case of Deloncle, or on the other hand they might simply be abandoned to the hopeless task of trying to justify themselves to the resistance. There was no alternative for those who had committed themselves publicly but to play out the collaborationist ordeal to the bitter end. Therefore they kept their courage up with hell-fire predictions; they were more fervent about German prospects than the Germans themselves were. They consoled themselves with the ever-visible police operations. In 1943 alone, as Abetz cabled to Ribbentrop, 40,000 people had been arrested for Gaullist, Communist, or anti-German activity. In March 1944 the Paris police made 4,746 arrests. Whatever the fear in their hearts, they boasted all over Paris about Hitler's secret weapons, and they took pride in flaunting their convictions—convictions which for the 100,000 or so Frenchmen in German uniforms were certainly sincere and for which they were prepared to brave death in fighting to the last hour against the Russian army advancing from the East.

Signs of faltering during the final year of the occupation were therefore few and far between. The usual speeches continued to be made, the usual articles written, the usual meetings assembled. On May 29, 1943, for instance, a banquet to celebrate the twentieth anniversary of an anti-Semitic sheet was held in the presence of Schleier, temporarily standing in for Abetz, and Darquier de Pellepoix, and Professor Labroue. Five days later, *Au Pilori* in its June 3 issue reported another luncheon given at the Ecu de France for "whoever in Paris is solidly anti-Jewish with a campaigning record to back it up": Darquier, Labroue, Montandon (soon to be killed by the resistance), Coston, Henri Lèbre, Ralph Soupault, Hérold-Paquis, Pierre Ducrocq, Alain Laubreaux, Jean Marquès-Rivière, Pierre Costantini, Jean Drault, Jean Lestandi. Still—a touch of gallows humor—on April 1, 1944, Oltramare organized at the Cercle Aryen yet one more honorific lunch, which he called "le Banquet des Condamnés à Mort." Paul Chack presided at the Cercle Aryen—the same Paul Chack who in *Le Matin* on May 4, 1944, was reported as speaking with emotion at a commemorative service in the Père Lachaise cemetery for the centenary of Drumont, whose pioneering anti-Semitism, Chack said, had amounted to genius. At this juncture, moreover, a brochure with the title *Je Vous Hais* was put together and published by Maurice-Yvan Sicard, Coston, Montandon, Bernardini, and the rest. This final propaganda effort managed to be uglier and more degrading

On March 5, 1944, a Sunday, Léon Degrelle, leader of the Belgian Fascists (here saluting the crowd), makes a speech in the Palais de Chaillot. On the right is General Karl Oberg.

in its photographs and text than anything of the kind previously.

"It really is the landing," wrote Charles Braibant in his diary on June 6. "Yet a concierge in my district remains skeptical. She told me, 'It's only a sideshow.' People hope, but are wary of being too optimistic. They are remaining calm." On June 7, "This afternoon Madame X. played bridge with the wife of an industrialist. Nobody passed a comment on events. Yesterday evening, tanks drove along the boulevard Suchet. It appears that the avenue de Neuilly and l'allée des Acacias in the Bois were swarming all day with troops marching off to Normandy. Butter has risen from 700 francs a kilo to 850 francs. A full professor therefore earns the equivalent of four pounds of butter a month."

On the tenth, Déat, as minister of labor, declared, "If I had to give a judicial interpretation of this country's situation this June 1944, as some people seem tempted to do, I would immediately request the honor of enlisting to fight in the uniform of the Waffen SS and I would leave my ministerial responsibilities to stand on that." Three days later, Déat, de Brinon, Paul Marion, Doriot, Bucard, and Knipping attended a conference with Abetz at the embassy, where it was observed: "According to evidence confirmed daily, the city of Paris seems calm but may hide a certain agitation which could blow up from one day to the next. In principle it has been agreed that preventive measures be undertaken in order to remove from circulation all influential Gaullist or Communist elements who might present a danger."

In *Cinquante Mois d'armistice* Pierre Nicolle recorded his impressions of Paris on July 5 and 6. "The capital's life is draining away in slow motion. Fresh restrictions; the metro is working on a schedule with a train every twelve or fifteen minutes; numerous lines are closed, and so are several more stations. Gas supplies are also severely limited; restaurants are now shut for three days of the week. Labor is harder and harder to find. The black market has broken all records. A kilo of new potatoes fetches 80 francs, peas are 60 francs, lines stretch outside bakeries. The population, outwardly calm, nevertheless shows signs of nervousness in everyday contacts. . . . The Stock Exchange is at a level which can be stigmatized as misery. Quotations are depressed by all the classical measures, but what cannot be concealed is a veritable flight out of paper money. The gold dollar on Wednesday was worth 1,100 francs."

The working class, Nicolle thought, was pleased by Soviet successes in the East. Just before the Normandy invasion the Communist party had declared its new slogan, "No liberation without insurrection." Were the middle classes justified in anticipating another bout of terror, or had they been listening too long to anti-Bolshevik talk? Was a Communist revolution about to be superimposed on everything else? The undoubted wish to hasten the collapse of the German occupation from within was bound up with the anxiety of the Communist leadership to be rid of political opponents who might challenge them in whatever the coming future might be. Renegades or PPF turncoats like Gitton and Clamamus and Clément and Fernand Soupé were early targets, already disposed of. But to this day it remains obscure how many radicals, socialists, and moderates were murdered in the closing period of the occupation by the Communists, in the almost certain knowledge that *miliciens* or Fascists could be made out to be responsible for the crime. One such case was Georges Barthélemy, mayor of the working-class district of Puteaux, a popular left-winger who was staunchly anti-Communist and who in elections had once defeated André Marty. The two "unknowns" who killed him on July 10, 1944, were obeying instructions to prepare as clear a field as possible for the Communist party after the liberation.

12 Departures and Arrivals

A month after D Day, Gerd von Rundstedt, commander in chief of the German army in the West, was replaced by Field Marshal Günther von Kluge, who was instructed by Hitler "to hold fast whatever the cost." Von Kluge found himself in immediate disagreement with the next most senior officer, Field Marshal Erwin Rommel, who during the first half of 1944 had an assignment from Hitler to strengthen coastal defenses against invasion. Rommel's chief of staff was Colonel Hans Speidel, posted back to France after a tour of duty on the Russian front. His headquarters were at La Roche-Guyon, in an old château belonging to the Duc de la Rochefoucauld. Rommel happened to be on holiday in Germany on June 6, so in the opening hours of the invasion Speidel had to make crucial decisions. Returning hurriedly, Rommel soon found the situation confirming his forebodings. Then on July 17 his car was strafed and it crashed, leaving him in hospital with head wounds.

The accident bore on the high drama of impending events in Germany: Colonel Claus Schenk von Stauffenberg was about to plant a bomb due to explode during Hitler's daily military conference. Stauffenberg and a few like-minded friends, though nationalists, had long been convinced anti-Nazis: other officers, once impressed by Hitler, had joined the conspiracy only as a means to stop a disastrous war. Rommel, they hoped, would support them. But time had passed in discussions and meetings, dangerous as these were to those involved. Two possible dates for planting a bomb had come and gone without success before July 20 was picked.

One of the leading conspirators was Count Fritz von der Schulenburg, and it fell to him to win as much backing as possible from the military staffs in France. In the last six months of 1943, he had been in Paris a good deal, sounding out opinion. On July 28, 1943, for instance, he had met Ernst Jünger, Eckelmann of the Kommandant von Gross-Paris's staff, and Colonel Kurt von Kraewel, who commanded a security regiment and who had recently been unfavorably impressed when he had had an interview with Hitler (Jünger referred in his diary to an appeal that he himself was drafting, but although this might have been useful to the conspiracy, Jünger in fact remained only on the margin). Then on October 4, Jünger and Marcel Jouhandeau happened to spend the afternoon with Braque in his studio, discussing among other things the origins of art and the lessons of old age, until it was time for Jünger to keep an appointment with von der Schulenburg in the Ritz. That autumn, von der Schulenburg enlisted the help of several men with power and influence, among them General Heinrich von Stülpnagel himself. The strain of being privy to the plot told on Stülpnagel, about whom Jünger was commenting on May 31, 1944, that he was "one of Kniebolo's [i.e., Hitler's] main adversaries since the first day. But he is tired, as one of his more frequent gestures reveals, when he slips his left hand into the small of his back as though to straighten his body. A sort of unease then falls across his face."

Caesar von Hofacker, Stülpnagel's aide-de-camp and a cousin of Stauffenberg's, was another central conspirator. Hofacker called on Jünger in his hotel, and Jünger's diary entry for March 27, 1944, recalls the atmosphere in which their talk took place. "Although he took the telephone receiver off the hook, he was not at his ease in my workroom and begged me to accompany him to the avenue Kléber so that he could speak freely. While we were pacing up and down between the Trocadéro and the Etoile, he confided a number of details coming from men he could trust. . . . It appears that Stülpnagel's entourage is suspected, and under the closest observation. Pastor Damrath and I are apparently considered unusually impenetrable and suspicious."

In Paris, an inner group around Hofacker consisted of von Falkenhausen, the nephew of the military governor in Brussels; Eberhard Finckh and Hans-Offried von Linstow, both colonels on the general staff; two members of the military administration, Walter Bargatzky and Freiherr Friedrich von Teuchert, both in the legal section; and Dr. Roland Thierfelder and Dr. Max Horst, Speidel's brother-in-law. Like most of the conspirators, Hofacker combined recklessness with indiscretion, but some of his friends and acquaintances—Dr. Michel, to give a striking example—were to declare after the war that they had had no inkling of what was being prepared.

Wilhelm von Schramm has described in his detailed study *Der 20. Juli in Paris* how many of the events leading to the day itself consisted of encounters with innuendoes and half-understandings, prone to become misunderstandings. On April 20, Speidel called on Stülpnagel in the Majestic, and then on Colonel Karl-Richard Kossmann, who had taken his place as chief of staff in Paris. On May 15, Stülpnagel and Rommel were godfathers at the christening by Pastor Damrath of Kossmann's child. Hofacker, as an emissary from Stülpnagel, confronted Rommel at La Roche-Guyon on July 9.

On the afternoon of July 20, at about four o'clock, Hofacker was telephoned in the Majestic by Stauffenberg in Berlin with the news that the bomb had exploded. Stauffenberg's assertion that Hitler was dead set in motion the conspirators' plan. Acting on Hofacker's information, Stülpnagel committed himself; he summoned to his office General Hans von Boineburg-Lengsfeld, who had succeeded Schaumburg as Kommandant von Gross-Paris, together with his chief of staff, Friedrich von Unger. He then ordered them to arrest the senior SS and SD officers in Paris and to keep their men confined to barracks. To provide an explanation for so unprecedented a measure, Stülpnagel told von Boineburg-Lengsfeld that the SS had apparently tried to stage a putsch in Germany, and the army had been ordered to step in. So it was that Oberg was surprised in his office in the avenue Foch, and Knochen was hauled out of a nightclub, to be held in custody along with their staffs and officials in the Hotel Continental in the rue Castiglione. Stülpnagel and Hofacker meanwhile hurriedly drove out to La Roche-Guyon in the anticipation of von Kluge's support. How Rommel would have reacted, had he not been in the hospital, remains uncertain. But von Kluge had learned from Berlin that Hitler had been only slightly hurt in the explosion; he refused to do more than invite the two conspirators to one last gloomy dinner and advise them to vanish afterward as best they could. Stülpnagel and Hofacker then returned to the Hotel Raphael, where in the officers' mess they had the odious experience of listening to Hitler on the wireless, his voice shaking with anger at what he called "a little clique of ambitious, criminally stupid officers without conscience."

Abetz, in an effort at diplomacy, entered the Raphael at about midnight. Boineburg-Lengsfeld was sent to release the SS and SD officers in the Hotel Continental and bring Oberg back to the Raphael. There, with Abetz prompting, Oberg and Stülpnagel shook hands and sat down to champagne until the small hours. So the army, the party, and the embassy—the three elements of the German occupation—were represented by their titular heads in person in this scene, as though at the curtain fall of a classical tragedy. The struggle for supremacy between army and party had been settled, but at a point when the decisiveness had lost relevance. The party could not replace the army on disintegrating fronts; it could only take revenge on those in its power.

At noon the next day, Stülpnagel, ordered back to Berlin, drove as far as Verdun. There, on the old battlefield, he put a bullet into his brain, but he succeeded only in blinding himself. The *Pariser Zeitung* published a false report that he had been attacked by the resistance. Eventually he and von Linstow and Finckh and Hofacker were among those who at Hitler's orders were tortured to death on meat hooks by the Gestapo. Rommel was permitted to shoot himself, although the public was informed that he had died of his wounds. Von Kluge swallowed poison.

For the consumption of any inquisitive Parisians, a story was circulated that the German garrison had been holding a maneuver. But as von Schramm and others have pointed out, the entire coup was made and unmade on the telephone, and to that extent the real news did not penetrate to the outside world until everything was over. Maurice Toesca's diary entry on July 21 revealed the ignorance of even someone as well placed as he was. "I had an appointment that morning at ten o'clock with a Captain Hüttemann to discuss cases of Frenchmen recently arrested. When I approached the place Beauvau, I observed German soldiers, grenades at their belts: they blocked off the rue des Saussaies. I left my car in the Faubourg Saint-Honoré, opposite the Elysée, determined to keep my appointment. . . . A soldier accompanied me to the captain's office. In the inner courtyard, on the way there, piles of still smoking ashes were everywhere. A smell of burning. The captain received me. His expression was serious. He was amazed to see me. Had I not been informed? No, about nothing. So he explained that the day before there had been an attempt on Hitler's life." It was quite impossible to discuss French cases, Hüttemann explained, adding that many dossiers had disappeared.

In the aftermath, Stülpnagel and von Boineburg-Lengsfeld were replaced by Generals Karl Kitzinger and Dietrich von Choltitz respectively. Kitzinger reached Paris in time only to turn around and leave again, his activity restricted to the Goering-like acquisition of last-moment booty. Until his appointment to Paris on August 3, von Choltitz had been commanding an army corps in Normandy. Before that, he had acquired a hard-driving reputation in Russia. Summoned to the so-called Wolf's Lair headquarters in East Prussia, von Choltitz was ordered by Hitler to defend Paris to the last and then destroy the city rather than surrender it. In the sleeper returning him to Paris, on the night of August 9, von Choltitz reflected on these orders: they seemed to him to emanate from a man who had lost possession of his reason, or so he was to write after the war. He knew from experience what little defenses stood between Paris and the advancing Americans. Wanton physical destruction of Paris could bring no military advantage, while also putting the army's security at risk, if the population was to react violently. Von Choltitz decided that his duty was only to defend positions keeping open the roads through or around Paris—bridges over the Seine included—along which the army could complete an orderly withdrawal. His courage in persisting in this was all the greater in that his wife and young children had remained in Germany and there could be no illusion of their escaping victimization.

Von Choltitz was a Prussian, a professional soldier in the stamp of every previous Militärbefehlshaber or Kommandant von Gross-Paris. He cut his hair very short and wore a monocle. As a child, he had been a page at the court of Saxony, and his sympathies were monarchist. The appointment to Paris at such a juncture of a man of this background suggests that Hitler was being rhetorical about destruction. For if that was what he intended as the final vindictive act to the occupation, then in Paris there already existed someone far more suitable for the purpose, someone who had the necessary will and the means at his disposal, namely General Karl Oberg. The Höherer SS und Polizeiführer had only to give instructions to the SS and SD. Von Choltitz's promotion was in all likelihood intended by Hitler to be a gesture toward the Wehrmacht, and so to rally the officer corps after its complete rout and demoralization at the hands of the party, especially now that maximum military effort in France was called for. So where Paris was concerned, perhaps a consequence of the July 20 conspiracy was the opposite of what might have been expected—Oberg did not come to exercise his powers at their most absolute.

Prior to von Choltitz's arrival, administrative and even military units had begun to prepare to leave. Archives were packed, papers from the military government were burned, civilian staff assembled at dawn at the stations where German troop trains alone continued to operate after August 10. On the eleventh, Angers and Alençon fell; on the twelfth, Chartres; on the thirteenth, Parisians attending the Sunday race meetings caught the sound of distant gunfire. The Americans were rumored to be about to arrive. Partly camouflaged German convoys returned from the front; exhausted soldiers were to be seen resting or camping in squares and parks.

Ernst Jünger lunched with Florence Gould on August 10 and wrote down, "Perhaps the last of these Thursdays. I talked to her, Madame Tharaud, and the Princesse de Sixte-Bourbon." (The brothers Tharaud, both members of the Académie Française, were prolific writers; among their joint books was *Quand Israel est roi,* the usual sort of diatribe against Jews.) On the way home, in the rue Copernic, where Jünger stopped to buy a little blue notebook, he ran into Marcel Arland, whose new novel he had been reading. The two shook hands. Then on the fourteenth, "Sudden departure at nightfall. In the afternoon, last meetings. I had tidied up the room and placed a bouquet on the table. I handed out tips. Unfortunately I forgot in a cupboard drawer some letters which are irreplaceable." There had been time to telephone Léautaud, who was much moved by the thought behind it and in his own diary turned introspective about right conduct during the occupation: "I kept intact my reason and free spirit, my candid speech, even in front of the two German officers with whom I had any dealings. . . . I showed myself courteous and polite, helpful when there was occasion to be, with 'enemies' who can remember at least this Frenchman in that light. I never said or did anything vile. So there! It's not so bad."

Drieu la Rochelle took stock with less self-satisfaction. He had finished correcting the proofs of *Chiens de paille,* and on August 11 handed them to Armand Petitjean, a young nationalist depicted in the novel. He then wrote letters to several people, including Malraux, before jotting in his diary, "How I would like to die tonight at the front, on either side: in a Scottish regiment, or in an SS regiment"—after which he took an overdose of sleeping tablets. But his cleaning lady, Gabrielle, arrived unexpectedly early, found him still alive, and called an ambulance. While the ambulance was on its way, Heller, the censor, arrived too, in his last twenty-four hours in Paris, with a passport that would have enabled Drieu to go to Spain. During the liberation Drieu remained convalescent in the American Hospital in Neuilly, then he hid out until the following March, when he combined another overdose of sleeping tablets with gas. "This time, Gabrielle, let me sleep," was the message found beside him. So he achieved the dramatic death around which he had stylized himself for so long.

Everybody was being swept along in the race of events. Time for consultation had run out; decisions were required on the spot, in an atmosphere reminiscent of the first fortnight of June 1940. One last scheme was to spring out of the agile mind of Laval. He had reached Paris from Vichy on the evening of August 9. If he, who had smashed the parliamentary democracy of the Third Republic, could now revive it, the day might be saved; at least Vichy might be presented as a German-enforced interruption to normality, and Laval might even be the man to bridge past and future. He called on Abetz, who appears to have endorsed the fantasy, for on the twelfth, Laval drove to Nancy to fetch Edouard Herriot, former president of the Assemblée, from the nursing home where he had been arbitrarily detained. Transported to Paris as a kind of totem, Herriot had no desire to save Laval from himself, and nothing came of the endeavor. Besides, ultras like de Brinon and Déat had noted that Laval was hoping to abandon the sinking ship; they seem to have intervened with Oberg to choke off the initiative.

The police went on strike on the fifteenth, in a move to prepare an alibi by dissociating themselves from their past collaboration and so curry favor ahead of time with the FFI. Consternation reigned on the assumption that law and order would be quite overthrown, but this proved unfounded. Once again, in the hastening collapse of institutions, the citizens of Paris were to be represented by the handful of civil servants and elected officials who were prepared to remain at their posts: Pierre Taittinger, the president of the Conseil Municipal in the Hôtel de Ville; René Bouffet, the *préfet* of the Seine; Amédée Bussière, at the Préfecture de Police; Victor Constant, the president of the Conseil de la Seine. These men were in touch with von Choltitz on urgent matters such as the absence of transport and dwindling food supplies. Stocks of essentials like flour were down to danger levels. The ten thousand tons of coal required each day for generating electricity did not arrive. Medicines were unavailable. The Swedish consul general, Raoul Nordling, a successful businessman who ran an international company making ball bearings, was among those contacting von Choltitz. His initial anxiety was that political prisoners might be butchered at the last moment by a defiant SD. On the fifteenth, a final trainload of 2,453 deportees was indeed loaded and dispatched from Paris to Germany. Von Choltitz agreed with Nordling that political detainees ought to be removed from risk, and in the circumstances Oberg could only consent. Prisoners held by the French were released when the police went on strike, and forty-eight hours later up to three thousand men detained by the SD were freed, all in fact except those at Compiègne, where the camp commandant refused. These men were put into a train but released during transit by the Wehrmacht.

"You could feel that everything was at an end." Brasillach, in his *Journal d'un homme occupé,* managed to strike a note of elegy about that interim week. "You could measure the catastrophe inch by inch, and yet the weather was marvelous, the women were delicious, and you caught your breath at the most magical sights—the Seine, the Louvre, Notre-Dame—the whole while wondering whatever would become of it all." During the occupation's finale, he wrote, "One watched the Germans departing: without malice but with prudent irony, crowds gathered outside the requisitioned hotels which were being packed up, and sometimes provisions or a pair of boots were bartered with the Fritzes. Materially the situation deteriorated with the speed of an avalanche. The electricity supply of one or two hours a day was cut short by breakdowns. The cinemas had closed. Sometimes audiences for music halls met in rooms lit only by the light of day, and a couple of theaters tried to keep the show running. Two dark and desperate plays were Jean Anouilh's admirable *Antigone,* running since the winter, and Jean-Paul Sartre's *Huis Clos,* two months old. On

Without electricity in August 1944, a photographer was obliged to work out in the open.

August 17, the final evening when Paris offered any public entertainment, I went to the latter with Maurice and Henri Bardèche. In spite of everything I still went to the Bibliothèque Nationale to put together my Greek anthology." A new restaurant opened in the rue Gay-Lussac; Brasillach dined out with Henri Poulain, Well Allot, and his wife, known as La Sirène; they saw Germans and waiters fraternizing. And then there was a farewell dinner at the Deutsche Institut. "It was a fine evening. In the garden we stayed out chatting for hours, evoking what had happened, and what might have happened. Grievances were laid aside, there were still delightful moments, for deathbed vigils have their attractions. The Institut was shutting next day. . . . Dr. Epting, at his friendliest, tried to persuade me to go to Germany to weather out the storm there. I explained the reasons why I did not want to take his advice. He told me he could not agree, then added, 'But if I were French, I am sure I would behave like you.'" The next evening, with the weather still glorious and the city tranquil, he was struck by the sight of thousands of boys and girls along the *quais* transforming the Seine into a swimming pool: "I saw them, happy, carefree, marvelous symbols of the city's *légèreté*."

August 17, a Thursday, was when the bulk of the German forces pulled out. To Galtier-Boissière, it was "the great flight of the Fritzes. From the Sorbonne to the Gare de l'Est and the Gare du Nord I watched their exodus, and then I returned by

198

Actors in the Théâtre Darnou keeping the show on by candlelight as electricity supplies failed in the days preceding liberation.

the boulevard Magenta and the rue Lafayette to the Opéra. On every thoroughfare, scores, hundreds, of trucks, loaded cars, mounted artillery, ambulances full of wounded on stretchers, were in file or overtaking and crisscrossing one another. At the carrefour Strasbourg-Saint-Denis and in front of the railway stations, feldgendarmes with their bailiffs' chains and signaling disks controlled the traffic, the Paris police being on strike. In the rue Lafayette a flash of monocled generals sped past like shining torpedoes, accompanied by elegantly dressed blondes who seemed more on their way to some fashionable beach. Near the Galeries Lafayette, in front of his broken-down truck, a bespectacled soldier was trying fruitlessly to be towed by either French or Germans: at each refusal he smiled without losing his temper or his confidence. On his belt were long-handled grenades. On the terraces of the cafés along the boulevards and the avenue de l'Opéra, men from every branch of the forces continued drinking their beer. In front of the Kommandantur, I passed three very old soldiers, filthy dirty and quite small. . . . At half past eight in the evening, trucks left, taking back to the Rhine the German personnel from the Trianon Hotel in the rue Vaugirard. . . . And suddenly, after the departure of the last truck, the SS sentries on duty, automatic weapons at the ready, moved out toward the spectators, who panicked and scattered in all directions."

That same day, Brünner, commandant of Drancy, organized his last convoy, number 79. He had to do so with unaccustomed improvisation as he commandeered three carriages of a train transporting antiaircraft batteries. When this train pulled out of Paris-Bobigny station, it carried with it Brünner, the Gestapo, and fifty-one more Jews, including Marcel Bloch-Dassault, who survived to reestablish himself after the war as an industrialist and manufacturer of aircraft. So Drancy was abandoned, its main gate hanging open, for anyone to wander in and see for himself what a German concentration camp was like.

De Brinon and Déat, Doriot and Darnand, with access to inside information, were able to drive off, ahead of everyone else, on the evening of the sixteenth. For most collaborators, especially those who hesitated to make a decision for as long as possible, evacuation became a matter of stampede. "Day after day Papa used to arrive home radiant, saying that everything was still fine," wrote Corinne Luchaire, "until one day, with no transition, it must have been around August 10, 1944, in the course of dinner as though he were raising the idea of some holiday trip, Jean Luchaire declared that, all things considered, he had decided to leave with us for a destination in Germany, and therefore we had to get ready and urgently pack our suitcases." For how long? Three or four months, Luchaire thought. So Luchaire, his wife, his other two daughters, Florence and Monique (Boby, his son, was already in Germany on Service de Travail Obligatoire), and an actor, René Arrieu, who was to marry Florence, as well as Corinne with her baby Brigitte on her knees, found themselves, on the seventeenth, beginning a train journey in the reserved half of a carriage, along with Costantini, Guy Crouzet and his family, Jacques de Lesdain, and Jacques Ménard (of *Le Matin,* and president of the Association of Anti-Jewish Journalists) and his family.

As late as the fifteenth, Rebatet and his wife Véronique had wandered along the Champs-Elysées. They were struck, like Brasillach, mainly by the dazzling looks of the girls. But: "Everything was decomposing. The metro no longer worked. Electricity was distributed only from half past ten to midnight." On August 17, "at about seven o'clock in the evening, I was trying to discover the latest news from Sordet's Inter-France Agency, in the Palais Berlitz building. I had it confirmed that the Americans were at Chartres, an hour's drive away. No time to be lost making up our minds. . . . The rout was falling back on Paris. Were we going to be raising anchor too late? We had only been back in the rue de Marignan for fifteen minutes when Ralph Soupault the Doriotist telephoned me: 'We're leaving tonight. Orders from the top. There's not a moment to be lost. Rendezvous in the rue des Pyramides, as quickly as you can.' In the rue des Pyramides, PPF headquarters was animated. There were faces I recognized. We waited for Wehrmacht trucks to take us east."

Everybody had been increasingly nervous throughout that first fortnight of August, according to Hérold-Paquis in *Des Illusions . . . Désillusions,* the memoir he wrote between this flight and his execution, "and kept on ringing up for news, Rebatet, Cousteau, Sordet, Charles Lesca. Sonderführer Haefs usurped a role for himself in the radio programs; temporary passports were issued at the embassy for those wanting to go to Germany; Dr. Bofinger, in charge of broadcasting in the Propaganda Abteilung, pushed off with the rest of the Majestic Hotel people." On the evening of the sixteenth, Hérold-Paquis gave his final broadcast, in an eerily abandoned studio. Afterward, "in Cousteau's house, the telephone never stopped ringing, the calls spaced out only by appeals from Rebatet in the Grand Hotel with his wife and his bicycle, demanding transport. At about three in the morning, a PPF car fetched us and drove us to the rue des Pyramides. And there we waited two or three more hours. To this day I do not understand how the convoy could have formed as it did, out on the open street, at night, without a single machine gun opening up on us to salute this noisy departure! As the night of August 17 drew to an end, an empty truck arrived from Saint-Denis, put at the disposal of the Radio on Doriot's orders. I had the Cousteaus climb in, the Soupaults—I emphasize—the families of a few militants, and hop, we were off along the Champs-Elysées . . . Alain de Berthois, chief editor of *Paris-Mondial,* took it into his head to refuse to come. The previous evening, Pierre Ducrocq had taken the same decision. Miramas gave way to his wife, and stayed put."

Miliciens and PPF members and other ultras, numbering between ten and twenty thousand, similarly piled into Wehrmacht trucks or military trains, only to find themselves inextricably caught up in the retreat eastward, exposed to Allied air forces as supreme in the skies as the Luftwaffe had been four years previously. Once they had entered the German orbit with mixed hopes and ambitions; now they had to seek exit from their own country in simple fear of their lives. Céline (who in *Au Pilori* had advocated suppressing the Radio altogether as an act of "mental hygiene") and his wife Lucette and his cat Bébert left too, and with him a friend, the actor Robert Le Vigan. So did Laval, after a last cabinet meeting with Maurice Gabolde (the minister of justice), Bichelonne, and Bonnard (the latter complained throughout the months of exile that he had had no time to pack up his collection of porcelain). At twenty past eight on the evening of the seventeenth, Laval was handed a letter from Abetz, to the effect that he had better come quietly if he did not want to be constrained. Not long before midnight, Abetz himself arrived with two SS officers to escort Laval away. Laval and his wife, watched by about forty friends and colleagues, said good-bye to their daughter José de Chambrun and left the office in the Matignon on the trek to Germany. Simultaneously, in Vichy, Pétain, claiming that he was a prisoner, was being driven off under armed guard. The destination of Pétain and Laval, of the remnants of Vichy and the ultras alike, was the former Hohenzollern castle of Sigmaringen, on the Danube about 80 kilometers south of Stuttgart and conveniently close to the Swiss frontier. The fiction of a French government-in-exile was maintained there until the end of the war—with Céline in the midst of the farce-cum-apocalypse of Sigmaringen, an author and a subject were perfectly matched, and the result was his extraordinary book *D'un château l'autre.* All of them, who had claimed so often and so stridently that Gaullists were mere tools of foreigners, had become the most hapless hangers-on of an enemy power they could not or dared not quit.

On the eighteenth, Oberg drove out of Paris with Knochen; the party had left the field to the army. The embassy closed. The Majestic Hotel ceased to function. No newspapers were published; no mail was delivered. Von Choltitz, in his headquarters in the luxurious Hotel Meurice in the rue de Rivoli, alone filled the vacuum. In his book . . . *et Paris ne fut pas détruit,* Taittinger wrote how the morning of the eighteenth had been marked by a gesture which was more than symbolic—the tricolor flag flew again on the Hôtel de Ville. This came about, he claimed, because an agreement had been reached the previous evening with Abetz, on the point of departure, and von Choltitz, "that Paris was to be neither defended nor destroyed, nor delivered to looting and arson." Von Choltitz's dispositions indicated that he would do nothing unless challenged, in the hope that he could hand everything over in good order to the incoming Allies. Since that spring, some thirty-two blockhouses known as *Stützpunkte* had been constructed to safeguard key positions like the Sénat and Chambre des Députés, the Ecole Militaire, the Ministry of Foreign Affairs, and hotels like the Crillon and the Continental, indeed the Meurice. Including office staff, clerks, and those who for one reason or another had not yet been withdrawn from the city, 16,500 men remained under von Choltitz's command. Some antiaircraft batteries could supplement a small number of field guns, and there were probably about thirty tanks, mostly light, though one almost certainly inflated estimate has seventy-eight. In addition, Luftwaffe bombers at Villacoublay could have been called upon had the situation deteriorated, and when the general commanding an SS division on its way to the front telephoned von Choltitz to inquire if he and his men could be of any use, the offer was declined as unnecessary.

Adrien Dansette in his *Histoire de la libération de Paris* has quoted an exchange revealing what the last eighteen months of preparation and deliberation among the factions of the resistance had actually achieved. A joint committee met on the eighteenth, and the Communist representative declared to the others, "The hour of insurrection has come; if you aren't with us, we will go it alone." "With what weapons?" the Gaullist representative asked. "We have six hundred," was the reply. Nothing more than small-scale skirmishing could be envisaged. Communist calls for insurrection continued to be issued in the face of reality over the next six days. Meanwhile the rue des Pyramides offices of the PPF, as well as those of *La Gerbe* and *Je Suis Partout,* were ransacked, their contents strewn in the streets.

The next day, Saturday the nineteenth, the striking policemen took over the Préfecture de Police, and on the twentieth the Hôtel de Ville was similarly occupied by the FFI (Forces Françaises de l'Intérieur). Dansette has described what he calls the FFI mobilization. "An officer was told by a double agent that two trucks were broken down at Levallois; they were attacked and their drivers killed; the spoils were fruitful: 4 machine guns, 12 submachine guns, 250 pistols, and some ammunition boxes. At Clichy, two German trucks collided at the angle of the boulevard Victor-Hugo and the boulevard Jean-Jaurès, and 9 machine guns, 15 submachine guns, and 8 Mausers were made away with. Next day, 20 submachine guns were taken from the Hotchkiss factory as well as a truckload of long-handled grenades on the quai de Saint-Ouen. So the insurgents, multiplying their stocks by a factor of four or five in six days, reached a strength of seven to eight thousand armed combatants for the liberation."

Since the main through roads were clear, and German patrols were able to pass freely up and down them, von Choltitz felt no call to intervene; the occupation of the Préfecture de Police and the Hôtel de Ville were without strategic significance. In any case, at the demand of the non-Communist resistance and through the good offices of Nordling, the Swedish consul general, a truce was arranged with effect from the twentieth. It so happened that once the truce was in operation three senior resistance leaders, including de Gaulle's *délégué général* in Paris, Alexandre Parodi, were caught at a roadblock, identified, and escorted to the Meurice. Dansette described how von Choltitz received them. "Let us understand the military governor's frame of mind. He knew nothing about the resistance. Nobody could tell him what it was, not even Nordling, for even he had only a very vague conception of it. . . . For him, von Choltitz, there was de Gaulle on the other side of the lines, and in Paris some civilians letting off shots in the streets, snipers violating the laws of war." The conversation finished with von Choltitz proposing the release of food stocks and offering to shake hands as between soldiers—which was refused. Then the resistance leaders were allowed to drive away.

"The Porte d'Orléans is black with people," André Thérive wrote, after observing the Germans and the resistance on August 20. "In side streets a few embryo barricades have been improvised with civil defense sandbags, old chairs, rusty iron-

One barricade improvised along the *quais* once the main German forces had pulled out.

work. But on the big arteries people are not playing at insurgents; they are once again spectators. No more shooting in the distance, no more threatening cars. Out on the open ground, there is a huge mustering of good-humored soldiers, clerks, and orderlies; beyond them trucks are being prepared for boarding and departure. Officers with goggles push back the idle gazers into lines. You could swear that the Queen of Queens is expected. . . . That's the heart of the matter: the return of peace and the ebbing, quite gently, of war."

Between Tuesday the twenty-second and Thursday the twenty-fourth, the reluctance of von Choltitz to engage his troops in battle encouraged those who wanted to be active against the Germans, so nullifying the truce. More and more insistent calls for insurrection were put out by the resistance, including the Communists' slogan *"Chacun son boche"* (To each his Boche). Verbal flourishes of the sort translated into an increased skirmishing with German patrols. Dansette gives the figure of a thousand wounded on each of these successive days, but offers no estimate of the dead except to say that funerals for resistants who were Protestant were held at the Oratoire, and for those who were Catholic at Notre-Dame-des-Victoires; in the latter case there were thirty to forty a day, as from the twenty-second. He also stated that a total of twenty thousand people (i.e., including the unarmed) had participated in the street skirmishes, which contrasts with Taittinger, who more realistically says that three thousand at most were involved in any fighting. (The myth-building and self-glorification which took place afterward, according to Taittinger, were so disproportionate that by January 1945 the Ministry of the Interior had received 123,000 letters from people demanding to be incorporated as bona-fide members of the resistance.) Taittinger estimates that altogether a thousand civilians lost their lives in the liberation. In Warsaw, where that same August there really was a general uprising against German occupation in almost exactly parallel circumstances, with the Russian army on the point of advancing into the city's outskirts, the casualties were of quite a different order, and they put the liberation of Paris into proper perspective. Warsaw, with 950,000 inhabitants, was about a third the size of Paris, yet 30,000 people died in the fighting within the Old City alone. The German historian Hanns von Krannhals, in his definitive *Der Warschauer Aufstand 1944,* accepted that what with air raids, shelling, disease, mass exterminations, and fighting, 166,000 Poles died before Warsaw was finally liberated.

For most Parisians, even the three days of skirmishing and barricading were spent in pleasurable excitement, picking up local gossip on the grapevine, occasionally hearing a ricochet or two, retreating to the safety of home. "Fighting in the streets is less risky and more picturesque than open campaigning," commented Galtier-Boissière; "one comes home to lunch carrying one's rifle; the whole neighborhood is at the windows to have a look and to applaud; the milkman, the greengrocer, and the man in the bistro won't chalk anything up on the slate. If only the cameras were turning, glory would be absolute." The underside of the resistance revolted him. A cobbler who had himself been denounced to the Gestapo was now in the resistance denouncing "collabos" as fast as he could. An elderly gentleman at present sporting a French naval uniform had not scrupled in the early part of the war to wear the swastika emblem in his buttonhole. The mother of a young girl was heard saying, "My little Josiane, it's too horrible. Her hair has been cut off, *monsieur.* Poor little Josiane! If she went to bed with Germans, it was because she's seventeen, *monsieur,* you follow me? But why ever cut off her hair for it? It's a crying shame, *monsieur.* She's just as willing to go to bed with Americans!"

General Eisenhower, commanding the American and Allied forces, had origi-

Young men wearing FFI armbands taking into custody some of General Dietrich von Choltitz's garrison.

nally planned to swing around Paris, to avoid fighting in the city and to be spared from having to divert food and supplies from his men to the civilian population. He was persuaded to change his mind and, for the sake of its prestige, to allow the French division under his command to enter Paris. The divisional commander was General Jacques Philippe Leclerc, and on the evening of the twenty-fourth, the first of his armored units reached the city. The next morning the rest of the division followed, accepting the surrender of one German blockhouse after another. At about one o'clock, a brief clash occurred outside the Meurice, and it was not before two more hours had passed that von Choltitz constituted himself a prisoner and then signed an act of capitulation. About twelve thousand Germans in all were captured, with some three thousand casualties, indicating that few of the garrison had attempted to break out. Some surrendering Germans were gunned down, notably in an incident when a grenade was thrown close to a column of prisoners marching around the Etoile, and a machine gun then opened up on them. At four o'clock in the afternoon, General de Gaulle drove in an open car into Paris and arranged to spend the night in the Ministry of War. The crowd, which just sixteen weeks earlier had been cheering Pétain, now cheered him.

Shots were still being fired from the rooftops, supposedly by collaborators who refused to surrender, but more probably by FFI snipers too hysterical to identify targets. Brasillach, in hiding under one of the roofs, was nearly flushed out by accident. Some days later he gave himself up on hearing that his mother had been arrested in his stead. He was tried and shot early in 1946. Among the few leading writers who refused to sign a plea for clemency on his behalf were Sartre and Simone de Beauvoir. Suarez was shot, and Paul Chack too, and so were those brought back from Sigmaringen: Laval, de Brinon, Luchaire, Hérold-Paquis, Darnand, Knipping, Bassompierre, as well as gangsters like Bonny and Laffont and Masuy, with one or two bureaucrats and some of the police inspectors who had helped the SD and Gestapo to be so effective. Anonymous small-time members of the Milice and the PPF were simply gunned down or were tied to stakes, their eyes bandaged, before they were shot. Pétain's sentence of death was commuted by de Gaulle to life imprisonment, which was served out. Doriot had been killed early in 1945 in Germany, when his car was strafed by aircraft. Alphonse de Chateaubriant, Lesca, Laubreaux, Darquier, and hundreds of others disappeared into Nazi twilight in Spain and South America, or even Italy in the case of Déat and his wife. As for statistics about summary executions, they cannot be reliably established. Robert Aron, who assembled probably as much evidence as remained, calculated that after the liberation there had been between thirty and forty thousand summary executions in France. Adrien Tixier, postwar minister of justice, offered the higher figure of 105,000 summary executions between June 1944 and February 1945. "National indignity" was a newly invented crime for which many thousands of former collaborators were imprisoned. Between August 21 and October 1, 1944, according to the specialist publication *Historia,* in its issue Number 41 entitled *La Justice sommaire de l'été 1944,* "There were apparently one million arrests, 100,000 of them in the Paris region." A small number of those Germans on whom responsibility lay for the crimes committed in the name of their country and their creed also served prison sentences: Oberg, Knochen, Abetz. More debatably, Epting went to prison, and so did Otto von Stülpnagel, the first Militärbefehlshaber of that name, who hanged himself in his cell.

The night which on June 14, 1940, had so terrifyingly set its stamp on the deserted streets of Paris could not simply be wound away, reversed like a film. What was to be done about the searing shame of it all? In particular, about the damage to the nation by its loyal serving of foreign interests and its complicity in genocide as well? In the face of these fundamentals of conscience, it was a reflex to sacrifice some for the sake of many. What the French did to themselves after the occupation was in some ways more painful than what the Germans had done to them during it. For the number of Frenchmen killed by other Frenchmen, whether through summary execution or rigged tribunals akin to lynch mobs or court-martials and High Court trials, equaled or even exceeded the number of those sent to their death by the Germans as hostages, deportees, and slave laborers. So liberation did not begin where occupation ended, but completed a cycle of violence and bloodshed.

Overleaf: **Resistance fighters dismantling the traffic signs erected by the Germans.**

II. INTERVIEWS

Ernst Achenbach

After the war Achenbach became a parliamentary deputy in Bonn. When he was proposed as German representative to the European Community in Brussels, his record came under scrutiny, and his nomination had to be withdrawn. A document quoted (CDJC Ref.: XXV-b-144) was a letter on embassy paper, dated February 11, 1943, and signed by Achenbach. Addressed to Roethke, Dannecker's successor, the letter confirmed the Foreign Office's instructions to proceed with anti-Jewish measures in the newly occupied Vichy zone. Difficulties were anticipated not from the French government but from the Italian government. Another document quoted (CXXVIa-92) was a telegram sent by Achenbach on February 15, 1943, from the embassy to Berlin, announcing that two German officers, Winkler and Nussbaum, had been killed in an ambush behind the Hotel Louvre, where they were quartered, and that consequently, "as a preliminary reprisal measure, it is intended to arrest two thousand Jews and deport them to the east." Klarsfeld has established in *Le Mémorial de la déportation des Juifs de France* that this operation took place and the Jews were sent to their death.

Achenbach's wife Margaret is American. She was present at the interview.

ACHENBACH: My father became a high school principal in Gelsenkirchen. I studied in Paris as a lawyer and spoke the language well. I was admitted to the Foreign Office as a third secretary in the spring of 1936; at first I was in the legal department. In the last days of 1936, I was sent to the Paris embassy under Count Welczek. When war broke out, we all had to leave. Paris was occupied, I was sent back, and I think I was the only one who had been in the embassy before the war. Sieburg and Grimm were private persons but belonged to the Comité France-Allemagne. Schleier, the minister, was the only one who was also a party member, but he let himself be influenced by the rest of us. Abetz later received a very high rank in the SS, but that was to give him equality with those he was negotiating with. Abetz was a subtle diplomat; he had a way of convincing others that they were right and yet he could maneuver them into thinking like him. I got on well with Abetz personally. I spoke openly with him. With Schleier less so, but he would not denounce a friend. Rahn was not a convinced Nazi. [*Achenbach's cigarette case, I notice, was a present from Rahn, his signature engraved on the silver lid.*] In 1940 I was thirty-one.

Paris was rather empty; it had a friendly atmosphere, however. In the first year of the occupation Franco-German relations were excellent. The atmosphere only gradually spoiled. I lived in the embassy, rue de Lille, and had my office there. I collaborated closely with Abetz; I was for political contacts. Quite a few people came to see me. Pretty soon we were in contact with Laval. I accompanied him to Montoire. De Brinon turned up, in his capacity as head of the Comité France-Allemagne: that group was always active. It was then too that I met Robert Murphy and Ambassador Bullitt. Murphy was intervening on behalf of some French people—there was some man who had locked away papers that should have been available, and he was going to be sent to prison, so Murphy asked if we could help. That was the embassy's specialty at the time.

Margaret came out for Christmas. We had had an apartment before the war, in the consulate building, rue Huysmans, off the boulevard Raspail. We found our furniture intact; the Swedes had taken care of it. This apartment was connected with the consulate, so we always had two German soldiers in front of it. We had a nanny for our eldest boy—he was born in 1938, so he must have been about two. The nanny was French and couldn't speak a word of German, and there was no arrangement for a *laissez-passer* for her. Whenever there was a new sentry, there was a good deal of trouble getting her through.

I only vaguely remember subsidizing the Maître du Feu, and his paper. I tried to help Freemasons; I had the reputation of being one myself. Somebody said I was a Communist, others that I was a liberal.

MARGARET ACHENBACH, *interjecting about the Maître du Feu:* I thought you were more patient with him than I would have been.

ACHENBACH: There was also Luchaire's paper, *Les Nouveaux Temps.* Luchaire was a charming man, I used to see him. And René Chateau, we founded a Club Européen together. There was also the Swiss Oltramare. Social life was very active. We were invited by some of the best society—they were very charming to us. Ninety percent of the so-called collaborators were French patriots who thought they ought not to do anything to annoy the Germans. As far as we were concerned personally, we didn't initiate much social life; we hadn't the means. We did take people out and invited them to meals. We saw the Beauvau-Craons, the Princesse de Polignac, and Dolly de Castellane—she was an aunt of Count Welczek. With ex-Queen Amélie of Portugal we had very nice contacts. When we left, she said, 'Doesn't Herr Hitler care for France anymore? Is that why he's removing Achenbach?' And we saw the Dubonnets and the Beaumonts. We knew Sacha Guitry. I knew Déat quite well; personally he was a very nice man. I must have known Costantini. Drieu la Rochelle was a friend, and so was Leroy-Ladurie, a very decent fellow. Doriot was a 150 percent Fascist. I met Pétain. After Montoire, I had to accompany him back to Tours.

The military was in charge, and the embassy was not nearly as important in wartime. According to my general belief, I was for Franco-German good understanding. We said friendly things, and that gained us a reputation for being too friendly. The embassy, and not only the embassy, was forced to work with the SS and the party and also with the hawks in the military. Some of them said why should we be so good to the French, and the only way to be rid of terrorist attacks is to punish the attackers. The embassy line always favored the French: it will be easier for collaboration if we treat the French decently and magnanimously. This argument was used to constrain members of the SS and the army, often with success. If you compare France with Belgium or Holland, the balance is in favor of France. The embassy earned a good share of credit for this. The military governor in later years, Stülpnagel, was in favor of magnanimity, but somehow he was forced to take measures that the embassy didn't think necessary, or anyhow he tried to reduce embassy influence. Of course instead of shooting hostages, it was better with the help of the French police to catch the attackers.

In February 1943, those two air force officers were shot to death. Stülpnagel announced that as reprisals he would ship two thousand Jews to the East. I reported this fact to the Ministry, and that is all there is to that telegram of mine. We all thought that shooting hostages did no good at all. Oberg was not the worst.

MARGARET ACHENBACH: Wasn't it at that meeting with Oberg, you came home, Dannecker had been there, and you said, "That man is mad"? You also had a conference with Abetz, and that was when Abetz said, "You mustn't have anything to do with conferences about Jews because you can't hold your tongue."

ACHENBACH: I had asked, "Do you think it's going to help the German war effort if we have all the Jewish groups against us?" Dr. Zeitschel was the embassy go-between with the SS; at the beginning he had belonged to the military police. He claimed somehow to be a Hohenzollern descendant. That was someone we didn't trust. Dr. Grosse, a trade unionist, worked with me; he had contacts with the French trade unions. Schwendemann dealt with the press, together with Feilh, a journalist. Schwendemann made the farewell speech for me. There were people who came later we didn't know. Gerstner: we treated him with a certain amount of caution, because he made the impression of being a thorough Nazi, but he turned out to be a Communist and became mayor of a sector of East Berlin. In March 1943, I was recalled, overnight, and received a posting in the Foreign Office. I learned from Baron von Steengracht that SS people thought I was too much of a collaborator.

MARGARET ACHENBACH: Oberg phoned once, and you were arguing with him and he slammed down the receiver. Ernst was the secret tip for French people who were in difficulties.

ACHENBACH: In my political group was Nostitz-Walwitz, son of Helena von Nostitz, a Berlin *salonnière*. Also von Böse. We were in touch with Laval throughout, and with his son-in-law, Chambrun. Laval once said to me, "De Gaulle and Laval are both necessary," meaning that France had to have representation with Germany as well as with the Anglo-Saxon world. De Brinon was very amiable, polite, but not a man you became friends with.

MARGARET ACHENBACH: We moved into an apartment at 102, rue de Grenelles. I was walking one day in the Palais Luxembourg and the windows there had been thrown open, and I heard a Frenchwoman say, *"Regarde moi ça, ils crevent de chaleur"* [*Will you just look at that—they're dying of heat*]. That was how they felt about us. A well-meaning Nazi woman came to me one day. She looked shaken, and she asked, "Can't the embassy do something? They are separating Jewish mothers from their children, and the scenes are dreadful." This woman worked in some welfare organization down at the station, and she had seen it for herself. I remember seeing Paris Jews marching through the streets when they had to wear stars. The best, most handsome of them, and in their medals, and I remember thinking that's right, that's intelligent of them. The embassy was furious about the order to wear the yellow star.

We had ration cards, on the same basis as the military. I was in the metro and there was this woman with a child who looked so terribly thin. I handed her my brand-new ration card. I realized only afterward that the authorities had stamped on the top: "A month's rations for occupying forces." We had a car with a diplomatic number, a *Dienstwagen,* a Citroën. After the war, our French maid went to see if Ernst was in the Cherche-midi prison, when she heard that Abetz had been arrested and taken there. She was afraid that all the embassy might be there, and in that case she wanted to take him packages.

Simone Mittre

For many years Madame Mittre accompanied Fernand de Brinon as secretary and confidante.

De Brinon's memoirs are all true, but there are things I'd rather not have seen in print. I was very shaken by his execution, and I didn't do the book. Jean Lasserre was a journalist who had collaborated with de Brinon; he did it from notes taken during the trial. I was on the *délégation générale* with de Brinon. Each time he came back from Vichy, he dictated notes to me. These we found in his papers, and we furnished them for the trial in the Haut Cour.

You can't understand de Brinon unless you go back to World War I. He had seen the dead on both sides in the battlefield, with their letters home lying on the ground where they had fallen. He thought that this must never happen again. I knew him in 1919; he was editor in chief of *Débats* at the time. From 1919 on, he devoted himself to Franco-German relations. Daladier sent him to interview Hitler. Hitler made a generous offer, and de Brinon was impressed. He was the only man who never changed his opinions—his politics during the occupation are explained by his politics between the wars.

He represented no party: he was independent. An article of his was suppressed in *Débats,* so in 1929 he resigned and took over the job of political correspondent of *L'Information,* until the start of 1939. The same thing recurred. He did an article on a strike, they didn't like the article, so he resigned. Then he went to a house belonging to his wife in the Pyrenees. It was Laval, as vice-president already, who telephoned de Brinon to be his Paris representative, since he knew Abetz had been appointed. He had been fetched by Angelo Chiappe, and together they went to Vichy. Representing the vice-presidency, he was installed at Matignon (in the rue de Varennes, where the prime minister now lives). We had a lot to do as everybody came to knock at the door. How right you are to take the job, they all said at the time. After December 13, the Marshal nominated de Brinon to represent him.

The Marshal gave him a big photo which I had framed in gold and green, and it carried the inscription: *"A Fernand de Brinon, le fidèle interprète de ma pensée auprès des autorités allemandes"* [*To Fernand de Brinon, the faithful interpreter of my thoughts to the German authorities*]. It stood on his desk for four years. In 1917 de Brinon had been on the Marshal's staff, and they had souvenirs to mull over. All the people at Vichy pushed de Brinon forward to take the brunt, but with the Marshal he had a good relationship.

In 1940, at Matignon, at first there were just de Brinon and me. He received the leading German personalities. I received people who had requests; we were in charge of those who had been arrested, and radio and press matters too. After a while Pierre Roussillon was appointed *chef de cabinet.* We stayed a year at Matignon. At first we had to deal through the embassy. Later with the other branches of the administration.

It was hallucinating to receive the callers. People just arrived, wanting to find a way to present their case; they formed a line. "Who told you to come to me?" I used to inquire. It's the *on dit,* was the answer. At our office *laissez-passer* to the Vichy zone were issued. Every day we had a quota of *laissez-passer*; every day I had the applications and the passes to make up. I couldn't be selective. I issued those I could on the principle of first come, first served. We made up the daily list—say I had twenty to grant—and Monsieur Moutarde, a man on our staff, then carried this list to the proper department in the Majestic. The Germans would authorize each *Ausweis* and Monsieur Moutarde would return with them. According to each case, when later people came to be arrested, de Brinon had to intervene with the army or the Gestapo. It was difficult, since these services were at odds with each other. We had more than one intervention a day—in the end we were doing nothing else.

Pardon often depended on how the case was presented. The dossiers that we assembled were fetched every day by a German and distributed to the Majestic, Knochen, or the embassy. You had better not make a mistake in whom you chose as your protector. And de Brinon had his other functions to perform, for everything concerning Paris passed through him. Telescript messages from Vichy arrived all the time. He had a bodyguard and a car from the garage of the Préfecture de Police.

We left Matignon because Darlan had decided to put Benoist-Méchin in and the service was his, so we had to requisition something to replace our office. Darlan said of Benoist-Méchin, "Now I've got a de Brinon of my own!"—which was his way of stressing the confidence existing between Laval and de Brinon. Darlan told de

Brinon to requisition something, so we visited two or three little private houses. Colonel de Corcelles was on friendly terms with Prince Amédée de Broglie, the son-in-law of Princesse de Faucigny-Lucinge, and it was he who proposed that we requisition the Princesse's house in the rue Rudé, which had been taken over for Himmler. I was against it because it was so big, but in fact the house was saved by the measure. De Brinon had it derequisitioned from the Germans and then requisitioned for himself by the Préfecture de la Seine. Afterward the Princesse resented it. We did an inventory, and she found her house intact again. Her secretary was called Gros; he kept two rooms on the ground floor. We held receptions in the rue Rudé, including a large one for Breker. De Brinon went to the eastern front in 1943; he was criticized for that.

We never took a day off. Sometimes we went to Chantilly, to a house requisitioned at Gouvieux, to be precise—it belonged to some Americans called Goddard. De Brinon liked horses. He had a thoroughbred and on a Saturday enjoyed riding it. We knew that the Communists had done the *attentat* at our house on the night of October 16, 1943. Some antitank mines had been placed on the windowsills, and they blew up the room.

His work essentially had to do with reconciliation. He thought he had to carry his mission right through to the end. Even at Sigmaringen, when he knew everything was lost. He asked for permission to enter Switzerland—I have a copy of the request—and he could have gone to Spain. He certainly had believed in the German victory. In 1940, listening to the news of the German offensive, he had tears in his eyes. He had thought that Hitler wanted to have a rapprochement with France. I went to the Nuremberg party rally in 1937 and 1938, with de Brinon and Brasillach and Cousteau. It was shattering. I was never political, but what de Brinon told me seemed logical.

He used to see Déat. At Sigmaringen, Déat and Luchaire and Darnand wanted to persist to the end, with the Charlemagne Division and so on—they were a bloc against de Brinon and General [*Eugène*] Bridoux. Leaving Sigmaringen, we ended in Innsbruck and there met a German we had known, who gave us a room in a hotel. On the wireless we heard that the Marshal's trial was about to begin. At that moment de Brinon said that he wanted to return. "They will shoot me," he said, "but at least I would like the chance to explain myself." He had a naïve side to him.

Jacques Benoist-Méchin

In one's own life there are things one cannot explain. I was pushed by events. Before the war I'd written the first two volumes in my history of the German army. It happened that I had not heard of the armistice, and so I was taken prisoner after it had come into effect, on June 27. I was in a camp for 6,700 men at Voves. We were not fed for twelve days and became groggy. It was harvest time, and all around us were wheat fields. I tried to write the next volume of my history of the German army and was then questioned about it by the camp commandant. I told him that we would die of hunger soon, and it was absurd to be surrounded by the unharvested fields. A deal was made: we would bring in the harvest, and they would send us home. I was allowed to take the camp in hand. I set up teams. When the harvest was in, I found that I had liberated everyone except the Moroccans and Senegalese, who could not go home. Marshal Pétain heard about it. I had met him before the war. We have two million prisoners leaving for Germany, Pétain said to me—would I look after them? I had some sort of conscience as a result of having freed myself, and so I agreed to become *chef de la mission diplomatique des prisonniers de guerre à Berlin.* I left for Berlin on December 11, 1940. Scapini was accredited with the rank of ambassador to deal with prisoners, and he and I were summoned together to the Wilhelmstrasse. I soon realized that if I wanted to get prisoners out, I had to be in Vichy, not Berlin. At Vichy I could give advice about avoiding shocks like the departure of Laval. Because the Marshal could not abide Laval, he chose Darlan, and then I became *secrétaire général du gouvernement* and Darlan's *secrétaire d'état.* I had offices in Paris and at the Hotel du Parc in Vichy. I was a politician, not a bureaucrat. When Darlan ceased to be prime minister, I stayed to complete some negotiations under Laval. Darlan was a great man, in my opinion; he trusted in me, for which I am grateful. My functions as *secrétaire général* were to oversee negotiations between France and foreign countries. We had diplomatic relations with America, North and South, Japan and the Axis countries, and the neutrals when I took up my job in February 1941.

The Germans never wanted to clarify peace conditions. Now I know why. Simply because they had no confidence in France. Going to meet Hitler in May 1941, I was prepared to examine anything they might propose on condition that they would tell us what they intended to do with us in the event of their victory. As of then, they were asking for the Luftwaffe to overfly Syria; we said we would look at it.

I thought Hitler was a very extraordinary man. I was impressed by him in the surroundings of Berchtesgaden—impressed by so much power. I believed in the New Europe, at least until that journey to Berchtesgaden. Then I could see for myself that Hitler did not believe in it. His position was as follows: either I win or I don't. If I don't, then all talk is useless; therefore I can wait to treat until I've won. Our position was: tell us your conditions. But he didn't want to tie his hands. In all disputed frontier zones he wanted plebiscites.

I was pro-German in the measure that it seemed pro-French to be so. I was not pro-German against Russia. Yes, in May 1942 I spoke at the Breker exhibition; I'd been a friend of his since 1924, when I went to Germany on military service, and was for Franco-German rapprochement. I had known all the German leaders since Scheidemann and had been on the Comité France-Allemagne since its start. To do the Breker exhibition was just to continue an old friendship. By 1942 I suspected that the Germans might lose, but I became sure by August 1943. Kursk was when the die was cast. The German army had picked the place and time for their counterattack, but it had been driven back, My mental evolution had not been lightning-fast. At Berchtesgaden I had speculated if he would win, and whether it was desirable that he should.

The collaborationist parties, I came to think, were engaged in dangerous politics. They were friends I wouldn't encourage. I was interested in Doriot, who had the only French party that amounted to anything. I was on friendly terms with writers like Drieu and Brasillach, who were sincere though I did not share their opinions. It was difficult, and more painful than you think.

It is hard not to be unfair about the role of Abetz, who was deeply and sincerely Francophile. Abetz used to ask: Was my appointment to the embassy a revenge because I had been expelled before the war, or did Hitler appreciate my feelings for France? His defect was wishful thinking. He knew but could not accept that Hitler was not in favor of rapprochement, so he put pressure on Hitler. His dispatches were not exact—they alluded to things that had not happened quite as he put them, in order to force Hitler's convictions. Fundamentally Hitler did not like France.

At the armistice, I much admired Laval's courage. At the time of the December 13 coup, I did the impossible to get him back. I provoked the Laval-Pétain meeting at La Ferté-Hauterive. When he was back in office, I did not get on with him. The defeat had traumatized me to work to transform ourselves. Laval was too old and set in his ways, accustomed to the Third Republic, and he did not believe that France could be transformed.

A totalitarian regime will always appear more seductive than a parliamentary mess. But in itself, a totalitarian regime is a hypertrophy of the role of the state. I was not a Nazi or a Fascist; my choice was based on realpolitik. I always said to the Germans: I am no enemy; give me something to convince my compatriots to think like me. If you concede nothing, what can I do? When I saw Hitler, I saw he was a Germanic European, but not a federator. The discussions of the Protocols of Paris lacked generosity. They kept on discussing whether we needed twenty-two, twenty-one, or twenty motorbikes when we had the chance to remake the world. We had a political annex stating that circumstances must be created in which we could make the Protocols a political reality. This they never wanted, so the Protocols were never executed. It was not a practical proposition to make France an outright ally of Germany, and I do not believe they would have wanted us on their side.

Arno Breker

Arno Breker has published a book of recollections, *Im Strahlungsfeld der Ereignisse, 1925–1965,* including much about Paris and his French friends during the war. Lifar, Cocteau, and Marais were among those he sculpted during the occupation, as well as Céline, whose bust is now at the entrance of his sitting room.

The beginning of the occupation was a dream, as I saw it. I was afraid of political action against us, but there was none. I was the first German civilian into Paris, when I came with Hitler. I spent a week at headquarters. I visited Rheims, and I was virtually the only person there. My book which recounts all this has been entirely boycotted. I was summoned by Hitler because I could speak French and had lived in Paris until 1934.

Hitler came only that once. Langeron is wrong when he describes in his diary a second visit—his successor was Bousquet, by the way, whose son was with me as a secretary during the war, and afterward I had to hide the boy. Hitler said to me, "I could have entered Paris at the head of my victorious army, but I didn't want to harm the soul of the population, to damage their national pride." The defeat was already felt strongly enough. Hitler wanted to visit my studio en route around the city. We were at Denfert-Rochereau. I was five minutes away on foot, but it was late, and he wanted to hurry, so we did not make the detour. He told me that his admiration of French culture had no limits. He did not speak of a degenerate people; he did not hate France. Politics had changed his path, he said, and if he had been able to continue his life as he had wanted, "I would have liked to live like you and continued my studies in Paris." I saw Hitler very moved before the tomb of Napoleon. He murmured that he wanted the ashes of L'Aiglon to be next to his father. Only he, as a Viennese, could have had that thought. After that visit, I had a long talk with Hitler in the evening, during a walk in the woods at headquarters. He felt my sensitivity to France and French culture, and he spoke only to me. I was very moved.

After the armistice, Benoist-Méchin, one of my old friends, came to see me in Berlin to ask me to collaborate in Franco-German rapprochement. He invited me to exhibit my work. I am an old *Parigot,* I said; in present circumstances I haven't the heart for it. A few months later Drieu visited me in Berlin and he proposed it too; he pushed me into exhibiting in Paris. While Drieu was with me, a stranger called, a Frenchman bringing a tiny bit of paper. It was a message from Rudier, who had cast all Rodin's bronzes. He had been arrested because he refused to make arms in his factory, and he had smuggled this message out of Fresnes asking me to do what I could to get him out. With that paper I went to Speer and asked if I could do casts in Paris, since no bronze foundries still worked in Germany. Speer lived with us during the war, at Jäckelsbruch, some 65 kilometers east of Berlin. I had moved there because all the glass panes in my Berlin studio fell in whenever there was a raid. Speer asked how much metal I needed. Thirty tons. That's nothing, he said. So I telephoned the embassy to liberate Rudier because I needed to work with him. Abetz was a friend. Suzanne, his wife, was fantastic, a sensation when she came to Paris.

At the beginning of 1941 I sent my works to Paris. My headquarters was in the Ritz; I had a suite there, and I paid nothing for it. I invited friends there. During the war, you could eat as well as in peacetime, or even better, only you had to know the right addresses. Rudier was a great gastronome, and he was always finding places for unforgettable meals.

I was very often in Paris. I'd take the Paris-Moscow train from the Gare du Nord, very comfortable too. I came all the time because of Rudier. He saved his equipment and team of ninety workmen, molders, cutters, *ciseleurs.* They did not want to lose their jobs. I paid them all the time. There were the usual exhibitions in galleries and museums, but I believe I was the only German artist with a public exhibition like that. For the opening, I gave a press conference in the Lido on the Champs-Elysées and said to the assembled journalists that I did not want them writing in admiration because they thought they ought to. I could guarantee that nobody who was critical would be harmed, and when I said that, frantic applause broke out. The exhibition was more or less as it would have been in peacetime.

Hitler's visit to Paris changed my standing. I was forty on July 19, 1940. That day I was invited to lunch at the Chancellory, and after lunch Hitler gave me the Golden Badge of the Party. The whole of his entourage saw what a part I played in his life. And then he was astonished by the success of my exhibition, and very proud. For him this was a certificate that he had found his best artist. Himmler noticed it. I told his aide that if ever an artist was in difficulty I would look after the matter. So I could address myself to General [*Heinrich*] Müller, head of the Gestapo. By that means I got Dina Vierny freed; she was sixteen or seventeen, a Russian Jew and mistress of Maillol. I was on very good terms with them. It was the same with many others. Including Picasso. I brought up the subject of Picasso with Müller in the Gestapo headquarters at the Albrechtstrasse. Picasso had been sending money to Russia via the Scandinavian countries. Cocteau had telephoned me to save him, saying I had to do something—Picasso was frightened. I knew his character—he was a great coward, he had the wind up. If the police were to lay hands on him, he might give up the ghost. I said to Müller that such a man could not be allowed to die, and that if he would not help, then I would ring up the Chancellory and tell the story there. That changed matters. He rang up Paris and gave the orders to stop all activity against Picasso.

After the defeat of France, the people were ready for unlimited reconciliation. This changed only when the Communist party no longer tolerated it. I was seeing

Freisz, Derain, Belmondo. I was against the trip of French sculptors to Germany on the grounds of security—I didn't want them to be victims of a raid. They did only one journey, in 1943, taking in Berlin, Düsseldorf, Munich, ending in Vienna. They drank and sang—Despiau, Dunoyer de Segonzac, Flammarion the publisher.

I was close to Laval. Before he was in office he wanted me to tell Hitler that he should be promoted to minister of foreign affairs. "I am worth forty thousand combat tanks," he said. Hitler did not speak French, and interviews through interpreters are no good. I saw Cocteau and Paul Morand; his wife was a Greek princess (my first wife Mimina was Greek too). At the Institut I met Céline. He was a dandy at the time—you can't imagine it. There were afternoon receptions with petits fours and champagne or beer or whatever you wanted. Epting was a serious man, grounded in French literature and philosophy. The French elite were to be found at the Institut.

French women were very much more courageous than French men. For the women, a battle had been lost, but not the war. In fashion, there was this fantasy about hats. My wife was lunching with Laval one day and on her hat she had a stuffed bird. Laval said that she had better hurry with her peas or the bird would eat them. Laval knew he would be shot. Nobody else had the courage to fight with the occupying forces to save France, to ameliorate and improve a difficult pass. I, as a German, would never have accepted Laval or any Frenchman merely because they were traitors, nor would Abetz have.

Georges Albertini

Under the pseudonym of Claude Varennes, Albertini published in 1948 *Le Destin de Marcel Déat,* containing much firsthand information. He had played an influential role in Déat's party, the RNP. In 1944, when Déat became a minister in the final reshuffle of the Vichy government and an ultra in his support of Germany, Albertini was his *directeur général du cabinet.*

Before the war my contacts with Déat had been infrequent. It was late in the day when he became a leader of pacifism, one of the numerous parliamentarians who thought that war ought to be avoided. Since 1925, and especially after 1933, he had been making a reputation in the Parti Socialiste, and as an orator in his own right. At the time, the rigid left-wing and right-wing contrast had recently ceased to correspond to reality. Those who were around in the Third Republic took attitudes toward war with Germany that cut across party politics. To simplify, there was a sort of peace party and a sort of war party. After June 1940, 99 percent of the population were in the peace party, a conjuncture which brought together such disparate elements as Déat and Deloncle—they simply found themselves on the same side of the barricade.

The two problems were (a) the defeat and (b) responsibility for it. It was our opinion that after the collapse a way of alleviating the occupation and the consequences of defeat had to be found, and that meant collaboration. (Too late, this was seen to be an illusion in several respects.) Déat was in this category; in his sympathies for Germany he was identical with many French intellectuals. The policy of collaboration had to last while the Germans were in France—there was nothing else for it. Sometimes it was discussed whether we would be shot afterward, but we remained convinced that it was more advantageous to restrain the damages of the occupation within France, and not from abroad. Neither the Gaullists nor we ourselves understood that these two functions were complementary. Nor did we want to leave France with the enemy, for that would have left us open to the reproach that we were disavowing our whole stance. We had not been to London either. It was only after the Normandy landings that I realized that the war had been lost for us.

Staying here with the Germans meant that even those who acted with the best of intentions were often exposed to getting their hands dirty—and they had to be aware of that fact. The whole problem lies here: we did it for respectable reasons, but we had to get our hands dirty all the same. I spent my time negotiating with them. Those who had the work to do were the ones to dirty their hands. One had to visit the Germans at the Majestic, or to deal with Sauckel, actually spend time fending them off.

Déat had illusions about the German regime. He had a lot of ideas in common with Hitlerism. The one-party state, we all felt, could not be worse than the parliamentary system which had led us into this pass. Déat was not exactly a partisan of totalitarianism, but he did not consider that our analysis of Fascism went far enough. It was a French version of authoritarianism, if you like, and in fact Déat laid the foundations for the de Gaulle state. Did his friendship with the Germans embarrass him at all? No, I don't think so.

From 1940 to 1944 I was secretary general of the RNP and devoted myself to it. Party offices were in the rue du Faubourg Saint-Honoré. Membership varied, being about twenty thousand in 1942, its best period. There were uniformed stewards who wore dark shirts and cross-belts. Composition was relatively varied. Politics were forbidden in the free zone, don't forget; the RNP was a party in the south only after 1942. RNP leaders like Goy and Vanor were nonentities. Déat chose them personally, but I threw the lot out. The party was all very inorganic, whatever it may have hoped for by way of one-party politics. I used to see Déat every day, but he did not bother with routine, the nuts and bolts of organization. He left that to me, and to our office staff, about twenty strong. *L'Oeuvre,* Déat's paper, received a subsidy, and it did more than any other paper to defend Laval's policies. *L'Oeuvre* and Luchaire's *Les Nouveaux Temps* both supported Laval, and in return Laval used money from secret funds for them, as happens in such cases, as everybody knows, my dear sir.

I did not know Doriot well, although I tried to arrange things between him and Déat pursuing an initiative of Henri Barbé's, former PPF *secrétaire général* but a RNP member since 1942. I thought there might prove common ground. Where collaboration was concerned, of course there was sincerity, and also a lot of opportunism, and sometimes sincere opportunism too. I reproach Déat most with leaving. His entourage stayed in Paris. I prevented them all from leaving. I did not see that anybody at RNP headquarters had any reason to flee his country. I can still see Déat, livid, his hat pulled down over his eyes as he got into his car, and we watched him go.

Lucien Combelle

I was born into a proletarian family and came to Fascism by reaction against my background, and through pride. I was twenty-five. I did not believe in natural equality, but that the best should win. To cultivate that is to be ripe for Fascism. When Gide said of me that Combelle's heart is on the left but his mind is on the right, he was perceptive. It prevented me from a being a Marxist but prepared me for Fascism. In 1938 and 1939 I was Gide's secretary and already a Fascist. I had started by reading Maurras, who gave me what I would call an instinctive aristocratic outlook on life. Then in Rémy de Gourmont I found a sort of French Nietzsche, who displaced Maurras for me. What with the outcome of the Spanish war and the 1940 German campaign, the old drama of my adolescence returned. The next influence was my meeting with Drieu. Where we met remains a trifle vague, perhaps with Gallimard at the *NRF* offices. Drieu and Bertrand de Jouvenal had founded a magazine called *Le Fait*; I dug up some interviews I published there. Then I began a long-term dialogue with Drieu, and all at once I had plunged into the thick of it. Drieu was as much a fantastic drug as Maurras or Rémy de Gourmont. Not really a militant, he was in some respects a dilettante, but receptive to the idea of French decadence. Toward me he had an older man's affection—I was this curious case of a boy with an odd itinerary.

From 1940 to 1944 I saw Drieu almost every day. I would visit him in the middle of the morning. He had mistresses, but none living with him. It was a sort of psychoanalysis to sit in his drawing room in the avenue de Breteuil. What carried weight was the matter of Germany and the Germans. The need for information and news was overriding, and Drieu knew what the American and English press was saying.

What did the Germans mean to a man like me? I won't make myself ridiculous by telling you that the army was correct, but it was. When you wrote something, it was submitted to censorship, but from that moment when you had chosen to be either for or against Vichy, for or against Laval, you had already selected the ideological tone. In the eyes of the Germans, we were already an intelligentsia on their side. Snags began only as the situation developed and people like Drieu and me asked whether Germany was not fighting a war of classical imperialism. Why shouldn't Germany have sought a compromise in the East with Marxism, in 1939? The censor started to worry about that, but Drieu had authority, and his theories did not provoke German reactions. Epting also found Drieu fascinating. To Epting you could say what you liked; he and his staff were all rather seductive. Epting particularly liked the marginal collaborationist intellectuals, and whenever there were upsets, like the arrest of Max Jacob, he was ready to do what he could. Achenbach at the embassy was helpful. One was obliged to be in contact with people like that; it was their duty to be taking the Paris temperature. They wanted a frame of mind within which they could work. What made me so useful to the Germans was exactly what Laval once reproached me for. He said, "Combelle, Fontenoy values you. He says you are sound, but that makes my task harder. You are an ideologue while I am empirical. For me politics is a question of negotiating ceaselessly with very demanding partners. And here you come at me with your Fascism."

I wrote in *Le Fait,* the *NRF* edited by Drieu, and *La Gerbe*. At the end of 1941, I was an editorial assistant at *La Gerbe*. Alphonse de Chateaubriant and his chief editor, Camille Fégy, a Doriotist, happened to go on holiday at the same time. So in the interim I had to fill the front page. On the very first day when I was responsible for this, I ran an article by Montherlant, and it was his usual article of collaboration in sub-Nietzschean style. Drieu then did his turn. The proofs were censored by the Propaganda Staffel. To censor Drieu was absurd, and I ran the article in full. The Propaganda Staffel reacted immediately. The paper was seized, banned for a fortnight, and I was summoned. People on the paper advised me to leave possessions like my watch behind. The German official listened to my explanation and told me that I would have to discuss my lack of discipline with Chateaubriant. Chateaubriant heard me out and said, "You have broken the ties between *La Gerbe* and Germany." I was fired.

Of all the writers with whom I had elective affinities, Jean Fontenoy was the most memorable—with Drieu and Céline, I suppose. Through Fontenoy I one day found myself with Deloncle's MSR. Fontenoy went sniffing for adventure. Meetings of the MSR took place at the house of a prominent industrialist, Eugène Schoeller, who had a cosmetics empire. On the Deloncle staff were Fontenoy and Georges Soulès, today known as the novelist Raymond Abellio. Fontenoy actually wanted to take his distance from the MSR, and Laval had some proposal for him, so he put his weekly paper *La Révolution Nationale* at my disposal. Once I was installed as editor, Drieu said he would write for me.

Fontenoy was someone I could spend hours with. One day we were eating couscous with Algerian nationalists who were pro-German, and after four or five glasses of wine I had to take Fontenoy home. He smoked opium too. In the middle of the occupation he translated three or four stories by Damon Runyon, which I published. Our circulation was thirty thousand. The notoriety of Drieu made of it a paper to which Brasillach and Déat gave their copy free. Of the four colleagues on my staff, one was Pierre Drouin, now on the editorial staff of *Le Monde*; another is at the United Nations; a third is at the Centre National de Patronat Français; and the last has vanished.

The history of the intelligentsia's collaboration has been distorted. There were the militants standing bail for everyone, intellectuals like Bonnard or Hermant, down to writers who were more or less committed, or else, like Montherlant, seduced but whose style was to stay uncommitted. They wrote because their profession was to write and because the German presence did not make them suffer. *La Révolution Nationale* went on right to the end of the occupation. In its last number Drieu published his famous *"Lettre à un ami gaulliste"*: "You too will be obliged to collaborate with the victors. I only hope that you will be luckier than we were." I saw the Germans as conquerors with an ideology that would allow for a new European order. I thought the West was exhausted, France at the end of her tether, England making a fantastic mistake in pursuing war. I saw Nazism as an aristocratic socialism. I went to Germany in 1941 and 1942 and 1943, invited by Epting, just to have a look around. I went and listened to the sound of the drums and then rushed back into my ivory tower and believed that I had understood the secret.

Henry Coston

Since the war, Henry Coston has been a most assiduous extreme right-wing journalist, publishing articles and books about the various conspiracy theories to which he has always devoted himself. His *Dictionnaire de la vie politique,* however, contains firsthand information about the collaborators and Fascists of the occupation.

The old political hatreds were aroused when France was occupied. I was a French nationalist. I wanted to bring out my paper *La Libre Parole,* which had been nationalist before the war. I had permission from the Propaganda Staffel, orally, but there was a delay as confirmation never came. The pages were composed, the galleys were in 52, Champs-Elysées. Then my printer had a visit from four soldiers. Why? Abetz was my opponent. Abetz was following in Bismarck's footsteps politically, holding that France would be less dangerous to Germany if she were busy in the Mediterranean and in Africa, and if the French had a republican form of government. Abetz protected Déat and the democrats in the RNP, but he countered everyone else like the French nationalists and the Action Française milieu, and he was very hostile to the PPF. He favored papers like Spinasse's *Le Rouge et le Bleu,* and *L'Atelier,* which had Masonic ties in that many of its contributors were Masons. Abetz was probably a Mason. Achenbach was worse than Abetz, continuously opposed to nationalist policies. The only German in the administration whom I knew from before the war was Schutz-Wilmersdorf, a journalist, who was now on the Propaganda Staffel.

After the armistice, then, I had no paper and no work. I entered *Paris-Soir* as assistant to Roger Capgras, who was the son of a Socialist deputy. Henri Jeanson was there. The Germans had found him in prison. I stayed there for twenty-five days. The paper was put together with a little bit here, a little bit there. The chief editor was François Gensen, who had covered racing for *L'Auto.* Langeron's famous letter in *Le Matin* declaring that newspapers must reappear had been published. Why shouldn't journalists be writing?

One day a friend of mine on the staff, Saint-Serge, told me that he had a cable from the DNB about the Iron Guard coup in Rumania. I pointed out that I had had correspondence with Codreanu. [*Leader of the Iron Guard, the most pro-Hitler and anti-Semitic grouping in Rumania, Corneliu Codreanu had been shot on November 30, 1938, "while trying to escape" from prison, where he was serving a ten-year sentence. The 1940 coup involved the flight of King Carol and the dictatorship of Marshal Ion Antonescu.*] I was invited to write an article about Rumania, and it appeared on the front page next morning. Upstairs was Schiessle, the elevator operator, the sole occupant of the building when the Germans had arrived, and so in some ways representing the previous proprietor. He had a glass eye and was rather a primitive specimen. As an Alsatian, he spoke German. Since he had been there a long time, he had acquired a flair, or at least could bluff it out now. When he saw my article, he telephoned me and had me come at eight in the morning. My article was exactly what *Paris-Soir* wanted, he said, and offered me a job as subeditor. This would have to be accepted by the German censors—at the beginning, that was true. So we went and talked it over with Schmidtke. He was not a very typical German—dark, not fair. He accepted and asked us to wait for two other men he was expecting. In came Roger Capgras and Henri Jeanson. Schmidtke informed us that we would all be working together.

While I was at *Paris-Soir* I received a visit from Maître Picard, whom I'd first come to know in 1938 at a meeting of Solidarité Française at the Salle Wagram. At this meeting were Georges Oltramare and Laurent-Celly, father of Jacques Laurent, who today writes under the name Cecil St. Laurent—the mother of Jacques was the sister of Eugène Deloncle. Picard asked how *Paris-Soir* suited me, since he was now in charge of *La France au Travail* and needed an editorial assistant. My wages were to be doubled and I would be free to write what I liked. Schiessle was understanding. So I moved, and worked under Oltramare. For meetings at five o'clock he would arrive at half past six—he was a womanizer. After a few weeks of this, I was at the press when a small fellow arrived, rather fat, with untidy hair, to say that he was the new editorial managing director. His name was Georges B. [*his name is withheld*]. Fifteen or twenty minutes later, Picard arrived to say, "The German embassy is imposing this person on me." It was difficult to go against that, although I told Picard that this person did not know his job. Could I do something else? So I took over the "A La Lanterne" column in *La France au Travail,* with contributions from others, like Picard and Saint-Serge.

Around October, people I didn't particularly like joined us: Jean Fontenoy, for instance, with Eugène Schoeller, and Jacques Dursort, who had been secretary general of the MSR until he rejoined *Le Pays Libre,* where he published very violent anti-Jewish articles and worked for Pierre Clémenti. After Fontenoy came Georges Daudet, and in June 1941 he replaced Picard, with the intention of transforming *La France au Travail* into a left-wing paper. Philippe Saint-Serge and I were thrown out with compensation, and the paper was renamed *France-Socialiste,* with René Chateau as editor. The paper had an income large enough to cover expenses. But Picard had always said that he had resources beyond the sales of 200,000. No doubt the Germans paid money to Oltramare and Picard. Throughout the occupation the paper was printed by Georges Dangon, who was in the resistance and in whose premises in the rue Montmartre, in August 1944, those responsible for installing the press after the liberation were to meet. He was a Mason, but a very liberal man. When I was sentenced to forced labor for life, Dangon intervened on my behalf. Coston never denounced me, Dangon said, when he was in a position to do so.

I had specialized in the struggle against Freemasons. I created a Centre d'Action et de Documentation in 1941, installed with the files and archives at 8, rue Puteaux. Actually with my friend Paul Lafitte, I had tried to form an anti-Masonic committee in 1940, but no organization of the kind was allowed to remain independent, so the authorities simply subordinated us to them. We published our *Bulletin d'Information Anti-Maçonnique* once a week, on a single sheet. Our objective was to publish fully the archives of the lodges. We came out every single week until August 1944, at the request of Vichy. We were a branch of the Ministry of Justice, so I was a sort of civil servant. Every month Vichy allotted me the sum of money necessary to pay for the bulletin and the two or three people on the staff. At that point we had two sets of censors, German and French, since the bulletin came out in both zones. I used to send it to Jacques de Boistel, who was *délégué des services anti-maçonniques,* in the rue Cadet. His superior, Bernard Faÿ, had orders from Pétain to supervise Masonic documents, but contributed nothing. The intervention of Faÿ was needed if we were to obtain information, as we should have done for the *Bulletin.* The anti-Masonic police services at the Square Rapp were directed by Inspecteur Moerschel, with a staff of about twenty, and other police inspectors to keep files. They were allowed to carry out raids and house searches in the occupied zone alone. I never once set foot in the Square Rapp. And in the German Service for Secret Societies the only man I knew was Stüber.

The warmongering that I uncovered in the lodges disgusted me. The Masons had been pressing for war in 1939. I gave *Au Pilori,* I think, the list of officers in the French army who were Masons. Some were Masons out of conviction, others as a means of advancement. They even became "collabos" or worked in Vichy, where their opinions evolved. *L'Oeuvre* and the RNP had many Masons. The Germans forbade the publication of the list I'd prepared. At one meeting, I told them that there were more Masons in collaboration than in the resistance.

When Laval was out of office, he said he would like to meet me. I went to his office in the Champs-Elysées. Paul Lafitte came with me; he had been the right-hand man of Marcel Bucard but had drifted away and helped me found the Centre d'Action et de Documentation. Laval kept us two hours. One thing which interests me, he said, is to have proof that Darlan is a Freemason, because the Marshal is very anti-Masonic. Laval didn't really care of course, but I understood that he was suggesting that I forge the proof. I had all the seals and stamps, and I could have. But I asked him whether he had ever addressed a lodge. In 1914, he thought. I didn't know about that, I replied; I was thinking of an address in 1923. Laval certainly wasn't anti-Mason. In fact Darlan's father had been a Mason, and I published that in *Au Pilori*. If the father was, the son must be too, Laval commented.

The Commission Judeo-Maçonnique was highly unofficial. It had been created by a former secretary of Bernard Faÿ, Gueydan de Roussel, a Swiss. He proposed a linking of the Jewish and Masonic questions. His commission met every fortnight in the rue Cadet. He had invited representatives from the Commissariat aux Questions Juives and Sézille's Institut des Questions Juives, as well as from the Service for Secret Societies. The only practical work—as opposed to lectures—was to prepare an onomastic file of the names of the Jews of France in 1943. It remained embryonic. Gueydan sniffed the wind, and fled to South America.

If Gueydan had been all worked up and frenzied like Sézille, I'd have understood, but he was cool and controlled, yet perpetrating these extravagances. We always suspected him; Bernardini said that he was an agent provocateur. In the archives found by the police after he had fled, the names of five hundred people were found numbered, and he was supposed to have been a Gestapo agent—the more subagents he could show the Gestapo he had, the more money he received. Armand Bernardini was the son of a Swedish diplomat, and his real name was Sjoested. His mother was Corsican. He stammered except when he spoke with emphasis. He was a cultivated man, with a passion for history. Once I sold him a collection of Masonic documents. He collaborated with Montandon at l'Ethnie Française [*Montandon's institute for determining racial purity along his own chosen lines*]. Professor Labroue was a former radical deputy for the Gironde, and had been a Freemason. I understood his evolution before the war. The chair of Jewish history at the Sorbonne had been created for him by Laval.

Au Pilori had appeared before the war under Henri-Robert Petit. He had founded it as a little monthly in the rue d'Argenteuil. He had been a colleague of Darquier in the Rassemblement Anti-Juif in 1937, but had had a row with Darquier and gone off to publish his own review. In 1940 he obtained permission from the Germans to have it reappear. Its first numbers have as editorial director Petit, and M. Tournaye, a financial journalist who became anti-Semitic because he used to keep company with financiers. He gave me articles for my *Libre Parole* but I never saw him once he was with Petit. After three or four numbers there was a palace revolution. Jean Lestandi de Villani had money, and he threw out the others. He was a highly colored personality, a loudmouth, very enterprising, but none too capable a writer. He preferred to take his money and run while the going was good. So Jean Drault became political editor.

The "Echoes" were put together from information brought to the paper by its readers. *Au Pilori* had Robert Jullien-Courtine, later of *Le Monde,* Robert Valléry-Radot, and Paul Riche, a filmmaker until 1940 as well as a Masonic Venerable and a pacifist. Riche was a Masonry expert—he exposed the *synarchie* affair. The *synarchie* was headed by [*Pierre*] Pucheu, the minister of the interior, and its members were equally divided between collaboration and resistance. Friends of Goering were in the *synarchie*. I had Riche's article in my hands, and I told him it carried his death sentence. He could publish it only in *L'Appel*. It was a much more secret organization than Masonry; the names of the *synarchs* are hardly known. The majority were liquidated—at the liberation the whole thing was suppressed. Paul Riche was the only anti-Mason to be shot.

Drault had been a colleague of mine at *Libre Parole,* so when he became editor of *Au Pilori* I did articles for him. I had had little or nothing to do with Lestandi.

The lists of Jews who had married into the aristocracy were compiled by Comte de L. (who would resent his name being published).

Je Vous Hais was a PPF publication, and true, they were anti-Semites there. I joined the PPF in 1942, and Doriot put me into the party's press office. The party press was directed by Maurice-Yvan Sicard. Since I was a specialist, Sicard asked me to help put together *Je Vous Hais,* although there were a good twenty of us in all, contributors like Bernardini. I wrote a long piece about finance. The pamphlet sold fifty thousand copies. The Germans refused us a larger paper allocation. We did not state anywhere that it was a PPF publication, since we feared that might harm sales.

Cahiers Jaunes was a monthly anti-Semitic bulletin put out by Sézille. I didn't contribute. I have done three different editions of the *Protocols of the Elders of Zion,* and some editions were done during the occupation by André Chaumet and the Institut des Questions Juives. Sézille was a racist. For me, anti-Semitism was not racism. Before being a journalist, I was a bank clerk, and my specialty was always finance and the press. I was the persecutor of Jewish societies and banks. I am an *anti-sémite d'état* [*for reasons of state*]; Sézille was an *anti-sémite de peau* [*instinctively*]. I was a member of the Association of Anti-Jewish Journalists. Its president, Ménard, came from *L'Auto,* as many of his kind did.

I left Paris at the same time as everyone else. We hired a gas-propelled car for the day, to transport us within Paris. At five in the evening, we said we would give him ten thousand francs to drive us to Vitry-le-François. We were with Bernardini and his wife, and Albert Vignaux. We got there at nightfall. Then we said we had to go as far as Nancy, where we bought him some more *gazogène,* and he set off home. We found Sicard and Cousteau. If we had stayed, we would have been dead. The resistance came to the house with machine guns, so we heard afterward.

Pierre Daix

In his autobiography, *J'ai cru au matin,* Pierre Daix has described in detail what he and a very few like-minded Communists did to oppose the occupation. In 1939 he was only seventeen. In a letter to me, he writes:

At the end of September 1939 the Comintern gave the PCF (Parti Communiste Français) the order to support Stalin's policy toward Hitler, and from that moment there were two lines within the party. The official line was applied essentially by the leadership, while the grass roots pursued an anti-Fascist line. As a student transferred to Rennes on account of the war, I was in contact with a region, Brittany, where the anti-Nazi line prevailed. When I returned to Paris in July 1940, the students were also pursuing this line, but the Communists in the red working-class districts, like Vitry where my parents were living, obeyed party instructions to come out into the open and to claim the town halls whose control had been wrested from them with the dissolution of the PCF in 1939. In August and September 1940, Rizo and Suret-Canal were arrested for anti-Nazi activity at the Sorbonne. [*Christian Rizo was a student whom Daix considered to have the best political brain in his group; Jean Suret-Canal was a professor of geography and an old member of the Central Committee.*] The Communist students played an important role in the demonstration of November 11, 1940, at the Arc de Triomphe. As a result of these events I was arrested a first time on November 26, 1940. This did not prevent the existence of the

PCF's other line. In my book *J'ai cru au matin* I examined these contradictions at length.

When I came out of prison, in March 1941, the Communist students were convinced that the USSR was on the point of entering the war against Hitler. We interpreted June 22, 1941, in an upside-down manner, convinced as we were that Stalin had obliged Hitler to reveal himself in his true colors! That explains the way we threw ourselves into *attentats* and became urban guerrillas, in the belief that we were helping the Red Army in its final assault. We could never have imagined that if we were henceforward receiving support from the party, which until that moment had turned its back on our anti-Nazi initiatives, this was because the party required martyrs to efface its policy from 1939 to 1941.

When the PCF allocated the description of Organisation Spéciale to our groups, it established an apparent continuity with the original OS [*the party youth movement*], and this was the basis of future claims that it had been preparing armed struggle from the autumn of 1940.

I was arrested for a second time on January 7, 1942, because of contacts with the first armed group; its members had been shot on March 9, 1942, and among them was my friend Rizo. Needless to say, in 1940 and 1941 I did not grasp a tenth of what I can now explain. [*He was deported to Mauthausen concentration camp.*]

In an interview Pierre Daix added that when he had returned to Paris on July 11, 1940, one of the first issues of *Humanité* he had seen contained a paragraph to celebrate fraternizing with the Germans. For most of the party militants, collaboration was fertile soil. Fernand Grenier, who had succeeded Doriot as mayor of Saint-Denis, was quite open in his support of the official party line that the Germans were allies of the Russians and the English therefore the warmongers. When the Germans carried out their roundup in October 1940, a few hundred militants were arrested. It is Daix's opinion that the German authorities were laying the ground for the Montoire policy, and dispensed with the neutrality of the Communists for the sake of arranging terms with Pétain and so safeguarding their rear while preparing to attack Russia.

In the spring of 1941, Daix judges, those effectively engaged with the party numbered 150 to 200 people, at most. The first year of the war had been catastrophic for the party. Membership had vanished, whether out of disgust with the party line or because members were held as prisoners of war in German camps. The first wave of activists to volunteer between November 1940 and January 1941 numbered about twenty. The following April, a second wave brought numbers up to fifty or sixty. Of these, only four or five still survive.

What was to develop into the resistance came from [*Georges*] Politzer, writing in *Pensées,* and [*Jacques*] Decour—a combination of Communist students and intellectuals, who had taken the position that Nazism was obscurantist and antiprogressive and so destructive of French principles that no compromise was possible.

We succeeded in our demonstrations in the streets of Paris twice, on July 14, 1941, and July 27, in the Faubourg du Temple. They were magnificent demonstrations; everybody managed to get away. The party wanted blood and got it finally on August 13. It was a crazy thing, but here was proof that the party had entered the war. But nobody was prepared for it. We had no arms and no training. The only men with experience of war were Fabien and Brustlein. Those of us who had wanted to fight had the inertia of the Russo-German pact until after June 22, 1941, and then we had hysteria. I remember Tony Bloncourt asking, "Is it really the party who is giving us orders?" We were obliged to improvise lodgings, arms, everything. When it turns out badly, we said, the Communist party will do something for us, until they did nothing at all.

In the autumn of 1941 the French police put up a better performance; instead of arresting a militant, they followed him; they then dismantled half the upper direction of the party. Politzer, Decour, and their families, about seventy people in all, were arrested, and twenty of them were executed in May 1942. I knew Politzer in prison. The French passed me to the Germans in their section of the Santé, but the Germans couldn't fit me into any group for lack of proof, so I was handed back to the French and shuttled through eleven prisons in all.

After a while, it became more important to kill PPF members like Gitton than Germans. The mask of the OS made it difficult to tell which of the party groups had killed him. Gitton was a man who had known the top direction of the party, the real direction which did not correspond to the official organization. Men like Gitton and Clamamus knew from the inside the exact relationship between the Comintern and the French Communist party. When they went into collaboration, the party couldn't touch them—after all, they were following Stalin's line. After 1941, it was essential to knock off those who could tell the truth.

"National Communism" became, in the eyes of Moscow, a term blemished with everything treasonable. Those who had attacked the Pact became people whom Moscow had to eliminate. It had trouble reaching those who were either in the collaboration or in the resistance—but some of them the party even had killed in the camps. There was a directive from Moscow, and in this matter the party was most rational, eliminating collaborators while ridding themselves of enemies who knew too much.

When I was arrested, the slogan was to mobilize everybody against the Germans. I think in the minds of the leaders we were all destined to disappear. I don't think Stalin thought there should be a resistance in France immobilizing German troops; he saw no need for social upheavals in France. There were prospects for revolution through the FTP, and some of the leaders, starting with Tillon, wanted to go further. My theory is that Duclos elbowed Tillon aside because he wanted to have a controlled revolution.

When I returned from Mauthausen and was with Tillon and had access to the secretariat of the party, then the battle was on for production and the renewal of France. We were a party of law and order at that moment. That was not the impression which I had had of the future from the Communists at Mauthausen.

Gitla Rosenblum

She is now Madame Szapiro. She was born in 1932. Half a dozen children, at most, survived the Grande Rafle of July 1942 and its sequel at Drancy, and she is one of them. Her sister Sarah is another. Her uncle, Haim Rosenblum, was present at the interview.

MADAME SZAPIRO: My parents came to Paris from Poland in 1930 and had twelve years of very difficult life. Mother had a grocery; at night she went to Les Halles, and in the morning she did her baking. My father worked in a butcher's. They each did an eighteen-hour day. I had a brother who was much older than I; he was twenty-five, married, with a child. He was arrested in 1941 and interned in Pithiviers. It began like that. Life was very perturbed. We sent him parcels—his wife and child had not been taken. I know my sister and I were due to go to a holiday camp by the sea. My parents had bought us each a little suitcase to pack our holiday clothes in, and those suitcases served us for our arrest. I was ten; Sarah was five.

On July 16 the French police knocked at our door and asked us to prepare. We'll be back to fetch you in two or three hours, they said; we're taking you for checking your papers. It is untrue that many people understood what this meant, did not wait for the return of the police, but escaped. It is probable that some policemen did not do it lightheartedly, but very few gave a warning that lives were at risk. My parents were very religious, observant; they were people of great probity. They decided they would wait—they had done nothing wrong and there was nothing to reproach them with. So they stayed, got dressed, and prepared a small bundle. My father went to the synagogue to fetch a scroll, the Torah, which a pious Jew ought to have on him if he is going away. The police returned and took us on foot, about 500 meters, to a collecting place in the rue des Rosiers. We lived in the fourth arrondissement, at 18, rue Saint-Croix de la Bretonnerie. There we were escorted into buses, along with thousands of children who were crying, and old people, some being dragged in pitiful states of health. We were driven to the Vélodrome d'Hiver, a big arena for bicycling races, and there we remained in the most atrocious conditions. There were a few Red Cross helpers, but we were under the French police. Rumor, and propaganda, was out of control. People screamed all night long. Women threw themselves off the top of the stands. I still hear the screams. I can see the scenes today. We stayed there eight days. The conditions were dreadful: the lavatories were the worst, blocked, and the smells and the filth were pestilential. There was no room; we were cramped together.

Then we were taken again in buses to the station and piled into cattle trucks, one on top of the other. The journey to Pithiviers lasted a few hours. There my father and another brother, age thirteen, were separated. My mother, a sixteen-year-old sister, the little one, and I were put into huts. After two or three weeks, there was an assembly, and my mother and sisters saw my father and brother. Their heads had been shaved. That was the departure for Auschwitz. We were separated again, this time just my little sister and me. I can see the roll call of the crowd. My father wore a beard and it had been cut off too—it was an atrocious sight. They were taken off in transports whose destination nobody knew. Not one of them came back.

My sister and I were born in Paris, we had French nationality, and this time they were taking foreign-born Jews. We stayed for weeks with a multitude of children at Pithiviers, until we were taken to Drancy, where we lived for some weeks in terrible conditions. I don't want to relate the horror of it—sleeping on disgusting mattresses, eating disgusting food which made everyone ill. The diet was a soup composed of things which had no nutrient value, and our intestines couldn't absorb it. We were overrun with lice and skin diseases. We must have looked a sight. But we continued to correspond with an uncle outside. He had an *Ausweis* and tried to free us. It sustained our morale. People did get out occasionally. Every morning there was a roll call. One day the roll call included us. We were terrorized. The uncle had said he'd fetch us, but we wouldn't be there for him. We climbed onto the bus. Then I had a reaction—I can't explain—I took my little sister by the hand and led her back into the camp. She was crying that they would come to shoot us. The miraculous occurred. A few days later the order to release us arrived. We were taken to the gate of the camp and told we were free. The order might well have come too late. My uncle crossed into the unoccupied zone. An organization coping with Jewish orphans had us placed in the Sarthe with peasants who were paid to look after us. We are among the very few who escaped.

As soon as we had been arrested, the French came into our apartment and looted it all. My sister remembers a detail from Drancy. One day I stole a carrot from the kitchen, and I was confined in the cellar. My sister came and shouted down the ventilation shaft, "I want you to get out—get the warden to let you out." At Drancy too, we had been searched that day. My mother had slipped me a little ruby before we got there—it must have been all she had. The French searchers found it and said, "Give it here—it's no business of yours to have a thing like that." It was miserable for me to hand over all I had left from my mother.

ROSENBLUM: On May 14, 1941, I was interned at Pithiviers. The Préfecture de Police had summoned me for a check of my papers. It was a swindle—they simply laid hands on everybody. If I'd suspected that they were capable of such behavior, I'd never have gone. After three months at Pithiviers, I got out. I escaped while on a pass. As an activist and a Zionist, I had a lot of contacts. At the Préfecture I knew an Inspecteur Henri. He got me an *Ausweis* to say that I was what was called a *Wirtschaftswertvoller Jude,* or economically valuable Jew, supposedly working in the fur trade. Some of my family were covered by that *Ausweis.* My brother had been arrested, and I tried to save him through two Jews who had been brought from Vienna by the Gestapo to supervise Jewish communal life, one of them a friend of mine since before the war. Then when the big roundup took place, I wanted to save my sister-in-law. I spoke to this man and he said that I was to telephone after tomorrow, which I did, to hear that the parents had already been deported but the two little girls were still there, and on this *Ausweis* I could get them out.

Jean Leguay

On March 12, 1979, Leguay became the only Frenchman so far indicted under a law promulgated in France in 1964 for "crimes against humanity." Documents in the Centre de Documentation Juive Contemporaire (CDJC) reveal the extent to which he was implicated in the measures taken by the French police against Jews, in particular on three separate scores: planning the Grande Rafle of July 1942, arranging the roundup of Jews in the Vichy zone for transfer to Drancy and so to Auschwitz, and finally in September 1942 supervising the arrest in Paris of a number of Jews from the Baltic countries, Yugoslavia, and Bulgaria. The documents show that on June 25, 1942, Leguay had a meeting with Dannecker, who reported afterward to Lischka, "I informed Leguay that between now and June 29 I need a concrete proposition concerning the arrest of a total of 22,000 Jews in the departments of the Seine and the Seine-et-Oise.... To Leguay's objection that it would be preferable to take more Jews from the unoccupied zone than from the occupied zone, I declared that I understood French interests ... but the security of the occupying forces necessitated the arrest of the fixed number in the occupied zone." How the operation was to be put into practice was discussed on July 4 at a meeting between Oberg, Knochen, Lischka and Hagen, and Bousquet and Darquier. Hagen's subsequent minutes note that Bousquet "will be represented by his delegate in the occupied zone, Leguay. It must be pointed out in this matter that Darquier de Pellepoix gave the impression of being almost overwhelmed by accepting responsibility." Leguay was present at meetings with Dannecker and Heinrichsohn on July 7 and 10 to discuss the technicalities of the Grande Rafle. On the seventeenth itself, while the arrests were proceeding, Hagen held another meeting, at which Leguay was also present. Roethke's subsequent memorandum refers to the fate of the children being arrested: "The representatives of the French police at several different times expressed their desire to see the children deported to a destination in the Reich."

On August 3, Leguay was writing to Darquier, "As arranged with them [*i.e., the German authorities*], I have taken the following steps so that the departures may take place on the dates indicated. The trains of August 19, 21, 24 and 26 will in principle be composed of the children...." On August 17, Roethke was sending a memorandum to Lischka; "Leguay let it be known that he had proposed to the French government to place at our disposal as from the end of August and into the first days of September the total number of Jews planned for the September program, since the occupied zone has enough room in the camps to receive the total number of Jews." On August 27, Heinrichsohn reported a further meeting with Leguay to discuss technicalities. "On September 1, 2, 3, and 4 there will be a train a day, each of one thousand

Jews. About the delivery of the total number of Jews for the September program Leguay is not at the moment in a position to be precise, since the arrests of the nights of August 26–27 and 27–28 are still proceeding. These police actions will be accomplished in the greatest possible measure, for Herr Bousquet takes the position that it is better to arrest in one big sweep the Jews in question than to start individual actions which once again might give the Jews the opportunity to hide or to flee into neighboring neutral countries. . . . Herr L. [*for Leguay*] will see to it that in the future the announced times of arrival of the trains will be strictly adhered to. . . . For the October program Herr L. asked to have a previously agreed conversation with SS Obersturmführer Roethke, but considers it would be preferable that SS Standartenführer Dr. Knochen and the secretary general of police, Herr Bousquet, hold a conference on the subject. . . . Herr L. then inquired whether the article which had appeared in the Paris press about the arrests in the unoccupied zone had been prompted by us. I explained to him that this was not the case and that to the best of our knowledge the Paris press had its information from the Commissariat aux Questions Juives. Herr L. expressed his great surprise, and declared that the work of the police as well as the plans of the secretary general of police Bousquet were made appreciably more difficult by press announcements of the kind."

After the liberation Leguay was relieved of his position within the *administration préfecturale* but did not have to face any charges. On the contrary, in 1945 he was entrusted by the de Gaulle government with a mission to Washington to promote industrial reconstruction. In 1957 he was restored by official decree to the *administration préfecturale* with all due rank and seniority, although by then he had embarked on another career and chose not to return to state service. Bousquet, however, was held in prison, tried, and sentenced to two years of "indignity" (which meant loss of certain rights). But this sentence was immediately revoked in the light of his "services rendered to the resistance"—a confusion of judgment quite characteristic of the time. There the matter might have rested as far as both men were concerned, had it not been for the publication in 1977 by Serge Klarsfeld of the CDJC documents referred to above, detailing how the Germans of the SS and SD had instructed the French services to arrest and deport Jews, and how French officials at all levels had complied.

Leguay had taken a law degree and entered the *administration préfecturale* in 1932. He had known Bousquet well before the war and had replaced him as a *sous-préfet* in 1939. In November 1940, when Bousquet became *préfet* of the Marne, Leguay was appointed *secrétaire général* of the Préfecture of the Marne. At the end of 1941 he was nominated to be *directeur du cabinet* in Paris for Ingrand, who was *délégué du Ministere de l'Intérieur* in Paris. When in April 1942 Laval was again head of the government, he selected Bousquet as *secrétaire général* of the police, whereupon Leguay was assigned to serve as liaison with Bousquet. Only thirty-two at the time, Leguay was evidently making a brilliant career for himself, but one which now might have imposed a severe moral strain upon another man. For whether he liked it or not, he could not fail to play his part in the machinery that was destroying the Jews in France. He was obliged to be in regular contact with Oberg and Dannecker and the rest; he does not deny that he attended the conferences recorded in the documents, though he claims to have no very clear memory of them. It was because so many thousands of people, some more influential than Leguay, others far more humble, accepted the SS and SD instructions and dispositions as all part of the day's work that the Jews went to their death. Leguay insists on the fact that he personally had no powers of arrest, and was unable to give orders to the Préfecture, whose men were actually rounding up the Jews. His responsibilities were administrative. It is his defense that the Germans were present as conquerors, somebody had to deal with them, and those who did, from Laval downwards, though they might have exposed themselves to misunderstanding, had in fact mitigated German policies and obtained worthwhile concessions. Why someone like Leguay did not resign or otherwise repudiate the official duties that he was performing, with whatever degree of conscientiousness, remains an open question at the heart of the Final Solution.

For the sake of clarifying the administrative structure within which Leguay worked, the following memorandum has been collected from a group of senior civil servants who lived through the period.

"The armistice, signed by France on June 22, 1940, had divided the country into two zones. Traffic between the zones was strictly controlled by the Germans. Telephone calls were practically impossible. Mail was restricted to open postcards printed in advance and limited to family news, in very few lines. Crossing the demarcation line, in either direction, required German permits that were hard to obtain.

"According to the Armistice Convention, the German authorities were granted 'all the rights of the occupying power' (Article 3). Yet within the Northern Zone, the French government retained full administrative responsibilities 'on condition of conforming to the regulations of the German military authorities and of collaborating with these authorities in a correct manner' (Article 3). France was then (and still is) divided into geographical units: the departments. Heading each department was a public official, the *préfet*, appointed by the government to represent all branches of executive power (finance, economy, education, police etc.). The *préfets* of the occupied zone were cut off from the Vichy government by the demarcation line. They could neither receive instructions nor report back. Facing the German authorities daily, they did not receive information with which to resist demands that were often excessive.

"Very soon, it appeared necessary to create in Paris the post of delegate general of the government, a position held first, briefly, by Léon Noël, one of the signatories of the armistice, then by General de la Laurencie, and afterward by Fernand de Brinon. Generally speaking, within the occupied zone a representative government staff had been created, having authority to discuss with the Germans the implementation of the Armistice Convention, which had merely formulated principles requiring interpretation and adjustment according to circumstances. Contact was also maintained in this way with the French administration in the occupied zone, ensuring the transportation of mail from the departments to Vichy, and vice versa. Along with the delegate general, and in principle under his authority, each Vichy ministry also appointed a staff in Paris whose importance varied considerably according to its objectives, upon which depended the number of officials detached from Vichy. Agreement from the German authorities had to be obtained in this respect too.

"Some ministries, for example the Finance Ministry, or the Ministry of Industrial Production, were able to operate mainly from Paris, with a skeleton staff in Vichy. The more political ministries faced a somewhat different situation. The Ministry of the Interior was authorized merely to establish a lightly staffed representative unit in Paris, with only basic administrative functions. Otherwise the Ministry's importance lay in its proposals to the government concerning the appointment of *préfets* to the departments, as well as in its responsibility for public order, including the management of the police in France.

"In 1942, when Laval again became head of the government, he also assumed the duties of minister of the interior. The Ministry was divided into two main Secrétariats Généraux. The one was the Secrétariat Général pour l'Administration (Secretary General Georges Hilaire), with sections for personnel, local government, and accounting. The other was the Secrétariat Général à la Police (Secretary General René Bousquet), which headed what was called the Direction Général de la Police Nationale, though it did not have authority either over the *gendarmerie* (which came under the Ministry of War) or over the *préfet de police* of Paris (who reported directly to the minister of the interior himself).

"Bousquet's Secrétariat Général was composed of a number of branches. Some dealt only with administrative questions, but others handled purely police matters and so were in charge of maintaining law and order, as well as for the detection of offenses and crimes and for the presentation of offenders to the courts. One branch consisted of counterespionage.

"When in 1940 a representative of all these branches (with the exception of the active police branches) was appointed in Paris, the official chosen for the post was Jean-Pierre Ingrand, who was to retain these duties until 1944. His exact title was "delegate of the Ministry of the Interior to the occupied territories." Under him, two small units were set up in Paris, the one to represent the Secrétariat Général pour l'Administration, the other to represent only those branches of the Secrétariat Général à la Police which were administrative. This small representative unit of the Secrétariat Général à la Police was managed by Jean Leguay, a civil servant who was a member of the *administration préfecturale*. Technically speaking, he was under Ingrand's authority, but he was also in direct contact with the secretary general of the police in Vichy. His functions can be summarized as follows:

> management of the unit in Paris of the Secrétariat Général à la Police, including the administrative branches of the Police Nationale;
> contacts with the German authorities in respect of these administrative branches;
> receiving messages from the Germans to be transmitted to Vichy;
> communication to the Germans of messages from Vichy;
> permanent contact, by telephone and in writing, with the *préfets* of the occupied zone;

> action, through repeated contacts with the German authorities,
> designed to obtain respect on the part of these authorities for the regulations
> governing Franco-German police relations.

"Neither the delegate of the Ministry of the Interior nor the representative in Paris of the secretary general of the police was entrusted with executive functions in police matters. Their functions were to liaise between the occupied zone and Vichy, and to observe.

"The position of the French administration became more difficult with every passing month in respect of the Germans. German demands were constantly increasing. At the same time, the French government and its administrative services were being violently attacked in Paris by the collaborationist political parties and the German-controlled press. They were accused of weakness, of playing a double game, of complicity with the Allied powers. In December 1943 the German authorities demanded the immediate dismissal of Bousquet. Both he and his Paris delegate, Leguay, left office on December 30, 1943."

Hans Speidel

Before the war, Speidel, then a captain, had been assistant military attaché in Paris. After the war, from 1957 to 1963, Speidel, then a general, commanded the NATO Land Forces Central Europe, in their Fontainebleau headquarters.

I was a colonel on the General Staff. On June 14, 1940, I was sent into Paris by General von Bock. I came through Le Bourget by myself; ahead of me were only some armored cars. I drove to the Hotel des Invalides, where a mixed French military unit was stationed. In the Hotel Crillon I established the office of the Militärbefehlshaber in Paris. There were Americans in the Ritz. In the Ritz communications were good, and I moved there later. How was Paris? A unique city, as it has always been. The population expressed some relief at our coming, because it meant that the city would remain undamaged. Stülpnagel was correct; for Hitler's and the party's taste too mild. Hitler reproached him with being too weak. In November 1941, I was sent to Hitler in East Prussia on Stülpnagel's behalf, to try to obtain a less harsh practice over the hostage question. I had to leave with only a partial success.

Abetz was a man of some breadth but not enough character. The role of the embassy was never clear in the tug-of-war between the party and the military government. Stülpnagel gave himself the greatest trouble, but of course the party won because that was what Hitler and Himmler wanted. I asked Ernst Jünger to write an account of this, and if it had survived it would have been a document of the greatest value.

The party wanted to take executive power away from the military. The crucial moment was the burning of the synagogues. There had been points of conflict before that but nothing on that scale. It is no exaggeration to compare the burning of the synagogues to the Kristallnacht. It was the first head-on clash btween the party and the military. It served to strengthen Knochen's position. Knochen was elegant, very adroit, cultivated too, but this did not prevent him from being a convinced party man. In the embassy Schleier was the important person, another uncompromising party man. Dr. Best was in disgrace—that's why he didn't play the part he might have. Minister Schmid also managed to keep him under wraps, to make sure that Best never had responsibility for anything outside his sphere. In March 1942, I went to Russia and returned only on April 15, 1944, as Rommel's chief of staff.

Darlan was a great personality. I used to see his aide Fatou, and General de la Laurencie. On the cultural scene Sacha Guitry got the theater going quickly, so that by August 1940 performances could be started again. I met Pétain only once, at the funeral of General Huntziger. After the funeral he received me alone. I had no time to leave Paris. I had to do everything the chief of staff generally does. Up early and working late. Lunch in the office in the Raphael. I was answerable only to the Militärbefehlshaber, and I had to advise him only on matters of policy related to the army. Dealings with the French collaborators were the embassy's affair, and I never met Doriot, Déat, or any of them. De Brinon I did know; he was inscrutable. The Préfecture de Police people I saw every now and then. They tried to be correct under the circumstances.

Albrecht Krause

In my family three generations had been students or teaching in Strasbourg University, my grandfather in 1871, my father from 1908 to 1911, his brother from 1911 to 1913, and I from 1941 on. I had commanded a company in Russia, and near Leningrad had a bullet in the heart, so for a year I was in a Strasbourg military hospital, the Diakonissen-Anstalt. I was twenty-one, and a *Leutnant der Reserve.*

In 1942 Freisler, the Nazi judge and president of the Volksgerichtshof [*supreme court*] came to Strasbourg to hold a tribunal for nineteen French Communists. As a law student I tried to sit in, which proved to be difficult, the indictment being high treason. Finally I was admitted because of my war injuries and decorations. Proceedings lasted from 9:00 A.M. to 1:00 P.M. with accusations shouted from the chair but no right of reply for the defendants or sufficient time for the defense counsels, who were outstanding Alsatian *maîtres* [*barristers*]—it was a mere farce. Immediately after, I joined the GOC Strasbourg for lunch in the Maison Rouge, at the time the Hotel Rotes Haus. The general and I were very surprised to see Freisler and his colleagues step in and enjoy a luxurious meal for almost three hours. By four thirty, back in court, Freisler pronounced the death sentence for eighteen of the Communists and one lifetime imprisonment for the only female defendant. It was clear to me that these judgments were prefabricated; I was stunned and ready to give up my law studies under such a legal regime.

A few days later, on August 14 to be precise, I took up a posting in Paris as Erster Ordonnanzoffizier beim Militärbefehlshaber in Frankreich, General d. Inf. Karl-Heinrich von Stülpnagel. He lived then in the avenue Malakoff, in the Palais Marbre Rose, which belonged to Mrs. Florence Gould but was used as Stülpnagel's residence.

In the Hotel Raphael, 17, avenue Kléber, I had an apartment, Number 103, consisting of sitting room, bedroom, and bathroom.

The chief of the general staff then was Colonel Kossmann [*succeeding Speidel*], with about fifty staff officers. I was in IA [*Operationsabteilung*]. Besides the normal general staff work, I had to write up the daily war diary.

The administrative staff [*Militärverwaltung*] was under Dr. Elmar Michel, a former Ministerialdirektor in the Reichswirtschaftsministerium, and after the war in the Bundeswirtschaftsministerium under Ludwig Erhard, author of the German "economic miracle," and finally, after his retirement, director general of the Salamander shoe company. Dr. Michel wore a general's uniform, but a special designation on the epaulettes showed his status as an officer of the military administration.

His second-in-command for the administrative side was Dr. Franz Albrecht Medicus, with the title Militärverwaltungsabteilungschef, and for the economic side it was Dr. Reinhardt, with the same rank.

Karl-Heinrich von Stülpnagel, a brilliant soldier and a most noble character, was a defender of human rights. Responsible for occupied France, he had to respect the Hague Convention and other international law instruments concerning prisoners of war and the consequences of occupation. He was a man of the highest intellect and education, with a particular interest in history and mathematics. He was married and had three children. His two sons were captains on the front in France and Italy. Frau von Stülpnagel lived in Bad Pyrmont, since families were not allowed in Paris. On weekends he used to invite interesting guests and some of us out to his secondary residence in the Vallée de la Chevreuse, to the old medieval abbey of Les Vaux de Cernay, rebuilt, I think, by one of the Rothschilds. Other than for duty reasons, he rarely saw French people.

I used to see French friends, some of them Alsatians with whom I had family contacts before the war. It was difficult, however, to make friends with the French upper crust; we were reticent about being invited. Many of them were accessible, though. They wanted to think that the war was over. Fern Bédaux invited Medicus and me to stay in her Touraine residence [*from where the Duke and Duchess of Windsor were married*]. With ordinary people, working people and peasants, contacts were normally nice and easy. A farmer couple in the Vallée de la Chevreuse very generously invited us to enjoy their excellent cuisine. Two or three of us junior officers used to go out there sometimes, even just before the Allied forces arrived, in July 1944, thus celebrating our departure in style.

We had a Deutsches Warenhaus [*military store*] in the avenue des Ternes, run by French staff, where we could buy provisions. If it came to rationed goods, a special license was necessary. If one wanted to buy silverware as a present for some official occasion, for instance, a license for fifty centigrams had to be asked for. You could find almost everything on the black market or in the Marché aux Puces.

Office hours started at half past eight. We were busy until 1:00 P.M. Then came a break until about three. From three to six we had routines. At around five or six, the subordinate headquarters would report, and then the front at seven. We had to follow up orders from OKW, OKH, and OB West; we had intelligence to sift, and the radio and foreign press to interpret. Then we had to do the ordinary daily general staff work, to write our orders and hold briefings. Between nine at night and one in the morning we were often at our busiest, after D-Day specifically. From time to time I had to go out to Versailles to see the LVF.

At meals Stülpnagel enjoyed the company of scientists, professors, and intellectuals. Among them was Eberhard Kessel, a former assistant of Meinecke's and Holzmann's at the University of Berlin. When Kessel got into difficulties with the Nazis before the war, Stülpnagel selected him as chief historian in the army archives, and now he had him posted to a regiment in the Paris area. That was how we first became friends; he married my sister.

Breakfast, lunch, and dinner were served in the cozy dining room of the Hotel Raphael by French personnel under the maître d'hôtel. There were only about eight tables; one, in the back to the right, was reserved for the "OB" (GOC); another, in the back to the left, was at the disposal of the "Chevaliers de la Table Ronde." This was a group of senior officers and military judges, among them General Speidel; Colonel Wilhelm Arendts, in private life director general of the Allianz Versicherung [*insurance company*]; Professor Max Braubach, historian from the University of Bonn, where he had been appointed at the age of twenty-eight; staff colonels Müller-

Arlès and Böttcher from the personnel division; Dr. Hans Bötticher, chief military judge; and Oberstrichter Schmeidler, another judge. On another table there were Theodor Volckmar-Frentzel, the Leipzig publisher; the writer Ernst Jünger, whom Stülpnagel protected from Nazi persecution; Professor Friedrich Schery, eminent musician and professor at the Heidelberg Konservatorium (on Tuesday afternoons he would give concerts; the daughter of the composer Glazunov was living in Paris, and she would play sometimes); as well as Dr. Hans Leo, IC [*G2 intelligence*] and a famous Leipzig barrister; Major Dr. Humm, liaison officer with the German embassy in Paris and the French government; Colonel Dr. Georg Bahls, chief legal adviser to the tobacco industry; Max Hattigen, attorney general at the high court of Bonn; Alfred Neuhaus, the cigar king of Schwetzingen; Max Horst, Speidel's brother-in-law. On the military administration table, next to Elmar Michel, Medicus, and Reinhardt, you saw Herbert Eckelmann, after the war legal adviser to the Horten Group; Dr. Caesar von Hofacker; Gotthard Freiherr von Falkenhausen, Essen banker and nephew of General von Falkenhausen, the GOC in Belgium [*dismissed by Hitler*]. Others were Freiherr von Teuchert, after the war the head of the Wittelsbach Fund; Walter Bargatzky; Botho Bauch, and Roland Thierfelder, German ambassador to Turkey. Many of them were involved in the July 20 plot against Hitler.

Stülpnagel took his meals with his personal aide-de-camp Professor Baumgart, who in private life taught the history of art in Jena and later Berlin. Guests were sometimes present as well, and often he called one of us to his table. He rarely accepted officers on his staff who didn't speak French. His staff was carefully selected, with a lot of outstanding men who could set an example. It was a unique phenomenon in that they all belonged to a certain intellectual and social layer, which was an elite. It was like a monastic order. Most of the officers had been born before 1900 and had served in World War I. For me, by far the youngest, they were significant and generous personalities—they called me *"Sonnenschein im Altersheim"* [*sunshine in the old folks' home*]. Speidel still refers to me as *"der kleine Krause,"* young, or little Krause.

For high-ranking guests we had apartments reserved in the Ritz, as well as the best boxes at the Opéra and seats in the theaters, which we could use ourselves if they were not occupied. We preferred not to be conspicuous and to go out in civilian suits. I remember having seen, among many others, Jeanne Manet, Charles Trenet, and Solange Schwarz, the premiere ballerina at the Opéra, in *Swan Lake*. Downtown there was an officers' casino and a *Soldatenheim* for NCOs and men.

The distinction between the police and us was clear-cut. Oberg and his staff were in the boulevard Lannes and in the avenue Foch. Oberg came from Hamburg, like me. He was rather distant, a man from a modest social background. From time to time Stülpnagel sent me to see him and to explain the situation in occupied France. I had also to interpret the GOC's standpoint, when infractions of the Hague Convention or other international legal instruments had been committed owing to SS or Gestapo actions, or were reported to us as imminent. Oberg was responsible for all police work, including hostages, actions against Jews, and all that; he tried permanently to extend his competences, even transgressed them, in affairs concerning the French resistance and intelligence. There were little or no social affiliations with the SS people, and if invitations were exchanged, then only on official occasions. Nor did we see Abetz much, except on social occasions. The permanent liaison officer between Stülpnagel and the embassy and the French government was Major Dr. Humm, who was very able and experienced. I had to assure liaison between us and HQ Heeresgruppe B under Rommel (whose chief of staff was Speidel), after D-Day and

238

throughout the period of invasion. I had many contacts with Winrich Behr, my opposite number on the staff, and with the war correspondents, Graf Clemens Podewils, Freiherr von Esebeck, and Hans Ertl, a famous climber in the Himalayas and the Andes. Colonel von Tempelhof was G3. We inspected the front lines in Normandy several times.

Our social life was much among ourselves, I suppose. The staff secretaries were nicknamed "Edeltippsen" [*literally, noble typists*] because many belonged to aristocratic families. They lived together in two-room apartments in the rue Copernic. Among them were Mädy Gräfin Podewils, Stülpnagel's personal secretary and sister of Clemens, Maria Josepha Baronin Rolshausen from Bavaria, Thesima von Kretschmann from Potsdam, Gertrud Karcher, daughter of the Saar industrialist, Ingeborg Schwerin, Erika Baronin Lüttwitz, Ruth Klöres, Mary and Jane Faber from Dresden, Dorett Kreutzberger from Upper Silesia. The Stabshelferinnen, as they were officially and somewhat awkwardly designated, had to wear a disagreeable gray housecoat of sorts, with a green ribbon, to protect their clothes; in reality it was a uniform. All staff personnel who were not living in the Raphael ate their meals in the Majestic's spacious dining room, but the girls ate on their own in the basement—separation of the sexes! The Edeltippsen sewed on our buttons, prepared meals for us and their friends *de passage,* coming from home leave or going to the front lines or on a U-boat in the Atlantic, or on an England-bound night fighter. Brothers and cousins were among them, so the girls were often afraid that they might never see them again. Among these men passing through, I remember, were Horst von Heymann, Eberhard Graf zu Dohna, Wilhelm Graf Finckenstein, Edmund Graf Clary from Austria, Kersten von Schenck, Friedel Wrede, Werner Hintze, Udo Klausa, Hans Möller, Kurt Thielmann, Günther Schauenburg. For all of them, and for us too, the girls organized visits to the opera and theaters and concerts, excursions to the beautiful châteaux near Paris or just a quiet chat for those who had something on their minds before going to the front—and this on top of their full-time and exhausting job around the clock. For us, it was an ersatz family life!

I used my limited spare time for studies at the Ecole des Langues Orientales at the Sorbonne. In school at the Gelehrtenschule des Johanneums in Hamburg, I had taken Hebrew courses, which were forbidden from 1936 on. Our professor was the famous Orientalist Bertheau, who continued Hebrew classes but called them Arabic and taught us introductory Arabic letters and grammar as well. Since Germans were not allowed to study at the Sorbonne, I got a Nansen pass to attend classes and went in plainclothes. One day I had no time to change my jodhpurs, and one or two people suspected that I was a German officer and didn't speak to me for six months. I also hired a teacher, who came originally from Alexandria, for lessons in Arabic. I worked two hours a day with him in the Raphael (he got a *laissez-passer*), and I paid him mostly in food and clothes for his ten children. They all lived in the cellar of a huge building with no furnishings except carpets and a cupboard.

From 1944 on, the Raphael and the Majestic were closed off by protective barriers. Everybody felt the thing could not last, not after Stalingrad. We had difficulties because Stülpnagel was known not to be a Nazi and to be surrounded by a considerable number of men of like mind. An officer could be charged officially with "weakening the power of the army." Jehle was the name of one section chief whom we suspected had been transferred to the staff to keep an eye on us. He was very able but nobody liked him. Sauckel, the *gauleiter* who ran the STO, had a liaison officer with us by the name of Glatzel, and in his presence we didn't say too much.

On July 20, during the course of the early afternoon, we heard the news that

Hitler was still alive. Stülpnagel realized the plot had failed but nevertheless decided on his own initiative to persevere in Paris and offer an armistice in the West to the Allies, in order to be able to send all available troops to Russia. He gave orders, in the evening, to arrest the SS, Gestapo, and leading Nazis, in all about eighteen hundred men. Top people were brought to the Salon Bleu of the Raphael, and we had wine and champagne with Oberg, Knochen, Abetz, Admiral Krancke, and others. Things developed rapidly. I answered the telephone at five in the morning on July 21 to take the message from OKW that Keitel was ordering Stülpnagel to report as soon as possible to Berlin. Stülpnagel refused to be accompanied by Baumgart or me and withdrew to his apartment in the Raphael. About six months after my arrival in Paris, toward the beginning of 1943, I'd first heard of the plot, and now Hofacker, exhaustedly, informed the participants about its complete failure. Oberg, promoted to SS Obergruppenführer, stood in instead, and then we had Kitzinger who arrived as a "satrap," with several officers, five wagons full of horses, goods and rationed food, and a Circassian boy and a Ukrainian cook in tow.

On the morning of July 21 I informed Walther von Stülpnagel, the general's younger son, and we hastened to Bad Pyrmont to inform Frau von Stülpnagel about the details of the drama, of which she had heard on the wireless. I then contacted a friend, the chief of police in Basel, who held out little hope that I might obtain asylum. Inquiries would last four weeks, there were few prospects of obtaining evidence, many German officers were trying to get asylum on grounds of Nazi persecution, and the loss of the war was in sight. I took my car, returned over the Schlucht-Pass in Alsace to Verdun, and stopped, as I had done eight days earlier, at the hospital to see Stülpnagel. It was July 30, and who should be there, sitting at the end of the hospital bed and talking to the blinded general, but Oberg.

Before being transferred to the south of France, and after a period of great danger and difficulty, I left Paris before dawn on the very last day of the occupation. During that final Paris week, I circulated between the Majestic and the Meurice hotels, and in the Etoile or Rond Point areas, but had no impression of any general uprising. When I left Paris in the direction of Meaux, via the rue Lafayette, in an old Opel P4, I heard shooting near the Gare du Nord. Of course I could no longer think of seeking shelter in the *"Haus der deutschen Angst,"* the six-floor bunker which had been constructed behind the Raphael and only recently has been replaced by buildings for better purposes.

Walter Bargatzky

Dr. Bargatzky is today president of the German Red Cross.

I was a *Landsgerichtsrat* in the Reich Ministry of Justice until a few weeks before the French campaign, when I was conscripted as a soldier. In July 1940, I was transferred to the military administration as a lawyer, in the Justizreferat, or Justice Department. Psychologically there was a certain antagonism between the military and the administrative staffs. Each French ministry was supervised by its equivalent department in our administration. The *préfets* came under the Ministry of the Interior. Tribunals, however, were under the Ministry of Justice.

Best coordinated all the civilian sections until he was succeeded by Michel. Best had an excellent relationship with the SD in the avenue Foch, and we never quite knew how far the relationship went. He wrote thousands of reports about the Breton independence movement, in which he had great faith. He was a *Vernichtungstheorist* [*a theorist of annihilation*], but he gave orders—he did not do the deeds himself. I often compared him to Robespierre. Within the administration he often amazed us. For instance, there was an interpreter who specialized in legal matters, a Dr. Leo, a young assessor from Hamburg, a *Sonderführer,* and not to be confused with Major Leo on the military staff. One day it came out that he was a Jew. We went to Best to appeal for Leo, and Best put out a helping hand. Leo was not allowed to continue as a *Sonderführer,* but he could remain in his company as an interpreter.

And another illustrative story of Best's unexpected character. Representatives from the French Ministry of Justice came around to see us about a Frenchman under arrest. Knochen had asked when this man was due to be released, and the French had supposed that this meant that the man would simply be arrested again and held although his sentence had been served. I drafted a decree to specify that police services, whether German or French, were forbidden to hold in custody men who had done their time. I explained this to Best, and my chief, Ministerialrat Belz, got it through. Best signed and promulgated it, well aware of what he was doing. Dr. Schlegelberger [*Staatssekretär in the Reichsjustizministerium*], who was visiting Paris, said that such a decree was inconceivable in Berlin.

Best was at his worst in the destruction of the synagogues. We heard of it the next morning. We had a signed statement from a witness certifying how Lischka had telephoned instructions to blow up one synagogue, and then the next, and so on. This was comprehensive enough for the Militärbefehlshaber to conclude that the synagogues might have been blown up by the French, but the initiative had come from the SD. The report, from Knochen and Lischka, that the French were wholly responsible was evidently false. Otto von Stülpnagel was arrogant, vain, somewhat of a caricature, but he did demand the dismissal of Knochen. This played an essential part in the reorganization that followed. Here we felt ourselves let down by Best, who was on such terms with Knochen—and with Abetz as well—that he let the whole thing drop. I had a remarkable last act to that whole affair. At the end of the war I was at Bad Reichenhall with all the files of the Paris administration. I found the report from Stülpnagel to have Knochen recalled, and in the margin was Keitel's comment in red pencil, *"Knochenerweichung, du Schwächling"* [*literally, softening of the bones, you weakling, but also a pun on Knochen's name*].

Our Justice Department had to supervise French justice. A representative from the Garde des Sceaux in the Place Vendôme would come to our department in the Majestic and show us the cases—the majority concerned *laissez-passer* into the unoccupied zone. In other cases the French asked us for guidance. Hostages came under the military staff IC or IA, and the Feldkommandanturs. The degree of French independence depended mainly on the personality of the French minister involved. I don't believe we interfered with French justice. In civil and criminal cases, of which there were thousands, we proceeded according to agreed formulas. Our section was never more than four people. We advised the military government on international law. Requisitioning of houses or hotels was done according to the Hague Convention. Each hotel had a German administrator to run it.

At some time in the summer or autumn of 1943, two members of our staff on a visit to Berlin were overheard making remarks to the effect that there ought to be an uprising against Hitler. They were members of the Price Control Commission, and their names were Seifert and Kleberg. Kleberg was a committed Christian. Both men had frequented the officers' mess in the Raphael, and the SD saw their chance to expose the spirit of opposition in that circle. A man with the party Golden Badge arrived with witnesses from Berlin on a special train. The two men were threatened with the death penalty, and Stülpnagel asked me to defend them. The tribunal met in the Raphael, in a room just to the left of the swing doors (in that little room Heydrich had once given us a lecture about what was really happening in the East). Opposite me, sitting at the table as an observer, was Lischka; it was the only time I saw him. We got a complete acquittal, thanks to careful coaching among those of us who were brought as witnesses.

I was in touch with Hofacker, who had testified for these two men, and with Teuchert, and on the grounds of this acquittal, I was asked if I would be the prosecutor on the day when charges could be brought against Oberg. We talked it through and decided to charge not only Oberg, but Hagen, Knochen, and Maulaz. We hesitated about Abetz, who had gone in for profiteering in the first weeks of the occupation. I spoke to Hofacker. I had no accurate evidence of pillaging. But I could prove how Oberg had weakened the war effort. He had given orders that deportees were to be deprived of their clothes, so that anyone escaping from these so-called *Nackttransporte* could be instantly recognized and shot down. Soldiers had to accompany the trains for the purpose, and Stülpnagel rightly said that he had none to spare. A second charge we could bring and prove concerned the uncompensated confiscation of property of those who had acted against the Reich, especially those tried before tribunals or held under *Nacht und Nebel* decrees. Dr. Maulaz, the economic affairs expert in the avenue Foch, explained that this property was inventoried and sent to the Reich, but we heard that some of it stayed at the avenue Foch.

The July 20 plot failed, the wave of arrests passed, and I saw that I would not be arrested. The Americans would soon arrive; we could not imagine it would last another winter. On July 29, I met the woman who was to become—and still is—my wife. She was a secretary at the Majestic. We decided to get married, in the English church that had been requisitioned by the Germans, in the rue Georges V. I went to see Pfarrer Damrath about it—he stayed in Paris to be taken prisoner. We had a last meal in the Raphael, with Teuchert, and the other Leo, and Horst, my witnesses, and then Major Leo arrived to say that we might be arrested any day. My wife left on the seventeenth, and we met up later in Germany.

Freiherr Friedrich von Teuchert

Until May 1942 I was in the Feldkommandantur at Saint-Lô. In Normandy the Germans were not the hereditary enemy; people did not know what exactly to make of us. We were soldiers. No SS, no resistance either. The cook in the mess, Adrienne, did her best. We had no weekend. Sometimes we went shooting and we played bridge. At Saint-Lô there was a stud and far more horses than in Paris, where only the best were kept, and then for racing. I think the French knew that the administration did what it could to protect civilians. Not that we were perfect. For a long time I kept a slip of paper brought by a Frenchman who wanted compensation for the loss of his car. The paper said, "Your car went off with me, Hindenburg." There was found to be no control of trichinosis, I remember, so in Berlin the veterinary department told us to introduce it. This landed on my desk. I sent for an official and he said the vets would be pleased, but there were more farmers than vets. We spent our time handling French bureaucrats, from Paris or Vichy, who came to protest or to congratulate.

In Paris, I lived in the Raphael but worked in the Majestic. We couldn't eat in the officers' mess except in uniform but with permission could go out in ordinary suits. Stülpnagel was strict. We received only what was our due. We were very preoccupied over what became July 20. One of the secretaries had a fiancé in the SS; she believed implicitly in Nazism. It was not easy to change anything, not even to hold a conversation—there were people who believed in *Endsieg* [*final victory*]. About a dozen on the staff were Nazis through and through, like Jehle. But the people in agriculture bothered about potatoes not politics, and so on.

General Viebahn, a corps commander at Saint-Lô, had said to me, "If you shake my hand, you are shaking a criminal's hand. I had the opportunity to shoot Hitler and I didn't take it." I knew that there was a camp at Compiègne for deporting people, mostly Jews, though not all. One day von Oertzen, on the staff, came to me and said, "You must go and see what von Behr is doing—if you haven't seen it, you can't believe it." So Professor Baumgart and I and someone else went to this warehouse with Jewish property being packed up—it was ghastly. When you saw it, you were charged with the ferocity to stay and do what we had to do on July 20.

How did I leave Paris? There were two green and white buses in front of the Royal Monceau. We were to be packed up and out by three in the afternoon. Then came a surprise. I went to the mess. White linen and silver were on the table. The French staff offered us a farewell meal. There were six or seven servants, and not one behaved as if we were anything except habitual guests. They said they hoped we'd be back. That made a lasting impression.

Ernst Jünger

At eighty-seven, Jünger is white-haired, but a trim and active figure. On one of his frequent visits to Paris, it so happened that I was able to meet him. *Routes et Jardins,* the 1940 section of his diary, has been reprinted—its original wartime publication had first alerted French intellectuals to the presence among them of this German writer, a brilliant observer, but one so self-controlled that in the circumstances he seemed too dispassionate and chill. His experiences of Paris in the war are to be discovered in their entirety in his diaries, entitled *Strahlungen,* and to read those two volumes is to be immersed in the drama of the period. Conversation added little, though he revealed one or two pseudonyms he had used—Merlin for Céline, for instance. Lady Orpington, described as an aristocratic English lady with whom he once had a drink at the Bristol, in fact hid the identity of Mrs. Florence Gould, at whose famous *jeudi* lunches Jünger and other like-minded Germans met their French counterparts. Pressed by me, he repeated the story of his arrival in Paris, in the interim between the conquest of France and the armistice, and how he had walked for over an hour from the place where he was billeted in order to have lunch at Prunier, that famous restaurant near the Madeleine, from where he proceeded to telephone his friends, Jean Schlumberger the writer, and Georges Poupet, a publisher. Speidel had been responsible for the subsequent presence of Jünger on the staff, in spite of a warning against having him from no less a person than General Keitel at Army Headquarters.

Jünger talked of topics still close to his heart: how a compromising correspondence between him and another German writer, Josef Breitbach, had been rescued from a safe-deposit box in the Crédit Lyonnais in Paris before any hostile person could read it; how the report that he had been commissioned by Speidel to write on the Machiavellian struggle between the army and other services had been lost, to the detriment of the historical record. In a moment of fear, after July 20, he had burned his own copy. He had come under suspicion, but had heard an SS man say of him, "Oh, he's a man I see every day at breakfast. He's a poet—you can safely let him go." Jünger had entered the war as a captain, and he emerged from it as a captain. In World War I he had done enough soldiering, he explained, and the second time around he wanted to write books.

Ursula Rüdt von Collenberg (today Frau Nottebohm)

I had an uncle, Baron Kurt Rüdt von Collenberg, who was a Luftwaffe general; he lived in Neuilly, in the villa of a Madame Mandel. He suggested that I become a *Blitzmädchen* [*as girls who worked for the German army were called*], but I did not accept. But I wanted to be in Paris more than anything else in the world. Wolfgang Windelband, the historian, was in Paris on the Archive Commission, and he took me onto it, thanks to my uncle. I came from Germany by train, in my ordinary clothes. I was twenty-one. It was a wonderful eye-opener right away that suddenly you could buy all the books you wanted, American, English, and French books.

I was in Paris from April 1, 1942, until October 1943. Only thirty people staffed the Archive Commission, mainly diplomats like Dr. Eugen Klee, some of them retired, or else historians like Dr. Michaelis. All except one were anti-Nazis. The head of the commission was Dr. Jagow, a charming man. We were in the Ministère des Affaires Etrange`res. One of the photocopyists, I remember, stripped the gold-embossed leather hangings off the walls and was sacked. We had at our disposal all the files of the foreign ministry since Richelieu. The diplomats and historians often used these files for their research—one of them wrote a biography of Marie Antoinette. We selected passages that served our war aims, for instance reports of French consuls, or colonial affairs, or what the English had done in Palestine, and how their occupation of countries compared to ours. We sent what we had extracted back to the Propaganda Ministry in Berlin.

The Auswärtiges Amt had requisitioned the Hotel d'Orsay, close to the Gare d'Orsay. We lived there. I had a wonderful huge room with a bath and a telephone— I never lived so well anywhere. We lunched in the canteen of the embassy, in the rue de Lille, but had vouchers for breakfast and dinner in the hotel. We worked until about four or five in the afternoon and then were free. I had special friends in Frau von Mauch, and Baronin Heyl (who married Dr. Klee). We went to the opera or the theater; we saw Jean-Louis Barrault and Sacha Guitry and the Grand Guignol; we visited exhibitions in the Orangerie and the Musée de l'Homme. Weekends were free, and we went everywhere sightseeing—off to Poitiers, down the Loire, to Amiens and Abbeville. By train. In Paris I can remember using the metro only; we knew nobody much with a car.

The Windelbands had an apartment in the Hotel Bristol. My uncle gave fantastic dinner parties in Neuilly, with all the right French guests, Marquis So-and-so and Comte Tra-la-la. We had good French friends—like Daniel-Rops, who translated Rilke. We had a young Frenchman come to give us language lessons. There was lovely material to be bought for clothes, and I found a little White Russian dressmaker. Fantastic deals were being transacted all around on the sly, for wines, food, shoes, what have you. We could buy what we wanted, much more than the French. It was the most wonderful and unforgettable time of my youth.

Hermann Eich

Dr. Eich, at the time of this interview, was editor in chief of a leading newspaper in Düsseldorf. In 1943, as *Leiter der Presse Gruppe* in the Propaganda Abteilung, he published *Wege der französischen Presse,* a guide to the French press.

In 1931 I had done a student exchange in France for six weeks, which had given me a taste for the country. Then, I was a journalist on the *Berliner Tageblatt,* a paper which was finally closed in 1939. I had tried to be attached to the Auswärtiges Amt as a press attaché, but Ribbentrop wanted his ministry to be recruited from circles without any bourgeois stamp. In mid-1939 I landed in a newly founded Auslands-presse-Abteilung der Reichsregierung [*department for foreign press relations*] in Berlin. That was the point of departure for my Paris mission. The campaign in France was under way when I was called to spend four or five days in a Potsdam barracks. Nobody knew what would happen in Paris. I flew off from Berlin with ten others. I remember that over Sedan the plane dramatically went down to a hundred meters above ground level, and the pilot told us that English fighters were approaching. But we reached Paris safely. It was June 20, 1940. I was in my mid-twenties, with this title of *Sonderführer.* Only at the end of 1942, as a Leutnant der Reserve, did I become a regular officer.

The first German officer who got newspapers going was Weber, a phenomenal organizer. He told us simply to make for the offices of *Paris-Soir*; we had nowhere else. Weber had requisitioned these offices on his own authority. And of course you know the fabulous story of the elevator operator Schiessle, who had been left behind to guard the place, only to find himself having to run a paper. I spent my first week somewhere in a barracks before I was billeted in the Hotel Berkeley, and then the Hotel Lincoln. Leutnant Weber was a maid-of-all-work. He inaugurated a big center for children of printers—I remember seeing him among hundreds of children at Clignancourt. The Germans arriving in Paris had some sort of a bad conscience, and he wished to ease strains all around. He was rather sympathetic, terribly fat, and didn't think only of himself. He married a woman who was the number-one dancer in the famous Lido, and they were still married after the war.

At *Paris-Soir* I remember a small machine, operated by a *Sonderführer,* which printed the news from Berlin. For those first weeks someone wrote out German radio bulletins, and copies were made for press publication. By September, however, I was properly installed at 52, avenue des Champs-Elysées. The Propaganda Abteilung was organized under the administration in the Majestic. Its head was Colonel Heinz Schmidtke. The Abteilung was divided into Staffeln, the head staff being in Paris, the others being in Angers and Bordeaux and so on. The Paris Propaganda Staffel was headed by Waechter, and it too broke down into subsections, for the theater, for the censorship, for paper distribution under Dr. Klecker, the film department, and a Gruppe Presse. From 1940 until mid-1942 I directed the Presse Gruppe at the Paris Staffel with Graf Podewils as my superior on the Presse Gruppe in the Majestic. Edith Piaf had a *faible* for Waechter, though their affair was platonic. She used to come sometimes to the hotel to check whether there were any chances of work for her colleagues or for herself. Waechter persistently invited her to sing to the troops, which she did on two or three occasions. He used to try to make a good impression on her with a turn of his, which he called *"Knabe mit Kelch"* [*lad with a tankard*]: he balanced a brimful glass of champagne on his forehead, jerked back his head, and caught the glass in his hand without spilling a drop. Edith Piaf found it entertaining, but in the long run Waechter bored her. In those first weeks of the occupation there were celebrations among the Germans of a victory that soon began to look ephemeral.

Within the Presse Gruppe there was a special section for military censorship, under Sonderführer Junges (after the war he became an ambassador). He was effectively head of censorship until one day in 1943 he was posted off to be editor in chief of the army paper in Salonika, and his place was taken by Dr. Moras. After the war Moras became editor in chief of the magazine *Merkur,* in the French zone of occupation in Germany. Waechter was eventually succeeded by Sonderführer Lucht. Sonderführer Hermes took over the French news agency Havas, which was then turned into AFIP and dealt with sport and culture and all that. Our French counterpart, the *chef de presse* in Paris, was Antoine-Marie Pietri, of the Ministère de l'Information, but seconded to the de Brinon delegation, where they were always struggling with Hermes.

In the first months of the occupation I was of dubious usefulness because my French was defective. I engaged a Frenchman from the Berlitz for lessons. I also engaged a Rumanian journalist who was secretary general of the Association of Journalists in Paris. Until the end of 1941 American journalists continued to work there, and their representative was Thomas Whitcomb, of the *Christian Science Monitor.* He had also run a small agency of his own, which was closed down, whereupon he resorted to Achenbach—after the war—to help him obtain indemnification. Whitcomb played the role of organizing the foreign press, obtaining their permits and *laissez-passer* and so on, and he had to liaise with me.

Initial press conferences at Number 52 were on such topics as supplies of milk and water, the state of roads and bridges, also measures taken to defend works of art. To introduce Graf Metternich on the subject, I wanted to say that the German army had received orders to protect works of art, but I stumbled on the wrong expression and some of the journalists looked around at each other with a wild surmise. Beumelburg, who was a sozzled old policeman, spoke about security.

Two or three times a week, we were in the habit of holding these press conferences to lay down the line for the French. Five or six of us from the Gruppe Presse sat together at a long table and guided the questions or exchanges. Dr. Arntz, who was an economist, handled specialist matters. Someone from the military administration always joined in. The journalists slowly dwindled in number, down to as few as eight, and often they were very visibly bored. Editors never came to these press conferences, and as the war dragged on, it was painful to us to see some girl jotting down our handouts for five papers simultaneously. Every day there was a mass of paper as well. In Berlin, half a dozen offices were manufacturing words for us, all blaming the Jews, et cetera, in idiotic journalese. The thin impact of German propaganda derived from the monotony of these words. Take the expression "plutocracy" which was supposed to be denigrating—the French were starved of everything and dreamed only of having a country which could be a plutocracy.

Editors in chief were by no means servile in their conduct. Jeantet, for instance, with his pretentious manner, made an impression on the younger members of the Presse Gruppe. I was once invited by him, and felt flattered. Sordet I knew as a *bonhomme,* and nothing but. I met Hibbelen once in 1944; he was a man between frontiers. Suarez, who had *Aujourd'hui,* was Abetz's man. He asked me once if I knew that before the war he had written articles in which Hitler was depicted as criminal and mad. I had read his four stout volumes on Briand and been impressed by them, but in fact I answered that what he had written before the war would not interest anyone. Lesca I saw only from time to time. Chateaubriant, with his limp and his beard and the venerable Madame Castelot in tow, was the incarnation all in one of goodwill, naïveté, and optimism. Because he could not bring himself to believe that his idol could commit crimes, he kept his eyes closed right to the end. Luchaire liked the good life, money and women. Already before the war he had been propagating Franco-German rapprochement, and so in that respect he was remaining consistent. He was a *Duzfreund* [*i.e., on intimate second-person-singular terms*] of Junges, which made it easy for the two of them to collaborate. I went to Corinne Luchaire's wedding, which was already stamped with forewarnings of the German defeat. I used to receive anonymous letters about how Luchaire's corruption was ruining the German image—but then every day we also received letters accusing French journalists of being Jewish, and sometimes accusing us too, in thoroughly anti-Semitic denunciations, always unsigned. Georges Prade, Luchaire's colleague on *Les Nouveaux Temps*, was also a friend—he was a magistrate in Paris, I believe. A score of journalists were helped by Luchaire to leave Paris at the end of the occupation, though some, like Jeantet, stayed. Had Brasillach been arrested a year later, I believe he would have been judged less severely. With Henri Jeanson, whom I knew, I always had the impression of a man who was a constant cabaret turn; he took nothing seriously, as though we were running an assembly of lunatics who by some misfortune had settled themselves in Paris. I can say that I know of no case of money going from our department to a paper or to a journalist. No editor or director or journalist came into my office to ask for a subsidy. My personal salary as a lieutenant was, I think, two hundred marks a month.

There was no precensorship. A military commentator would send in proofs in order to be on the safe side, however. In general, the system was to invite journalists along if they had any uncertainty, so that we could decide together what to allow through, and in fact a censor always remained on duty at Number 52 until midnight. Most of the Propaganda Staffel were reasonable and on the friendliest terms with the journalists, though a few believed in displays of power. Our line was simple: show us anything about which you are doubtful. Journalists and editors had their own sensible idea of what should be done. My activity was more one of coordination. Suppose that there had been a bombing raid. I would give a press briefing, with directions on how the story was to be reported, and then allow the journalists to go out to see it for themselves. The next day I would check through their accounts. I might find that my half-hour briefing had been cut down to four lines, but that was all. The pressure of our apparatus was sufficient.

A concrete example: at the beginning of 1942 Sacha Guitry telephoned me to say that he had written a light-hearted exposé for *Aujourd'hui* of the dangers of *doryphores* [*literally, Colorado beetles*], but to his amazement, the censor had forbidden publication. Now *doryphores* was one of the nicknames for the Germans, and Guitry was winking at the public, no doubt about it. I telephoned Moras and explained that Guitry was certainly having fun at our expense, but that the papers were dry and dull and stuffed with communiqués, so therefore this piece ought to be allowed to run. The editor in fact pruned down the final version, and Sacha Guitry afterward wrote me a thank-you letter in that huge handwriting of his.

Weber founded a press club in the cellar of the Lido—later on, gatherings were held in a building on the avenue Henri Martin. We met once or twice a month, as a rule, to listen to French speakers. There were little tables for guests, and food and drinks were served. Pierre Fresnay addressed the club, and so did Jean-Louis Vaudoyer, director of the Opéra. On one occasion I invited Jünger and Speidel, on another occasion Sieburg, who was giving an address next day at Les Ambassadeurs.

Sieburg was a great friend; he often lamented to me that German conduct was ridiculous.

In 1942 I was posted to Russia, but people with special qualifications were hard to replace, and I was back at the end of the year. I returned to the Hotel Lincoln, in the rue Lincoln. Graf Podewils was promoted to be a war correspondent in Russia, and later with Rommel, so I stepped into his shoes, with the title of *Leiter der Presse Gruppe*. To wear uniform was embarrassing, and I put it on solely for military appointments. One had to run the gauntlet, because people stared so. It was the moment of *attentats*. Outside the Hotel Lincoln sentries were now permanently on duty. Where professional and private relations with the French were concerned, I noticed the difference. One day I was sitting on the terrace of the Café Colisée, when I was greeted by the man with whom I'd done the exchange in 1931. He said that his parents would be delighted to see me. I called at their apartment in the boulevard Saint-Germain. I shall never forget the sad and distressing atmosphere. I saw that the much-abused word "collaboration" was being destroyed when it came to old ties. The generous and widespread reception of Germans by French families became rarer, and as a German, one was inclined to understand the reasons.

From the beginning of 1942, the German embassy started to hold press conferences of its own. From then on, all political questions were treated by the embassy, with the exception of purely military matters, which continued to be handled through the Presse Gruppe. Schwendemann was the counselor who handled the embassy press conferences. He and Achenbach also received the top management of the French press for confidential discussions. The death of Bunau-Varilla, owner of *Le Matin,* made such an impression on Schwendemann that he made himself ill, weeping at the funeral. Schwendemann was twenty years older than me; I respected his seniority and his professionalism. I grew accustomed to these personality disputes, but never suffered curtailment of my role in the Presse Gruppe. Schmidtke was a soldier, a square-head; he had no knowledge whatsoever of France, and nobody took him or his rages too seriously.

My book aimed to show to a limited public what exactly the Presse Gruppe was, and to that extent to bolster it. Our work was somewhat restricted by an attitude within the military administration, which held that it was not profitable to allot so much paper to newspapers that had a very mixed readership. People did dip into the papers, but what they needed most was something to wrap their cabbages in. To coincide with the book, we staged an exhibition in the avenue Henri Martin to display the work of the Presse Gruppe. Dr. Michel opened this exhibition with a speech. On the second page of my book you will find a note to explain that paper for the publication was taken from the contingent allocated to French newspapers. Only one hundred copies were published, in a numbered edition. The book was printed in German on one of the French presses we used, whose compositors by then were skilled in the German language.

A week before my departure, I was ordered to report to the Majestic. Schmidtke issued instructions to recruit a squad to destroy the printworks of every newspaper. I asked him for technical clarifications, and he indicated some specialist who could give advice. By chance, Schmidtke was ordered to leave Paris and rejoin some other staff, which was why the departure of the Presse Gruppe was not marked by this idiotic act. Each press remained intact, and a dozen hours after our departure the rotaries were turning again. We just packed up in a truck and drove out under hundreds of Allied planes.

Gerhard Heller

Gerhard Heller studied romance languages in Toulouse during the academic year of 1933. Epting, at the time head of the Deutsche Akademische Austauschdienst, the bureau for the exchange of scholars, had arranged this. Then, in 1935, Heller was in Paris on another exchange program. There he met Abetz, with whom he became on second-person-singular terms of familiarity. At the end of that year, he took a job as a broadcaster on the German radio. In the summer of 1940, a friend in the Propaganda Ministry told him that someone with good qualifications in French was required in Paris to run the Referat Schrifttum, or literature section, of the Propaganda Staffel. Heller brought to his job excellent contacts, therefore, as well as expertise, fitting him for the important part he was to play in French literary history. *"Notre cher Gérard,"* as Brasillach and others were to Frenchify him, quite appropriately, featured as a kind of honorary colleague, or superpublisher, in the careers of writers who had to submit their manuscripts to him for the *bon à tirage,* or authorization to appear in print. A wide range of writers, from Malraux and Jean Paulhan, to Léautaud and Fabre-Luce and Georges Blond, left favorable comments on him in memoirs or articles written at the time, as well as later.

Heller kept a diary, but on August 13, 1944, he buried it somewhere on the esplanade des Invalides and so lost it. He has been able to reconstitute fragments only, which some years ago were set in type for publication in the *NRF.* But Gaston Gallimard, then old and ill, felt that this might cast too many reflections—and so the wartime censor of literature in Paris was himself censored in peacetime in Paris.

In June 1941, Heller wrote, "François Mauriac is signing at Grasset's advance copies of his novel *La Pharisienne.* I ask Henry Muller and André Fraigneau whether I might take advantage of this opportunity to pay my respects to the writer. The latter gives me a copy, with the inscription, 'To Lieutenant Heller, who has taken a great interest in *La Pharisienne,* and its fate, with gratitude, François Mauriac.' Indeed, I need to justify myself toward my compatriots who are of the opinion that I ought not to have authorized the publication of this book." After the war, the Communist press was to take this inscription as evidence of Mauriac's collaboration—and no doubt the example prompted Gallimard to decide that discretion was the better part of valor where he and his firm were concerned, even though in November 1940 Heller was commenting that the publishing house "is considered Judeo-Bolshevik and anti-German." Other fragments of this lost diary depict Heller in November 1940 calling for the first time on Drieu, climbing nine flights of stairs in the darkened house on the avenue de Breteuil, in order to crack Drieu's last remaining bottle of whiskey. "I told him that it is impossible for me to believe that Hitler and the Germans will create the kind of Europe that he is imagining." Again, August 1941, "Marcel Jouhandeau and Marcel Arland arranged the meeting with Jean Paulhan. We met on the first floor of a small restaurant in the rue de Ponthieu.... Conversation turned to German poets, and I said some inept things yes, real stupidities, on the subject of Jews in Germany. As a sequel to the talk, he (Paulhan) sent me a magnificent old edition of Voltaire's life of Frederick II of Prussia."

Heller's wife, Marie-Louise, was present at the interview.

GERHARD HELLER: November 8, 1940, was my thirtieth birthday, and on that day I drove into Paris to take up my job with the Propaganda Staffel. I found I had a smallish room at 52, avenue des Champs-Elysées, and plenty of manuscripts lay there already. The first books I read were Benoist-Méchin's *La Moisson de quarante* and Jean Baroncelli's *Vingt-six hommes*—he writes film criticism for *Le Monde* now. I read day and night, to get rid of the pile. My instructions were simple: to read everything and decide what could appear. The very next day, November 9, there was a celebration in the Chambre des Députés, and I sat there and thought that though I was only a little cog in the machine, I did have an aptitude for my job and could show how grateful I was for everything I had learned in France—after all, as a boy I'd been awarded a scholarship by the French Republic. On November 11, students demonstrated in the Quartier Latin and on the Champs-Elysées. We were ordered to go downstairs and sort them out. My colleagues seized some students and brought them up on the elevator to the fifth floor. I shared the ride with four young Parisians, and when we reached the top I told them to hop it fast. I then went down again and got lost in the crowd. Later when I was asked what had happened to my four students, I answered that they'd already been taken care of.

I had a uniform like every soldier's—it reeked of barracks. I was wearing it when Drieu first came into the office, about mid-November. A little later, I remember seeing heaped up in a vast garage on the avenue de la Grande-Armée the thousands of books proscribed on the so-called Otto list. They were going to be carted off for shredding. One day when I was still a new boy, I had to accompany another *Sonderführer* to the Presses Universitaires de France, in the boulevard Saint-Germain, to instruct the director, Paul Angoulvent, to remove Jewish authors from his list. To underline the gravity of the order, the other man laid his revolver on the desk. I saw Angoulvent as white as the wall.

Jacques Bernard at the *Mercure de France*—where Léautaud spent a lifetime— had published a book by Georges Duhamel, who was considered an anti-German writer. Bremer, at the Institut, waged war on Duhamel, though the Institut had no right to ban a book. I was ordered to the *Mercure de France* to tell them to destroy the stock of Duhamel's *Lieu d'Asile*. I'd read it, and I said to Jacques Bernard: Look, take a dozen copies, make a parcel, and write on it "Property of Lieutenant Heller" and that way you can keep it until the day when you can republish. Two days later, Ingrid, the Danish wife of Jacques Bernard, with her daughter Mimi, arrived to invite me to dine on Saturday night. I used to go there very often afterward, with another secretary who was anti-Nazi, Annie Hackenberg.

One day in 1941, a friend told me that Marie-Louise Bousquet wanted to invite me to a concert at which the cellist Pierre Fournier was to play. My first French friends were André Fraigneau and Henry Muller, at Grasset's. They wanted me to go, but I was not allowed to be in civilian clothes. There was nowhere to sit, and I was looking about when someone spoke to me. It was Jouhandeau. "We'll sit on the floor," I said. Everyone had a look at this odd German officer squatting on the floor. Mrs. Florence Gould happened to be there and afterward invited me to have a drink with her at the Bristol. We stayed up late. I met Pierre Benoit. Mrs. Gould's lunches began that way—I introduced Jünger to her. Jouhandeau was teaching and was free only on Thursdays, so Thursday it had to be. Also in my office, I'd given orders that if a French publisher called, his hand had to be shaken and he had to be offered an apéritif. Word was getting out in a small circle that here was this German who was a bit of a card.

In 1941 and 1942 I organized the trips to Weimar. I chose which writers ought to come, and naturally they were "collabos"—Ramon Fernandez, Chardonne, Drieu, Brasillach, Fraigneau, Thérive, the critic of *Le Temps*. I was the guide. We journeyed across Germany, accompanied by some Belgians and Italians, including Elia Vittorini. The German writers whom we met at Weimar were under the sponsorship of the Ministry of Propaganda. Then in July 1942 the Referat Schrifttum was removed from the Propaganda Abteilung and reconstituted as a section of the embassy's, under Wilhelm Knothe, the consul general. I could no longer sign authorizations on my own. I had to run to my superior to have something done.

MARIE-LOUISE HELLER: I'd come to the literature section before Gerhard, in August. Dr. Kaiser, head of it then, had said that we had to send a telegram to Berlin, in order to have help. We sent the telegram, he would later add, and that's how we acquired Heller. My functions were transferred with the Referat Schrifttum to the embassy. I couldn't carry my typewriter, so I took a velo-taxi, the only time I ever did so. All the embassy rooms were full. So Heller and I and the Musik Referat arrived to find no space. Our bureau was relocated in the Deutsche Institut, in two rooms. I had a private room in which to sleep in the stable block at the embassy. Gerhard was always away from morning till night.

HELLER: Propaganda Abteilung personnel had a whole house reserved for them in the rue Spontini. We were on the fourth floor. I took an apartment nearby in the rue Casimir-Périer. A lady called Virginie looked after me. Marie-Louise and I married in 1945.

MARIE-LOUISE HELLER: I had a *Haushaltszuteilung,* permission to keep a house, issued from the embassy. One lined up and got food from the stores. Once at the embassy, I had several bosses. I was on permanent stand-by, to answer the telephone.

HELLER: I took advantage to meet Marie-Louise as often as possible. I would also run into Abetz and tell him things confidentially. He promised to cover me, but I could never be sure if he would back me up. For instance, in the case of Gérard Boutelleau. He was the son of Jacques Chardonne and had an English wife. He went to Tunisia and became Gide's secretary. When the Germans captured Tunisia, they arrested Boutelleau because his diary was found to contain aggressive anti-German remarks. He was deported to Sachsenhausen. Chardonne roped me in. One could save people, but it cost a year of hard work. I spoke to Breker, to the Ministry of Propaganda, to the Foreign Office, and I had Gérard Boutelleau liberated to Paris. He had promised that he would do nothing more, but in fact he entered the resistance and was arrested again, which was highly dangerous for me who had guaranteed him. Brasillach, at the lunch to say good-bye to Bremer, said in his speech that Heller is a liberal—well, the SD were there, and it was as good as a denunciation.

To my way of thinking, we had to lose the war in order to be rid of Hitler. I was influenced by Jünger, with whom I could speak openly. We made it a point of honor not to give the party salute. It was a narrow path one had to walk because of the risk of being sent to the Russian front. I had a weak heart and was unfit, but during the war I started to develop a nervous disease. Céline happened to be the one who diagnosed it—a terrible man, but a genius in his way.

In the Hotel Berkeley, on the avenue Matignon, I had a room, and I kept it, and paid for it, even when I was at the Deutsche Institut. After curfew one day, I was walking down the Champs-Elysées when I saw something stirring in the bushes. It was a girl with a ponytail. I brought her into the hotel, where she had to spend the night in the lobby. She was called Claudine, Martine, Aline, something like that. She kept on coming back; she made me take her out into the countryside; we went on walks. She liked to show herself topless to me. I never touched her, of course. Her parents, she explained, did not like Germans. Jacques, a boy of fifteen, also propositioned me; he adored me. It was a taste for strangers in both cases, I think.

Drieu in his *Journal* called me cowardly. I imitated him, I even had his hat copied, he was so elegant. One day we lunched in the embassy, and I can see Drieu, with tears in his eyes, explaining that he wanted to advise the enemy without being on their side. He was a Fascist. That's the drama. He might have been a great writer. At the Théâtre Edouard VII, Racine's *Britannicus* was being put on, I remember, and Laubreaux stood in the crowd. A siren went off, and there was Laubreaux ranting aloud about Jews and Freemasons. I used to talk a lot to Brice Parain and his Russian wife. I'd met them at a swimming pool. In a bathing costume, nobody has a nationality. If anyone asked about my accent, I would say I was Alsatian. I spoke openly to Montherlant; I was a great friend of the dealer Carré. I went to see Marcel Arland at Brinville, and Bernard Grasset at Garches. I used to lunch out with great ladies as well as concierges. I simply wanted to know all the French.

Already in 1941 we had seen that it was impossible to exercise censorship on the whole output of literature. We gave a good quantity of paper to publishers, and they were very active and never complained. I concluded a pact with editors and publishers: they could produce what they liked as long as paper was available, except on a few themes, like the war or security, and no works by Jews, and nothing anti-German. Auto-censure was best. The agreement we had with the Syndicat d'Edition in the first half of 1941 was on my initiative.

Otherwise I gave my signature to approve the publication of Eluard, Aragon, Elsa Triolet, everyone. I was the first member of the public to read Camus's *L'Etranger*. Madeleine Boudot-Lamotte, the secretary of Gaston Gallimard, brought the manuscript to me—she married a German—and said that Ramon Fernandez and Paulhan had given favorable opinions upon it, and would there be any objections from the German authorities. She handed it over to me at six in the evening. I took it home, read it until four in the morning, and was carried away. Next day I telephoned Madeleine to say that there was no objection, that it was a highly original work and would provide a point of departure for new fiction. I authorized it, but then the Propaganda Abteilung criticized me because objections were coming from the French side. How could the Germans, the French were asking, allow something like this to be published?"

Helmut Rademacher

Within the German administration in Paris there were, confusingly, other men with this surname, notably Erich Rademacher, a Foreign Office official, and a Sonderführer Rademacher at the Majestic, who was (I take it) the man whom Lifar referred to in his memoirs as "Bernard Rademacher, announced as Goebbels's representative ... a former actor who spoke French well."

At the outbreak of war I had the rank of Ministerialrat in the Prussian civil service, working in the Reich Finance Ministry. The Ministry of the Interior then selected me for a crash course lasting a fortnight at Marburg-an-der-Lahn, during which we were instructed in what our duties would be in the event of the occupation of France. We received a booklet in which the administrative skeleton was already set out, though it incorporated France only as far as Lille. The Higher Command had not anticipated that France would fall so quickly. From mid-May to mid-June I had my first experience of occupation. I had the rank of Kriegsverwaltungsabteilungschef [*equivalent to a colonel*] in the military administration of Liège. On June 14 I received the order to report to General von Briesen, the Stadtkommandant of Paris, though he had been *en poste* only a matter of hours. I drove to Paris and found him in the Place de l'Opéra, and on the fifteenth I stood at his side as he took the salute of the troops marching down the Champs-Elysées. I then had to start the preliminaries of the administration. I was appointed city commissioner, Stadtkommissar, the civilian equivalent of the job held by Speidel on the military side.

Turner had selected me. He was running von Briesen's Verwaltungsstab and was a capable man, a lawyer, in the party and the SS, but with a mind of his own. He was opposed to anti-Semitism, which was why they chucked him out. With him was Ermert, who had the Golden Badge of the party. On the sixteenth or seventeenth I went with Ermert to see Langeron. Turner was already there, to establish control

252

of the police. Langeron was very reserved. We took our compass bearings of the overall situation. Every evening there was a conference with Turner in the Prince de Galles Hotel, which I had requisitioned for the military administration staff, already several hundred strong. In the Georges V there was a general with some reason for wanting the Prince de Galles, so we moved out. An Office of Locations had been set up at once under the Stadtkommissar, and von Briesen gave orders to take over the hotels. So I requisitioned them as offices and lodgings for the administration; I requisitioned the Chambre des Députés.

Preparations to administer what we called Stadt-Paris had been predetermined in that booklet at Marburg, but the Marne and the Oise departments had to be improvised out of what resources we had. My task was to take over from the army. Every day we had to supply food, fuel, transport. An immediate problem that June was milk for the children. Industry was at a standstill. I was responsible for the two million inhabitants of Paris, and the two million more in the Marne and the Oise; I was also responsible for the waterworks, the underground, gasworks, three thousand buses, public utilities of all sorts. At about ten o'clock each morning, in the Chambre des Députés, either the *préfet* Magny would see me or I would go to him for a discussion of these problems. For each branch of the French administration we had to draft in a German administrator, not a military man but a specialist of rank and experience. In fact, these were people of international caliber. The Frenchman in charge of the metro already knew his opposite number in Berlin. Paris was famous for the canals under the city, which could be navigated. The director of the Berlin canals came.

To begin with, the Militärbefehlshaber-Paris was divided into an administrative section, an economic section, and a *Sonderstab der Stadtkommandantur*. I was the chief of this Sonderstab until April 1941, when as a result of reorganization the Kommandantur von Gross-Paris was established under General von Schaumburg, and Turner, hitherto his chief of staff in the Chambre des Députés, was posted off to Yugoslavia. After April 1941, though I remained Stadtkommissar, I also took over as Schaumburg's Chef des Verwaltungsstabs, or chief of his administrative staff. Oberkriegsverwalter Lippert headed the actual administrative section, and Fischer its economic section. My people were not in the Chambre des Députés, as Turner's had been, but instead actually in the offices of the French—that was the difference. It made for greater control and efficiency. I myself kept a permanent bureau in the Préfecture, and Magny and I were on the best of terms. Both of us minded our manners. One day he came to me, and the next I went to him. He had the title "Excellence," and I stressed that fact heavily, so that my people treated him as politely as he treated them. Taittinger was his subordinate.

From the standpoint of organization and planning, the French were better than us, but they could not put their plans into practice as well. The apportioning of oil and gasoline was always difficult. I remember when coal supplies were deficient one winter, and we were not sure what we could get from Lille or Longwy. There were freight cars of coal to be unloaded at one of the stations, and Magny asked me how he was to set about the task. The Parisians lacked initiative. My essential job was to see that Paris was systematically and adequately supplied. I toured Normandy and Brittany to organize provisions of meat, butter, and cereals. Foodstuffs came from too few departments, and deliveries were insufficiently varied. I had to visit industrialists and their factories. When a factory employed over two hundred people and was fulfilling a German order, I decided to allocate special rations to it, and I carried this through as though there were no war. That is a contribution of which I am proud.

The French came to the Chambre des Députés for permits and requests of all sorts, especially for cars. Sacha Guitry, to his credit, came to me with pleas for Jewish actors.

Schaumburg shared quarters with his chief of staff. He was a confirmed bachelor. His aides were Major Prince Ratibor and Oberleutnant von Dühring. Wives were not allowed to come to Paris; when one of the staff members fixed his wife a job with the navy and she arrived in Paris, Schaumburg did not like it. He ordered me to start a soldiers' shop, where coffee, tea, chocolates, and clothes could be bought without tickets. German soldiers only, mostly on transit. The French assistants there had to speak German. Schaumburg was very stiff and formal, busying himself with parades and military details. Once I had to do a tour of inspection of French brothels with him and his adjutant, Rittmeister Graf Waldersee. The girls had their certificates issued by my office, and they were all French of course. In Paris there were one hundred and twenty brothels in all, forty of them reserved for German soldiers, four for our officers, and one for the generals. Schaumburg held me responsible for seeing that Germans frequented only those brothels reserved for them. All at once, on our tour, we heard a cry from one of the rooms—we'd caught a German officer in a French brothel. "Report to me in the morning," said Schaumburg.

One day Speidel telephoned me to say that hostages were being shot and to ask me what ought to be done about it. We met to discuss it and went for a walk, as it happened, in the zoo. Stülpnagel and Schaumburg were both there, and the latter asked what I was doing joining in such a discussion. As a matter of fact, I knew Stülpnagel well, but Speidel answered for me that I had been consulted as a lawyer, and could therefore give advice. Schaumburg was for shooting the hostages, and somehow after that scene our relationship deteriorated. As for the first Stülpnagel, he used to go around Paris incognito and then he would call me to ask some question, like, Why does cheese cost so much? He had just seen it at twenty francs for 500 grams, say, and considered the price exorbitant. He was more human than he is credited with. In April 1941, Hans Frank (in charge of the Government General, as Poland was now called), visited Stülpnagel, and Speidel gave a small supper party in the Majestic. Toasts were drunk, and finally Frank lifted his glass to Stülpnagel: "I, King of Poland, drink to you, King of France." Speidel kicked me under the table.

Medicus, who took Best's place, spoke excellent French. He had wanted to succeed Turner, but Stülpnagel appointed me instead. Medicus and Ermert had the rank of general, with a red stripe down their trousers. I had no red stripe. Best had said that I ought to be a *Standartenführer* but Himmler and Heydrich were against it. Shortly after our entry into Paris, I was in the Ritz with Turner and Ermert when Himmler came in. He could not stand the sight of me; we had run up against each other when I was in the Reich Finance Ministry. "What are you doing here?" he asked. "I am Stadtkommissar for Paris," I was able to answer. I had to show Rosenberg around Paris. And Milch. And Goering, whom I already knew. Then I had to spend evenings with these bigwigs. I had to take Goebbels to the theater. I showed Speer around the *boulevards périphériques* and heard him say that the führer had appointed him minister in order to make Berlin the world's most beautiful city and I hadn't the right to make Paris its competitor.

I was often in the Majestic arguing for hours on end with Dr. Michel. Debré, the representative of the Hotel Association, ate with us often. Among my friends were Dubonnet, maker of the famous apéritif, and his American wife. Of Bousquet I have only delightful memories; he was jovial and didn't take it all too seriously. Hotels and restaurants whose ownership had been English were taken over, and many of them, including Maxim's, were then managed by the Berlin restaurateur Otto Horcher, who was my right-hand man for a while in Paris. Another well-known restaurateur, Walterspiel, took over the running of bistros that had been enemy-owned, perhaps thirty or forty in all, out of a total of four thousand in the city. Restaurants and nightclubs would put in to me for their allocation of wines and champagne. The owners of these places would claim to have a monthly consumption of twenty thousand bottles of champagne, say, at a cost of five marks, but then would sell off a portion of their allocation at twenty marks a bottle on the black market.

Big business came to me, Krupp, Daimler-Benz, who had branches dealing with the French. We arranged contracts for the French through my economic section. Its head, Fischer, one day told me of a French industrialist who had had his third lunch with him, bringing a different woman every time—he was aghast. I wanted laborers to go to Germany of their own free will, not compulsorily, as Sauckel planned. In each factory, I instituted a place where men could enlist if they so chose. In the factories it was too easy for SS officers to rush in and pick out anyone. I resisted that, and wrote critical reports on the subject to the military administration, so much so that Sauckel one day came into my office and had a shouting match with me. That was the reason for my dismissal. On January 15, 1943, I had to leave Paris. One last thing I recall: just before my departure, I was dining in the Ritz with Frau von Stohrer, wife of our ambassador in Madrid. It must have been November 8, 1942, for that night we heard of the Allied landings in North Africa, and I said that the war was lost. Knochen was present, and though he was easily put into a rage, on that occasion he made no comment.

Dr. Herbert Eckelmann

I had been an *Oberregierungsrat* in the Reich Ministry of Economic Affairs, until I was suddenly transferred into uniform and in the space of eight days became a soldier. We were stationed at Giessen, with the brief of considering economic aspects of the German army and those areas which it might occupy. In the event of the occupation of France, preplanning had to be done—we were working out what it would be essential to take over, what kind of special staffs would be required, and so on. We had designated officials for those spheres in which they were already specialists, for instance Freiherr von Mahs from the Reichsbank to head the economic section, or Reinecke to be in charge of agriculture. Men like these were selected from the civil service or from industry on the basis of their skills or their knowledge of France. Without a doubt it was thoroughly professional. We tried our best to bring our conclusions to the attention of the soldiers, but they were preoccupied with war games. From the start, our intention was to make the occupation of France as bearable as possible for the French, while fulfilling our own aims for Germany and the war. We thought, we hoped, that this was compatible.

When war broke out, I was transferred to Lille to join the staff of General von Blaskowitz, whose instructions were to prepare for military government in France. Blaskowitz then moved from Lille to Compiègne, but was not himself appointed military governor, as had been expected. He was billeted in the château of the Comte de Vienne, and I shall never forget how Blaskowitz and he greeted each other with the chivalry of an age long gone. Furthermore, the Comte's son had just been taken prisoner. Every evening Blaskowitz invited one or more of his staff officers to dine with him, and I happened to be next to him when the news reached him that advance army columns had reached Paris and would enter on the following morning. He ordered me, as an economist, into Paris to report on questions of supplies and traffic control and so on. So in I went, with an intelligence officer, in a military car. We were distressed to observe how frightened the French were of the Germans. Corn was ripening in the fields, but the farms had been abandoned. I saw soldiers milking bellowing cows with distended udders. The roads were blocked with returning refugees.

On that first day, June 14, I reported to General von Bockelburg, and I met with Colonel Speidel and Hasso von Etzdorf, the Foreign Office liaison officer, in the Crillon. The last two were discussing what should be done about the American embassy, and on their own initiative they had cabled Washington that the ambassador was safe. I was placed under the command of General von Briesen, and he asked me to accompany him to Versailles for the presentation of campaign medals to the soldiers—for me that was the most impressive moment of that whole week. The next day, when we came to give an account of ourselves, the military commander said that the von Briesen division had to evacuate Paris immediately, thanks to the disastrous influence upon them, in a bare twenty-four hours, of French womanhood.

I was quartered at first in the Ritz. The French could not have been more helpful; they were anxious to restore normality. Once they realized that we were paying, tradesmen were thankful that we were there to buy in the shops. The older generation found it hard to go against the propaganda they had been fed about us, and the first successful contacts were established through the youth. At that stage I had no dealings with the French administration. On the other hand, the SS, under Knochen, had its own men and offices already being prepared; there you could see the first of the distinctions and rivalries set up by Hitler, which were later to tell so much against us.

I started off on the staff of Streccius, the first military governor. My office was in one of the hotel rooms of the Majestic. I was in the Wirtschaftsabteilung, or Economic Section, which employed eight men, and my responsibility was for employment, wages, and salaries. To begin with, unemployment was acute. It was up to the French to restart things. We sent for the men from the relevant French ministries, asked them what their procedures were, and what instructions we could give which might be helpful. Weekly consultations were instituted. Labor was always a thorny question—we were to have a clash with Hitler on sending French workers to Germany. We never believed they should be sent on a compulsory program. Stülpnagel, who took over from Streccius, was a stickler for detail; we called him "Habakkuk" and did not think very much of him. He brought on himself all sorts of trouble with the administration. His cousin and successor was a most intelligent man, who spoke good French. Every Wednesday he put on civilian clothes and wandered off on his own through Paris, looking into cinemas, shops, workplaces, poking his nose into things. The French have much to be grateful for where he is concerned.

At the beginning of 1943, I succeeded Rademacher as Stadtkommissar. Turner, before him, had been a major in the reserves but had also held the rank of SS general; he had made a scene because the sentries had only stood to attention for him when he thought they ought to have presented arms. Schaumburg, retiring on account of his age, was followed by a cavalry general, von Boineburg, whose chief of staff—my military counterpart, therefore—was Colonel Jay. On Boineburg's orders, Jay was the man who actually arrested the entire SS leadership on July 20. Boineburg, like me, lived in the Hotel Raphael, although the Villa Coty was at his disposal.

Under me were twenty-three men, all experienced, all French speakers. During the occupation there were very few modifications of personnel. I was responsible for all economic affairs to do with Paris, such as supplies of coal, oil, gasoline, the means of provisions, down to traffic and such things as forestry. Thus the official government shoot at Rambouillet came under me, and we had trouble with the head keeper one day when Field Marshal Hugo Sperrle shot a doe in season. Food supplies were my worst headache. And also how to create the political atmosphere in which to allow French industrial plants and factories to have an unimpeded output. We needed peace and quiet in Paris—that is to say, conditions of security in which German orders could be fulfilled. Armaments for the Wehrmacht were supervised by my representatives in French factories. General Thomas, in the Majestic, was responsible for arms procurement. For the French, it was not without its dangers to know me, so it was better to stay out of their company socially. I loved Paris. I went for long walks by myself through the streets, I went to the opera, but looking back on it, perhaps I was too desk-bound.

My opposite number was Taittinger, a distinguished man, an industrialist from Lorraine. I owe a lot to Taittinger. *"Monsier Eckelmann,"* were his opening words, *"je suis français et vous êtes allemand."* [*In Taittinger's book,* . . . et Paris ne fut pas detruit, *compliments to Eckelmann are reciprocally to be found.*] I decided to pay him a formal visit, with Boineburg, and though this was forbidden in principle, Stülpnagel gave us leave to do so. It was in the Hôtel de Ville. On each step of the ceremonial staircase stood a Garde Républicaine. At the top was Taittinger, in a tailcoat. Boineburg had insisted on the correct protocol, and Taittinger had promised that we would be received exactly as the Prince of Wales had been. Taittinger stuck to his line, which was: I will never do anything against the interests of this city and its inhabitants. Your interests must be to keep Paris safe and orderly, and in that respect, I'm your man.

Of course Paris was far more of a normal city than anywhere in Germany. Taittinger argued that if we closed down the horse racing, Parisians would only grumble about us instead of grumbling about the race results. The greatest obstacles we had were with coal deliveries. Hitler had placed the Pas-de-Calais and the Nord under the administration of Brussels. No coal from these sources came to Paris. We had to try to thrash it out with the Lille Feldkommandantur. Taittinger's advice was to try to obtain sufficient coal to heat at least the cinemas, so that audiences there were all right. The maintenance people came up with a generator in the cellars which was pedaled, as though on a treadmill. The Sèvres factory had to have special coal rations to fulfill an order for Goering.

To build the Atlantic Wall, we needed a massive French work force, and I went to see the minister of labor to procure it. No problem at all. We also had to see Pétain in that connection, and as I was then about to go on a trip to North Africa, the old gentleman said to me, *"Bon voyage, mon cher."* I saw him again, that last April, when he came to Paris and was greeted at the door of Notre-Dame by Cardinal Suhard, Boineburg, and me. It was unforgettable. The cathedral was dark, but a tricolor hung there. When we came out, the whole crowd went wild with enthusiasm and could not be held back by the police.

In my experience there was hardly any sabotage. Ritter was shot. I was sorry about that but could understand French feelings. Attacks on personnel, or on goods and services, were not on any scale that can properly be called sabotage. Cooperation was the order of the day. Take the work force. Designers, engineers, and specialists would come from Germany to supervise French production so that our effort was satisfied to the greatest possible extent. Nobody and nothing in France undermined our programs. Even with the French workers in Germany there was peace right to the end. We thought we could not impose our habit of *Eintopfgericht* [*all dishes served as one course*] on workers in factories; they had to have separate courses in their canteens. But our men ate in these canteens too, and the French adopted one-course meals—well, in the end, everybody swapped around! In Paris, it became a little more problematic to cater to the immediate needs of the population as the occupation drew to its close. French trucks convoying the goods in from the country-side began to be attacked by the resistance, so we had to provide German escorts.

Then my new—and last—commanding officer, von Choltitz, received his scorched-earth orders that Paris was to be destroyed: gas, electricity, power stations, metro, the lot. Choltitz summoned me to hear my opinion, and I answered that on military grounds such destruction was pointless, it would not help our soldiers, and the means of destruction were lacking. [*Von Choltitz in a memoir explained that on August 15 he had received a delegation headed by Eckelmann and composed of the officials responsible for services such as gas, water, electricity, and the post. If there were dynamiting, the officials hoped that it might be performed in such a way as not to jeopardize living conditions. "I let each of these gentlemen speak his mind, and was deeply impressed by the tact, intelligence, and courage with which they presented their requests."*] On the seventeenth, Abetz came to Choltitz to explain that he was removing the Vichy regime. With Choltitz I inspected the *Stützpunkte* [*fortified blockhouses*] we had built, and saw how they were manned by dear old daddies. As luck would have it, nobody bothered them. On the twentieth, Speer came, we talked it out openly, and we agreed that it was too late in the day for any destruction. Had we simply marched out of Paris along with the rest, however, we would certainly have been condemned to death by a military tribunal. So we remained at our post in the Meurice, in the Kommandant's lodgings there.

On the twenty-fifth we ate luncheon in the dining room of the Meurice. Jay asked Choltitz what orders he had to give, for the soldiers could not be expected to continue fighting after their senior officers had been captured. Choltitz replied that he had no new orders to give. The Americans had allowed French tanks in first, and down the rue de Rivoli came three or four heavy American tanks and some lighter armor and a couple of soldiers—we could watch from the windows. Choltitz's bed-room and sitting room were on the fourth floor, and he and Colonel von Unger and Jay and I and a few orderlies had retired up there. Then in came an older man in a German uniform with the insignia of the resistance on it, and a hammer and sickle on his helmet. He manipulated the bolt of his Sten gun, and that was too much for Choltitz, who told him to rip off his badges. At that point there came a French lieu-tenant who saluted and asked whether he had the honor to be speaking to General von Choltitz. Jay recognized the fellow; they had competed against each other in international riding events before the war. I used to win then, Jay reminded this man, now you are the winner. To Choltitz the Frenchman said, "Will you give the order for a cease-fire?" And Choltitz answered characteristically, "Since you are in my bedroom, it's a little late for it."

We were led off to Leclerc. Out in the street a huge mob had already assembled, and they screamed and spat at us, which was none too good [*nicht so furchtbar schön*]. A French Red Cross van with two high-society ladies in it then drove us through Paris to the Préfecture de Police where I was preparing myself to be sen-tenced to death. Instead, the behavior was perfectly correct. About ten of us German officers were driven to the Gare Montparnasse, and on the way the resistance men were polite. De Gaulle had arrived, and was with other officers, when Leclerc and Choltitz turned up. They agreed that fighting at the *Stützpunkte* should be broken off. It fell to me and an escorting French officer to make the arrangements. We drove out toward Vincennes, which was where I knew there were German troops. I told the Frenchman that he might be shot at and should therefore wave a white handkerchief. We crossed into the German lines and there my French officer was held prisoner, though really he had come under a flag of truce. My conscience still bothers me a little about this. But I was free. I had been in the hands of the French only during that one day. And I'd lived through the occupation of Paris from the first day to the last.

In our own interests we had tried to be on the best of terms with the French. Once we had left, our French partners were badly in the lurch, accused of being collaborators. They tried to exculpate themselves, telling tales of how wretchedly they had been treated. In fact, as I saw it, the French administration had been excellent, their civil servants highly professional, the *préfets* first-class, one and all conscientious men.

Werner Zachmann

The four million inhabitants of the region known to the Germans as Gross-Paris could not commute to work on foot. Public transport had to be maintained as efficiently as circumstances allowed. Werner Zachmann had been a transport engineer since 1926, with the Dresden tramway system, before his transfer to the relevant section of the military administration. Some aspects of public transport, however, were not purely administrative. The buses in which the Jews were driven away during the Grande Rafle, for instance, were the property of the state-owned bus company. On the metro Jews were allowed to travel only in the rear carriage. On points like these Zachmann had no light to shed, claiming that he had been merely a technician, and adding flatly that he did not even remember seeing such a thing as a yellow star on anyone.

I spent a couple of days in Marburg, the clearing station for all personnel posted into the various military administrations within the Reich. I was to report to the Kommandantur in the Place de l'Opéra, but I had no idea what my job in Paris was to be. I arrived by train in July 1941. Someone in the Kommandantur checked my papers and sent me on to the Majestic. I took the metro. Then I was told that I had to find Rademacher in the Chambre des Députés, and so I learned that I was to be in charge of the metro, the omnibuses, and oddly the Eiffel Tower, because of its elevators. In addition to this first responsibility for *Personen-Nahverkehr* [*public transport*], I also took over the running of the Nahverkehrsbevollmächtiger section [*issuing authorizations to regional traffic, notably the permits for private cars*] in 1943. A private car could be driven only if there was some overriding reason and the owner could not use the metro—the fire brigade, industrial transportation, and the like.

First I called on Paul Martin, director general of the metro. Among the directors of the metro and the state-owned bus company, which was incorporated into the metro in 1942, were several with whom I had regular personal contacts: Pons, Devillers, Mariage, and others whose names now escape me. Baron de Neuville ran a privately owned bus company with almost three hundred buses. He invited me to dine. The butler wore white gloves. At this huge table, laid with silver, the Baron and I sat toasting each other, just the two of us. Every day I was in contact with French specialists and interpreters. The liaison man from the metro was Boissier; the man from the bus company was called Duleau. I had the advantage of having been appointed by the Germans to do a job benefiting the French. The metro functioned almost like in peacetime, from five in the morning until midnight. Only a few stations were closed down. I had ten thousand men working in the metro. I could support the French in their petitions for electricity, workshops, gas, steel for the repair of tracks, and of course permits for them to keep their personnel. I could prevent men from being deported for the STO. The men would receive their requisition order, the directors of the metro or the bus company would ask me to intervene, I would apply to the Sauckel Dienststelle, and it worked. Sometimes there would be the odd dispute or fight between members of the the Wehrmacht (who were entitled to use the underground free of charge) and employees of the metro. In the interests of those working for the metro I used to intervene, usually with success, putting the case to whichever was the competent German military department. Nothing ever came of such incidents. Acts of sabotage were unknown. More dreadful things happen today in peacetime Cologne than ever on the metro in wartime Paris.

Bus traffic was limited in the city center; there was little or none. Buses ran where there was no metro. Buses used these gas cylinders which could drive for 30 kilometers and be tanked up again at fixed points beside the road. We laid the pipes. Whenever a German *Dienststelle* [*any department of the administration*] wanted buses, the request came through us. For example, there might have been an air raid and workmen were needed to clear up. Several thousand buses were kept in readiness, able to leave the garages only with my authorization. Only a thousand buses operated regularly. We also ran a new trolley-bus line and laid a stretch of metro. German experts visited us, and we would go out inspecting with our French colleagues. [*He shows me a photograph of himself, in breeches and boots, with General von Boineburg and three directors of the metro, on an official visit to the metro sports ground.*] And a delegation of French transport engineers came with me on a big tour in Dresden, Munich, Salzburg, where there was also a new trolley-bus line, and Berlin, where the Burgermeister laid on a big reception for them. Our concern on this journey to Germany was to study transport problems and to exchange ideas between technicians, both French and German. Meetings took place in a very friendly atmosphere, and the best of spirits prevailed. They were all very nice people.

It is quite correct that the average Frenchman lived a virtually normal life. Naturally the supply of some provisions was curtailed, as happens in all countries at war. As I saw for myself in the circle of my French acquaintances, there were some tight squeezes, for instance in the delivery of fuels to heat apartments and houses. But my colleagues in the Wirtschafts-Abteilung of the military administration had taken good care to make certain that no Frenchman had to go hungry. We had the framework for good relationships all around. In ordinary shops I bought things like coffee and chocolate for my wife which I could never have found in Germany. The restaurants were full, but expensive. In our hotels we were well catered to, though on account of the war we could not have exactly what we wanted. I was in the Hotel Prince de Galles, then in the Hotel Wagram by the Tuileries metro station. Four or five big theaters showed good German films. We went to the Lido and the Folies-Bergères. I looked up a French doctor I knew before the war and met plenty of friends, married couples—we took trips together on the Seine. I can't complain. I'm glad to have lived through that period while being able to continue my profession.

On about August 20 the girls on the staff, the *Stabshelferinnen,* left Paris on trucks. After the capitulation, those of my colleagues who had remained behind, as well as members of other sections, fell prisoners to the Americans. I was ordered to stay. The only soldiers about belonged to one of the garrison battalions. The metro had ceased to run. I moved into the Crillon. Two tanks came first. A few shots were fired into the Crillon, and we gathered in the big dining room to see what would happen next. The streets were wide open, empty. Then trucks arrived, and some French soldiers, and after them a crowd of thousands, all yelling. We were escorted from the Hotel Crillon to the Préfecture in French trucks. Next day we were taken in French police cars to a police barracks in Paris, and then transferred by American soldiers to a camp in the French countryside, and so, via England, finally to the United States.

Maurice Bardèche

Since the war Bardèche has engaged in polemics on behalf of Vichy and the extreme right in general. He is also the editor of the collected works of Robert Brasillach, with whom he once cooperated on a history of the cinema. He is married to Brasillach's sister.

I published my thesis on Balzac in 1940 and became a professor at the Sorbonne until 1941, when I taught at the University of Lille. At the Sorbonne I was thirty. Most of my colleagues knew I was the brother-in-law of Brasillach, but I was never in any way embarrassed by the relationship. The occupation changed life materially because of privations of every kind: the street scene had changed, what with using a bicycle instead of a car. Throughout the war, the conduct of the German soldiers was correct and even cordial: the German forces behaved as though on garrison duties and gave fine concerts in the Luxembourg or paraded at the Tomb of the Unknown Soldier. Difficulties began with the winter, and with queueing, but even the latter was accepted courageously as the price of defeat.

The Rive Gauche bookshop was one of those generous but clumsy ideas the Germans came up with. On the advice of the Institut, the Germans put my brother Henri in to manage what was intended to be the best bookshop in Paris for French and German books. After 1942, the Rive Gauche had the monopoly of books for prisoners of war. The name commemorated a friend of Robert's called Annie Jamet, who before the war had founded a Rive Gauche group that committed itself to a policy of rapprochement and friendship between France and Germany. Her husband, Henri Jamet, was one of the friends of Otto Abetz, the German ambassador to Paris; Jamet had turned down official jobs that had been offered to him and only, under the Administration of Jewish Property, took over the publishers Calmann-Lévy. From time to time receptions were held at the German embassy in the rue de Lille, and Abetz used to say that if he had a million collaborators he could hope to obtain peace terms favorable to France.

Je Suis Partout had a sort of anarchy about it, and the crisis in 1943 came about in part because Robert wanted to put a stop to that. He also thought he no longer had the right to engage the young in an adventure that might well stamp the rest of their lives. The Germans had launched into an enterprise that might have been ill-advised, but since they had done so it became a matter of choosing between them and the victory of bolshevism. In my heart of hearts I approved of collaboration, both as a necessary rapprochement between our two countries and as the only safeguard of Europe against the USSR. We all had the impression that our policy was systematically undermined by resistants, whether the Communist or the Gaullist variety. Their provocation made it difficult for the French, and we saw them as saboteurs and traitors. Our conviction was that the war had been wanted by the Jews. Contrary to what was said after 1945, during almost the entire occupation the majority of the French people looked with indifference on what was happening to the Jews. The Grande Rafle passed almost unnoticed. Only foreign Jews were involved. Many Jewish shopkeepers who had set up in Parisian districts seemed to be continuing to do their business. The wearing of the Jewish star did not appear to be persecution. I remember walking one day to the Place du Luxembourg, and we saw how many were wearing the yellow star. How amusing, we thought, how odd that there are so many of them, whom we simply did not know about in our district. Everybody in France thought that the concentration camps were analogous to the prisoner-of-war camps, and only Jewish leaflets circulated secretly to give news of some other camps.

Véronique Rebatet

I came to Paris in 1931 to do a doctorate in law, and met Rebatet at the time. We married in Galati in 1933. I was not interested in politics. The man I married was a film critic under the pseudonym of François Vinneuil for Action Française and *Je Suis Partout,* as well as a critic of music and art for the *Revue Universelle.* He lived simply—actually when I married him the rent on his apartment had not been paid for some time. I had to settle the backlog and have furniture sent to us from Rumania.

He had been influenced by Maurras. We went to Italy in April 1936, with Paul Achard [*she draws my attention to* Les Mémoires d'un fasciste, *Vol. II, p. 115: ". . . the elegant Alfieri, minister of Popular Culture, had received us in Rome, with the most refined courtesy, for a film congress . . ."*]. The *Je Suis Partout* team as a whole admired Mussolini and Degrelle. Democracy rubbed Rebatet up the wrong way; he thought France might have to be conquered before it could pull itself up. He went to Cologne and was struck by the Hitler Youth. He liked their songs. In 1938 he went on a walking tour in Germany, and he applauded the Munich Agreement. So he evolved out of the anti-German ideas of Action Française. And of course he agreed with them about the Jews. He was first put on to the Jews when Pierre Gaxotte asked him to write an article on foreigners in France.

When he saw how the front was collapsing in June 1940, he sent me to his family house in Moras, in case Paris was bombarded. After the armistice, when he had been demobilized, he came to find me there and to start writing *Les Décombres.* Then he received the telegram from Laubreaux to come to Vichy, which he did. So we returned to Paris a couple of months later. It was easy to make the journey—and why not? The Germans did not disturb the public. The population easily accepted the occupation. Paris had never been so brilliant culturally. Jacques Becker, Chomette and the brother of René Clair, Autant-Lara, Grémillon, a Communist, Marcel Carné, were all making films after Rebatet's heart. He was also on the edge of the Céline circle, with Marcel Aymé, Gen Paul the painter, Ralph Soupault. His close friends included Brasillach, with whom we often went out, Georges Blond, Dr. Paul Gúerin, who wrote the medical column in *Je Suis Partout,* and Emil Vuillermoz. Monsieur Nasenta, the director of the Galerie Charpentier, put on the most fascinating art exhibitions. The *esprit français* had plenty of scope. I never saw a better performance of *Tristan* than the one with Germaine Lubin as Isolde [*in 1941, at the*

Opéra]. Rebatet loved Wagner. And he went on the trip to Germany with musicians like Honegger and Schmitt, during which they met Richard Strauss and Léhar. Jean Bérard, director of Pathe-Marconi, was with them [*he was an advocate of collaboration, a strong anti-Semite, with a mistress, Vera, who was Rumanian-Jewish*]. My maiden name was Popovici; the rumor that I was Jewish was false. The Germans mostly bored Rebatet—he found them heavy—and the only friend he had among them was Moras of the Propaganda Staffel; our country house was at Moras, and the coincidence of name pleased him.

The row at *Je Suis Partout* had complex motivations. [Mémoires d'un fasciste, *Vol. II, gives Rebatet's version: "I must admit that I could hardly decipher Brasillach's reaction to the drama. I could have understood it had our friend said, 'The fall of Mussolini marks the beginning of the end of Germany, who will lose the war in a catastrophic fracas.' We had believed in her victory, and based all our actions on that quasi-certitude. . . . Robert sent me letter after letter to Moras, trying to convince me most affectionately that we could no longer write political articles in* Je Suis Partout. *. . . I saw that Robert had changed his objectives. It was no longer a question of transforming* Je Suis Partout *into a purely literary magazine—which was chimerical, as I had at once spotted—but of abandoning it wholesale. Robert all of a sudden did not wish to work any longer with Charles Lesca . . . whom he accused of fast footwork on the financial side. . . . That was a way of warding off accusations of cowardice, which troubled Robert. . . . Our friend persisted in the quarrel, supported by Georges Blond and especially by Henri Poulain, our subeditor and the only member of the team without talent as a writer. . . ."*] Rebatet used to hold Poulain responsible for the death of Brasillach. *Je Suis Partout* had a dinner once a month, but women were not allowed. Once Madame Blond and another wife sat on purpose at an adjoining table in the restaurant, but the men sang such vulgar songs that they had to leave. Rebatet was sober, he had a lovely voice too, but when he started to drink he turned into a stentor. I wasn't in Paris at the time; I was with my father in Bucharest. At some point Brasillach wanted to provoke a duel with Lesca. Laubreaux was full of himself, quick to take offense, and immoral—he was always bringing along any little bit of a girl.

Denoel said that there was not enough paper for *Les Décombres*. Perhaps a million people read it in the war. Afterward Rebatet started to write his novel *Les Deux Etendards*. [*It was finished when Rebatet had served his prison sentence, and published by Gallimard in 1952. The 1,312-page epic is dedicated "to Véronique, my dear wife. For her love, her courage, and her fidelity."*] We used to receive phone calls at three in the morning to call us *salauds*. So at the end we went to live in a hotel, before leaving for Sigmaringen. If we had stayed, there would have been a settling of scores—they came with a machine gun to our house in Neuilly after our departure and sacked the place. [*Denoel, the publisher, did stay and was murdered.*]

Charles Filippi

I met Philippe Henriot in 1932, when I was a law student in Toulouse, and I was dazzled by his character and oratorical skill. I had complete confidence in him. By 1939 he was a pacifist, arguing that we were not materially prepared for war. Afterward he was straightforwardly for Pétain. He lived in Bordeaux but came to Vichy and wrote a weekly article for *Gringoire* as well as being speaker for the Ministry of

Propaganda. After June 22, 1941, he took the line that this was a struggle against communism and bolshevism, and he became a collaborator in the full sense of the word. He was a good Catholic; anti-Semitism of his kind derived from church doctrine.

I had been an officer and was in barracks when I heard de Gaulle's broadcast. If somebody had then suggested that we ought to join him, I might well have agreed, but nobody did. I returned to being a lawyer in Toulouse and took up regional propaganda for the Milice—it was Henriot who first asked me to enroll as a *milicien,* and later to become his private secretary. I wore a blue uniform with the gamma emblem on it. At the outset the Milice consisted of professionals, landowners, and squires, the bourgeoisie, those who had followed Maurras.

Collaboration paid better dividends than resistance. We tried to choose the lesser evil. In June 1944 I accompanied Henriot on a six-day visit to Germany. In Frankfurt and Leipzig the houses might have been destroyed but the factories were in good order. We visited Arno Breker; it was a Sunday, and the promenaders were out on a sunny afternoon. In Berlin we called on Goebbels; he had a bust of Napoleon in his antechamber. And while we were in Berlin we heard that the Allies had landed in Normandy. Henriot spoke in a factory in which there were French workers. The way he handled them much impressed the Germans. He talked to Sauckel and to Dr. Ley of the Arbeiterfront in an attempt to improve facilities like writing letters and receiving parcels. I realized only very late that the Germans would lose; they had impressed me with their talk of secret weapons.

On about June 25, Laval in Vichy asked Henriot to attend a cabinet meeting in Paris, to help restrain the ultras who wanted to declare war on England. He told me he would attend and catch the night train back in order not to have to sleep in Paris. The cabinet meeting was postponed for a day, so he had to stay. His bodyguard, Pantalacci, was a cousin of mine who had been invalided out of the LVF and couldn't return to his native Corsica. On the night of the attack he was on duty. Henriot had gone to the Gare de l'Est to see off his son, who was returning to Germany in the NSKK [*German motorized labor force*], and then went with his wife to a cinema on the Champs-Elysées. Getting back to the Ministry, he dismissed Pantalacci, who had not wanted to leave, offering instead to sleep on a camp bed by the door. Twice Henriot's personal telephone rang in the night. Later his killers denied that they had done this. Madame Henriot was nervous and wanted to telephone Darnand for protection—he had only to pick up the telephone and some *miliciens* would have come around. If Henriot had not been murdered, he would have gone to Germany and, as I knew him, followed Laval's path. He would consequently, like Laval, have abstained in Germany from any intervention into politics.

Robert Soulat

The events of February 6, 1934, politicized me. I was fourteen. The PPF did not yet exist, so I came to *francisme.* My party number was 21,193, though there weren't that many of course, probably not half. It was easy to approach them. I went to three or four meetings, and then in 1936 meetings were banned. In 1937 I was in Germany, on holiday in a youth camp. The following year I enlisted in the army, in the 24th Regiment de Tirailleurs Tunisiens; I didn't think there would be a war, but I wanted to be a soldier. I was in Belgium with the First Army in May 1940 and taken prisoner. One day in February 1943 I was in a working party unloading sacks of sugar at the camp in Glogau, in Silesia, where I had been sent from my own camp at Sagan, when I was told to report to the office. As part of the *Relève,* I was free.

A train took me back to Compiègne. To get one's ration card, one had to register, and so I learned that the class of 1940 had to go to Germany for the STO. So although I'd just been released from Germany, the French authorities were proposing to send me straight back. They agreed to a delay and dispatched me to work in a foundry at Puteaux. To hell with it! I went instead to the Organisation Todt [OT], at 33, Champs-Elysées. I was given a course for three months, with about seventy others, learning telephone engineering. I lived in a hotel requisitioned in the rue de Cévennes in the fifteenth arrondissement. We had tickets like everyone else, and a recreation center in the rue de La Boétie. I was initially allowed to eat in the OT Heim in the rue de Berri. Later on, the French and other *Ausländer* had to eat in a less smart restaurant in the rue de La Boétie. I was paid three thousand francs a month. I wore uniform all day, and people mistook me for a German. The things I overheard about myself—how I laughed! I had no sense of being in a minority. I felt that I was part of the German army, which had occupied the whole of Europe. I thought I was only a small cog, but still . . . this was the right thing for me. What mattered was that I was anti-Communist; the Russian danger was far worse than the German danger. I never liked Jews, but the Bucard party before the war had not emphasized anti-Semitism. Others with me in the OT were mostly PPF and we didn't like the PPF, which was a mistake since it had the greatest chance of success. It was political cadres which Bucard lacked. In September 1943 I took part in a march of Bucard people in Paris. At the end of that year I was stationed in the Sarthe, still repairing telephone lines for the OT.

In May 1944 I volunteered for the German navy, but after training we were all sent to the Waffen SS. I wanted to go right to the very end. I didn't see how it would end, but I was in it right up to my neck. You are like a marble on a slope; you just roll down. There were Frenchmen, Walloons, Letts—we went to Greifenburg, where the Charlemagne Division was being formed. Then we went to Komitz in Poland, to Wildflecken, and so to Pomerania at the end of February 1945. Speaking German by then, I was an interpreter at staff headquarters. Otherwise I might have been with the others in Berlin at the end.

III. EPILOGUE

October 23, 1979, was briskly autumnal in Cologne. By half past six in the morning I was standing on the steps of the courthouse in the Appellplatz. The trial of the Paris Gestapo—as the three accused were labeled, for the sake of simplifying—was to begin that day: in all probability the last of the trials of Nazi war criminals. But a courtroom had been provided with seats for about sixty people, and there were hundreds of journalists lining up. Furthermore, by about eight o'clock, about a thousand Jews arriving from Paris had marched from the railway station into the Appellplatz. They chanted, *"Lischka Mörder, Hagen Mörder, Heinrichsohn Mörder."* As many of them as possible sought to enter the small courtroom and had to be excluded. Passions rose.

An uneasy conscience was visibly at work among the Germans present. The police, the court attendants, did not enjoy holding back and coercing people wearing yellow badges that proclaimed "Auschwitz" or *"déporté"* or *"Juif de France."* A bigger courtroom was in fact available, but some luminary had decided to try to make this trial as invisible as possible. Shouting and scuffling with embarrassed policemen were the result. I obtained an entrance pass. Photographers and television crews squeezed and swarmed into the court; they stood on the benches, on the judge's desk.

Toward eleven o'clock the judge at last appeared, pale and tense, but firm. He had the moral authority to control the situation in the room. Proceedings began, although outside the window the syllables of the chant fell hard and regular: *"Lischka Mörder, Hagen Mörder, Heinrichsohn Mörder."* And the accused were brought into the dock.

For some time I could not take my eyes off Kurt Lischka: he, I noticed, averted his. A powerfully built, sharkish man, for all his seventy years. His head seemed molded around brutality. His hands were huge, the fingers like implements. So this was the man who had taken over the Jewish Affairs section of the Gestapo in 1938 and organized the Kristallnacht, a pogrom the like of which had not been seen in Europe for many a century. So this was the man who with Knochen had arranged to blow up the seven Paris synagogues and had brought down the first Stülpnagel, and who had directed the Grande Rafle, the man who on July 2, 1942, wrote, "One must accelerate and bring to its conclusion the Final Solution of the Jewish problem in Europe, according to the directives issued in the Reich." Bargatzky, when he was a defense counsel at the military tribunal in the Hotel Raphael, had seen this man in the uniform of an SS *Obersturmbannführer.* Leguay had sat in on conferences with him. He must, one supposed, have been proud to shake hands with Himmler.

Hagen, I recognized from a photograph taken during the summer of 1942. In that photograph, he is standing every inch the eager young SS *Sturmbannführer,* poised, energetic, looking at Laval, who is drawn into himself like a creature of the underworld and an epitome of creepiness, sucking at the usual cigarette, while between them stands Oberg, arms akimbo, like a patronizing schoolmaster. In the background is some dimly classical Paris façade. It is a fearful document. Hagen was so much brighter than Oberg that he was less his deputy than his mentor. A successful company director since the war, he had not changed much, though at sixty-six he had filled out. He looked pink and fresh; he favored polo-necked jerseys. Now and again his expression drooped as if the shadow of his past were passing over it. So that was the man who went to Palestine before the war and taught Eichmann, his traveling companion, the meaning of Zionism.

269

And Heinrichsohn. A somewhat weak, self-indulgent, possibly self-pitying, face. A conventional appearance, but with aging once-blond hair a trifle wispy, to add an individuality of style. For the last good many years he had been a respectable lawyer and mayor of his small town in Bavaria. In 1940, however, when he was only twenty, he had volunteered for his tasks. This was the man who day after day went out to Drancy, inspected that camp, and believed it to be right and proper. He looked at victims but saw only his own power. One witness, Madame Marie Husson, remembers the contrast of his appearance at the time—she uses the classical word *ephebe* to describe him—and his sadism. Another witness, Madame Odette Daltroffe-Baticle, confirms it: "Every night there was a deportation Heinrichsohn was there; it was astonishing to see this young and handsome man, elegant in riding clothes, maltreating us and taking such pleasure in brutalizing children, nearly all of them recalcitrant. His presence was useless; he came because he enjoyed it. I think that among the SS he was one of the most sadistic." On the railway siding at Drancy–Le Bourget, this man must have been the last sight that the deportees had before they were sealed into their cattle trucks on the way to death. He was eager to please now, and of the three in the dock the only one to make the least effort, the only one, what is more, to wheedle. To know how his mind had worked, I remember feeling, would be to collide head-on into evil. Meeting one's eyes, he lowered his at once.

Lischka that first day declined to be cross-examined, but in principle, he told the judge, he had no objection to answering questions. *"Lischka Mörder, Hagen Mörder, Heinrichsohn Mörder,"* the French Jews were still shouting as they finally marched away from the Appellplatz through the streets of Cologne, to the evident bafflement and annoyance of the bystanders. No, their blank shut-out faces seemed to declare, this event had nothing to do with them, nothing to do with Germany, with their lives and society, not even with the question of what it means to be a human being. Other people were concerned, and in another country, at another time. One appreciated what kind of an emotional process had gone into ensuring that the courtroom was too small.

Inside that courtroom, the defense lawyers were to put into words exactly this rejection of the truth. Their arguments were the equivalent of the dumb and insolent stares on the faces of the general public. Their clients were innocent, they maintained. Internment had to be distinguished from deportation, and deportation from extermination. Their clients happened merely to have been engaged on certain social policies whose ends had been unforeseeable. Their clients had known nothing of genocide; their clients had personally lent no hand to the Final Solution—if these sad things occurred, then others had been responsible, for their clients were first and foremost dutiful SS men, good citizens and kind parents. It is always the fault of someone else. But there are the documents, signed Lischka, Hagen, Heinrichsohn: there are their cables to Berlin, to Eichmann, the deportation orders, the train details, the convoy lists, the memoranda, the dossiers. To listen to the prevarications and misrepresentations, the downright subterfuges being fudged up in that court, was to be torn between pain and rage. I never left without a headache.

In other trials of war criminals in Germany, every conceivable legal device has been used to stall, to extend, and finally to frustrate a judgment. In this particular case, attempts to see justice done have dragged on since 1945. It was not for want of trying that thirty-four years passed before the trial could proceed. Immediately after the war Lischka was handed over to the Czechs to answer for his involvement in the murder of two Czech generals. By 1948 he was back again in internment in the British zone of Germany. Hagen too was held by the British. By 1950 both had been handed over to the German authorities, who were then responsible for bringing charges against them. So poorly drafted were the relevant treaty clauses between the Allies and the Germans that the latter were under no legal obligation to return Lischka and Hagen for trial in France, although warrants were out there for their arrest. Almost a decade passed while the German government sheltered behind this legal imbroglio. In the event, a tribunal in Paris could do no more than sentence Lischka and Hagen *in absentia* to life imprisonment.

In 1956, Heinrichsohn was similarly sentenced *in absentia* to death. The French charge against him specifies how on August 15, 1944, he had been a member of a killer squad which had gone to the Paris station of Pantin, to take five Frenchmen off the deportation train already at a platform. One of them was Colonel André Rondenay, de Gaulle's military representative in Paris. The killer squad had then driven the men out to a village, Domont, in the Seine-et-Oise, shot them there out of hand, and ordered the local feldgendarmerie to bury the corpses. Commanding the killer squad was an SS officer, Count Alexander de Kreutz, who was actually born in Petrograd in 1907. Back they had all gone to the rue des Saussaies, "to quaff champagne," in the words of Heinrichsohn's official accusation, "in accordance with a custom then prevailing among the German police of an 'executioners' banquet,' as it was significantly known."

Perhaps they really have managed to erase from their consciences the memory of their deeds. Perhaps they really have come to imagine that they sat in the SS and SD offices in Paris passing around meaningless paperwork, like so many genial businessmen. Looking at the accused in the dock, I came to believe that they did not fully realize what it was they were charged with. They listened to the defense lawyers with interest; they absorbed the casuistries which would make others responsible for what they did. The alternative demanded that they look into themselves and ask whether it would not have been better, for the sake of humanity, had they never been born.

It is pointless to interview them. Corrupting, too. A former Nazi, or a French Fascist, come to that, can perhaps provide firm facts or testimony, but they find it too hard to face their own reality. All, down to the humblest, who participated in genocide share the same psychological impluse to use an interview to explain away their responsibilities, dodging off behind someone else. An interviewer therefore is invited to accept being the mechanism for certifying those lies which these men need to believe in if they are not to find themselves alone with the dreadful facts. Knochen, no less, is still alive and well, though naturally able to provide a doctor's certificate exempting him from being a witness at this trial. Quite recently, when Knochen was interviewed by a French writer, he stated, "Let me say that the greatest crime in history was the extermination of the Jews by Hitler. And the greatest tragedy of my life was the fact that in an indirect way, and quite without being aware of it, I was mixed up in it. At no point did I know, or even suspect, that the Jews of France, deported to the East, were murdered." By the standards of the Lischka-Hagen trial, this rates as a full and frank confession. Knochen was prepared to admit that his work had facilitated Hitler, who was otherwise apparently on his own in his crime, the sole exterminator. Plenty of others who were in the Paris Gestapo are still at large and untroubled by justice in Germany: Dr. Illers, for instance, who once was head of the section, the Peter Hüttemann whom Maurice Toesca called upon in the rue des Saussaies after the July 20 plot, Rudolf Weinberger, who was with Heinrichsohn in the killer squad on that day of August 15, 1944. But to seek them out in an interview is to propose complicity in moral contamination.

Then is it wrong to sit in that court, and listen to the very selfsame fictions which would be trotted out in an interview? Is it futile to bring these men to justice, or on the contrary, is prosecution that special kind of futility which is heroism? And if them, then why not all the others, officers and guards, train conductors, clerks, not only German but French, without whom the mass murdering would have been inconceivable? The desire for justice, I was well aware as I sat in that small court, is vain, but to abdicate it is to concede their moral contamination, to become infected oneself by inaction. The verdict must be imperfect; what matters is that a judge has reached it.

I went back to the court on the day that judgment was supposed to be pronounced. Naturally the defense had found some ingenious way to spin out proceedings, and there was no sentencing. Letters were read out from former SS *Standartenführers* in occupied countries to the effect that they too had known nothing about genocide. So guilt is shuffled around and around in Germany, and the courtrooms grow smaller and smaller, and the faces of the bystanders outside become more and more sullen, dead. The country's Nazi experience has drained character out of it, has exhausted morality. Where is the challenge to come to terms with it, if someone else is always responsible? I found myself powerfully seized by the image of that child's hand which a Red Cross helper had seen waving through the bars of a cattle truck at the start of a long last journey, until struck by a Drancy policeman. In fact Lischka, Hagen, and Heinrichsohn were sentenced respectively to ten, twelve, and six years in prison. No doubt the defense has not said its last word, and quite spontaneously, all manner of exemptions and certificates of ill health will be to hand. Public opinion was hardly touched. Perhaps it really did signify little, for there is no atoning for what these men and their kind did. And that child's hand—is it the image of innocence betrayed or of the human condition?

Flags change outside the lately vacated German staff quarters and hotels in the rue de Rivoli.

Bibliographical Notes

Anyone interested in France during the Second World War will be in debt to two writers in particular, Henry Amouroux (*La Vie des Français sous l'occupation* and *La Grande Histoire des Français sous l'occupation,* of which I was able to consult the first four volumes) and Robert Aron (*Histoire de Vichy* and *Histoire de l'épuration*). Both writers extensively interviewed participants in events and collected much firsthand testimony while it was still possible to do so. Since it is unlikely that the official French archives will have survived without successive weedings, and unlikelier still that any researcher will have access to them in the foreseeable future, the works of Amouroux and Aron will probably not be superseded, nor even much supplemented. Aron does not always give his sources, but Amouroux provides a bibliography which it hardly seems necessary to duplicate here. Among other general books, also with useful bibliographies, are Pascal Ory's *Les Collaborateurs 1940–1945* and Robert O. Paxton's *Vichy France.* Michèle Cotta, *Collaboration 1940–44,* is a good introduction, with emphasis on the collaborationist press. In the absence of archives, the press remains an invaluable source, and one of the most complete and accessible collections is at the Centre de Documentation Contemporaine of Nanterre University. In 1943, Dr. Hermann Eich published *Wege der Französischen Presse* under the auspices of the Propaganda Abteilung. *Histoire de la collaboration* by Saint-Paulien (the pseudonym of Maurice-Yvan Sicard) justifies collaboration with the sleight-of-hand that might be expected of Doriot's former press officer, but is informative as well. Also informative, and from the extreme right, is Henry Coston's *Dictionnaire de la vie politique française.* A series in magazine format, *Les Années Quarante* (published by Tallandier), carries eyewitness reports of the period, and the magazine *Historia* has regularly published the kind of material which is usually kept from the light of day, notably in its special numbers 26 and 27, entitled *La Gestapo en France,* and numbers 39, 40, and 41, entitled *La Collaboration, La Milice,* and *L'Epuration.*

Chapter 1:   The Harvest of 1940
Page
3   A French colonel with two or three of his men . . . : Georges Benoit-Guyod, *L'Invasion de Paris.*

3   In the skeleton of the captured open city . . . : Roger Langeron, *Paris, Juin 40.* As *préfet de police,* Langeron had access to information not available to the public; he also experienced the initial contacts with the incoming German administration. In matters of descriptive detail he can generally be trusted. In 1941 he was removed from his post by the Germans, and his book was thereupon published in London under Gaullist auspices. Allowance must be made, therefore, for the need for self-justification.

5   "there had never been anything like the eerie atmosphere . . .": Robert Murphy, *Diplomat Among Warriors.*

6   Why should Paris be defended . . . : Military developments in France during May and June 1940 have been variously and thoroughly described, notably by Alastair Horne, *To Lose a Battle;* Jacques Benoist-Méchin, *Soixante Jours qui ebranlèrent l'occident;* Henri Michel, *La Seconde Guerre Mondiale,* and *La Drôle de guerre.*

6   "I felt the German advance like a personal threat . . .": Simone de Beauvoir, *La Force de l'age.*

8   "Hitler has played the hand in a magisterial way" and subsequent quotations: André Gide, *Journal 1939–1942.*

8   "Oh! I did not do it . . .": Abel Hermant, *Le Matin,* June 23, 1940.

9   "Along the entire length . . .": Paul Léautaud, *Journal.* In this lifelong work, Volumes XIV, XV, and XVI are devoted to the war years.

10 Clogging the roads westward and southward . . . : The exodus is nowhere better depicted than in Henri Amouroux, *La Vie des Français sous l'occupation,* and his *Le Peuple du désastre 1939–40.*

10–11 The government, doomed already to bear responsibility . . . : Robert Aron, *Histoire de Vichy,* reconstructs these events in a manner which has come to be generally accepted by all parties.

12 Hitler calculated . . . : For Hitler's attitude toward France in 1940, and later, see *Frankreich in Hitlers Europa,* by Eberhard Jäckel, which also has a complete bibliography; also, *La Délégation française auprès de la Commission allemande d'Armistice,* five volumes of documents published by the French government.

12 Breker has described how he had been summarily fetched . . . : Arno Breker, *Im Strahlungsfeld der Ereignisse.*

12 The itinerary . . . : Hans Speidel, *Aus Unserer Zeit.* See also accounts by others present, Gerhard Engel, *Heeresadjutant bei Hitler,* and Otto Dietrich, *The Hitler I Knew.*

12–13 The janitor, Pierre Théodore, known as Glouglou . . . : Serge Lifar, *Ma Vie.*

14–16 In the huge Pétain-Laval literature heat easily triumphs over light, and no single study of either man can be wholeheartedly recommended, unless Geoffrey Warner, *Pierre Laval and the Eclipse of France* and Richard Griffiths, *Marshal Pétain.* A defense of Pétain is *Pétain a sauvé la France* by his lawyer, Maître Jacques Isorni, while Alfred Mallet's *Pierre Laval* is another skillful piece of special pleading. See also Louis Noguères, *Le Véritable Procès du Maréchal Pétain;* Admiral Auphan, *Histoire élémentaire de Vichy;* and the three-volume Hoover Institution *La Vie de la France sous l'occupation* (also available in translation).

Chapter 2:   *Deutschland Siegt an Allen Fronten*

19 "It had no effect . . .": Léautaud, *op. cit.*

19 In his diary he told . . . : André Thérive, *L'Envers du décor 1940–44.*

19 *"Eh bien,* it's most odd . . .": André Halimi, *Chantons sous l'occupation.*

19 "There I was having shared . . .": Yuki Desnos, *Les Confidences de Yuki Desnos.*

22 The Germans, as amorphous as they were busy . . . : For details of the German entry into Paris, see Pierre Audiat, *Paris pendant la guerre,* and Jean-Marc de Fovelle, *L'Entrée des Allemands à Paris.* For posters during this period, see Pierre Bourget and Charles Lacretelle, *Sur les murs de Paris.*

22 Education, suspended just before . . . : Langeron, *op. cit.*

23 "so much so, indeed . . .": De Beauvoir, *op. cit.*

23–24 Sacha Guitry happened to return . . . : Sacha Guitry, *Quatre Ans d'occupation.*

24 During the autumn, when the theater . . . : Hervé le Boterf, *La Vie parisienne sous l'occupation.* This book devotes an entire chapter to the theater, another to the music hall, a third to the cinema, and for the period in general leaves no stone unturned.

24 Marie-Laure de Noailles . . . : Lifar, *op. cit.*

25 "The largesse he dispensed . . .": Arthur Goll and Robert Fizdale, *Misia.*

25 "Fortunately he was sidetracked . . .": Ristelheuber's diary is quoted in Goll and Fizdale, *op. cit.*

26 "Since the armistice . . .": Jean Bérard, *Jean Bérard vous parle* (Inter-France, 1941).

28 For the performance of *Tristan,* see Speidel, Unserer, and Alfred Fabre-Luce, *Journal de la France,* 3 vols.

28 Joliot-Curie's wartime activity is described in Maurice Goldsmith, *Frédéric Joliot-Curie.*

28 "When Bourdet had his bicycle accident . . .": Léautaud, *op. cit.*

29 Sylvia Beach, friend of James Joyce . . . : Sylvia Beach, *Shakespear and Company.*

29 Beckett remained in Paris until 1942, and was eventually decorated "as an

	information source in an important intelligence network." See Deirdre Bair, *Samuel Beckett.*
30	Salle Druout sales figures from Le Boterf, *op. cit.*
30	Paris's best-known brothel: Fabienne Jamet, *One Two Two.*
30	"One could have one's fill . . .": Le Boterf, *op. cit.*
31	After the armistice, the entire occupied zone: Hans Umbreit, *Der Militärbefehlshaber in Frankreich,* has the most thorough account of the machinery of the German occupation, with some analysis of policies and personalities as well.
31–32	The summary of Werner Best's career and his comments on his colleagues are from his unpublished memoirs, which are in Tübingen University, with a copy on microfilm at the Bibliothèque de Documentation Contemporaine at Nanterre.
34	One book mistakenly asserting that Schaumburg was assassinated is Gerard Walter's *La Vie à Paris pendant l'occupation* (p. 215). Le Boterf unfortunately repeats the fiction.
35	The requisitioning of hospitals, prisons, and the post office is discussed in Audiat, *op. cit.*
36	Otto Abetz published a partial autobiography, *Mémoires d'un ambassadeur, histoire d'une politique franco-allemande,* as well as *Pétain et les Allemands,* and, after his trial and imprisonment, *D'une prison.*
37	Relevant books by Friedrich Grimm include his memoirs, *Mit Offenem Visier,* and *Frankreich Berichte 1934–1944.* Sieburg's books are in a style of cloudy rhetoric which is almost impenetrable.
37	Such, then, were the associates . . . : Karl Epting, *Frankreich in Widerspruch* (Epting's postwar *Generation der Mitte* is also revealing, if only for its self-pity). See also Abetz, *Mémoires.*
37	"Slowly we turned . . .": Grimm, *Mit Offenem Visier.*
38	"The armchairs in the salon . . .": Georges Oltramare, *Les Souvenirs nous vengent.* For Oltramare in general, see the stenographed transcript of his trial in the Centre de Documentation Contemporaine Juive.
39	"You will always arise . . .": Robert Brasillach, *Oeuvres complètes,* 12 vols., ed. Maurice Bardèche. The occasional journalism of the prolific writer has been collected almost in its entirety into the twelve volumes.
39	"was wide open . . .": Lifar, *op. cit.*
39–42	Alice Epting-Kullmann, memoir, *Pariser Begegnungen,* was privately printed at Hänner über Säckingen in 1952.
42	"the only time in my life . . .": see transcript of trial, *Les Procès de trahison devant la cour de justice de Paris. Paquis, Bucard, Luchaire, Brasillach.*
42	"She was very eager . . .": Epting-Kullmann, *op. cit.*
43	The role of the Abwehr in Paris is described by a former Abwehr officer, Oscar Reile, in two books, *Geheime Westfront* and *Treff Lutetia Paris.* See also Hans A. Eckart, *Der Gefesselte Hahn.*
43	For an interview with Knochen by Lucien Steinberg, see *Historia,* Hors Serie No. 26, *La Gestapo en France,* p. 26. See also *Historia,* Hors Serie No. 27.

Chapter 3:	**From the Camp of the Conquered into the Camp of the Conquerors**
44	"The renewal of contact . . .": Fernand de Brinon, *Mémoires.* Further exculpation is to be found in *La Vérité sur Fernand de Brinon,* a pamphlet published by his friends in 1947 after de Brinon's execution.
45	Lunching in the Rue Rudé . . . : Ernst Jünger, *Strahlungen,* entry of October 8, 1941. The diary has been published in a French translation, entitled *Journal* (two vols.).
46	"How could it conceivably have happened . . .": General Martin in Hoover Institution, *op. cit.,* vol. 1.
46	"I am anxious to know . . .": Maurice Toesca, *Cinq ans de patience,* entry of September 6, 1942.
47–48	For Grote and Weber, see Robert Aron, *Histoire de l'épuration,* whose second volume carries the subtitle *Le monde de la presse, des arts, des lettres . . .* Specialist studies of the press as an instrument of collaboration include Jacques Polanski, *La Presse, la propagande et l'opinion publique sous l'occupation;* Mar-

cel Baudot, *L'Opinion publique sous l'occupation;* Jean Quéval, *Première page, cinquième colonne.* See also Umbreit, *op. cit.*

48   For *La Victoire,* see Quéval, *op. cit.,* and Amouroux, *La Grande Histoire.*

49   For Bunau-Varilla, see Breker, *op. cit.*

49   For an analysis of the role of Luchaire and his papers, see Claude Lévy, *Les Nouveaux Temps et l'idéologie de la collaboration.*

49   "He told me that . . .": Corinne Luchaire, *Ma drôle de vie.*

50   The letter from Luchaire is quoted in Jacques Chabannes, *Paris à vingt ans.*

50   For Hibbelen, see Aron, *Histoire de l'épuration,* vol. 2.

50   "I watched . . .": Simone Signoret, *Nostalgia Isn't What It Used to Be.*

50   For Fontenoy, see Lucien Combelle, *Péché par orgeuil.*

51   "The embassy dreamed up a plan . . .": Oltramare, *op. cit.*

51   "Châteaubriant is proceeding . . .": *The Goebbels Diaries,* translated and edited by Louis P. Lochner, entry of September 28, 1943.

52   For Henri Jeanson, see his *70 Ans d'adolescence.*

53   For Jacques Galtier-Boissière, see his *Mon Journal pendant l'occupation.*

53–55   For Pierre Drieu la Rochelle, see his *Récit Secret,* as well as his *Journal.* For the Drieu-Paulhan-NRF imbroglio, see Frédéric Grover, *Six Entretiens avec André Malraux;* also Dominique Desanti, *Drieu la Rochelle ou le séducteur mystifié;* and Tarmo Kunnas, *Drieu la Rochelle, Céline, Brasillach ou la tentation fasciste.* For more information on Drieu la Rochelle, the most recent and comprehensive biography is *Drieu la Rochelle,* by Pierre Andreu and Frédéric Grover.

56   For Céline, see the several books by Frédéric Vitoux, notably his *Céline.*

57   "Large, bony, robust . . .": Jünger, *op. cit.,* entry of December 7, 1941.

58   "Don't you agree . . .": Epting-Kullmann, *op. cit.*

58   Céline's pseudo-Hitler fantasy related in Vitoux, *op. cit.*

58 ff   For a very complete account of *Je Suis Partout,* see Pierre-Marie Dioudonnat, *Je Suis Partout 1930–1944.*

59   "The only hope left . . .": Lucien Rebatet, *Les Décombres.*

62   "It seems to me . . .": Brasillach, *op. cit.*

63   Unobtainable since the end of the war, *Les Décombres* was reprinted in 1976 carrying the additional subtitle *Les Mémoires d'un fasciste* with the following *avertissement* ("warning to the reader") pasted on to its flyleaf: "Some readers will be shocked by the republication of *Les Décombres,* a fascist and racist polemic. This book, published thirty-four years ago, under the German occupation, is nonetheless a historical document of first importance. As for the doctrines which inspired it, and against which the struggle is perpetually required, their perpetuation justifies a new reprinting to instruct and warn those who did not live through the original drama." To conform to these sentiments, the more extreme anti-Semitic passages had been bowdlerized. At the same time, the publisher, Jean-Jacques Pauvert, took the opportunity to add Rebatet's sequel, written after the war, with the title *Les Mémoires d'un fasciste Volume II.*

63 ff   Communist party policy, inevitably the subject of much subsequent obfuscation and wishful thinking, has been minutely traced by A. Rossi, *Les Communistes français pendant la drôle de guerre* and *La Guerre des papillons,* books as invaluable as they are scarce, needless to say. The version of events which the party has tried to pass into history—in vain, it must be said—is found in Germaine Willard, *La Drôle de guerre et la trahison de Vichy.*

64   "We and our interpreters . . .": Charles Tillon, *On Chantait Rouge.* Tillon's books also explains the position of those Communists guilty of "national deviation."

64   "The Paris police is collaborating . . .": Langeron, *op. cit.*

66 ff   Someone so controversial as Doriot might be thought to have provoked a lengthy bibliography, but such is not the case. There is *Histoire de la Collaboration,* a partial, not to say eulogistic, book by Saint-Paulien (in reality, Doriot's press officer, Maurice-Yvan Sicard). *Die Doriot Bewegung,* by Dieter Wolf, is excellent. Its French translation, *Doriot, du communisme à la collaboration,* for some reason has been deprived of its notes. See also Jacques Doriot, *Je suis un homme du maréchal,* 1941, and his *Realités,* 1942.

67   "France must pass . . .": Victor Barthélemy, *Du communisme au fascisme.*

67–68   Marcel Déat has been even less discussed in print than Doriot. The standard work remains *Le Destin de Marcel Déat,* by Claude Varennes (real name, Georges Albertini; see interview page 221). See also Déat's own wartime pamphlet, *Le Parti unique,* and his *Pensée allemand et pensée française.* Pascal Ory, in *Les Collaborateurs 1940–1945,* has a bibliographical note that "the memoirs of Marcel Déat remain to this day unpublished and can be consulted only with difficulty," and indeed the trace of this manuscript seems now lost altogether. Ory adds, "Other autobiographical manuscripts of personalities of secondary importance will no doubt never be published." For *L'Oeuvre,* see also Quéval, *op. cit.*

69   For lesser French Fascists, see Ory, *Collaborateurs,* and the same author's anthology, *La France allemande.* Also J. Plumyène and R. Lasierra, *Les Fascismes français 1923–1963;* and Paul Serant, *Le Romantisme fasciste.*

69   "As I looked . . .": J. Hérold-Paquis, *Des Illusions . . . désillusions.*

69–70   For a close account of the events of November 11, 1940, see Pierre Bourget, *Histoires secrètes de l'occupation de Paris.* Bourget's *Paris 1940–1944* is a useful general account of the occupation and is illustrated.

70   The fine, dignified ceremony . . . : Rebatet, *op. cit.*

71   The account of the ball at the Château de Bouffemont is from Luchaire, *op. cit.*

Chapter 4: The Spread of Terror

72   For Breitscheid and Hilferding, see Kurt Kersten, *Deutsche Rundschau,* September 1958, p. 843.

72   Friedrich Grimm, *Der Grünszpan Prozess,* 1942; see also the article by Maître Weill-Goudechaux in *Le Monde Juif,* May 1949.

73 ff   Freemasonry in France has a specialized bibliography going back to Voltaire. The length and strength of this pedigree speaks well for its fantasy. Two solid general histories are Pierre Chevallier, *Histoire de la Franc-Maçonnerie française;* and J. A. Fauchon and A. Ricker, *Histoire de la Franc-Maçonnerie en France.*

73   *Au Pilori* began publishing these lists of Freemasons in the issue of August 28, 1941.

73   "Interiors of the lodges . . .": Thérive, *op. cit.*

76 ff   The destruction of French Jewry, and Vichy complicity with the Nazis in this matter, continues to be contentious. A definitive study is Joseph Billig, *La Solution finale de la question Juive.* Serge Klarsfeld, ed., *Die Endlösung der Judenfrage in Frankreich* is a telling selection from the German documents housed in the CDJC. See also Léon Poliakov, *La Breviare de la haine;* David Diamant, *Le Billet Vert.* On the German bureaucracy of the Final Solution in France, Umbreit has surprisingly little to vouchsafe.

76   "For the time being . . .": Langeron, *op. cit.*

82   The role of Dannecker and the cooperation of the relevant sections of the French police is fully elucidated in Claude Lévy's *La Grande Rafle du Vél d'Hiv.*

82 ff   For the history of the CGQJ, there is a standard work of comprehensive scholarship: Joseph Billig, *Le Commissariat générale aux questions Juives,* 3 vols. See Vol. 1 for story of Dr. Blanke, Vol. 3 for the Michel memorandum.

83   "a frenzied Nazi . . .": Xavier Vallat, *Le Nez de Cléopatre.*

83   For Fournier and Regelsberger, see Billig, *Commissariat.*

86   "Laurent with his limp . . .": Georges Wellers, *De Drancy à Auschwitz.* See also his *L'Etoile jaune à l'heure de Vichy.*

86   Sézille is quoted in *Le Pitre ne rit pas,* documents ed. by David Rousset.

86   The Institut's program is quoted from the advertisement in *Au Pilori.*

87   "In provincial town halls . . .": Guitry as quoted in Amouroux, *La Grande Histoire.* See also Guitry, *op. cit.*

87   "a Jewish marriage . . .": Comte Bruno de Franclier in *Au Pilori,* July 8, 1943.

87   "At no moment . . .": *Au Pilori,* July 15, 1943.

Chapter 5: Spoils of War

88   "At the Casino de Paris . . .": Thérive, *op. cit.*

88	Goebbels first visited . . . : Lifar, *op. cit.*
88	"A tapped telephone . . .": *The Goebbels Diaries,* translated and edited by Louis P. Lochner, entry of April 22, 1943.
88	Text of Rosenberg speech in *Le Matin,* November 29, 1940.
89	Hitler's instructions to Abetz are quoted in Rose Valland, *Le Front de l'art.* See also Jean Cassou, *Pillage par les Allemands des oeuvres d'art.* Umbreit, *op. cit.,* discusses spoliation of works of art.
92	Goering's address to the Reich commissioners has been widely quoted, e.g., in Mallet, *op. cit.,* Vol. 2.
92	"We were all aware . . .": Eitel Lange, *Der Reichsmarschall im Kriege.* Besides Eitel Lange, another friendly German journalist was Kurt Lothar Tank, *Pariser Tagebuch.*

Chapter 6: *Système D*

94	"For the second time . . .": Benoit-Guyod, *op. cit.* Amouroux, *La grande histoire des Français sous l'occupation* has much information on food and rationing in each of the four volumes published to date. See also J. Debu-Bridel, *Histoire du marché noir 1939–1947.*
95	For food restrictions and diets, see *Paris sous l'occupation, documentation photographique* ed. by Claude Lévy and Dominique Veillon. Statistics for children's heights taken from M. Reinhard, A. Armengard and J. Dupâquier, *Histoire générale de la population mondiale.*
95	"I sewed and planted . . .": Maurice Toesca, *op. cit.*
95	The weekly menu is in Micheline Bood, *Les Années doubles.*
95	Rahn's conversation with the *préfet* is in Rudolf Rahn, *Ruheloses Leben.*
96	"The room was crowded . . .": Galtier-Boissière, *Journal.* His *Mémoires d'un Parisien* also contains spirited observations of the kind.
96	"One has the impression . . .": Jünger, *op. cit.*
97	The letter about his mother is quoted from Jean Bourgoint, *Retour de l'enfant terrible.*
98	The repercussions on ordinary . . . : Jean Dutourd, *Au bon beurre.*
98	"Economy and hygiene . . .": Colette, *Paris de ma fenêtre.* See also Maurice Goudeket, *Près de Colette.*
99	"The friend who is expecting you . . .": Alfred Fabre-Luce, *op. cit.* When these diaries were republished after the war, they were found to have been lightly but skillfully edited to accommodate the turn of events. All following quotations on this and the next page are from Fabre-Luce.
100	"As silent as the country . . .": Charles Braibant, *La Guerre à Paris.*
104	"People no longer invite . . .": Edmond Dubois, *Paris sans lumière.*
104	For statistics about shoes, see Le Boterf, *op. cit.* Also see his chapter on fashion.
105	*Zazous* are discussed in several works, including Amouroux, *La Grande Histoire,* and Audiat, *op. cit. Les Zazous,* by Jean-Claude Loiseau, appears to be the only book solely devoted to the phenomenon, and it is the source of the quotation from Jonny Hess.
105	"It was no small hardship . . .": Janet Teissier Du Cros, *Divided Loyalties.*
106	"Photographs of Pétain . . .": Maurice Sachs, *La Chasse à courre.*
111	Details of Sachs's last few years can be found in André du Dognon and Philippe Monceau, *Le Dernier Sabbat de Maurice Sachs.* Monceau knew Sachs in Germany and was in a position to report at last on his otherwise unexplained disappearance and death.

Chapter 7: **A Change of Direction**

112	"France's interest lies . . .": Léautaud, *op. cit*
113	"One of the Reich's . . .": Henri Clerc, *La Collaboration, Conference à Paris,* April 24, 1941.
113	"We dawdled in the Bois . . .": Jean Guéhenno, *Journal des années noires 1940–1944.*
114	"Beforehand, muster . . .": Jünger, *op. cit.*
115	"Many German officers . . .": Léautaud, *op. cit.*
115	For Doriot meeting, see *Le Cri du Peuple,* May 26, 1941.

116 "In the Salle Wagram . . .": Jean Guéhenno, *op. cit.*

116 The Communist slogans are quoted in Rossi, *Guerre.*

116 "Parisians are famished . . .": Pierre Nicolle, *Cinquante mois d'armistice.*

116 "Don't forget to listen . . .": Fabre-Luce, *op. cit.*

117 For the LVF, and later the French Waffen SS, otherwise the Charlemagne Division, see André Brissaud, *Les Agents de Lucifer;* Jean Mabire, *Les S.S. Français;* Henri Charbonneau, *Les Mémoires de Porthos;* Christian de la Mazière, *Le Rêveur Casqué;* Mathieu Laurier (pseudonym for Pierre Vigouroux), *Il reste le drapeau et les copains.*

117 "In the boulevard des Italiens . . .": Jean Guéhenno, *op. cit.*

117 "Russia's entry into the war . . .": De Beauvoir, *op. cit.*

118 "The Paris region . . .": Tillon, *Chantait.* The same author also wrote a general account of the Communist partisans, *Les F.T.P.*

120 "The news of the assassination . . .": Benoit-Guyod, *op. cit.*

120 "One or two more German soldiers . . .": Léautaud, *op. cit.*

120 "We are not used . . .": *La Semaine* quoted in Halimi, *op. cit.*

124 The destruction of the synagogues is the subject of a chapter in Bourget, *Histoires.* See also Umbreit, *op. cit.*

125 "In him, delicacy, . . .": Jünger, *op. cit.*

126 "January 10, 1942. Claude Blanchard . . .": Galtier-Boissière, *Journal.*

126 The Militärbefehlshaber's report is quoted in Umbreit, *op. cit.*

127 "Heydrich must have had . . .": De Brinon, *op. cit.*

128 Statistics are from Charles Rousseau and Roger Céré, *Chronologie du conflict mondial 1935–1945.*

128 *Le Peuple reveillé,* the fourth volume in Amouroux's series, is as comprehensive an account as any of the origins of the resistance. His bibliography lists all and more than need be read on the topic. For Henri Frenay, see his memoirs, *La Nuit Finira,* and his controversial *L'Enigme Jean Moulin.* See also Henri Michel, *Les Courants de pensée de la résistance.*

129 "People knew each other . . .": Marie Granet, *Ceux de la résistance.*

129 For the CNR, see Jean Moulin, *Premier Combat;* Laure Moulin (his wife), *Jean Moulin;* and René Hostache, *Le Conseil National de la résistance.*

134 "You have only to look . . .": Léautaud, *op. cit.*

135 "Met young B . . .": Benoit-Guyod, *op. cit.*

Chapter 8: Pitchipoi

136 "had registered a paid attendance . . .": Sézille quoted in Billig, *Commissariat,* Vol. II.

136 "in front of numerous local people . . .": Wellers, *Drancy.*

138 "Only last month . . .": *Je Suis Partout,* May 31, 1942.

138 "The yellow star . . .": *Je Suis Partout,* June 6, 1942.

138 "Some Jews left without hope . . .": *L'Appel,* October 22, 1942.

138 "In the rue Royale . . .": Jünger, *op. cit.*

140 "Optimism remained . . .": De Beauvoir, *op. cit.*

140 "Believe me, my dear fellow . . .": Jeanson, *op. cit.*

140 "Since you are taking care . . .": Anonymous letter reproduced in Rousset, *op. cit.* p. 39.

142 "President Laval has proposed . . .": Dannecker's telegram, July 6, 1942, CDJC document XLIX-35.

142 "Bousquet, secrétaire général . . .": Billig, *Commissariat,* Vol. 3.

142 "They were dumped . . .": Wellers, *Drancy.*

143 "The gendarmes tried . . .": Annette Monod quoted in Lévy, *Grande Rafle.*

143 "Yesterday . . . a large number . . .": Jünger, *op. cit.*

143 "Many of the vehicles . . .": Claude Mauriac, *Les Espaces imaginaires* (also the source for the Mauriac quotation on p. 144).

144 These operations in Paris . . . : Details of deportations from Serge Klarsfeld, ed., *Le Mémorial de la Deportation des Juifs de France.*

144 Brünner "was small . . .": Wellers, *Drancy.*

145 Statistics for Action M in Billig, *Commissariat,* Vol. 3.

146 "From 1940 onward, it seemed . . .": Guitry, *op. cit.*

146   "While I was making . . .": Guitry, *op. cit.* The incident finds confirmation in the fey memoirs of Arletty, *La Défence.*

146   "I am writing this . . .": Max Jacob's letter quoted in Francis Steegmuller, *Jean Cocteau.*

146   "On February 22, 1944 . . .": Desnos, *op. cit.*

147   "I was led to defend . . .": Desnos, *op. cit.*

Chapter 9:   **Underground**

148   "with such languid grace . . .": Fritz Molden, *Exploding Star.* For Ulli Rüdt von Collenberg, see interview page 244.

148 ff   For details of the Bureau Otto, and German trafficking generally, see Jacques Delarue, *Trafics et crimes sous l'occupation.* For Szkolnikoff and Ioanovici, see *ibid;* Aron, *Histoire de l'épuration;* and *Historia,* Number 39. Also Le Boterf, *op. cit.*

149   Details of Sainrapt and Brice in Aron, *Histoire de l'épuration (Le monde des affaires).* For Bickler, see *Historia,* Number 39, pp. 146 ff.

150   The Laffont-Bonny gang has been extensively described. See in particular Philippe Aziz, *Tu Trahiras sans vergogne;* Delarue, *op. cit.*

151   Karski's journey is related in Walter Laqueur, *The Terrible Secret.*

151   "Inter-section jealousies . . .": M. R. D. Foot, *The SOE in France.* This is the official history of SOE by the one and only historian so far allowed access to the relevant secret files. See also Bruce Marshall, *The White Rabbit,* for information about Yeo-Thomas father and son; Jean Overton Fuller, *The German Penetration of SOE;* Marie-Madeleine Fourcade, *Noah's Ark.*

151   For examples of counterintelligence work in the Avenue Foch, see *Hugo Bleicher: Colonel Henri's Story,* ed. by Ian Colvin.

153   "Must I stay . . .": *ibid.*

153   "In front of the door . . .": Edmond Dubois, *op. cit.*

153   "There were two daily rendezvous . . .": Anne Guéhenno, *L'Epreuve.*

154   "Footsteps were always coming . . .": Christopher Burney, *Solitary Confinement;* see also his *Dungeon Democracy.*

155 ff   Details of the Red Orchestra taken from Leopold Trepper, *The Great Game.*

Chapter 10: *Tout-Paris*

157   "Just look at the German officers . . .": Raymond Ruffin, *Journal d'un J3.*

157   "It is terrible to say so . . .": Bood, *op. cit.*

160   "You know everything . . .": Luchaire, *op. cit.*

160   Guéhenno thought so too . . . : Jean Guéhenno, *op. cit.*

160   "'Hitler is a saint,' . . .": Léon Werth, *Journal 1940–44.*

161   "Who displayed a flamboyant Hitlerism . . .": Galtier-Boissière, *Mon Journal pendant l'occupation.*

161   For Maurice Toesca's confrontation with his German friend, see Toesca, *op. cit.*

161   "The two of us . . .": Jünger, *op. cit.*

162   For Breker's exhibition, see Breker, *op. cit.*

164   "The facts speak . . .": Le Boterf, *op. cit.*

164   "in spite of shortages . . .": Abetz, *Mémoires.*

165   For incidents surrounding the premieres of Cocteau's plays, see Steegmuller, *op. cit.*

165   "obliged me to accompany . . .": Bourgoint, *op. cit.*

165   "A few months ago . . .": Toesca, *op. cit.*

166   "How bizarre it is to find . . .": Brasillach, *op. cit.*

167   For *Le Soulier de satin,* see Jean-Louis Barrault, *Souvenirs pour demain.*

168   "Cuzin, Desanti, three or four . . .": De Beauvoir, *op. cit.*

168   "people were cheerful . . .": Boris Vian quoted in Halimi, *op. cit.*

168   For Picasso's play, see André-Louis Dubois, *Sous le signe de l'amitié;* also de Beauvoir, *op. cit.*

169   See Herbert R. Lottman, *Albert Camus,* for the fullest account of Camus' career.

172   "The public at the opening night . . .": The critic, Henry-René Lenormand, quoted in *ibid.,* p. 319.

Chapter 11: To Each His Own Laws

173 "We were returning . . .": Galtier-Boissière, *Journal.*

173 "The Hitlerian savages . . .": Rebatet, *op. cit.*

173 "There are still many French . . .": The informer is quoted in Umbreit, *op. cit.*

173 "I noticed that these buildings . . .": Benoit-Guyod, *op. cit.*

174 "The sky is alive . . .": Fabre-Luce, *op. cit.*

174 For statistics on the PPF congress, see *Le Cri du Peuple,* November 4–8, 1942.

174 "It is impossible . . .": Wolf, *op. cit.*

178 "at times fearfully resembling . . .": Saint-Paulien, *op. cit.*

178 "We found a large demonstration . . .": Braibant, *op. cit.*

180 "You will never achieve . . .": Darnand is quoted in J. Delperrié de Bayac, *Histoire de la Milice.*

180 "On September 6 . . .": Barthélemy, *op. cit.*

181 "Professor Debré and . . .": Braibant, *op. cit.*

181 "On October 17 . . .": De Brinon, *Mémoires.*

187 "The death of Henriot . . .": Gertrude Stein, *Wars I Have Known.*

188 "All Paris turned up . . .": Lifar, *op. cit.*

Chapter 12: Departures and Arrivals

193 ff The authoritative account of the plot of July 20 in Paris is in Wilhelm von Schramm, *Der 20. Juli in Paris.* For Rommel, see biographies by Desmond Young and by David Irving. Also see Hans Speidel, *Unserer* and *Invasion 44.*

195 For Dietrich von Choltitz, see his *Brennt Paris?* and *Un Soldat parmi les Allemands.*

196 ff An enormous literature has arisen around the liberation of Paris, most of it having less to do with events than with the need to recover morale and national poise after the war. Adrien Dansette, *Histoire de la libération de Paris,* duly lists some of these works in its bibliography. Though itself written in *tricolore* prose, for which allowance must be made, it can be relied on for facts.

196 "I kept intact my reason . . .": Léautaud, *op. cit.*

196 For Drieu from August 1944 until his death, see Andreu and Grover, *op. cit.*

197 Though also self-justificatory in tone and in intention, Pierre Taittinger, *. . . et Paris ne fut pas détruit,* can be relied on for facts.

197 "You could feel that . . .": Brasillach, *Oeuvres complètes,* vol. 6, *Journal d'un homme occupé.*

198 "the great flight of the Fritzes . . .": Galtier-Boissière, *Journal.*

200 For Convoy 79, see Klarsfeld, *Mémorial.*

200 "Day after day . . .": Luchaire, *op. cit.*

200 "Everything was decomposing . . .": Rebatet, *op. cit.*

200 "and kept on ringing up . . .": Hérold-Paquis, *op. cit.*

202 "The Porte d'Orléans . . .": Thérive, *op. cit.*

204 For statistics on the Warsaw Uprising, see Hanns von Krannhals, *Der Warschauer Aufstand 1944.*

204 "Fighting in the streets . . .": Galtier-Boissière, *Journal.*

Part II: Interviews

239 Jehle, says Umbreit, *op. cit.,* p. 272, was an SS Standartenführer and the Gestapo man in the Majestic Hotel.

Index

French youth, 157–58; effect of German attack on Russia on, 116–18; embassy activities re, 38–39; and Franco-German relations, 214; by French youth, 158–60; Goering on, 92; of intellectuals, 223, 224; justification of, 46, 55, 58, 145, 233; moral question in, 145, 146, 161, 162, 206–07; in press, 47–64; in radio, 35–36; by socialites, 39–42; term, 44; by Vichy government, 221–22

Collaborators, 8, 30, 88, 181, 214, 236, 264, 272; Benoist-Méchin on, 218; Communists as, 64, 66; fled Paris, 200–201; Freemasons as, 226; Laval as, 126; party of (proposed), 68; power of, 50; punished after liberation, 206–07; replaced government, 183; and resistance, 121, 125–26, 128, 188, 190, 261–62; special privileges of, 100; ultras, 188–90, 197, 201, 264; when German defeat seemed possible, 135, 188–92; writers, 250

Collenberg, Baron Kurt Rüdt von, 244

Collenberg, Ursula Rüdt von (Ulli, now Frau Nottebohm), 148, 244

Colonna, Judas, 87

Combat, 128

Combat (underground paper), 172, 180

Combats (newspaper), 180, 181–83

Combelle, Alex, 104

Combelle, Lucien, 190, 222–24

Comité France Allemagne, 37, 44, 213, 218

Comité Nationale d'Ecrivains (CNE), 172

Commissariat Générale aux Questions Juives (CGQJ), 83, 86, 127, 136, 140, 227, 233

Commission d'Etudes Judéo-Maçonnique, 86, 227

Communications, 35

Communist party (France), *see* Parti Communiste Français (PCF)

Comoedia (journal), 104, 165, 168, 172

Composers, 26

Concentration camps, 38, 59, 85–86, 142, 147, 197, 262; *see also* Drancy

Conseil Nationale de la Résistance (CNR), 129–34

Constant, Victor, 197

Contrôle des Administrations Provisoires, 83

Cooper, Duff, 38

Copeau, Jacques, 28

Correze, Jacques, 183

Cortot, Alfred, 26–28, 42, 146

Costantini, Pierre, 69, 87, 117, 190, 200, 214

Coston, Henry, 48, 73, 183, 190, 224–28; *Dictionnaire de la vie politique,* 224

Coty, François, 34

Counterintelligence (German), 149, 151–52

Cousteau, Pierre-Antoine, 99, 200, 201, 217, 228; *L'Amerique juive,* 62

Craig, Edward Gordon, 26

Cri du Peuple, Le (newspaper), 67, 116

Crouzet, Guy, 183, 200

Cuny, Alain, 164

Curfew, 122, 104, 167

Daix, Pierre, 228–30; *J'ai cri au matin,* 228, 229

Daladier, Edouard, 17, 216

Daltroffe-Baticle, Madame Odette, 270

Damrath, Pastor, 194, 242

Dangan press, 64

Dangon, Georges, 226

Dannecker, SS Hauptsturmführer Theo, 82–84, 86, 136, 144, 213, 214; deportation of Jews, 141, 142; and Leguay, 232, 233

Dansette, Adrien: *Histoire de la liberation de Paris,* 46, 202, 204

Dantas, Souza da, 26

Daquin, Louis, 164

Darlan, Admiral Jean, 71, 73, 112, 126, 216–17, 218, 226–27, 236

Darnand, Joseph, 179–80, 183, 186, 187, 200, 206, 217, 264

Darquier de Pellepoix, 83, 85, 86, 127, 141, 142, 190, 206, 227, 232

Darrieux, Danielle, 26, 164

Daudet, Georges, 226

Daudet, Lucien, 42

David, Jean, 180

David-Weil [art] collection, 90

De Brinon, Fernand, 50, 62, 71, 127, 135, 150, 178, 181, 192, 197, 234, 236, 246; and Achenbach, 213, 215; and appeals for leniency, 145; at Breker exhibition, 162; fled Paris, 200; Laval's representative in Paris, 44–46; on Milice, 180; Simone Mittre on, 215–17; shot, 206; at Wagner exhibition, 115

De Brinon, Madame (née Lisette Franck), 45

De Gaulle, General Charles, 8, 11, 59, 64, 115, 157, 202, 215, 222, 259; BBC broadcasts, 16, 36, 69, 116, 129, 264; entered Paris, 206; had Pucheu shot, 17–18; lack of information re, 129; and resistance, 129–34; sent agents into France, 118, 129

De Luquerica, Felix, 11, 188

Déat, Marcel, 58, 174, 180, 188, 197, 214, 224, 225, 236; arrest of, 70–71; assassination attempt on, 117; collaboration by, 116, 117, 221–22; and de Brinon, 217; disappeared, 206; fled Paris, 200; pacifism of, 67–68; plan for national revival, 183; in Vichy government, 183, 192

Debats, 215, 216

Debré, Professor, 181, 254

Decour, Jacques, 118, 229, 230

Défence de la France, 150

Degrelle, Léon, 62, 262

Delannoy, Jean, 164, 165

Delarue, Jacques: *Histoire de la Gestapo,* 128

Delaunay, Charles, 104

Delaunay, Maurice (alias François-Henry Promethée; Le Maître de Feu), 48, 213, 214

Delfanne, Georges (alias Christian Masuy), 149, 150, 206

Delforge, Lucienne, 26

Deloncle, Eugène, 68, 124, 174, 221, 224, 225; collaborationism, 115–16, 117; murdered, 183, 190

Delorme, Danièle, 164

Delperrié de Bayac, Jacques: *Histoire de la Milice,* 186

Demonstrations, 69–70, 134, 229; student, 249–50; *see also* Resistance

Denizot, Gaston, 39

Denoel, Robert, 63, 87, 263

Denouncing *(Délation)* and denunciations, 74, 83, 87, 105, 138, 140–41, 247; *see also* "Echos"

Derain, André, 26, 162, 221

Desmarets, Sophie, 164

Desnos, Robert, 19, 30, 52, 140, 146–47, 164

Desnos, Yuki, 19, 146–47; *Les Confidences de Yuki,* 147

Despiau, Charles, 26, 42, 143, 221

Destouches, Louis, *see* Céline, Louis-Ferdinand

Deutsche Beschaffungsamt in Frankreich, 148

Deutsche Institut (Paris), 37, 38–42, 89, 110–11, 148, 250, 251

Deutsches Nachrichten Büro (DNB), 43, 47

Devillers (transportation director), 259

Dietrich, Otto, 12

Dieudonné, Charles, *see* Oltramare, Georges

Dior, Christian, 26

Dioudonnat, Pierre-Marie, 62

Diplomatic corps, 25–26

Dohna, Eberhard Graf, 239

Doriot, Jacques, 54, 68, 121, 125, 144, 179, 180, 183, 188, 192, 200, 214, 218, 222, 228, 229, 236; collaborationism, 115–16; death of, 206; enlisted in LVF, 117; fled Paris, 200; on Laval's dismissal, 70; leader of PPF, 66–67, 174–78; on number of PPF killed, 181

Dormoy, Marie, 115

Dorsay (pseud. of Pierre Villette), 62

Drancy (concentration camp), 85–86, 169, 230, 231, 232, 270; Jewish children at, 142; Jews interned at, 136, 141, 142, 144–45, 146, 199–200

Drault, Jean, 55, 190, 227

Dreyfus, Alfred, 29, 115; trial, 72, 76, 83

Drieu la Rochelle, Pierre, 38, 53–55, 56, 66, 172, 188, 218; and Breker, 220; *Chiens de paille,* 196; and Combelle, 223–24; friend of Achenbach, 214; and Heller, 249, 250, 251; *L'Homme a cheval,* 55; *Journal,* 251; suicide of, 196

Drouin, Pierre, 224

Drumont, Edmond, 190

286

A Note About the Photographers

André Zucca was born on May 18, 1897, in Paris. The illegitimate son of an Italian dressmaker and a French father, he had French nationality. Part of his Italian family had emigrated to America, and he himself spent World War I there. Returning afterward to Paris, he got a job as assistant to a photographer specializing in theatrical work. He soon branched out and was published in prewar papers, including *Le Matin, L'Illustration,* and *Paris-Soir.*

At the outbreak of World War II, he was working for *Paris-Soir* as well as for *Paris-Match,* which had been launched only for a short while. With the occupation, the Germans took over the *Paris-Match* printing works, where they proceeded to publish their own illustrated magazine, *Signal.* Zucca worked for *Signal,* where a number of his photographs were published. The Germans provided him with Agfa color film, and he used a Leica. Since he had been a friend of Céline, Robert Le Vigan, and other outright Nazi sympathizers or collaborators, he was afraid of reprisals at the time of the liberation and went into hiding in the countryside. Many of the color photographs in his archive remained unpublished. He himself died in Paris in June 1973. Thanks are due to Magnum Photos through whom the Zucca photos were first found and who have the rights to their distribution which were so kindly granted for this book.

Roger Schall worked before World War II for the Ullstein press, and his photographs appeared in the *Berliner Illustrierte* and in many fashion periodicals, German and French. In 1938 he covered the Nuremberg party rally for *Paris-Match.* Meanwhile he ran his own small agency. It was only natural, therefore, that the Germans would contact him in due course. According to Schall, Otto Abetz himself persuaded him to work, holding out the promise of being allowed to photograph the entry of German troops into Moscow. Obliged to join the official union or *syndicat* of photographers, he held card number 135 and did free-lance assignments in black and white, many of them in the fields of fashion and entertainment. He did not work for *Signal.* For his nightclub sequences, taken after midnight, he had a special permit, or *Ausweis.* Immediately after the liberation he published a selection of his wartime photographs in *A Paris sous la botte des Nazis.* Retired now, he lives in Paris.

Graphic Credits

Typefaces: Times Roman, Century Schoolbook, and Block Condensed, set by University Graphics, Inc., Atlantic Highlands, New Jersey

Color Separations: J & L Lithographics, Inc., Northbrook, Illinois

Color Insert Printing: Rae Publishing Co., Inc., Cedar Grove, New Jersey

Text Paper: 70# Patina from Alling and Cory, New York, New York

Text Printing and Binding: The Murray Printing Company, Westford, Massachusetts

Designer: Michael Rand

Design Coordinators, New York: Robert Reed and Constance T. Doyle

Production Editor: Trent Duffy

Production Manager: Tricia West